MOVIES *of the* FIFTIES

MOVIES *of the* FIFTIES

EDITED BY ANN LLOYD
CONSULTANT EDITOR
DAVID ROBINSON

ORBIS PUBLISHING
LONDON

Acknowledgments

Many of the illustrations come from stills issued to publicize films made or distributed by the following companies: Allied Artists, American International Pictures, Les Artistes Associés, British Transport Films, British Lion, Samuel Bronston, Cineriz, Cinés, Columbia, Daiei, Dansk Kulturfilm, Dino de Laurentiis, Ealing Films, EMI, Excelsa-Film, Federiz/Francoriz, Filmways, Francinex, Franco-London Films, Gaumont, Hungaro Films, Stanley Kramer, London Films, Lux Films, Les Films Marceau, Marianne Productions, Memorial Films, MGM, Mirisch Corporation, Monogram, Mosfilm, Nordisk Tonefilm, Palomar, Paramount, Pathé, André Paulvé, Paris Film, PEA/PPA, Film Polski, Rafran, Rank, Remus, Republic, Rizzoli Film, RKO, Rusconi, Sandrews, Satyajit Ray Productions, Selznick International, Seven Arts, Shochiku, Specta Films, Svensk Filmindustri, Titanus, Toho, Tokyo Eiga, 20th Century-Fox, Two Cities, UGC/CICC, United Artists, Universal International, Vides, Warner Brothers, Woodfall. Although every effort is being made to trace the present copyright holders, we apologize in advance for any unintentional omission or neglect and will be pleased to insert the appropriate acknowledgment to companies or individuals in any subsequent edition of this publication.

Atmosphère, Kingsley Canham, Peter Cowie, Arnold Desser, Greg Edwards Archive, Barry Edson, Joel Finler Collection, Dennis Gifford, Ronald Grant Archive, Sally Hibbin, David Hine, Ciné Images, Japan Film Library Council, Robert Kingston Films, Kobal Collection, Museum of the City of New York, Museum of Modern Art, National Film Archive, National Film Theatre, Firoze Rangoonwalla, David Robinson Collection, Swedish Film Institute, Talisman Books, John Topham Picture Library, Tise Vahimagi, Bob Willoughby.

Abbreviations used in text

add: additional; **adv:** advertising; **anim:** animation; **art dir:** art direction; **ass:** assistant; **assoc:** associate; **chor:** choreography; **col:** colour process; **comm:** commentary; **cont:** continuity; **co-ord:** co-ordination; **cost:** costume; **dec:** decoration; **des:** design; **dial:** dialogue; **dial dir:** dialogue direction; **dir:** direction; **doc:** documentary; **ed:** film editing; **eng:** engineer; **ep:** episode; **exec:** executive; **loc:** location; **lyr:** lyrics; **man:** management; **mus:** music; **narr:** narration; **photo:** photography; **prod:** production; **prod co:** production company; **prod sup:** production supervision; **rec:** recording; **rel:** released; **r/t:** running time; **sc:** scenario/screenplay/script; **sd:** sound; **sp eff:** special effects; **sup:** supervision; **sync:** synchronization; **sys:** system.
Standard abbreviations for countries are used. Most are self-evident but note:
A = Austria; AUS = Australia; GER = Germany and West Germany after 1945; E.GER = East Germany.

Editor
Ann Lloyd
Consultant Editor
David Robinson
Editorial Director
Brian Innes
Deputy Editor
Martyn Auty
Chief Sub Editor
Jonathan Groucutt
Senior Sub Editors
Alastair Dougall, Graham Fuller
Editorial Assistant
Lindsey Lowe
Research Consultant
Arnold Desser
Picture Researchers
Dave Kent, Sue Scott-Moncrieff, Sandy Graham
Research
Kingsley Canham, Paul Taylor, Sally Hibbin
Designers
Ray Kirkpatrick, John Heritage

CONTENTS

INTRODUCTION

If one could not exactly say of the Fifties as Dickens said of the French Revolution 'it was the best of times, it was the worst of times . . . ' at least for the cinema it was a period full of contradictions. In many ways it seemed like a beginning, where in other, unforeseen ways, it proved to be an end. Elsewhere, what looked dangerously like delivering the *coup de grace* turned out quite unexpectedly to be the saving grace. At the beginning only those gifted with prophecy could have imagined that television, a cloud no bigger than a man's hand on the horizon, would rapidly become the big menace to the seemingly invincible Hollywood machine. At the end of the decade nearly everyone was so panicked by what television had become that the possibilities of fruitful combination and collaboration were hardly remarked on at all. And as for those highbrow European movies that had begun to nibble away at American cinema, well, how could something so small-time possibly be either a threat or an aid?

Looking back from the Eighties, the Fifties seem to be characterized above all by a naive belief in gimmickry. As television made its first noticeable inroads on the movie-going public, the answer was sought increasingly in technical innovation. There was, of course, a certain logic to that: give the public what it could not get at home from a small screen. And what could it obviously not get? Size, grandeur, spectacle, overwhelming personal involvement. Hence the giant triple-screen process Cinerama, which made psychological involvement in, say, a filmed roller-coaster ride seem physical in a way hardly known since Lumière's audiences had run for the door at the sight of a train heading towards them on screen. Hence the smaller, cheaper one-camera versions of the same idea, like CinemaScope and VistaVision. Hence, for that matter, 3D and 'a lion in your lap'.

These new processes were all very well as the sensation of a moment. But once the surprise had worn off we were back with the old, perennial question of what was *on* the many-splendoured screen. What people still wanted was, above all, stars. And as it happened history was conspiring to deprive them of this prime need. Partly it was the inscrutable workings of human nature, which had seemed during the first two decades of the century to produce an amazing glut of colourful personalities who could be shown off to their maximum advantage on screen, and then had drastically cut down the supply. The classic stars who had survived from silent days or came in with the first blossoming of the talkie were now maturing towards character roles, and not so many had arisen during the Forties to replace them. Moreover, it had not been clearly realized how much the star system had to do with the whole back-up structure of the Hollywood studio, managing and directing every detail of the contract player's professional life. If Marilyn Monroe and James Dean were the last superstars to be created in the old mould, it was not so much because the raw material was necessarily lacking as because the breakdown of the study system meant that the mould also was broken.

So, Hollywood found itself more and more in a bad way as the decade progressed, and its first inspirations on how to stem the tide of television proved temporary palliatives at best. It was clearly necessary to look elsewhere. And that elsewhere was the dangerous and unmanageable territory that lay beyond the borders of the United States – perhaps, horror of horrors, in some place where they did not even speak English. Since the early Twenties, Hollywood had been in the habit of regarding Europe as a great reservoir of talent; but what could not be recruited could be happily ignored. Now things were different. The Italian neo-realists, shooting their stories on the streets where they had really happened, made a deep impression in America after the war and led to a certain amount of imitation, with location shooting gradually becoming the norm. But much more psychologically significant was the defection, in 1950, of a major Hollywood star, Ingrid Bergman, attracted first by the talent, then by the person of Roberto Rossellini. Her departure was a nail in the coffin of traditional Hollywood; her return to win an Oscar for *Anastasia* in 1957, despite having lived openly with Rossellini and borne him illegitimate children – and got away with it – was another and even more significant nail.

In any case, it was evident that European cinema was something which would have to be met on its own terms; no longer was it possible just to enlist or dismiss. Economic considerations too were favouring the 'runaway' production: moneys frozen in Europe, local colour aplenty, and the greater cheapness of practically everything connected with film production kept film-makers coming to Europe to make their films, and even if the intention was still to make a hundred-per-cent Hollywood film, something still rubbed off. And Europe could be relied upon to provide something else which those tempted by television could not get in their own homes: the 'mature' subject treated in a suitably 'adult' way. Mature and adult were, naturally, relative terms, but the immense box-office as well as critical success of films like *Room at the Top* and *Blow-Up* helped to drive the lesson home.

But whichever way you looked at it, the tigers were at the gates of Hollywood. Early in the Fifties the major companies were still huffing and puffing and backing a no-collaboration, no-surrender policy towards television. No old movies were to be shown on television, no major star or director from the movies proper would dream of sullying himself by appearing on or working for television, and so on. But not everyone saw things that way. When his agents, MCA, went into television production in a big way, canny Alfred Hitchcock followed suit, and far from discrediting him, *Alfred Hitchcock Presents*

(1955–62) made him more than ever the director-as-superstar. Stars such as Loretta Young who felt their movie careers to be fading or, like Lucille Ball, had never quite reached their full potential in the cinema, moved over to television and had gigantic successes. By the end of the decade the jibes about the amateurishness and anaemia of television which were a staple of movie comedy in the mid-Fifties had taken on a decidedly hollow ring. When MCA, on the strength mainly of its television interests, became outright owner of Universal, and Lucille Ball's television company Desilu took over lock stock and barrel the old RKO studios where she had once been a starlet, the revolution was symbolically complete.

What the revolution meant was that there was no longer one vast, uniform movie-going public which went ritually and regularly to see movies outside their own homes. Instead there were many different publics, and among the most important, and certainly the most faithful, was what had formerly been the negligible specialist group of movie buffs who went to see foreign-language movies, non-commercial and avant-garde movies and revivals. The rise of the French New Wave of critics-turned-film-makers, and all their romantic ideas about the classic Hollywood cinema, summed up in the notorious *auteur* theory, gave a new impetus to this new way of looking at movies: Hollywood companies found that there was gold in their long-neglected vaults and specialist distributors found that they might be handling the surprise hit of the season. In the great days of the movie, those involved were too busy doing what they were doing to think too much about it. During the Fifties practice was supplemented by, or sometimes gave way to, theory. It was then that the kind of interest was born which has made publications like this a practical possibility today.

John Russell Taylor

New channels for movies

Changing life-styles affected moviegoing in post-war America and attendances declined. Hollywood figured: if you can't beat the TV companies, then either make films for them or sell them old ones

Afterwards, the victims of the late Forties and early Fifties in Hollywood remembered the panics. They remembered Jack Warner screaming into the studio, pointing to contract artists one by one, bellowing: 'I can do without you! And you! And you!' They also remembered that the columnist Hedda Hopper, in a moment of uncharacteristic shrewdness, had warned in *The Hollywood Reporter* (May 1950):

'Television is the one medium that I don't believe Hollywood can give the old run-around; so we might as well take the TV producers by their hot little hands and cooperate.'

They remembered the obdurate studio heads, and the long process of convincing them that Hollywood was really changing, that the studio machine had cracked, that television mattered, both as a rival and as a potential source of revenue for the film industry, and that new and damaging forces were abroad.

The adjustment was painful, and the studios managed to mask it and evade it for a while by introducing wide-screen processes and big, splashy hits. But the industrial structure of Hollywood, already rocked in the Forties by the antitrust laws and by social changes, was radically altered in the Fifties by a declining demand for movies and the increased independence of stars, directors and writers, all striking out their own to save on income-tax bills.

In place of the comfortable process of making assembly-line product for tied houses, uncertainties abounded. A movie might disappear soon after shooting or make a wholly unexpected profit. Nobody knew. The panic of men like Jack Warner may have reflected the more visible threat of television, but it also testified to an unformed awareness that the industry was becoming a game of chance.

The simplest reason for the panic was the steady but inexorable decline in audience figures since the astonishing highpoint of 1946. Hollywood managed to fool itself about the full extent of America's loss of interest in regular moviegoing. Official estimates from within the film industry had proved too pessimistic, by tens of percentage points. The economic panic of the Forties came largely from banks and boardrooms where financiers believed the movies were doing even worse than they actually were. In the Fifties the movie industry gained resilience because those figures had been discredited as a result of closer analysis.

As movies slipped, television grew, but that is very far from the whole story. Film attendances declined from 1947, long before most American cities had television. For a while, TV expansion was frozen while manufacturers solved problems of interference. By 1948, a million TV sets had been sold in the USA, but the average weekly cinema attendance showed a decline to 90 million. America was losing the filmgoing habit before television was an established substitute.

By 1951, the decline in movies and the rise of

television were indissolubly linked in Hollywood's panicky mind. Cities that were part of TV networks were losing their movie audience – by as much as 40 per cent. Cinemas began to close down: 51 in New York since the war, 64 in Chicago, 134 in Southern California. Yet the moguls ignored some other factors which might have made them take a less simple view of the phenomenon. Cities receiving TV tended to be the expanding cities, the fattest markets, the most affluent communities.

After the Depression and its necessary, if hysterical, emphasis on work, the post-war years carried a sort of liberation. As the home and the immediate community became more and more important, two things happened. Physical barriers came between Americans and the movies – many

Top: Virginia Grey and Dan Dailey in Hullabaloo *(1940), one of the first films to show a TV set as home furniture. It was to be another ten years, however, before television presented a genuine challenge to cinema as the prime public entertainment medium. Above: by 1959, the film industry's somewhat desperate attitude to TV was typified in this scene with David Niven from* Happy Anniversary

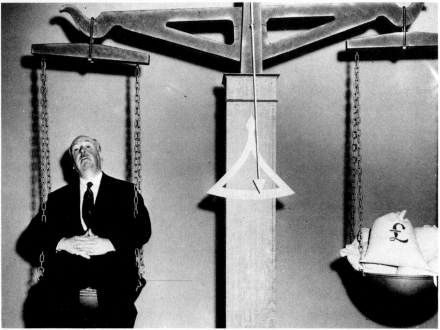

Top: television meets the movies; at the 1953 Academy Awards ceremony Frank Sinatra receives his Oscar for From Here to Eternity (1953). Top right: Warner Brothers TV shows from the Fifties (clockwise from bottom left): Sugarfoot, Hawaiian Eye, Cheyenne, Lawman, Maverick, 77 Sunset Strip, Bronco, Alaskans, Bourbon Street Beat, Colt 45. Above: a typically jokey opening to the Alfred Hitchcock Presents TV series

lived in suburbia and the big cinemas were in the downtown areas; young children made demands on young parents and the new affluence meant that the big Saturday-night escape was less of an event than it had been during the Depression. Cinema was becoming an occasional diversion.

Such social changes meant that Hollywood's emphasis on battling TV with bigger, better pictures would not work in the long run. Drive-in theatres and, in the next decade, cinemas in suburban shopping malls were much more important in bringing back audiences.

As far as Hollywood was concerned, something had to be done about TV. One film from 1959 (Happy Anniversary) even showed David Niven kicking in a television set, and Jack Warner forbade the sight of a TV set in a single frame of Warners film.

For all their fundamental differences, however, movies, radio and TV had a long history of alliance. Radio Corporation of America founder of the NBC networks helped found RKO Radio Pictures; in 1929 it was Paramount's money which staked the struggling radio company CBS; in the Forties 20th Century-Fox agreed to release its Movietone News on TV five nights a week; even MGM, the most conservative of the majors, bought into a Los Angeles TV station. In 1949, Columbia established Screen Gems, a subsidiary that would handle films for television. By the early Fifties, the first important deal between a studio and a network took place: Disney sold a family-entertainment series called Disneyland to ABC-TV.

The terms and the publicity surrounding the Disney deal finally convinced Jack Warner to join

the game. He sold Warner Brothers Presents, a series of 50-minute dramas to which were attached 10-minute trailers for Warners stars and movies currently on release. The Warners series contained shows entitled Casablanca, Kings Row and Cheyenne. The latter was perhaps the most influential series ever. Warners made a profit on the $75,000 spent on each show, plus a bonus of $37,500 for each summer re-run. Jack Warner got publicity and ABC-TV came out of the deal with 40 hours of guaranteed glossy programmes for the year 1955–56.

The new TV movies bore a reassuring resemblance to the old product of Poverty Row. Films were made on low budgets with five-day schedules and limited ambitions. These were industrial products, pre-sold (as movies had been to chains of cinemas) with a built-in profit margin. They did not require huge publicity budgets, since the TV habit guaranteed their audience. Other studios joined the rush:

In the uncertain climate of the early Fifties, Hollywood was forced to make overtures to TV companies

MGM Parade and 20th Century-Fox Hour followed the Warners lead in mounting TV shows with some of their top contract players in 50-minute featurettes.

Then in 1955, the unthinkable happened. RKO was in grave financial trouble. The corporation had suffered grievously as a result of being divorced from its cinema circuits. The bankers looked at the books and discovered that RKO's movies made only thirty cents in every one dollar of company profit. The rest of the revenue came from the cinemas – huge assets that were barely maintained and cheap to run. RKO without their cinemas were a bad bet. Their bankers lost confidence and RKO needed cash. They earned it by selling out their movies (shorts and features alike) to television.

Significantly the deal was struck not with a TV network, but with an intermediary company that was in business to distribute movies for TV. The total price of the RKO package of films was $5 million – an average per feature film of barely $20,000.

The deal opened up the lucrative territory of screening old movies on TV. In time, TV sales came to constitute a source of revenue that was the salvation of the film companies. Television determined the basis of whole production programmes and was considered a kind of fail-safe device. Screen Gems rented pictures from Columbia and also televised some pre-1948 Universal films. Sales of movies to TV inevitably gave rise to contractual problems with artists, writers and directors who claimed fees for the rescreening of their work.

Anyone distributing movies to TV made a fortune, and television companies suddenly saw how they could fire most of their staff, run movies round the clock and have guaranteed audiences for minimal effort. The TV deals by major studios probably did more than any other single factor to boost the uninventiveness of American TV. They discouraged the evolution of a tradition of TV drama: movies for TV provided the networks with easy programming and gave the studios an illusion of a business which had found its stability again.

Between 1948 and 1959, all the major studios were forced by antitrust law to enter into 'consent decrees' whereby film-production companies were required to sell their cinema chains, and to stop block-booking. They could no longer sell all their

movies to some country cinema, with the implicit threat that the cinema would get all or nothing at all. These decrees had radical effects: they reinforced Hollywood's post-war emphasis on the notion of hit films. Instead of gearing their studios to assembly-line production, the moguls aimed for single, one-off successes. Darry F. Zanuck declared this policy for 20th Century-Fox in 1946; Columbia and Universal followed suit. MGM talked about economizing on budgets by trimming the length of their movies. Theirs was the most traditionally organized studio, but by 1958 MGM had also switched to a 'single hit' policy.

It had become clear that a movie with certain key

elements which augured success was more likely to be booked by independent cinema owners and could be sold at higher prices. Big stars, thousands of Nubian slaves and a Cole Porter score – or any combination of the above – became the means of selling films to choosy cinema owners as well as to the public.

In the course of the Fifties, the studios realized that the cost of maintaining staff contracts for high-volume production was uneconomic in the face of declining revenue. Furthermore, once the cinema chains had been divorced from the major production companies, the hidden subsidies (whereby profits from cinemas had been channelled into productions) were no longer available. Stripped of their cinema assets and the profits that accrued from them, the studios were themselves less bankable and needed formulas for success that would convince accountants and loan officers. Suddenly, big screens and spectacle were promoted and helped make cinema movies the sort that 'Can never be seen on TV'.

At this point in Hollywood's history, the tested formulas of the Thirties (star-teaming, serials, and so on) were thrown aside and movies became a chance game. The industry needed only a slight setback to topple into serious trouble although it could still be wildly successful.

Hollywood remained cheerful. For a while, it seemed as if wide-screen processes might save the business and take it to new heights. One Cinerama documentary (whose finest moment was a point-of-view shot from a roller coaster) grossed more than $20 million in only 13 cities and ran for more than three years. But Cinerama was an expensive process to install and guaranteed no flow of product.

Also in the early Fifties, 3-D came and went. Hitchcock used it brilliantly in *Dial M for Murder* (1954) but other directors simply heaped flying objects into the audiences' laps. 3-D required awkward technology and uncomfortable glasses for its viewers. VistaVision, another wide-screen process, was introduced and *White Christmas* (1954) became a commercial success for Paramount on the strength of it. The rival was CinemaScope. In retrospect it was hard to distinguish between the success of the process itself and the success of the production programme used to launch it.

The new Hollywood optimism of the mid-Fifties was derived from gimmicks and single hit films. In this new climate, talent was no longer automati-

Above left: tall in the saddle, Clint Walker and Andrew Duggan as the US marshall in an episode from Warners' made-for-TV Western series Cheyenne. *Left: Ray Milland and Grace Kelly in Hitchcock's* Dial M for Murder, *a thriller in which a man frames his wife for a murder. It was notable for Hitchcock's experiments with 3-D. Below left: Paramount's* White Christmas *was the first film to be released in the new VistaVision wide-screen process*

Top: Charles McGraw as Humphrey Bogart's successor in the role of Rick in the Warners TV series Casablanca. *Top right: the construction of a drive-in cinema in California, a sign of the changing pattern of film exhibition in the Fifties. Above: James Stewart in the title role of* The Glenn Miller Story, *a film whose box-office take proved that Universal ranked among the major studios of the Fifties*

cally contracted to one studio, although Universal and MGM were reluctant to give up their roster of stars. Actors went freelance and agents were beginning to exploit the fact. American tax laws made it sensible for the stars to appear to be independent; rather than sell their services and their labour, it suited actors better to be associated with completed movies. In this way they would pay 25 per cent tax on a sum which, had it been paid as salary, would have been subject to 70 per cent.

As a result of this new independence, stars whose names alone might encourage banks to lend money, cinemas to rent movies and audiences to attend, could begin to state their prices.

They may not have known it, but Hollywood majors were becoming dependent on independent productions. In 1949, for example, only 20 per cent of the movies released were made independently of the major studios; in 1959, almost 60 per cent of American movies were made by independent companies. Of course, independence is an equivocal term; major studios still put up large sums of money – and sometimes all the money – for independent films, thereby exerting a powerful influence over what was made. But the fact remains that the movie marketplace had become disorganized. The passion for hits meant that 'name talent' (leading stars) placed a high premium on their skills. As the demand for movies continued to drop, production costs began to soar. Agent power supplanted studio power. The majors became increasingly passive.

Among the big companies, power balances had already shifted. Once the antitrust laws had finally divorced cinemas from film production, the smaller studios could compete in the market to produce main features. Columbia released *From Here to Eternity* (1953), United Artists put out *High Noon* (1952), Universal, once a studio dominated by serial and sequel production, produced *The Glenn Miller*

Story (1953) and *Magnificent Obsession* (1954). The position of the older, undisputed majors (MGM, Paramount, 20th Century-Fox and Warner Brothers) was less solid. The most spectacular success story of Hollywood in the Fifties was the turn-around in the fortunes of United Artists. In the late Forties, United Artists had been torn apart by

As the old studio system crumbled, independent production became the new battle cry. Maverick producers and wealthy stars formed one-off partnerships with the Hollywood majors to make block-buster films

disputes among the stockholders, but after re-organization during 1950–51 it thrived in its new role as a financing and distribution arm for independent movies.

Independent producers grabbed a new power in Hollywood and seemed to make films more efficiently, possibly because they did not have studio overheads to worry about. Hal Wallis, Norman Krasna and Jerry Wald survived brilliantly as producers, even after they had been fired or encouraged to leave by panicky studio bosses. Thoughtful movies from Stanley Kramer, and his quieter partners Carl Foreman and Richard Fleischer, and brasher stuff from Wallis and his peers, all kept the Hollywood distribution machine at work. A new structure was established in which the independent producers still had to sell their product through the existing networks of the Hollywood majors. The strict discipline of the old studio system was undermined by greed and wilfulness on the part of stars and producers. But the consent decrees did not bring an end to the oligopoly the majors operated in film distribution and exhibition, nor did they put an end to the restrictive practices of the huge cinema chains.

Hollywood's new customers were fickle and highly selective about what they went to see, but a single hit could keep a major studio financially safe for a year. Studio economics had changed radically but studio structures had not. The majors were still major.

As Hollywood entered the Sixties, the film business had such basic problems that the studios would not even think about them. In short, the studio system made less and less sense. If Hollywood gambled and lost, the industry might dissolve. That story is for the Sixties. But its roots were in the Fifties – the decade when the production of motion pictures went from an industry to a gamble in a mere ten years.   MICHAEL PYE

Zanuck's formula worked, and the company recorded a healthy profit every year from 1935 onwards, thanks to such top hits as *In Old Chicago* and *Alexander's Ragtime Band* (both (1938), *Jesse James* (1939), all starring Tyrone Power, and the Technicolor productions of *Kentucky* (1938) and *Drums Along the Mohawk* (1939). These last two films were part of an ambitious programme in Technicolor which Zanuck embarked on in 1938. It was also during the late Thirties that Zanuck decided to turn his efforts toward raising the prestige of 20th Century-Fox to match its commercial success. He hired a number of top creative talents who helped to boost the quality of production: lighting cameraman Leon Shamroy, art directors Boris Leven, Richard Day and Wiard Ihnen; costume designer Travis Banton; and music director Alfred Newman. Finally there was the director John Ford, who was reaching the peak of his career and averaged two films per year from 1939 to 1941.

During the early Forties prestige productions were divided between two main categories. The first was the 'serious' black-and-white film – John Ford's *The Grapes of Wrath* (1940) and *How Green was My Valley* (1941), Henry King's *The Song of Bernadette* and William Wellman's *The Ox-Bow Incident* (both 1943). The second group comprised costume action pictures and Westerns in colour – Fritz Lang's *The Return of Frank James* (1940) starring Henry Fonda; Rouben Mamoulian's remake of *Blood and Sand* (1941), his first colour film since *Becky Sharp* (1935); and Henry King's *The Black Swan* (1942), the first Technicolor swashbuckler on the high seas.

The high quality of 20th Century-Fox Technicolor continued during the mid-Forties but then, after Henry King's *Wilson* (1944) and John M. Stahl's *Leave Her to Heaven* (1945), it lapsed into a conventional pattern. Musicals most often had a cast headed by Betty Grable, whose two biggest hits were in *The Dolly Sisters* (1945) and *Mother Wore Tights* (1947). Another

20th Century-Fox will always be associated with prestige productions and big budgets. But even the success of their Technicolor and CinemaScope movies did not spare the studio its ups and downs

The origins of 20th Century-Fox can be traced back to the beginnings of the American cinema during the early years of this century. In 1904 William Fox, a Jewish Hungarian immigrant, sold a profitable clothing company and first entered the arcade and nickelodeon business. He gradually developed an interest in film exhibition, distribution, and finally production, leading to the formation of the Fox Film Corporation in 1915. His first star of note was the legendary Theda Bara who appeared in almost forty pictures from 1915 to 1919.

Fox continued to grow during the Twenties and was close behind Warners in adapting to sound. In 1929 William Fox bought control of Loews Inc, the parent company of MGM, but after a Federal antitrust investigation and prolonged litigation the deal was reversed. In the reorganization that followed, William Fox was forced out of the company he had founded and which continued to bear his name. But soon afterwards the studio was hit hard by the industry-wide Depression 1931–33 – and it lacked the strong leadership which Fox had provided.

At about this time Darryl F. Zanuck had resigned from his position as production head at Warners-First National. He convinced Joseph Schenck, president of United Artists, to join him in the formation of a new independent production company, Twentieth Century Pictures, in 1933.

Although Fox recovered during 1933–35, the studio was still weak, and had only three major stars – Janet Gaynor, Will Rogers and Shirley Temple. As a first step towards revitalizing the company, Fox was merged on May 29, 1935 with the smaller, but healthier Twentieth Century, which remained the dominant force in the new company. Its two leading executives – Zanuck and Schenck – took over and brought with them the Twen-

tieth Century logo with its beaming searchlights and fanfare music to introduce the films of 20th Century-Fox.

Zanuck also brought with him one established name, Loretta Young, and immediately began to develop a new group of potential stars – Sonja Henie, Tyrone Power, Alice Faye, Don Ameche. Meanwhile Shirley Temple continued to perform as the company's biggest box-office asset. The emphasis was on romance and musical comedy in an American setting, on entertainment and on success at the box-office.

Below: Huston, Zanuck, Welles and Hedda Hopper on the set of Roots of Heaven *(1958)*

with a number of less-than-memorable musicals, the prestige works tended to stress romance and adventure, and were generally adaptations from popular novels set in exotic or foreign locations.

After the departure of the two leading post-war directors, Elia Kazan and Joseph L. Mankiewicz, and of Howard Hawks who had contributed three films of note between 1949–53, the studio obviously suffered from a shortage of creative film-makers. Added to this was a lack of executive leadership, particularly after the resignation of Zanuck in 1956. Director Henry King had also passed his peak: he had first been under contract to the old Fox company from 1930 and then at 20th Century-Fox ever since. His career had ranged from the Will Rogers – Janet Gaynor *State Fair* (1933) up to *Tender is the Night* (1962) starring Jason Robards and Jennifer Jones, and along the way he discovered Tyrone Power, who played some of his best roles under King's direction. Possibly King's most successful collaboration was with Gregory Peck during the early Fifties

Left: Tyrone Power in Captain from Castile. *Right: Marilyn Monroe starred in this successful 1955 comedy. Below: one of the long line of musicals,* The Dolly Sisters *starred Betty Grable and June Haver as the musical-comedy stars Jenny and Rosie Dolly*

formula for success was the horsey-doggie picture – *Smoky* (1946) and *Thunder in the Valley* (1947) – or else the occasional lavish costume picture like *Forever Amber* and *Captain from Castile* (both 1947).

While the colour pictures continued to do well in terms of receipts, the quality and variety of the black-and-white productions provide a clear indication that the studio was at its peak. There were Westerns – *My Darling Clementine* (1946) and *The Gunfighter* (1950); war pictures – *A Walk in the Sun* (1945) and *Twelve O'Clock High* (1949); socially conscious films – *The Snake Pit* (1948), *Pinky* (1949), and *Gentleman's Agreement*, which won the Best Film Oscar in 1947; thrillers filmed on authentic exterior locations – *Call Northside 777* (1948), *Panic in the Streets* (1950); and two delightful Cary Grant comedies from Howard Hawks – *I Was a Male War Bride* (1949), and *Monkey Business* (1952) which provided Marilyn Monroe with one of her first featured roles. Then there was *All About Eve*, the top Oscar winner in 1950 with two awards going to writer-director Joseph L. Mankiewicz. In addition the studio continued to distribute the highly successful *March of Time* series and the cartoon shorts – *Terrytoons* – from producer Paul Terry, starring Mighty Mouse and the talking magpies Heckle and Jeckle.

In fact, film revenues held up well through the late Forties, and a moderate decline in the early Fifties was decisively reversed by the introduction of CinemaScope; *The Robe* (1953) went on to become the studio's biggest hit of the decade. The company also pioneered the introduction of an improved magnetic stereophonic sound. Yet when they announced that all future productions would be in colour and CinemaScope, their policy failed to take account of the fact that not all subjects were equally suited to this format; and although it was not strictly adhered to, it gave the studio a particularly glossy and perhaps superficial image throughout the rest of the Fifties. Along

on such movies as *The Gunfighter* (1950), *David and Bathsheba* (1951) and *The Snows of Kilimanjaro* (1953).

In addition, the studio was slow to recognize that it had under contract the biggest star to emerge in Hollywood during those years – Marilyn Monroe. She had made her first big impact in 1953 as the star of *Niagara* with Joseph Cotten and Jean Peters. Following this came Howard Hawks' *Gentlemen Prefer Blondes* (1953) with Jane Russell, and the early CinemaScope picture *How to Marry a Millionaire* (1953) which also featured Betty Grable and Lauren Bacall. But Marilyn did not really triumph until two years later with the Billy Wilder production of *The Seven Year Itch* (1955), scripted by George Axelrod from his own play, and her success was soon confirmed by *Bus Stop* (1956) – again scripted by Axelrod, but this time under director Joshua Logan.

Clearly, the company still had its fair share of stars during the Fifties, and these top names

boosted the box-office value of otherwise unremarkable products – though they could not save them altogether.

With the income from *The King and I* (1956), *Peyton Place* (1957) and Joshua Logan's *South Pacific* (1958) the company continued to record a small profit, but none of these could compare with the receipts from *The Robe* – the original CinemaScope release. The company was in the red by 1959–62; major losses in feature-film production were partially disguised by income from the sale of 260 acres of studio land. A loss of over $60 million during 1961–62 included expenditure of over $30 million on the disastrous *Cleopatra* (1963) and a $2 million write-off on Marilyn Monroe's last, unfinished picture *Something's Got to Give*.

A remarkably large number of the most interesting and successful films continued to be in black-and-white – *The Three Faces of Eve* (1957), *Compulsion* (1959), *The Diary of Anne Frank* (1959), *Sons and Lovers* (1960), *The*

Above: the studio back lot with parade from
Hello, Dolly! Top right: the recent box-office
success Star Wars. *Above right: the studio head*
Sherry Lansing as an actress in Rio Lobo.
Right: Hope Lange confesses her murder to
Lana Turner in Peyton Place

Hustler (1961) and *The Longest Day* (1962). This
latter was the last in a series of films independently produced for 20th Century-Fox by
Zanuck, who was suddenly brought back to
replace Spyros Skouras as president of the
corporation in the crisis year of 1962. (Skouras
had led the business side of things since the
death of Sidney Kent in 1942.)

Zanuck ruthlessly set about reducing studio
staff and overheads, scrapping unlikely projects, and most important of all, completing
Cleopatra. It was revenues from this (finally
released in 1963) and from *The Longest Day* that
helped put the company on the road to re-
covery. Furthermore, the incredible success of
The Sound of Music (1965), along with such hits
as *Those Magnificent Men in Their Flying Machines* (1965) and *The Valley of the Dolls* (1967)
managed to counterbalance expensive flops
like *Dr Dolittle* (1967) and *Star!* (1968). Nevertheless the studio was in trouble once again
when *Hello, Dolly!* (1969) and *Tora! Tora! Tora!*
(1970) failed to recoup their substantial costs,
and massive losses caused the final departure
of Zanuck in 1971.

In spite of their setbacks 20th Century-Fox
did come up with some interesting films during
that period. They restored a measure of their
former prestige with a group of tougher, male-
orientated genre movies – *Planet of the Apes*
(1967), a science-fiction entry starring Charlton Heston, and *Butch Cassidy and the Sun-
dance Kid* (1969), an entertaining Western by
George Roy Hill. In 1970 came two excellent
but contrasting war pictures – the Oscar-
winning *Patton* and Altman's *M*A*S*H* – and
finally William Friedkin's award-winning
thriller *The French Connection* (1971). It was

this film, along with Ronald Neame's *The
Poseidon Adventure* (1972), that first helped the
company to move back into profit.

Between 1975–77 a run of hits boosted
revenues further, and the phenomenal popularity of George Lucas' *Star Wars* (1977),
followed by Ridley Scott's *Alien* (1979), confirmed once again the studio's position as one
of the most successful film companies in the
States. Early in 1980, 20th Century-Fox appointed the first woman to head a major
Hollywood studio – Sherry Lansing, who had
appeared in small roles in *Loving* and Howard

Hawks' last Western *Rio Lobo* (both 1970).
Thanks to the achievements of Irvin
Kershner's *The Empire Strikes Back* (1980), the
expensive and long-awaited sequel to *Star
Wars*, she has had some breathing space to
develop her own projects.

The ups and downs experienced by the
entire film industry during the Sixties and
Seventies could be seen at their most extreme
in the case of 20th Century-Fox. No other
company demonstrated so clearly the un-
predictable nature of the industry, yet managed to survive so well.   JOEL FINLER

The Wilder side of life

'They say Wilder is out of touch with his times. Frankly I regard it as a compliment. Who the hell wants to be in touch with these times?'
                                                    Billy Wilder in 1976

In Mitchell Leisen's *Hold Back the Dawn* (1941), a gigolo, played by Charles Boyer, has fled war-torn Europe and waits impatiently at the Mexican border for an entry-visa so he can get into the USA. He and the other refugees gaze longingly at the checkpoint, which consists of a wire fence, an immigration office and, beyond that, an extraordinary archway of welcome and promise with the legend 'The United States' emblazoned across it. The archway resembles nothing less than a cinema marquee on Sunset Boulevard.

Hold Back the Dawn was written by Charles Brackett and Billy Wilder and was one of several films of the period designed to influence American opinion about the war in Europe. It is the most overtly biographical of Wilder's films. Wilder was part of the artistic and intellectual exodus from Europe in the early Thirties, and for film-makers like Fritz Lang, Max Ophuls, Otto Preminger, Robert Siodmak and Wilder, America *was* Hollywood, as the *Hold Back the Dawn* set amusingly suggests. Appropriately, at the end of the film, the gigolo sells his story to Paramount Pictures.

The Europeans on the run from Hitler were to exert a profound influence on the American cinema, just as earlier emigrés like Ernst Lubitsch and Victor Sjöström did in the Twenties. Their cultural heritage and recent traumatic experience brought a visual exoticism, a sophistication and wit, a sourness and a pessimism lacking in the more homespun,

Below: Don Taylor and William Holden as POWs in Stalag 17. *Below right: the romantic comedy* Love in the Afternoon *starred Gary Cooper as a playboy and Audrey Hepburn as the young girl who beguiles him*

optimistic visions of native American directors like Howard Hawks and King Vidor. The European sensibility permeated all genres and Wilder's contribution – his unrivalled series of satires, thrillers and romances – was to be as significant as any.

Not just a gigolo

He was born Samuel Wilder in 1906 in Sucha, Austria (now part of Poland), into a fairly rich Jewish family. After completing his studies in Vienna, Wilder entered journalism and scored a few notable coups, interviewing Freud, Richard Strauss and Arthur Schnitzler. He moved to Berlin in 1926 where he gained a reputation as a crime reporter who specialized in daring exposés. He also claims to have been a gigolo, entertaining well-to-do ladies at the Adlon Hotel. Berlin was then the world's cultural centre and its expression of decadence; the German cinema, based at the Ufa studios, was technically and stylistically more advanced than any other. Apart from *Menschen am Sonntag* (1929, *People on Sunday*), made as a kind of challenge to the glossy Ufa style, Wilder's early films as a scenarist were mainly zestful comedies and light romances which, despite their limitations, contain glimmers of the Wilder to come – particularly in their Viennese humour, the play with deception and mistaken identity, and the lure of America and Hollywood.

Wilder packed his bags for Paris the day after the Reichstag fire in February 1933. (Many of his relations who stayed behind were to perish in concentration camps.) He had a rough time in Paris – though it would later be the setting for some of his most enchanting films – but was able to direct his first feature

there, the recently rediscovered *Mauvaise Graine* (1933), a freewheeling comedy-drama about car thieves. The film ends as the hero and heroine are about to set sail for America. Wilder's own departure soon followed, his route taking him via Mexico.

Within five years of arriving in Hollywood, Wilder had attained a position of some eminence. His scripts with Brackett, notably *Bluebeard's Eighth Wife* (1938), *Midnight, Ninotchka* (both 1939), *Hold Back the Dawn* and *Ball of Fire* (1941), were models of their kind and made the pair the highest-paid writers in the industry. (Their partnership was dissolved in 1950 and since 1957 Wilder's collaborator has been I.A.L. Diamond.) Wilder's first four features as a director in America – *The Major and the Minor* (1942), *Five Graves to Cairo* (1943), *Double Indemnity* (1944) and *The Lost Weekend* (1945) – demonstrated his versatility and were all critical and commercial successes. Wilder also

Above: Billy Wilder and Marilyn Monroe arrive at the press reception for Some Like It Hot. *Above right: in the film Monroe was Sugar Kane, a tipsy band-singer involved with a musician (Tony Curtis) and his buddy who dress in drag to escape from gangsters*

promoted himself effectively, and rapidly became one of Hollywood's most celebrated wits, his picturesque insults and wisecracks entering folklore and forming the basis of three hagiographies.

Despite the occasional dispute at Paramount, the 'Europe in Exile' studio where he worked from 1937 to 1954, Wilder could do no wrong. He provided intelligence and entertainment in equal measure. Sadly, Wilder's position today is very different from that of, say, the early Sixties when he collected three personal Oscars for *The Apartment* (1960) and could name his own price. His most recent film,

Fedora (1978), was financed with German tax-shelter money and only received limited distribution. The archway to Hollywood was no longer welcoming, Universal terminated his contract after *The Front Page* (1974), and Wilder found himself behind the wire again, making his film in Europe. But *Fedora* is Wilder's testament, arguably the greatest film of his entire career.

Memories of old Europe

It is important to stress Wilder's background for it appears in his films in the fundamental structural opposition between Europe and America. Inevitably, Wilder's feelings about both are deeply ambivalent and this accounts for much of the tension in his work.

His evocations of Europe are tinged with melancholy, the humour being a safeguard against emotional indulgence, as in the pre-Occupation Paris of *Ninotchka*, the re-creation of Lubitschean Vienna in *The Emperor Waltz* (1948), the devastation of Berlin in *A Foreign Affair* (1948) and that city's East-West partition in *One, Two, Three* (1961). In Wilder's Parisian films the tone is always romantic and in the Berlin films the tone is astringent; both are nostalgic.

Nearly half of Wilder's output is set in some expressive European location and in using places with autobiographical associations – Vienna, Berlin, Paris – Wilder is obviously lending a certain authenticity to his films. But a closer examination reveals that he is exploring a geography more psychical than physical that has less to do with place than moral values. Paris, for instance, rarely registers as a location in the filmic sense – Wilder prefers to set his scenes in hotel rooms and, for *Irma La Douce* (1963), rebuilt Les Halles in Hollywood – but it is intensely felt as a spiritual influence. Europe, in the romances at least, functions as a place of rehabilitation, educating New Worlders in a manner reminiscent of Henry James.

Time and time again Wilder despatches Americans to Europe where they undergo a process of humanization. The purest example of this is *Avanti!* (1972), in which a harassed

Filmography
1929 Der Teufelsreporter (sc. only); Menschen am Sonntag (co-sc. only) (USA: People on Sunday). **'31** Der Mann, der Seinen Mörder Sucht (sc. only) (USA: Looking for His Murderer); Ihre Hoheit Befiehlt (co-sc. only) (co-sc. only on French version: Son Altesse Ordonne/Princesse à Vos Ordres, 1931; and USA version: Adorable, 1933); Der Falsche Ehemann (co-sc. only); Emil und die Detektive (sc. only) (USA/GB: Emil and the Detectives). **'32** Es war Einmal ein Waltzer (sc. only); Ein Blonder Traüm (co-sc. only) (USA: Blonde Dream) (co-sc. only on British version: Happy Ever After, 1932; and French version: Un Blond Rêve, 1932); Scampolo, ein Kind der Strasse (co-sc). only) (GER-A); Das Blaue von Himmel (co-sc. only). **'33** Madame Wünscht Keine Kinder (co-sc. only) (GER-A); Was Frauen Traümen (co-sc. only) (USA: What Women Dream) (co-sc. only on USA version: One Exciting Adventure, 1935); Mauvaise Graine (co-dir;+co-sc) (FR). *All remaining films USA unless specified*: **'35** Music in the Air (co-sc. only); Lottery Lover (co-sc. only). **'37** Champagne Waltz (co-sc. only). **'38** Bluebeard's Eighth Wife (co-sc. only). **'39** Midnight (co-sc. only); What a Life (co-sc. only); Ninotchka (co-sc. only). **'40** Arise My Love (co-sc. only); Rhythm on the River (co-sc. only). **'41** Hold Back the Dawn (co-sc. only); Ball of Fire (co-sc. only). **'42** The Major and the Minor (+co-sc). **'43** Five Graves to Cairo (+co-sc). **'44** Double Indemnity (+co-sc). **'45** The Lost Weekend (+co-sc). **'48** The Emperor Waltz (+co-sc); A Foreign Affair (+co-sc). **'50** Sunset Boulevard (+co-sc). **'51** Ace in the Hole (+prod; +co-sc) (GB: The Big Carnival). **'53** Stalag 17 (+prod;+co-sc). **'54** Sabrina (+prod;+co-sc) (GB: Sabrina Fair). **'55** The Seven Year Itch (+prod;+co-sc). **'57** The Spirit of St Louis (+co-sc); Love in the Afternoon (+prod;+co-sc); Witness for the Prosecution (+co-sc). **'59** Some Like It Hot (+prod;+co-sc). **'60** The Apartment (+prod;+co-sc). **'61** One, Two, Three (+prod; +co-sc). **'63** Irma La Douce (+prod;+co-sc). **'64** Kiss Me, Stupid (+prod;+co-sc). **'66** The Fortune Cookie (+prod;+co-sc) (GB: Meet Whiplash Willie). **'70** The Private Life of Sherlock Holmes (+prod;+co-sc) (GB). **'72** Avanti! (+prod;+co-sc). **'74** The Front Page (+co-sc). **'78** Fedora (+prod;+co-sc) (GER).

Baltimore executive (Jack Lemmon) goes to Italy to reclaim his father's corpse. Because of bureaucratic complications he is delayed and consequently discovers a potential for life he never knew existed. This may sound trite or overly schematic on the page but in the context of a long career and as performed by Lemmon, Wilder's regular and most brilliant interpreter, *Avanti!* becomes a deeply moving personal pilgrimage and a masterpiece of discreet exegesis. This strand of Wilder's career, which also includes the underrated *Sabrina* (1954) and *Love in the Afternoon* (1957), in which the all-American personas of Humphrey Bogart and Gary Cooper are reconstituted in the light of European experience, contains some of Wilder's most elegant and characteristic work, demonstrating his high regard for Lubitsch. However, it is the more caustic side of Wilder, the Stroheim side, which has received more general critical acclaim.

It is significant that in *A Foreign Affair* and *One, Two, Three* the occupying American forces – GIs in the former, Pepsi Cola in the latter – signally fail to impose their set of values on the Europeans. The transformation process never works in reverse. When they are denied access to Europe and its life-enhancing potential, Wilder's Americans are the victims of paranoia, motivated by greed and sexual enslavement, and either wind up dead or, just as

disconcertingly, renouncing secure material values at the call of personal, moral principles. Wilder's heroes have to choose between money and happiness and the mark of the hero's maturity (and Wilder's esteem) is in his choosing of the humanist rather than the materialist option. Films in this group include *Double Indemnity*, a classic *film noir* co-scripted with Raymond Chandler, *Ace in the Hole* (1951), *Stalag 17* (1953), which uses a German POW camp as a microcosm of the civilian rat-race, *The Apartment*, *Kiss Me, Stupid* (1964) and *The Fortune Cookie* (1966).

Playing his ace

Wilder's tendency in these films is to sympathize with the individual rather than the group but he stops short of actually endorsing his hero's attitudes or actions. A character like Chuck Tatum (Kirk Douglas) in *Ace in the Hole* will enliven a sterile community but the cost in personal and moral terms is unaccountably high. Tatum is a 'yellow' journalist who prolongs one man's suffering in order to whip-up human interest. The site of this modern morality play is a remote desert area, as arid as its inhabitants, and immediately the crowds

Above: Shirley MacLaine as the French whore who captivates the gendarme (Jack Lemmon) in Irma La Douce. *Above right: Lemmon, as an aspiring executive, and MacLaine, as the elevator girl sleeping with his boss, in* The Apartment. *Right: Wilder's courtroom drama starred Dietrich as a treacherous wife*

arrive seeking some kind of vicarious excitement. Although Tatum investigates the story (and dies for his trouble), Wilder's hatred is reserved for the mob, perhaps even for his own audience and, indeed, *Ace in the Hole* played to empty cinemas and upset Wilder's relations with Paramount.

Love American-style

Similarly, an important Wilder film like *Kiss Me, Stupid* presented such a bleak picture of middle-America that Wilder was the victim of a sustained press campaign against him. Only *The Apartment* received wide acclaim, its devastating critique of the American success ethic seemingly diluted by the growing love between its victims, C.C. Baxter (Jack Lemmon) and Fran Kubelik (Shirley MacLaine). Yet · *The Apartment* is not a glossy comedy but a disturbing portrait of urban loneliness and at the end Baxter and Miss Kubelik are homeless and jobless. It is not exactly the happiest ending in movies.

But if these films are variously virulent hate-letters addressed to America, Wilder has also written two love-letters as well, unequivocal tributes to American innocence and exuberance but both significantly 'distanced' by being set in the Twenties: *The Spirit of St Louis* (1957), an almost Fordian biography of Lindbergh, and the classic comedy *Some Like It Hot* (1959).

Some Like It Hot is probably Wilder's best-loved film and its daring plot contrivance – Lemmon and Tony Curtis play Jerry and Joe, two musicians who disguise themselves as girls after they witness the St Valentine's Day Massacre and have to escape – lies at the heart of Wilder's preoccupation with role-playing and transformation. There are outrageous impersonations in *The Major and the Minor* (Ginger Rogers as a 12-year-old), *Witness for the Prosecution* (1957, Marlene Dietrich as a cockney tart) and *Irma La Douce* (Lemmon as an elderly English Lord) but the point is not the effectiveness of the disguise but its very transparency. The comical identity crises of characters like Jerry, when his female self takes over in *Some Like It Hot*, are lighter versions of the torments of characters like Fedora, Norma Desmond in *Sunset Boulevard* (1950) and Sherlock Holmes in *The Private Life of Sherlock Holmes* (1970). This last is perhaps Wilder's most deeply moving study of the psychological split between private lives and public personas.

Some like it Hollywood

There is a cinematic allusiveness in all of Wilder's films (*Ace in the Hole*, for example, can be approached as an allegory concerning Hollywood methodology; *Kiss Me, Stupid* is certainly that) which is expressed through various homages and the use of specific performers. James Cagney in *One, Two, Three*, applying gangster methods to international trade; William Holden and Jack Lemmon playing virtually the same roles in successive films; Marilyn Monroe in *Some Like It Hot* playing herself in all but name; appearances by real-life directors like Cecil B. DeMille and Erich von

Above right: Avanti! *cast Lemmon and Juliet Mills as strangers who go to Italy to collect the bodies of their respective (and recently deceased) father and mother, who had been lovers; they then embark on an affair of their own. Right: William Holden as the ageing film producer Barry Detweiler in* Fedora

Stroheim – these devices all reveal an acute awareness of Hollywood mythology. This allusiveness is most intensely realized in *Sunset Boulevard* and *Fedora*, two explorations of Hollywood image-making that have as many intriguing points of confluence as divergence. *Fedora* is a rich summation, the poignancy of the occasion oddly transcended by the exalted expression. A film of constantly shifting moods and perspectives, *Fedora* – in which a washed-up film producer attempts to lure an elderly star out of retirement – casts a nostalgic eye over the old Hollywood and a rueful eye over the

new. Its very defiance of modishness – its concern for narrative and character – makes it one of the most beautiful of modern films.

Wilder's wittily sardonic views of the American Dream gone sour, of Europe, Hollywood, and of manners and morals in general do not lose their sharpness – or their poignancy – with the passing of time. Norma Desmond, talking of silent pictures in *Sunset Boulevard*, says, 'Still wonderful, isn't it?' Thirty years later the words apply equally well to Billy Wilder's classicism and to *Fedora* in particular.
ADRIAN TURNER

The Blonde Gentlemen Prefer

The trials and tribulations and the incendiary mixture of wide-eyed innocence and sumptuous sexiness have often obscured the fact that Marilyn Monroe was a supreme talent, 'as near genius as any actress I ever knew' said Joshua Logan who directed her in *Bus Stop*. There was certainly no-one else like her . . .

Hollywood's great stars seldom seem to have been the products of happy homes and stable childhoods. Chaplin's father walked out on the family when his son was one year old, and Fairbanks' when Douglas was four. Mary Pickford's father died when she was four, Valentino's when he was eleven, Garbo's when she was thirteen. Marilyn Monroe was never even certain who her father was: he may have been a mechanic called Mortensen or a film-laboratory employee called Gifford, or a Mr Baker who was the father of her elder brother and sister. For safety's sake, early publicity gave it out that whoever he was he had been killed in a car crash shortly after the birth of his daughter.

Like Chaplin again, Marilyn was committed to an orphanage after her mother retreated into madness. In her case the legacy of mental instability was more terrifying: her maternal grandfather and grandmother – a fanatical disciple of the evangelist Aimee Semple Mac-Pherson, in whose temple Marilyn was baptised Norma Jeane Mortensen – ended their lives in mental institutions.

Unlike the other great stars, however, Norma Jean (the final 'e' only appears on her birth certificate) was a child of the movie capital. She was born, on June 1, 1926, in the Los Angeles General Hospital. Her room in the

Los Angeles Orphan home is said to have looked directly onto the neon sign over RKO studios, and Marilyn later told interviewers that one of the most wonderful memories of her childhood was a Christmas party given by RKO for the orphan children, when she was nine. None of her biographies or interviews reveal at what age this apparently lonely, shy and introverted girl conceived the determination to become a movie star; but that determination must have been single-minded and steely to survive the inevitable years of disappointment and frustration that she was to experience after her first arrival at 20th Century-Fox.

At the time World War II ended she was working in an aircraft factory, testing parachutes, when a photographer taking official propaganda pictures spotted her potential and introduced her to an agent, Emmeline Snively. By 1946 she was launched as a pin-up and cover girl, and a smart publicity stunt secured a test at Fox. Ben Lyon, the actor, who was then the studio's talent scout, advised her to change her name: Monroe was her grandmother's married name; Marilyn was Lyon's suggestion – a tribute to an earlier star, Marilyn Miller. She was signed by Fox for a year and went through the familiar processing of potential starlets: she was photographed; given

a couple of small parts – one of which, in *Scudda Hoo! Scudda Hay!* (1948) was entirely cut out – but the studio did not renew her contract.

By this time, however, Marilyn seems already to have been actively organizing her career. She kept up her classes at the Actors'

'Hollywood's a place where they'll pay you a thousand dollars for a kiss, and fifty cents for your soul. I know, because I turned down the first offer often enough and held out for the fifty cents'

Laboratory where she had been enrolled by Fox; acquired the first of the personal drama coaches who were later to try the patience of her directors; and made good use of the admirers, advisers, patrons and protectors – the most significant of them was the agent Johnny Hyde, thirty years her senior – whom she readily attracted. She won a featured role in a Columbia musical, *Ladies of the Chorus* (1948), was chased by Groucho Marx in *Love Happy* (1949), and received her first small but favourable critical attention for the role of a crooked lawyer's girl in *The Asphalt Jungle* (1950). Its director John Huston – who some 11 years later was to guide her patiently and painfully through her last completed film, *The Misfits* (1961) – told her, 'You know, Marilyn, you're going to be a good actress'.

She had already had half a dozen small parts when she walked through *All About Eve*

had advised the film business, 'Don't fool yourself. This girl is a coming star'. Much later, on Laurence Olivier's *The Prince and the Showgirl* (1957), there appears to have been a touching mutual admiration and affection between Marilyn and the veteran Dame Sybil Thorndike.

The three years between *Niagara* and *Bus Stop* (1956) were the peak of her professional career, a period comparatively untroubled by the personal problems that were eventually to dog her. A keen judge of material – her intelligent rejection of scripts often caused friction with the studio – she regretted Otto Preminger's *River of No Return* (1954) as a miscalculation, a crude exploitation of her sexual attractions.

It is almost inconceivable now that so many of Marilyn's contemporaries were sceptical about her technical achievements and about her ambitions to be a serious artist – her touchingly demanding literary pursuits and her work with Lee and Paula Strasberg at the Actors' Studio in New York. Her performances in *Gentlemen Prefer Blondes* and *How to Marry a Millionaire* show a refined and precious comic talent; in the latter she plays an acutely myopic beauty forever crashing into walls when, from vanity, she discards her enormous spectacles. In *There's No Business Like Show Business* (1954), developing her endearing, funny, baby singing voice, she parodies the conventions of the stage musical star. In *The Seven Year Itch* (1955) she proves an altogether equal comedy partner to old hand Tom Ewell and outstrips the director Billy Wilder with the subtlety of her comic effects. The climax of this period of her career, however, is reached in Joshua

Above left: Marilyn Monroe – 'a beautiful profile all the way down' – with Yves Montand (in tails) in Let's Make Love. *Top: Marilyn's look and Groucho's leer in* Love Happy. *Above and below: dramatic roles in* The Asphalt Jungle *and* Don't Bother to Knock. *Right: as Lorelei Lee in* Gentlemen Prefer Blondes, *with Jane Russell*

(1950), leaving behind one of the first authentic 'Monroisms'. As Miss Caswell, a starlet, she arrives at a party on the arm of stage critic Addison DeWitt (George Sanders) who suavely introduces her to Margo Channing (Bette Davis), 'You know Miss Caswell, of course?' 'No', Margo mercilessly snaps back. 'That', smiles Miss Caswell guilelessly, 'is because we

never met.' Marilyn became well known for such deceptively artless and worryingly enigmatic ripostes.

The public had already noticed her, and her parts became bigger and more significant. In 1952 Fox made the mistake of casting her in a dramatic role – as a psychopathic girl in *Don't Bother to Knock*. The notices and the box-office returns were bad, but in retrospect it is a creditable performance, with moments of intuition and intensity which may well have been stirred by the parallels to her own childhood.

The three Marilyn Monroe films that were released in 1953 – *Niagara*, *Gentlemen Prefer Blondes* and *How to Marry a Millionaire* – definitively established her as a star and a new sex image for the age. *Niagara*, Henry Hathaway's tongue-in-cheek handling of a torrid melodrama of passion, teamed Marilyn's own natural splendours with the Niagara falls – and introduced 'The Walk' with a 70-foot shot of Marilyn undulating away from the camera in uncomfortable high heels across cobble-stones. Her unique ambulation was a celebration of her sensuous physique, a positive percussion and choreography of limbs, buttocks and the thighs that seem to have an extra curve (she always gave out her *upper* and *lower* hip measurement). In *Gentlemen Prefer Blondes* she was teamed with Jane Russell, and in *How to Marry a Millionaire* with Betty Grable and Lauren Bacall. It was no doubt Monroe's presence that made both films major box-office hits; but she always seemed to work well with other actresses of character and intelligence and to inspire their liking. Working with her on *Clash by Night* (1952), Barbara Stanwyck

Above: Marilyn as a saloon singer in River of No Return. *Right: as gold-digger Pola with Mr Denmark (David Wayne) disproving that men never make passes at girls who wear glasses in* How to Marry a Millionaire

Logan's *Bus Stop*, with a comic performance of flair and charm and pathos that transcends the stage-bound screenplay.

Already Marilyn was regarded as a 'difficult' actress. Her attendances on the set became more and more erratic. For a while she abandoned Hollywood for New York and her mentor, Lee Strasberg. At this time too she acquired Paula Strasberg, his wife, as a new

> *'I want to be an artist . . . not an erotic freak. I don't want to be sold to the public as a celluloid aphrodisiacal'*

drama coach to replace Natasha Lytess. First married at 16, Marilyn later became the wife of the baseball star Joe Di Maggio in 1954, but the marriage foundered after a year. A third marriage to the playwright Arthur Miller and her appearance alongside Olivier in *The Prince and the Showgirl*, her only British film, seemed the culmination of her cultural ambitions.

Her private life had begun to darken, however. Already there was the horrifying dependence on drugs, and prolonged periods in mental clinics. The unpunctuality and absenteeism which had first seemed a caprice were revealed as symptoms of sickness. She

became hard to work with. She is charming and funny in Billy Wilder's *Some Like It Hot* (1959), but her co-star Tony Curtis said, 'Kissing Marilyn Monroe was like kissing Hitler'. Curtis wears women's clothing for most of the film and Marilyn serenely retorted to his ungallant remark, 'He only said that because I had prettier dresses than he did'.

Let's Make Love (1960) was the most insignificant film of her later career, despite George Cukor's direction and the lift to her morale provided by her affair with co-star Yves Montand. Finally she struggled through *The Misfits*. Her marriage to Arthur Miller – who

had scripted the film and had clearly based the character of Roslyn on his wife – was breaking up. She was sick, frequently quite incapacitated by narcotics, and repeatedly hospitalized. Still Marilyn's performance is one of the finest of her career: she seemed only to gain in depth and insight. Some of her most touching scenes are those when Roslyn expresses her horror at the inhumanity of the men to the mustangs they are catching: Marilyn always revealed an extreme and even neurotic empathy with animals and children.

She began work, again with Cukor, on *Something's Got to Give* in 1962. But she

appeared on the set only 12 times in the first month of shooting. Fox fired her and sued for compensation. Seven weeks later, on August

'Talent is developed in privacy . . . but everybody is always tugging at you. They'd all like sort of a chunk of you. They'd kind of like to take pieces out of you'

5, she died from a drug overdose. She was 36. The few brief sequences that she had shot for *Something's Got to Give* showed a new and metamorphosed Marilyn. There was little trace of the round-faced pin-up of the early days in this woman of breathtaking grace, beauty, luminosity and awful fragility. In a series of costume tests she walks and walks again (and by this time she no longer undulates, but floats); and the hieratic, ritual magic of the rushes is haunting and unforgettable.

Marilyn belonged to the last years of the studio system and the last real generation of stars. Her contemporaries included Grace Kelly, Audrey Hepburn, Marlon Brando, James Dean, Kim Novak and the grown-up Elizabeth Taylor. She hated being a sex symbol ('I thought symbols were something you clash'); yet she was one of the most potent embodiments of sexuality the screen has ever known. It seemed to emanate from her own exultation and fascination with her physique and sexuality. 'I'm very certainly a woman and I enjoy it,' she said. She was said to wear her dresses two sizes too small so that she was always conscious, from their clinging, of every part of her body. She liked to look at herself in mirrors. When she moves or stands or sits, she gives the impression that she is unconsciously feeling and testing and *enjoying* every limb and nerve. The nude bathing scene filmed for *Something's Got to Give* survives, an act of solitary devotion.

With the sexuality, however, there went a refined comic technique. We can never know to what extent it was instinctive and to what extent developed by her very intense and serious studies in the studios and with her drama coaches. Certainly there is nothing accidental about her management of the cabaret scene in *Bus Stop* as she struggles through 'That Old Black Magic', and there is something almost mystical about her ability to

Above left: as the bruised, bewitching Sugar in Some Like It Hot. *Above: the serene beauty of Marilyn Monroe – caught in a relaxed mood while filming* The Misfits

shift mood from low-comedy to the heart-touching pathos of which she was uniquely capable.

'I'm not interested in money,' she told a somewhat surprised early producer, 'I just want to be wonderful'. That ambition she achieved, triumphantly.   DAVID ROBINSON

Filmography
1947 Dangerous Years. '48 Ladies of the Chorus. '49 Love Happy. '50 A Ticket to Tomahawk; The Asphalt Jungle; The Fireball; All About Eve; Right Cross. '51 Home Town Story; As Young As You Feel; Love Nest; Let's Make It Legal. '52 Clash by Night; We're Not Married; Don't Bother to Knock; Monkey Business; O. Henry's Full House *ep* The Cop and the Anthem (GB: Full House). '53 Niagara; Gentlemen Prefer Blondes; How to Marry a Millionaire. '54 River of No Return; There's No Business Like Show Business. '55 The Seven Year Itch. '56 Bus Stop. '57 The Prince and the Showgirl (GB). '59 Some Like It Hot. '60 Let's Make Love. '61 The Misfits. '62 Something's Got to Give (unfinished).

Burt Lancaster:

Whether working in Hollywood or in Europe, Burt Lancaster has always sought challenging roles and shown an interest less in conventional stardom than in professional fulfilment

the quixotic actor

Burt Lancaster is the acrobat who turned film star and then serious actor, and his most memorable film work has probably been that which came easiest to him. There were the tongue-in-cheek adventures like *The Crimson Pirate* (1952), in which he peformed his own stunts, and other films in which he could be equally uninhibited playing charlatans and rogues, larger-than-life figures who cast a spell over their audience, such as *The Rainmaker* (1956) and *Elmer Gantry* (1960). He won an Oscar for portraying the fiery preacher in the latter film, but claimed: 'Elmer wasn't really acting – it was me.' Because it came so naturally to Lancaster, it was a powerful and convincing portrayal. The actor sought out more demanding parts and was keener to extend his acting range than to chase box-

office popularity. He even went to Italy to work with Visconti in *Il Gattopardo* (1963, *The Leopard*) and *Gruppo di Famiglia in un Interno* (1975, *Conversation Piece*) and with Bertolucci in *1900* (1976).

Lancaster has been shrewd and realistic about his screen career, as well as stubborn and demanding in his often quarrelsome relationships with directors. Laurence Olivier, for example, found him unmanageable on *Separate Tables* (1958) and quit the picture. But his accomplished work with Robert Siodmak, Robert Aldrich, Richard Brooks, John Frankenheimer and Sydney Pollack testifies to his ability to work with talented directors more than once (five times, in fact, with Frankenheimer) when he sees eye to eye with them.

Born in 1913 in a poor section of New York,

Top: early, swashbuckling Lancaster in Crimson Pirate. *Above left: one of his first roles was in the family melodrama* All My Sons *(1948). Above: he was unhappy playing an alcoholic in* Come Back, Little Sheba

Lancaster discovered his talent for gymnastics as a boy. He and a friend, Nick Cravat, became circus performers during the Thirties until a finger infection compelled Lancaster to seek less athletic work. In 1942 he was drafted and toured Europe entertaining servicemen. In 1945 his looks and manner earned him a part in a Broadway play, even though he had never studied acting; his performance impressed the critics and Hollywood talent scouts.

He showed the first signs of an independent streak in retaining the freedom to choose

outside film work when he signed up with producer Hal Wallis. In fact, it was the films of another producer, Mark Hellinger, which gave his screen career such a strong start.

In *The Killers* (1946) Lancaster played the brooding Swede whose passive acceptance of a violent death was the puzzle the film unravelled; in *Brute Force* (1947) he was one of the tough convicts set on breaking out; in *Criss Cross* (1949) he was an armoured car driver – with a double-crossing ex-wife – who gets involved with a gang of crooks. In films like these, with their strong visual styling and consistent dark mood, it did not matter whether Lancaster had much acting ability or not: his virile looks and muscular figure were enough to see him through.

Although Lancaster had made a late start as a screen actor, he quickly went into production for himself in partnership with his agent Harold Hecht. They made the lurid and unconvincing *Kiss the Blood Off My Hands* (1948), then more wisely embarked on a costume romp, *The Flame and the Arrow* (1950), in which Burt (joined by his old partner Nick Cravat) could climb, leap, swing, swash and buckle with an exuberance that recalled Fairbanks Sr and Flynn in their prime. Other such zestful entertainments quickly followed – none more delightful than *The Crimson Pirate* (1952), in which Lancaster deftly prepares us for the

fantastic happenings at the start by welcoming us aboard his pirate vessel and telling us, as he swings between the masts: 'Ask nothing! Believe all that you see! No, believe only *half* of what you see.'

In *Vera Cruz* (1954) Lancaster brought the same heady excess of roguish high spirits to the Western, which showed again when he revived his career in 1966 with his colourful portrayal of a mercenary in *The Professionals*; told by the woman he has abducted to go to hell, he lightly responds: 'Yes, ma'am, I'm on my way.'

Lancaster was attracted to parts in which he could express his concern over racial oppression. In *Apache* (1954), he played the role of an Indian in lone resistance to the army; in *The Unforgiven* (1960) he was the rancher who stood up for his half-breed foster sister (Audrey Hepburn); in *Valdez Is Coming* (1971) he was the Mexican-American lawman who refused to stay in his place; while back in 1951 he had portrayed a celebrated real-life Indian athlete in *Jim Thorpe – All American*.

In several films where the actor played villains, his quiet-spoken, calm but intense manner made them all the more menacing: he was memorable as the evil gossip columnist J.J. Hunsecker in *The Sweet Smell of Success* (1957), while in *Seven Days in May* (1964), *Executive Action* (1973) and *Twilight's Last*

Above left: Lancaster in a rare love scene – with Deborah Kerr in From Here to Eternity. *Above: portraying Robert Stroud the murderer/ornithologist in* Birdman of Alcatraz. *Below: he won an Academy Award for his portrayal of the fiery preacher* Elmer Gantry. *Bottom: as a French Resistance leader saving art treasures he confronts Paul Schofield in* The Train *(1964). Bottom left: he tries his hand at political intrigue in* Seven Days in May

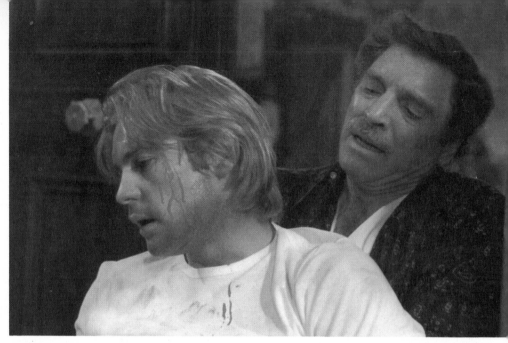

Gleaming (1977) he was a political intriguer against the President and the State.

These parts needed the authority and power that Lancaster embodied, although at other times he tried to suppress this aspect of his personality. He succeeded in *Birdman of Alcatraz* (1962) with his portrayal of convicted murderer Robert Stroud, who becomes a noted ornithologist from his cell; but he was uncomfortable in roles like the middle-aged, tempted ex-alcoholic of *Come Back, Little Sheba* (1952), the failed writer of *Separate Tables* or the German judge on trial in *Judgement at Nuremberg* (1961). One could admire the effort, but one could sense the strain. Similarly one could respect the actor for denouncing the agreeable but lightweight *Airport* (1970) as 'the biggest piece of junk ever made' and preferring to star in such offbeat films as *The Swimmer* (1968).

There were disappointments. The actor's production company wound up after losing money making the kind of films Lancaster preferred; his ventures into direction – *The Kentuckian* (1955) and (with Roland Kibbee) *The Midnight Man* (1974) were not well received; and in *The Gypsy Moths* (1969) he was unfairly ridiculed for his love-making scenes with Deborah Kerr because of their age, compared to the sensational affair they had conducted in *From Here to Eternity* 16 years earlier.

If recently Lancaster has not found the right parts to suit a performer of his advancing years, he remains an actor who cares about the work he does and the meaning it has, and is unusually conscientious about the responsibilities of screen stardom. ALLEN EYLES

1946 The Killers. '47 Brute Force; Desert Fury; Variety Girl (guest); I Walk Alone. '48 All My Sons; Sorry, Wrong Number; Kiss the Blood Off My Hands (GB: Blood on My Hands) (+co-pc). '49 Criss Cross; Rope of Sand. '50 The Flame and the Arrow (+co-pc); Mister 880. '51 Vengeance Valley; Jim Thorpe – All American (GB: Man of Bronze); Ten Tall Men (+co-pc). '52 The First Time (co-pc only); The Crimson Pirate (+co-pc) (GB); Come Back, Little Sheba. '53 South Sea Woman; From Here to Eternity; Three Sailors and a Girl (guest); His Majesty O'Keefe (GB). '54 Apache (+co-pc); Vera Cruz (+co-pc). '55 Marty (co-pc only); The Kentuckian (+dir.; +co-pc); The Rose Tattoo. '56 Trapeze (+co-pc); The Rainmaker. '57 The Bachelor Party (+co-pc only); Gunfight at the OK Corral; The Heart of Show Business (short) (guest); Sweet Smell of Success (+co-pc). '58 Run Silent, Run Deep (+co-pc); Separate Tables (+co-pc). '59 The Devil's Disciple (+co-pc) (GB); Take a Giant Step (co-pc only). '60 The Unforgiven (+co-pc); Elmer Gantry; Summer of the Seventeenth Doll (pc only) (AUS) (USA: Season of Passion). '61 The Young Savages; Judgment at Nuremberg. '62 Birdman of Alcatraz (+co-pc). '63 A Child is Waiting; The List of Adrian Messenger (guest); Il Gattopardo (The Leopard) (IT-FR). '64 Seven Days in May; The Train (FR-IT-USA). '65 The Hallelujah Trail. '66 The Professionals. '68 The Scalphunters; The Swimmer. '69 Castle Keep; The Gypsy Moths. '70 King, a Filmed Record . . . Montgomery to Memphis (retitling for TV: Martin Luther King) (doc); Jenny is a Good Thing (doc) (narr. only); Airport. '71 Valdez is Coming; Lawman. '72 Ulzana's Raid. '73 Scorpio; Executive Action. '74 The Midnight Man (+co-dir; +co-sc; +co-prod; +co-pc). '75 Gruppo di Famiglia in un Interna (Conversation Piece) (IT-FR) (+Eng. Lang. version+It. Lang. version); Ali the Man; Ali the Fighter (doc) (guest). '76 Moses; Moses – the Lawgiver (IT-GB); 1900 (IT-FR-GER); Buffalo Bill and the Indians, or Sitting Bull's History Lesson. '77 The Cassandra Crossing (GB-IT-GER); Twilight's Last Gleaming; Victory at Entebbe; The Island of Dr Moreau. '78 Go Tell the Spartans. '79 Zulu Dawn (USA-NETH). '80 Cattle Annie and Little Britches.

Top: again Lancaster finds himself defending art treasures as a battle-weary soldier in Castle Keep *(1969). Top right: his excursions to Italy include a role as a professor whose privacy is invaded by Helmut Berger in* Conversation Piece. *Above: as an ageing Indian fighter he leads a bloody counter-attack on Apaches in* Ulzana's Raid *(1972). Below: as a Mexican bandit Lancaster shows little concern for privacy in* Valdez is Coming

Cold war cinema

At the start of the Fifties, America was in the grip of anti-communist hysteria. Hollywood found new dramatic material in the McCarthyite purges: the 'Reds' were the latest villains of the piece

The speed of the Allied victory against Japan was only made possible because of the success of the Manhattan Project, the operation based at Los Alamos, New Mexico, which manufactured the first atomic bombs. The capture of Iwo Jima, less than eight square miles of volcanic ash, had cost the lives of 6000 US marines with a further 17,500 wounded. The casualty list at Okinawa ran to 49,151. If the Japanese decided to defend their five principal islands with that sort of tenacity, the American Joint Chiefs of Staff estimated that Japan could probably hold out until well into 1948. America would, therefore, incur losses greater than the sum total of those killed since Pearl Harbor.

In the event two A-bombs were enough. On August 6, 1945, one bomb containing the equivalent of 20,000 tons of TNT was dropped on Hiroshima. In one minute a thriving city was obliterated; over 70,000 people were killed. On August 9, 39,000 people died in a second nuclear explosion at Nagasaki. Five days later, in the face of extreme opposition from fanatical militarists, the Emperor Hirohito publicly announced Japan's capitulation.

Far from being a 'war to end all wars', World War II had been terminated in a manner that everyone acknowledged could prove merely the harbinger of a future holocaust.

The concept of a nuclear Armageddon seemed to stultify film-makers. MGM approached their story of the making of the bomb in the traditional glossy manner, but reduced its budget when they realized just how fraught with danger the production was. *The Beginning or the End?* (1947), a studio-fabricated account of the Manhattan project, seemed at first to be an echo of *Madame Curie* (1944) and other

scientific-discovery films. It had a fictional framework and a romantic sub-plot involving a young scientist and his bride. However, whereas radium, the electric light bulb and other such advances had been of benefit to mankind, the value of the atomic bomb was clearly dubious.

Other films, like *Seven Days to Noon* (1950) and *Strategic Air Command* (1955), toyed with the theme but similarly failed to reconcile the idea of a nuclear holocaust with entertainment. Stanley Kubrick's black comedy *Dr Strangelove, or How I Learned to Stop Worrying and Love the Bomb* (1964) was probably the most successful film on the subject.

In February 1946, after only nine months of

Above left: Senator Joseph McCarthy uses the new medium of television to further his fanatical purges of alleged communists in American society. Above: in the second round of HUAC investigations into Hollywood, Robert Taylor was among the actors who testified to J. Parnell Thomas. Below: the acting chairman of HUAC in 1950, Senator Karl Mundt, reading the news of the conviction of Alger Hiss, an alleged communist spy

'peace' in Europe, demobilization of the Soviet army was halted and the emphasis in the current five-year plan was switched from consumer goods back to armaments. The Cominform (Communist Information Bureau) was established in 1947 to replace the Comintern (an earlier international organization of Communist Parties) and the spy system in the western world was significantly strengthened. The Cold War had arrived.

The war was fought not only in Europe and Asia, but also on the home front where the House Un-American Activities Committee (HUAC) continued its work. It is possible to measure the change in temperature of the Cold War by comparing HUAC's work in Hollywood in 1947 with its investigations into the film industry three or four years later.

After the Ten were jailed, a certain amount of witch-hunting in Hollywood was apparent. In the early Fifties the practice became enshrined in an actual blacklist, but in 1947 the vetting was negative rather than positive. The trade paper *Variety* reported quite openly that Katharine Hepburn had been discarded as a possibility for the lead in Leo McCarey's *Good Sam* (1948). McCarey told

Top: Janet Leigh as a ballerina being deported by the communist authorities in The Red Danube. *Above:* The Iron Curtain, *directed by William Wellman, was one of the first anti-communist propaganda films and starred Dana Andrews in a dramatization of the case of a Russian defector who sold secrets to the Canadian government. Above right: the arrest of a communist agitator in* The Red Menace. *Right: an action scene from Anthony Mann's* Strategic Air Command *(starring James Stewart), the story of the planes that carried America's atomic bombs during the Cold War*

Variety's reporter that in view of Miss Hepburn's political sympathies, he would offer the role to Ann Sheridan. Similarly, unconfirmed reports that Dalton Trumbo was working on a script for Sam Goldwyn, and that John Howard Lawson was writing one for Walter Wanger, were quickly denied by the respective producers. In 1947–48 the atmosphere in Hollywood, as in the country at large, was fiercely anti-communist but not yet paranoid.

In the autumn of 1949 came the announcement that the Russians had closed the missile gap by exploding their first nuclear bomb. The triumph of the Berlin airlift, which only six months previously had persuaded the Russians to call off their blockade of the city, now seemed futile. Fear of communism spread like a contagion.

In the wake of the unpalatable investigations conducted by HUAC in 1947, the American film industry had already decided to show how clean its hands were by producing anti-communist films. The disease which gripped the country in 1949 served only to strengthen that resolve. Darryl F. Zanuck, produced the prototype of the burgeoning genre: *The Iron Curtain* (1948). This was followed

Movies in the cold war traded on *film noir's* paranoia and sci-fi's fear of being taken over by aliens

rapidly by such memorably titled but artistically negligible films as *The Red Danube*, *The Red Menace* (both 1949) and *I Married a Communist* (1951).

In 1949 the Republican congressman Richard Nixon secured the conviction of the former State Department official, Alger Hiss, on a charge of espionage, and politicians of both major parties were convinced that America's major institutions were swarming with communist traitors. A primary list seemed to include Roosevelt and Truman, the labour unions, Alger Hiss, Secretary of State Dean Acheson and the entire State Department. The rising tide of anti-intellectualism was also useful to the witch-hunting factions. HUAC was the most publicized aspect, but the years 1949–50 saw the mushrooming of various committees dedicated to the elimination of all communist propaganda. Mostly they concentrated on stalking local libraries and bookstores for books they considered to be pro-communist. *The Grapes of Wrath* was one of the first books designated for burning.

Ironically, in 1949, reports reached the West that the John Ford film *The Grapes of Wrath* (1940) was doing wonderful business behind the Iron Curtain. Performances were preceded by a lecturer who pointed out that the picture of dispossessed Okies was an accurate portrait of general conditions in present-day USA.

Zanuck modified the story somewhat when he told *Variety* that the Russians had re-dubbed and re-edited a print of *The Grapes of Wrath* to prove that the Okies were typical Americans, but when the print reached Yugoslavia it had to be hastily withdrawn from circulation because the living standard of the Joad family was seen to be better than that experienced by the Yugoslavian people at the time.

One US politician benefitted from the hysteria even more than Richard Nixon. On February 9, 1950, Senator Joseph McCarthy, the junior and almost unknown Senator from Wisconsin, delivered a speech to the Women's Republican Club in Wheeling, West Virginia, in which he claimed to have a list of 205 employees of the State Department who were known to Dean Acheson (the Secretary

of State) as being members of the Communist Party.

McCarthy never managed to make any of his charges stick – but then he didn't need to. He was talking to a country that was seemingly desperate to prove him right. In Wheeling, West Virginia, where it all began, a violent controversy started when it was discovered that inside packets of US bubble gum were certain give-away cards informing unwary children that the USSR, with its population of 211 million, had its capital in Moscow and was 'the largest country in the world'. The corrupting cards were removed from circulation.

Mrs Thomas J. White, a member of the Indiana State Textbook Commission, charged: 'There is a communist directive now to stress the story of Robin Hood . . . because he robbed the rich and gave it to the poor. That's the communist line. It's just a smearing of law and order.'

The incidents piled on each other, progressing from the comic and the bizarre to the sinister and the tragic. Fearing the wrath of the new HUAC investigations, Monogram Pictures cancelled a projected 'biopic' on Henry Wadsworth Longfellow on the grounds that Hiawatha's peace activities might be construed as propaganda for a communist peace initiative. HUAC, now under the chairmanship of

Above: the patriotic Robert Walker starred in The Beginning or the End? *MGM's tribute to the scientists and troops who developed and tested America's atomic bomb. The film's title was taken from a speech by President Truman. Below: Barry Jones as Professor Willingdon in the Boulting Brothers'* Seven Days to Noon, *the major British contribution to the Fifties wave of films about the potential for nuclear war. The professor threatens to explode a bomb in London unless the world powers sign a nuclear weapons ban. Suddenly he is a wanted man and all London is looking for him*

NEW BOXOFFICE POWER

ALLIED ARTISTS

...the new major company explodes into ACTION...not plans or promises...but a powerhouse line-up of COMPLETED top "A" pictures packed with CINEMASCOPE, TECHNICOLOR and BIG STAR CASTS! Our answer to your product shortage is on the following pages. Allied Artists is on the move, in the news, ready for boxoffice action!

Above: the film distributors Allied Artists chose the most potent image of the day to boost their launching campaign. Below: the Russians had their own spy dramas as Secret Mission *testified. Below right: the Soviet film* Conspiracy of the Doomed *showed envoys of the Vatican plotting with the CIA to bring about the downfall of communism in Europe*

Senator John Wood from Georgia, was even more iniquitous than it had been under the rule of J. Parnell Thomas (who was by then serving a prison sentence for padding the Congressional payroll with his relatives).

This time the Committee headed straight for the actors. Sterling Hayden, Will Geer, Lee J. Cobb, John Garfield, Gale Sondergaard, José Ferrer, Karen Morley, Howard da Silva and Larry Parks, amongst others, were subpoenaed. Some recanted and some didn't; all were asked for 'names'. This second series of investigations, which ran parallel with

McCarthy's own 'inquiries', resulted in the infamous blacklisting of all people whose views were in the slightest way suspect. The talent that was thus expelled might not have been especially important, but the climate of fear and suspicion these investigations engendered in the film business led to a near-fatal sterility of ideas in Hollywood in the Fifties.

Meanwhile the anti-communist films continued to roll off the production line. No fewer than 13 were made in 1952. Even such clean-cut, all-American figures as Robert Taylor, in *Conspirator* (1949), and Robert Walker, in *My Son John* (1952), were apparently salaried employees of the Kremlin. Sam Goldwyn, with a glove-maker's eye for a bargain, ordered the re-editing of his pro-Russian war film *The North Star* (1943) and the addition of a new commentary to suggest that the little Russian village under attack from the Nazis was really a little East European village under attack from the Russians, who were carrying on in the tradition of barbarism.

Not that the Russians were any less unscrupulous in their own anti-American propaganda films. *Secret Mission* (1950) also recast history in Cold War terms, depicting the attempts of an American intelligence agent and a Senator to effect a separate peace with Hitler in 1945. The film ends with the Americans preparing to launch a new offensive against the Soviet Union. *Meeting on the Elbe* (1949) revealed more of the anti-Soviet policies of US forces in post-war Germany. *Court of Honour* (1948) exposed a network of Russian scientists passing secrets to the Americans and *Conspiracy of the Doomed* (1950), in a plot of bizarre imagination, revealed, for the first time, the sordid conspiracy between the Vatican and the CIA to undermine communism in Eastern Europe.

The comic-book approach of such films gives only a faint indication of the suspicion and hysteria aroused by the Cold War. It should be remembered that McCarthy had warned of a North Korean invasion months before it happened in June 1950 and that General MacArthur had been proved wrong when the Chinese entered the war six months later.

Though it took considerable time for the American public to accept the fact, the two super-powers to emerge after 1945 were of fairly equal strength. If the USA claimed nuclear superiority, the Russians could point to the increasing spread of communism around the world. World War II had neatly labelled the two warring sides 'Right' and 'Wrong' and ensured the correct result. In the Cold War of the Fifties, the Americans re-labelled the opposing sides but the battleground for this war of propaganda was now on the airwaves and in the media, and film would continue to play its influential role in the conflict.

COLIN SHINDLER

Olivier's Heights

Laurence Olivier's towering achievements in the theatre have overshadowed his work in the cinema. Yet whether in his own daring adaptations from Shakespeare, or in his many superbly realized romantic and character roles, Olivier has time and again proved his great talents on film

Spencer Tracy once called Olivier 'the greatest screen actor of them all', a tribute that is particularly remarkable in that it comes from the one actor who could legitimately lay claim to the title. Yet because Olivier has always considered himself first and foremost a stage actor (a consideration for which he was rewarded with the first peerage ever given to an actor), critics have been inclined to regard his screen career as of secondary importance.

It comes, therefore, as something of a surprise to realize that Olivier has thus far made nearly sixty films. The list is dominated by his three major Shakespeare adaptations – *Henry V* (1944), *Hamlet* (1948) and *Richard III* (1956) – but his screen work began as far back as 1930, in which year he played in a 'quota quickie' called *Too Many Crooks*.

His career can be divided into four phases. First, in the Thirties, came his films as a romantic juvenile lead: there are roughly fifteen of these, leading up to William Wyler's *Wuthering Heights* (1939) which was the first production to give Olivier any real respect for the cinema. Until then it had been on his own admission a place to make money in between the stage appearances that were his *raison d'être* as an actor. After some early and best-forgotten comedies, such as *The Temporary Widow* (1930) and *Potiphar's Wife* (1931), he had been ignominiously sacked by Greta Garbo from *Queen Christina* in 1933, thereby confirming his own belief that he was not cut out to be a film star.

Despite one early attempt at screen Shakespeare (as Orlando in Paul Czinner's *As You Like It*, 1936, opposite the enchantingly miscast Elisabeth Bergner) the Thirties were not a very happy time for Olivier; although his prestige as a stage actor continued to grow, he was generally only ever considered for film roles that Leslie Howard or Ronald Colman were unwilling or unable to accept. Not until the meeting with Wyler did he find a director who could teach him the basic techniques of film acting. Until then, 'stagey' is the word that best describes much of his screen work, even in such acknowledged successes as *Fire Over England* (1937), the first of the three films he made with his future second wife Vivien Leigh.

But then came Wyler and *Wuthering Heights*, though again Olivier only got to play Heathcliff after Ronald Colman proved unavailable and Robert Newton had done a poor test for the role. Olivier's acting won him the first of nine Oscar nominations.

'Looking back', he said later, 'I was snobbish about films until *Wuthering Heights* . . . then, gradually, I came to see that film was a different medium and that if one treated it as such and tried to learn it humbly, with an open mind, one could work in it. I saw that it could use the best that was going; it was Wyler who

Left: Olivier, sporting a medieval haircut, studies the script of Henry V, *which he directed and starred in. Above: Henry at the siege of Harfleur*

gave me the simple thought – "if you do it right, you can do anything". And if he hadn't said that I'd never have done *Henry V* five years later.'

In the meantime came *Rebecca*, *Pride and Prejudice* (both 1940) and *That Hamilton Woman!* (1941) as well as one or two guest appearances for the war effort in Britain. There is little doubt that had Olivier stayed in Hollywood he could have become another of the screen's great romantic Englishmen. But, as he was once quoted as saying, somewhat uncharitably. 'I don't wish to become just another film star like dear Cary'; if he were going to act in front of a camera again, it would be on his own terms and those terms were now Shakespearean.

Rooted in an English classical tradition (Olivier was born, the son of a clergyman, in Dorking on May 22, 1907) he began to look upon the filming – and therefore the popularizing – of Shakespeare as something of a personal crusade. He initially hoped to involve Vivien Leigh (whom he had married in the USA in 1940 after divorcing his first wife, the

Above: Olivier with Mina Burnett in his first film, Too Many Crooks. *Below: Olivier's*

every word and gesture bespoke malevolence in his portrayal of Richard III

actress Jill Esmond) in his plans. Their acting partnership had established them both at the head of their profession, though there was always to be some doubt about her strength in his company on stage. On the screen, however, they were sadly never to work together again after *That Hamilton Woman!*; Leigh's triumph as Scarlett O'Hara in *Gone With the Wind* (1939) led the owner of her contract, David O. Selznick, to refuse to allow her to appear in 'insignificant' roles. When compared to Scarlett, even Ophelia was deemed 'insignificant'.

For this reason Olivier was unable to cast Leigh as Princess Katherine in his first attempt to film Shakespeare, *Henry V*. In addition he was unable to obtain the services of Wyler as director; this setback led him to take on the mantle of director as well as the lead role. Indeed, as film historian Roger Manvell has noted, the film might never have been made at all had it not been for a volatile Italian lawyer called Filippo del Giudice, who had earlier persuaded Noel Coward to make *In Which We Serve* (1942) and was now looking for another patriotic classic to coincide with the D-Day landings in Normandy.

Working to a budget of £300,000 (which was only exceeded by one-third) Olivier cut Shakespeare's text by about one-quarter, adding to it only a spectacular Agincourt battle sequence (shot in Ireland) and the death of Falstaff, which he lifted from the end of *Henry IV Part II* to serve as a kind of soundtrack-flashback to explain the old man's disgrace. The decision to start and end the film within the confines of Shakespeare's Globe Theatre, and to cast the celebrated music-hall comedian George Robey as Falstaff was an indication of considerable courage in a producer-director making his first film.

Though the print cost of *Henry V* was not to be recovered for several years, its critical success encouraged Olivier to make *Hamlet*. He had doubts about his suitability for the lead, commenting that his style of acting was 'more suited to stronger character roles rather than the lyrical, poetic Hamlet'. These feelings were echoed by some critics, although James Agee thought that 'a man who can do what Olivier does for Shakespeare (and for those who treasure or will yet learn to treasure Shakespeare) is certainly among the more valuable men of his time'. The film won a total of four Oscars.

Richard III, the last of Olivier's major Shakespeare films, and his own personal favourite,

was made in 1956 for Alexander Korda. This had been one of Olivier's greatest stage successes, but he again only took on the direction after a more experienced man (in this case Carol Reed) had declined the challenge. The film opened to considerable critical acclaim on both sides of the Atlantic. In the USA, following an unprecedented deal with American TV, the film was first shown by NBC, who interrupted it for three General Motors ads, one for a car battery 'more powerful than all the horses in *King Richard*'.

Sadly, however, none of the Shakespeare films had done well enough at the box-office to encourage production companies to provide Olivier with the money to make an adaptation of *Macbeth*.

The two final periods of his film-making career can best be divided into the films in which he played sizeable parts and those in which he guest-starred. In the former group are nineteen post-war films, of which only five were original, modern-dress screenplays: Peter Glenville's *Term of Trial* (1962), Otto Preminger's *Bunny Lake Is Missing* (1965), Joseph Mankiewicz's *Sleuth* (1973), John Schlesinger's *Marathon Man* (1976) and Franklin Schaffner's *The Boys From Brazil* (1978). This statistic may help to explain why Olivier is still thought of in primarily stage terms though many years have elapsed since his last theatrical appearance.

Carrie (1952) reunited Olivier with Wyler, who had originally wanted 'dear Cary' for the role. Nonetheless, Olivier's performance, as a man inadvertently destroyed by the woman he loves, indicated the kind of screen actor Olivier could still be if he chose to put his mind to it. Of his subsequent features *The Entertainer*, which he made for Tony Richardson in 1960, represents Olivier at his absolute non-Shakespearian best. The part of Archie Rice, a down-at-heel pier comic, was one that he had first created on stage three years earlier. At that time the notion of Britain's leading classical actor allying himself with the playwright John Osborne, a well-known 'angry young man', caused considerable press disquiet. However Olivier had recognized that in *The Entertainer* Osborne had created one of the great roles of all time:

'You see this face? It can split open with warmth and humanity. It can sing, and tell the worst, unfunniest stories in the world to a great mob of dead, drab erks and it doesn't matter, it doesn't matter because – look at my eyes. I'm dead behind these eyes, dead, just like the whole inert shoddy lot out there.'

Olivier's performance in this film remains convincing proof of his greatness on camera. Since this film, Olivier has appeared in *Term of Trial* (1962), a kind of latterday *Carrie*, and starred in some film versions of famous National Theatre productions, such as *Othello* (1965), *The Dance of Death* (1969) and *Three Sisters* (1970) – all of which hovered, in Dilys Powell's phrase, 'on the very margin of cinema'. He then made a return to major screen roles as a player of macabre practical jokes in *Sleuth*, the two-handed thriller with Michael Caine (who said that acting with him was like acting with God), a sadistic Nazi dentist in *Marathon Man*, and an Austrian Jew on the track of a Nazi war criminal in *The Boys From Brazil*.

On the guest-starring front his performance as the Mahdi in *Khartoum* (1966) was perhaps

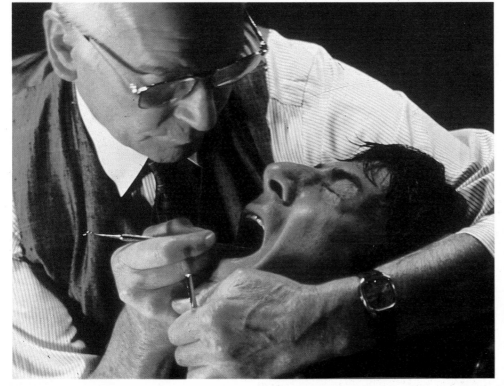

returning home, but not Olivier. How many other actors could have gone from Shakespeare to Harold Robbins on screen and survived the descent in reasonably good shape?

'Between good and great acting is fixed an inexorable gulf which may be crossed only by the select, whose visas are in order: Olivier pole-vaults across it in a single hair-raising animal leap', wrote Kenneth Tynan, while another critic has commented:

'Olivier looks like a man who could lynch a crowd; he resembles a panther – just when you know where he is and that you've got him cornered, he springs out at you from some totally different direction.'

And that, in essence, is also the story of his screen career.   SHERIDAN MORLEY

Filmography

1930 Too Many Crooks; The Temporary Widow (GB–GER). '31 Potiphar's Wife (USA: Her Strange Desire); Friends and Lovers (USA); The Yellow Ticket (USA). '32 Westward Passage (USA). '33 Perfect Understanding; No Funny Business. '35 Moscow Nights (USA: I Stand Condemned). '36 As You Like It. '37 Fire Over England; 21 Days (USA: 21 Days Together). '38 The Divorce of Lady X. '39 Q Planes (USA: Clouds Over Europe); Wuthering Heights (USA). '40 Rebecca (USA); Conquest of the Air; Pride and Prejudice (USA). '41 Words for Battle (narr. only) (short); That Hamilton Woman! (USA) (GB: Lady Hamilton); 49th Parallel (USA: The Invaders). '43 The Demi-Paradise (USA: Adventure for Two). '44 Henry V (+dir; +prod; +co-sc). '48 Hamlet (+dir; +prod). '51 The Magic Box. '52 Carrie (USA). '53 A Queen Is Crowned (narr. only) (doc); The Beggar's Opera. '56 Richard III (+dir; +prod). '57 The Prince and the Showgirl (+dir; +co-prod). '59 The Devil's Disciple. '60 The Entertainer; Spartacus (USA). '61 The Power and the Glory (USA). '62 Term of Trial. '63 Uncle Vanya. '65 Bunny Lake Is Missing; Othello. '66 Khartoum. '68 Romeo and Juliet (narr. only) (GB-IT); The Shoes of the Fishermen (USA). '69 Oh! What a Lovely War; The Dance of Death; Battle of Britain; David Copperfield. '70 Three Sisters (+dir). '71 Nicholas and Alexandra. '72 Lady Caroline Lamb (GB-IT). '73 Sleuth. '75 Love Among the Ruins* (USA). '76 Marathon Man (USA); The Seven-Per-Cent Solution (USA). '77 A Bridge Too Far. '78 The Betsy (USA); The Boys From Brazil (USA). '79 A Little Romance (USA-FR); Dracula (USA).
* shot as TV film but shown in cinemas

a deliberate reminder of his then-current stage Othello, also very gutteral and way over the top, and here as in *Spartacus* (1960), in which he plays a homosexual Roman general, it seems fair to assume that for Olivier, epic acting means overacting. His other guest-starring work has been only occasionally distinguished (Richard Attenborough got a remarkable performance out of him as the old Dutch doctor in *A Bridge Too Far*, 1977) and lately Olivier has taken to admitting in interviews that he is making films more for his still-young children's bank balances than his own sense of pride as an actor.

'As long as I can stand', Olivier has said, 'I'll go on doing my job'. Even after a decade in which his physical health has been tested to the uttermost by three crippling illnesses it remains impossible to think of him in total retirement. Joan Plowright, his third wife and the mother of his three younger children (there is an elder son by Jill Esmond), once said that she somehow could not visualize her husband in an orchard working on his memoirs, and he added that he knew of no greater pleasure in life than setting off to work each morning and looking back over his shoulder to see the children waving from the window.

Other men already past their seventieth birthdays might have talked of the pleasures of

The Evergreen Gregory Peck

Gregory Peck's integrity, dignity and sincerity have always brought him success, particularly during the Fifties when the threat of a nuclear holocaust gave Hollywood a new range of material

He was born in La Jolla, California, in 1916, and after finishing High School he enrolled at San Diego State College with the idea of pleasing his father by becoming a surgeon. However, finding that medicine didn't appeal he dropped out. A year or so later he entered the University of California at Berkeley and there he discovered his interest in drama.

The sideshows at the New York World Fair gave Peck his first taste of 'showbusiness'. His break, however, came while he was working as a Radio City guide, with a scholarship to the Neighborhood Playhouse School of the Theater, which was very keen on promoting promising young actors and actresses.

Peck began making his way in summer stock companies. Then in 1941 he made a screen test for David O. Selznick, who commented to one of his talent scouts that he didn't see how they could use Peck, and thought that most studios would have similar problems as he photographed like Abraham Lincoln and had little apparent personality. However, Broadway was not proving as successful as Peck might have hoped and he signed for the screenwriter Casey Robinson's short-lived production company, well aware of his limitations, and eager to learn his craft:

'On my first film, *Days of Glory* (1944), [Jacques] Tourneur taught me something I had to learn. He would criticise my precise diction and say "Common it up." . . . the microphone was just a few yards away, and I didn't need to project.'

Days of Glory, in which Peck played the leader of a Russian guerrilla group, was not a box-office success, but audiences came away with the memory of a large, loose-limbed actor with the gaunt, bony features that are a cameraman's delight – raw, a little awkward but unmistakeably an actor. Even then there was in his screen playing a hint of the quality that separates the artists from the players.

During Peck's theatrical days the Leland Hayward Agency had represented him. With new interest being shown in their property by Hollywood, Hayward set up a shrewd multi-package deal, contracting Peck to four companies over a six year period with a commitment to make 12 films. This enabled him to ring the changes on his image without being typecast or having to undergo the slow build-up to stardom in one studio's vehicles. In short succession Peck was a priest; a romantic lead opposite Ingrid Bergman and Greer Garson; a rakish, despicable but irresistible heavy; a stern but loving father; a big-game hunter; a barrister besotted with his client; a reporter experiencing anti-Semitism; a Western gunfighter, and a wartime bomber-squadron commander. He emerged as a highly bankable star, carefully tailoring his talent to the projection of the quintessential Hemingway hero, displaying pride without vanity, forcefulness without brutality and passion without sentimentality.

Above: Peck as MacArthur *(1977). Below: Peck and William Wyler in front of the star-laden cast of* The Big Country. *From left: Alfonso Bedoya, Charles Bickford, Jean Simmons, Charlton Heston, Carroll Baker, Burl Ives and Chuck Conners*

Popular literary and stage successes provided the core of Peck's work, and by 1951 David O. Selznick had revised his judgment:

'Peck we know to be the new rage, and if any further proof were needed, it was to be found in what happened at the previews of *Spellbound* (1945). We could not keep the audience quiet from the time his name first came on the screen until we had shushed the audience through three or four sequences, and stopped all the dames from "ohing" and "ahing" and gurgling.'

Serious roles – like the reporter posing as a Jew in *Gentleman's Agreement* (1947), who is sceptical of his assignment to investigate anti-Semitism because he feels it is none too apparent in its most blatant form, and assumes the manifestations are too subtle for non-Jewish folk to comprehend – authenticated the impression of dignity and intelligence. These were complemented by his roles for veteran director Henry King, as the martinet commander in *Twelve O'Clock High* (1949) and as *The Gunfighter* (1950) trying to live down his past reputation. They were exceptional in that they were 'character' roles, divested of glamour and sentimentality, projecting him as a loner – although the former was flawed by the insubstantial position the script takes on the moral nature of the task he is performing.

From 1950 Peck freelanced, always the star of the show and maintaining a strictly private life off-screen. However, in talking about his career he projects a slight insecurity – especially after one of his films fails – claiming that he doesn't think he is dull, just undemonstrative, and that his emotions are constantly being wrung by his work. Nevertheless, his choice of scripts has not always been sound. In *David and Bathsheba* (1951), for instance, Peck's David grew into a credible individual – proud, anguished, with a wry streak of humour and the recognizable vices and virtues of most human beings – but much depended on Peck's strength of portrayal to rise above the shortcomings of the script. Equally, *Night People* (1954) – about an exchange of political prisoners in Berlin – fails to convince because of the hysterical anti-Red feeling it portrays.

Gregory Peck is a very methodical worker, writing notes on his scripts and asking himself questions as a means of finding his way into a character. After his first three or four pictures he used to sit in on story conferences and make helpful comments. Sometimes his suggestions were accepted and he was soon allowed to approve the director, co-star and script for his films. Sheilah Graham was Scott Fitzgerald's mistress during the last depressing years of the author's life and was dismayed at 20th Century-Fox's portrayal of their affair in *Beloved Infidel* (1959). She cited a number of instances in which Peck's extraordinary insistence on being so involved with the production reflected a concern less for the film itself than for his being the star of the show. During the filming of *Beloved Infidel* Graham commented on her memory of the moment when she realized that Scott had begun drinking again: '"Oh, no," said Greg, "I don't see it like that. I'll say something pleasant and smile."' Graham also notes that Peck took his status very seriously:

'As a tax advantage, Greg co-produced *The Big Country* (1958) with Willie Wyler directing. As in most of these deals, Greg's co-producership was more of an honorary title . . . Wyler will not take interference from anyone. There was a close-up and Greg wanted it one way and Willie wanted it his way. After some arguing the star drew himself up to his over six feet and said: "I'm the producer." "Shit", replied Wyler. They didn't speak to each other for years.'

A serious-minded man, Peck is politically active as a Democrat and is a successful fund-raiser for the Motion Picture Relief Fund and the Building and Endowment Campaign. As a former president of the Academy of Motion Picture Arts and Sciences his most spectacular

achievement, in the civic field, came after Dr Martin Luther King's assassination five days before the Oscar ceremony in 1968. All the coloured presenters withdrew, and the following day Peck decided to postpone the ceremony until after the funeral – the only time the awards have ever been delayed. He convinced the NBC, the sponsors and the performers to fall in line and this persuasive dignity and sincerity are the cornerstones of his two best performances: *On the Beach* (1960) and *To Kill a Mockingbird* (1962).

In *On the Beach* – as the commander of a nuclear submarine which survives the Bomb by being submerged – Peck gave a powerful performance. His wife and children having died when the Bomb dropped, the commander heads for Australia as the Southern Hemisphere has temporarily escaped contamina-

Top: I Walk the Line (1970) was not a box-office success but Peck's performance as the sheriff, who ruins himself by falling for the daughter of a moonshiner, is moving. Left: Captain Horatio Hornblower (1951) was originally meant for Errol Flynn. Below: Deborah Raffin, Joseph Bottoms and Peck the producer during filming of The Dove.

tion. He falls in love with an attractive woman – played by Ava Gardner – but although they enjoy each other's company he finally decides to return to America so his men can die on home ground. In *To Kill a Mockingbird* – for which he won an Oscar – he plays Atticus Finch, a small-town lawyer defending a negro, quietly courageous, sharp in business but tender and loving towards his children. The action of the film is counterpointed by the elegiac recollection of childhood and the portrait of a very human father dedicated to the pursuit of truth and justice.

During the late Sixties and the Seventies Peck appeared less frequently, turning to the production of the controversial *The Trial of the Catonsville Nine* (1972) – which dealt with the sensitive political issue of Vietnam – and the vapid *The Dove* (1974):

'It wouldn't have been my wish to go on making three or four films a year as I did for so many years, but, on the other hand, I'm not offered as many as when I was say 35. That's natural, and I knew that time would come. I've no feeling of regret about it.'

He has continued to pick varied roles, reviving his career by playing the American ambassador to Britain in the highly successful

Filmography
1944 Days of Glory; The Keys of the Kingdom. '45 The Valley of Decision; Spellbound. '46 The Yearling; Duel in the Sun. '47 The Macomber Affair; Gentleman's Agreement; The Paradine Case. '48 Yellow Sky. '49 The Great Sinner; Twelve O'Clock High. '50 The Gunfighter. '51 Only the Valiant; Captain Horatio Hornblower (GB: Captain Horatio Hornblower RN). '51 David and Bathsheba. '52 The World in His Arms. '53 The Snows of Kilimanjaro; Roman Holiday. '54 The Million Pound Note (USA: Man With a Million) (GB); Night People. '55 The Purple Plain. '56 The Man in the Gray Flannel Suit; Moby Dick. '57 Designing Woman. '58 The Big Country (+ co-prod). '59 Pork Chop Hill (+ prod); Beloved Infidel. '60 On the Beach. '61 The Guns of Navarone (GB). '62 Cape Fear; To Kill a Mockingbird; How the West Was Won. '63 Captain Newman MD. '64 Behold a Pale Horse. '65 Mirage. '66 John F. Kennedy: Years of Lightning, Day of Drums (doc) (narr only); Arabesque. '68 The Stalking Moon. '69 MacKenna's Gold; The Chairman (GB: The Most Dangerous Man in the World); Marooned. '70 I Walk the Line. '71 Shootout. '72 The Trial of the Catonsville Nine (prod only). '74 Billy Two Hats; The Dove (prod only). '76 The Omen. '77 MacArthur (GB: Mac-Arthur the Rebel General). '78 The Boys from Brazil. '80 The Sea Wolves.

horror film, *The Omen* (1976) – who else could have made such a role believable? He followed this with a portrayal of the Nazi doctor, Mengele, in the fictionalized biography *The Boys from Brazil* (1978).

When asked about his tremendous scope he explains that most of his characters are not close to his own personality – giving *Duel in the Sun* (1946), in which he was a rascal, a rich man's spoiled son, as an example. But in the main he plays heroes who are beset by difficulties imposed upon them by circumstances beyond their control or by 'evil' people. Arguably the less pleasant characters have

stretched him, and are more memorable than roles such as the journalist in *Roman Holiday* (1953), who falls in love with a runaway princess, or the businessman in *The Man in the Gray Flannel Suit* (1956), where the moral is that the acquisition of power and wealth is not necessarily desirable.

Peck sees his talent for communicating sincerity as an expression of his concentration. As the film historian and biographer Tony Thomas has noted, he projects his own integrity in his work:

'The image is that of a good man. It may not be a terribly exciting or stimulating image but

in its strength and in its implied virtues it is an image of value, particularly for Americans.'
KINGSLEY CANHAM

Above: based on a real event in Korea, Pork Chop Hill *(1959) starred Peck as the colonel in command of an attack on a hill that was of questionable strategic value. Below left: Ava Gardner and Peck in* On the Beach. *Below: Peck, as Atticus Finch, guards his jailed client in* To Kill a Mockingbird

Space invaders

Cold War paranoia made its mark on the cinema in a variety of ways, most spectacular of which was the science-fiction boom of the Fifties with its topical theme of being taken over by aliens

Left: the classical science-fiction landscape of dunes and mountain ranges in Forbidden Planet *was given a new visual appeal through George Folsey's mellow, CinemaScope photography. The plot was a free adaptation of Shakespeare's* The Tempest. *Below: the rocket ship designed to carry a select group of humans away from their planet which is on a collision course with the planet Bellus. The designer George Pal won an Oscar for his apocalyptic special effects*

To look back at the science-fiction cinema of the Fifties from a 30-year vantage point is to identify, with some surprise, a golden decade. It's not that the films were masterpieces. Far from it. In technical ingenuity, not one of them could match ten minutes of *The Empire Strikes Back* (1980). In dramatic values, they alternated between the steely gaze (signifying incredulity, determination or lust) and the dropped jaw (defeat), with a tremulous grin occasionally permitted for the end credits. In storyline they were, by the dozen, what has since become recognized as first-generation schlock – a term which appropriately evokes the sound of rotting garbage hitting the bottom of a bucket.

They deserve their reputation. As bad films go, Fifties schlock movies achieved magnificent depths, plumbing the all-time low at the end of the decade. This was the era of *Invasion of the Saucer-Men, The Brain from Planet Arous, I Was a Teenage Frankenstein* (all 1957), *The Astounding She Creature, The She Demons, Colossus of New York* (all 1958), *Teenage Zombies*, and *Plan 9 From Outer Space* (both 1959). The last film is arguably the worst ever, but the foregoing titles give a fair indication of the artistic standards in question.

The title role in *The Astounding She Creature* (also known as *The Astonishing She Monster* and *The Mysterious Invader*) was played by Shirley Kilpatrick under the direction of Ron Ashcroft. A silent wayfarer from the skies, she wandered the Sierra Madre in lurex pyjamas, creating a ripple in the

WHEN WORLDS COLLIDE

PRODUCED BY GEORGE PAL
MAKER OF 'DESTINATION MOON'
DIRECTED BY RUDOLPH MATÉ
COLOR BY Technicolor
A PARAMOUNT PICTURE

advised by rocketeer Hermann Oberth, the film proclaimed its authenticity in every detail. It even avoided the extremes of Heinlein's original (in which Nazis are discovered plotting away on the moon), by translating his precocious schoolboy astronauts into average American adults, all courage and good humour, such as would capture a hill in Korea or carry the flag into space with equal resourcefulness.

Destination Moon showed firmly that space-flight opened a new frontier, offering fun, sacrifice, and fresh subjects for the amateur photographer, plus a place in the history books and a long-distance call from the White House. The film also observed that the Moon offered strategic advantages and that if the Americans didn't get there first some other nation would.

It wasn't a message to be ignored. Since 1947, the torrent of UFO reports had led to keen speculation about the Moon as a base for flying saucers. If the Earth was under surveillance, it was time to repay the interest. If national security was also at stake, nothing could be permitted to stand in the way of

Above: Roger Corman's Attack of the Crab Monsters, *a quintessential piece of schlock science fiction: a group of scientists are studying marine life on a remote island, when suddenly . . . Right: in* The Alligator People *Bruce Bennett plays a disabled man who takes a special serum and turns into an alligator to the surprise of his friends and family. Below right: a distinctly paranoid fable,* Invaders From Mars, *showed aliens taking control of their victims' minds. Below: a scientist transplants his son's brain into a giant robot who goes on the rampage in New York*

camera lens and snarling radioactively at other members of the cast. The She Demons, on the other hand, were an all-girl dance ensemble on a nuclear testing-site where they were caged by Nazis whose leader conducted facial transplants. Hard to beat, that one.

Notable monstrosities were to follow. With the approach of the Sixties, however, the mood changed and the zestful innocence of schlock was overshadowed by darker complexities. Before considering these, we should return to the start of the golden decade, launched as it was by the film that changed the face of science-fiction cinema, *Destination Moon* (1950). George Pal's production was pure technology, the giant leap for mankind, pre-staged as simple, stirring prophecy. The fantasies of the Forties had tended to be macabre and gloomy, even vaguely unhealthy like *The Beast With Five Fingers* (1946) or the equally creepy *House of Darkness* (1948). And while Superman, Captain Video and Batman marked the return of good, old-fashioned heroism in the movie serials of 1948 onwards, their comic-book image trivialized them.

There was nothing trivial, however, about *Destination Moon*, with its majestic space-flight and super-spectacular lunar surface. It made science fiction on the screen respectable, even if the magazines persisted in disguising themselves as lurid nonsense. Derived from a Robert Heinlein story, designed by the space-artist Chesley Bonestell,

THE SUPREME EXCITEMENT
OF OUR TIME!

2½
YEARS
IN THE MAKING!

THIS
ISLAND
EARTH

STARRING
JEFF MORROW
FAITH DOMERGUE
REX REASON

COLOR BY *Technicolor*

Screenplay by FRANKLIN COEN and EDWARD G. O'CALLAGHAN
Directed by JOSEPH NEWMAN • Produced by WILLIAM ALLAND

Above: an allegory of the human race torn apart by nuclear war: the story of This Island Earth *was actually set on the planet Metaluna where superintellectuals had enslaved a race of gruesome mutants. Below: women exile the men and rule the planet Venus until the Queen decides 'vimmen cannot live vizout men'. Below right: more powerful images of female dominance in* Attack of the Fifty-Foot Woman

the space programme, which thus merged conveniently with the American Dream.

Thanks to *Destination Moon*, the 'good guys' were the riders to the stars; thanks to the Cold War and the McCarthy hearings, the political leanings of the 'bad guys' were seldom in question. They were either leftovers from the last war or instigators of the next. In the films immediately following *Destination Moon* they made their treachery felt in a remarkable variety of ways.

The three classic science-fiction films of 1951 were *The Thing*, *The Day the Earth Stood Still* and *When Worlds Collide*, and they demonstrate how quickly the film-makers and their public recognized that a simple moonshot would do little to restore domestic security. The ending to *The Thing*, with its famous warning 'Watch the skies!', illustrated that teamwork and wisecracks can burn one bloodthirsty alien but there are plenty more available, ready to propagate their seed-pods at the drop of a severed hand. And if they don't arrive as chilly foreign agents, they'll turn up as Michael Rennie accompanied by his giant robot, ready to burn *us* to a crisp by way of chastisement. Mankind must learn its lesson, or God will surely intervene once more; the gospel according to Philip Wylie's script for *When Worlds Collide* shows a new Ark leaving for a Technicolor Eden.

God retreated from the struggle very early in the Fifties, having appeared in William Wellman's *The Next Voice You Hear* (1950) and in *Red Planet Mars* (1952), although the divine presence was invoked from time to time – most notably in *War of the Worlds* (1953), where the Martian desecration of a church is promptly followed by the invaders' deaths. God's part is taken over by the figure of the scientist, wandering uneasily in a borderland between exile and acceptance as a consequence of having brought one hideous war to an end by inventing the weapon that could start another.

From 1953 (when *Quatermass* began on British TV), screen eccentrics settled down in earnest to the task of pumping hypodermics and spraying noxious fumes, their experiments unleashing a menagerie of destructive mutants. For the rest of the decade, cinema audiences had a choice of being taken over by *Invaders From Mars*, *It Came From Outer Space* (both 1953), *Invasion of the Body Snatchers* (1956), *Invisible Invaders* (1959); squashed flat or otherwise intruded upon by *The Beast from 20,000 Fathoms* (1953), *Them!* (1954), *Gojira* (1954, *Godzilla*), *Tarantula* (1955), *The Monolith Monsters* (1957); confronted by the surgically unspeakable, as in *Donovan's Brain*, *The Magnetic Monster* (both 1953),

The Fly (1958), *The Alligator People* (1959); or being driven back from space in a nasty condition as, for example, the protagonists of *The Quatermass Experiment* (1955), *The Brain Eaters* (1958), *The First Man Into Space* and *The Hideous Sun-Demon* (both 1959).

Although Byron Haskin's 1955 epic *Conquest of Space* sought to restore some charisma to the solar system, it seems that the new age heralded by *Destination Moon* was quickly taken over by fear and cynicism. The dominant image of the rocket, a symbol that could be directed either upwards to explore fresh mysteries, or downwards to punish the unrepentant, was habitually taking the latter course. Not until Kubrick's *2001: A Space Odyssey* (1968) did it seem that man could return to the stars with an easier conscience.

The second half of the Fifties saw the world brought to an end with increasing frequency – most depressingly with *The World, the Flesh and the Devil* (1959), and *On the Beach* (1960) and most intriguingly with *The Last Woman on Earth* (1960) and *Rocket Attack USA* (1961). The Cuban missile crisis was just around the corner, and for students of science fiction it would be no great surprise.

The most consistent message of the period, as we now look back on it, was one of helplessness. William Cameron Menzies' film *Invaders From Mars* was an early example: a melancholy account of a small boy's discovery that his parents have been taken over by aliens. The takeover theme returned in the mid-Fifties with *The Quatermass Experiment, 1984* (1956) – two very different sides of the same coin – *Invasion of the Body Snatchers* and Roger Corman's trilogy of compulsion: *It Conquered the World, Not of This Earth* and *Attack of the Crab Monsters* (all 1956).

Each film shows society being eaten away from within. In dramatic terms, a few individuals gradually become aware of the developing cancer and make futile attempts to arrest its progress, often sacrificing themselves in the process. In *Attack of the Crab Monsters*, the struggle actually takes place on an island where malignant forces gain in power by absorbing the intellect of their victims. The culprit, as usual, is the all-purpose potency of radioactivity, the ultimate scientific obscenity which mocks the ageing process by accelerating it.

More complex fears are exposed by the films dealing with changes in size. *The Incredible Shrinking Man* (1957) was an almost Orwellian exercise in paranoia that was promptly echoed by *Amazing Colossal Man* (1957); *Attack of the Puppet People* and the near-legendary *Attack of the Fifty-Foot Woman*

26 Million Miles Through The Unknown Universe -- To The Indescribable Terrors and Beauties of Planet VENUS!

QUEEN OF OUTER SPACE

PRINT BY TECHNICOLOR CINEMASCOPE

starring
ZSA ZSA GABOR ERIC FLEMING • LAURIE MITCHELL • LISA DAVIS

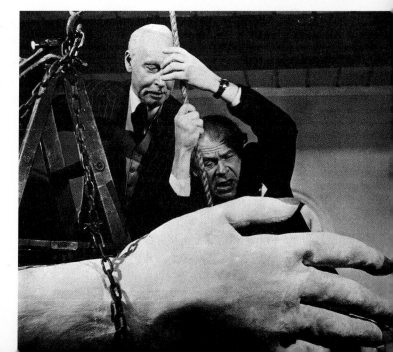

Above: urban destruction in War of the Worlds. Below: a typical alien from Invasion of the Hell Creatures. Bottom: in far-off Sumeria, deep under ground lived The Mole People, a race of slaves

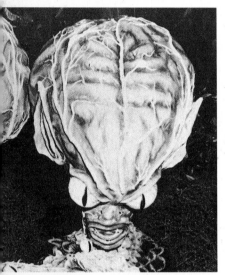

(both 1958). Since the days of *King Kong* (1933), it had been apparent that a solitary anthropoid could capture an audience's affection, but in the era of schlock – typified by the cheapest possible special effects – the idea tended to be unsupported by visual clarity and precision.

The Fifty-Foot Woman is no exception; she is either revealed merely as a papier-maché hand or she is glimpsed transparently drifting about on another piece of celluloid (thanks to the rather crude matte-work), in a charmingly styled two-piece. What makes her predicament strikingly memorable is precisely that there is no incentive at all to see it in other than metaphorical terms. A wife is driven to distraction by her unfaithful husband and her passion destroys them both. The science-fiction aspect is almost irrelevant except that it serves to heighten, so to speak, the struggle between the characters. But what spectacular melodrama it makes!

The three greatest science-fiction films of the decade date from the mid-Fifties. They had widely different origins, but were alike in the care with which they were produced and their special effects were excitingly successful. Coincidentally, they illustrate the same theme of disenchantment. In Disney's *20,000 Leagues Under the Sea* (1954) Jules Verne's volatile recluse, Captain Nemo, cruised

bitterly into the twentieth century to demonstrate that the perpetual struggle between nations was a meaningless waste of planetary resources and a neglect of the magical powers that science could reveal to men. Ultimately, the vessel *Nautilus* may have achieved more influence than all the Cape Kennedy launchings, but the scorn expressed by Jules Verne's hero remains valid today.

In Joseph Newman's *This Island Earth* (1955), the fragility of our own planet is demonstrated through the story of a bright young scientist recruited to save the distant world of Metaluna from destruction by interplanetary warfare. Quite how he will achieve this when his hosts (who have much larger foreheads) have failed, is perhaps unclear but our hero and heroine (played by Jeff Morrow and Faith Domergue) did their best to make themselves useful while homicidal mutants patrolled the corridors and meteors bombarded Metaluna from neighbouring Zahgon. Lacking the focal character that, for example, Verne's Nemo would have provided. *This Island Earth* is too bland to inflict any bruises, but what it does offer is distinctly discouraging: the greater the science, the mightier the destruction.

With *Forbidden Planet* (1956), the triptych is completed. Jules Verne's Nemo character becomes Shakespeare's Prospero, alias Morbius, a castaway on Altair-4. This planet contains, in mile upon mile of storage chambers, the accumulated knowledge of the Krell race, long since disappeared. Again mankind is offered scientific wealth that could bring, if anyone is interested, the key to the universe. Again mankind proves incapable of looking further than his immediate hungers, and Morbius is unable to prevent himself from using the Krell power simply to attack his fellow creatures. It wasn't a lesson to take too seriously at the time. The hit of the film was Robby the Robot, not the star, Walter Pidgeon, and while critics made passing allusions to *The Tempest*, it was overlooked that Shakespeare's play had also dealt with disenchantment and the collapse of a once-stable system.

Viewing *Forbidden Planet* in context, however, it looks above all like the first 'inner space' story, cancelling the cheery optimism of *Destination Moon* with one elegant, anarchic sweep and opening the way for a spate of brash, trashy, truthful parables. Other contemporary allegories included *Fiend Without a Face* (1958), where brain power became a form of lethal parasite, and *Queen of Outer Space* (1958) in which the costumes and props of *Forbidden Planet* were used once again, though here to parody the whole idea of anyone or anything being brighter than a terrestrial. Together these films shook science fiction every which way, like a cinematic kaleidoscope.

At the end of the golden decade, comedy entered the genre. Jerry Lewis paid a *Visit to a Small Planet* (1960) and Fred MacMurray played *The Absent-Minded Professor* (1961) in Disney's fantasy film. A more serious tone was struck in *The Time Machine* (1960) where the scriptwriter David Duncan and the director George Pal dispensed with H.G. Wells' evolutionary background and patched together an amiable love story between Rod Taylor and Yvette Mimieux. Just over the horizon were Joseph Losey's *The Damned* (1962) a merciless tale of omnipotent children and Val Guest's *The Day the Earth Caught Fire* (1961) a contemptuous account of how nuclear testing knocks the world off its axis and sends it careering towards the sun. After Antonioni's *L'Eclisse* (1962, *The Eclipse*) and Stanley Kubrick's *Dr Strangelove, or How I Learned to Stop Worrying and Love the Bomb* (1964) – two contrasting accounts of nuclear paranoia – it looked more and more as if the future, should we survive to enjoy it, would be rather less than fun.   PHILIP STRICK

FROM A LOST AGE... HORROR CRAWLS FROM THE DEPTHS OF THE EARTH!

THE MOLE PEOPLE

STARRING JOHN AGAR · CYNTHIA PATRICK
with HUGH BEAUMONT · NESTOR PAIVA · ALAN NAPIER
Directed by VIRGIL VOGEL · Written by LASZLO GOROG · Produced by WILLIAM ALLAND · A UNIVERSAL-INTERNATIONAL PICTURE

The City of Dreams and Nightmares

Over the years Universal City – sited on a sprawling ranch five miles north of Hollywood – grew into a vast and hugely successful studio, famed for its horror movies, thrillers, comedies and science-fiction classics

Film companies today tend to be great, faceless corporations. In the early days the studios took their character from the moguls who founded and ruled them. Of these Carl Laemmle (1867–1939) was, from every available account, the most appealing, the archetype of the good Jewish businessman – bold, tenacious, loyal, fair, whose word was his bond. To all Hollywood, as well as to his own staff, he was known, with real affection, as 'Uncle Carl'.

He was born in Laupheim, Germany, the child of a poor Jewish estate-agent. Eight of his twelve brothers and sisters died in infancy, and his mother died when Carl was in his middle teens. He always retained a sentimental loyalty to his family and, when he had become a rich man, refurbished the family home for use on his regular visits to Germany. Throughout his career he showed a weakness for giving jobs to relatives (among them his nephew the gifted William Wyler) and at one time a dozen Laemmles were on the Universal executive.

Laemmle was apprenticed to a stationer at 13, and quickly proved himself the perfect bookkeeper. In 1884 he emigrated to America and did a variety of clerical jobs before rising in 1898 to become manager of the Oshkosh, Wisconsin, branch of the Continental Clothing Company.

The Universal dawn

In 1905, because he felt that his services were not being adequately rewarded, Laemmle resigned and invested his savings in a nickel-odeon. Fortunes were made rapidly in the picture business then. Soon he had a chain of cinemas and a distribution organization – the Laemmle Film Service. In 1909 he was invited to join the new Motion Picture Patents Company, a monopolistic trust intent on gaining total control of the industry. But his natural independence revolted against such restrictive practices, and instead of aligning himself with this power he set himself to fight it. So, to supply films to theatres boycotted by the trust producers, he went into film production. Laemmle's Independent Motion Picture Company (IMP) was the centre and spearhead of a vigorous campaign that eventually brought down the trust.

Out of the battle emerged the Universal Film

Above: part of Universal City in the Hollywood hills in the early Twenties – the grandiose sets on the right re-created Monte Carlo at great expense for Stroheim's Foolish Wives. *Inset: the familiar globe logo. Below: Carl Laemmle (second from left) at the opening of Universal City in 1915*

Company, formed in 1912 from an amalgamation of IMP with Powers' Picture Plays, Bison Life Motion Pictures and several lesser companies, including Nestor, Champion and Eclair. The new company's first release was *The Dawn of Netta* (1912). Classics figured large among early productions with versions of *Robinson Crusoe, Uncle Tom's Cabin* (both 1913), *Jane Eyre* and *The Merchant of Venice*

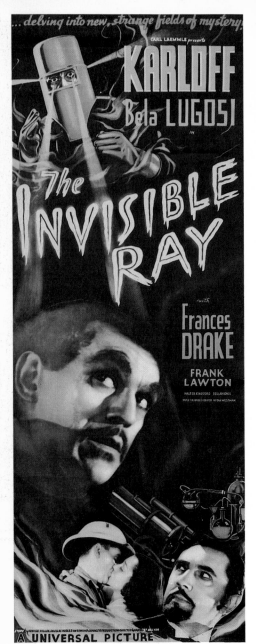

Above: Lois Weber (in dark glasses) – here directing an unidentified silent – was given a free hand by Laemmle to produce and direct her own feminist subjects in the early days of the studio. She was also Mayor of Universal City. Left: an early foray into science fiction, directed by Lambert Hillyer in 1935, teamed the studio's two outstanding horror stars

(both 1914). Universal's first outstanding success was *Traffic in Souls* (1913), a sensational five-reel 'exposé' of white slavery, made for a few thousand dollars by a group of technicians under the direction of J. Loane Tucker – allegedly in secret and without the knowledge of Laemmle (who did not like 'unpleasant' subjects) or his executives.

In 1915 Laemmle, perhaps emboldened by the large profits of *Traffic in Souls*, astounded Hollywood with the inauguration of Universal City, a 230-acre lot transformed into a true film-making city, with its own schools, police and hospitals as well as permanent sets for all occasions. Laemmle also jolted a hitherto somewhat secret industry by opening up Universal to sightseers, a policy which, he rightly estimated, was of considerable publicity value.

Laemmle's basic principles in business were that it pays to advertise, and that the best-selling policy is to offer value for money. Universal believed in stars. In his IMP days Laemmle, who had employed Mary Pickford, initiated the policy of naming stars when he organized publicity stunts to whip-up fan fever for Florence Lawrence and King Baggott; until that time the companies had carefully concealed the names of the stars from the public for fear that 'named' artists might demand higher salaries commensurate with their drawing power.

In the silent era Universal stars included, at various times, Annette Kellerman, the first aquatic star; Wallace Reid; Westerners Francis Ford (brother of John), Harry Carey, Hoot Gibson and Jack Hoxie; Rudolph Valentino; Conrad Veidt; and, above all, Lon Chaney. Although Chaney and Tod Browning, the brilliant director of the bizarre and macabre, did most of their work in collaboration at MGM, the success of Chaney's films at Universal, notably *The Hunchback of Notre Dame* (1923) and *The Phantom of the Opera* (1925), gave the studio a lasting taste for horror.

The promotion of two of Universal's greatest silent directors may have had something to do with Laemmle's own German origins. No doubt sympathy for a fellow immigrant helped his decision to allow Erich von Stroheim to direct his first film, *Blind Husbands* (1919). Its success led to a second Stroheim film, *The Devil's Passkey* (1920). When costs on Stroheim's next picture, *Foolish Wives* (1922), escalated alarmingly, Laemmle characteristically turned it to advantage by featuring the record-breaking (and potentially company-breaking) expenditures in a publicity campaign. Laemmle's newly appointed production chief, the 22-year-old Irving G. Thalberg, was less indulgent. *Foolish Wives* was given to other hands to cut and *Merry-Go-Round* (1923), Stroheim's last Universal film, was finished by one of the studio's other directors.

Another significant European engaged by Laemmle was Paul Leni, who completed three stylish horror films for Universal – including the masterpiece *The Man Who Laughs* (1928), starring the German star Conrad Veidt – before his early death. National or family connections were not essential for success at Universal, however. Laemmle had the sort of intuition and impulsiveness that often seemed to characterize immigrant moguls. Accordingly he promoted John Ford from stunt man and general hand on Westerns, reputedly saying, 'Make Jack Ford a director. He yells the best.' Universal was also one of the first studios to employ women directors, among them Lois Weber, Ida May Park and Cleo Madison.

Showcases for sound

Universal entered the sound period triumphantly. Its first musicals included *Show Boat* (1929) – remade in 1936 by James Whale – *Broadway* (1929) and the part-colour *King of Jazz* (1930). The most prestigious production of this time, however, was *All Quiet on the Western Front* (1930). Laemmle's apparently altruistic gesture in financing this costly picture – he even presented copies in gilded and sealed containers to the major libraries of the world – may have been something to do with a reputed yearning to win a Nobel Peace Prize. In the Twenties Laemmle had worked indefatigably for German relief; and in 1930 the distinguished British author John Drinkwater was induced to write a hagiography that unequivocally promoted Laemmle's claim for a Nobel Prize – conceding only that it might be shared with Erich Maria Remarque and Lewis Milestone, author and director of *All Quiet*. Laemmle was never to get his prize, however.

The last of Mr Chaney

In the early Thirties Universal entered its second great horror cycle, thanks to the British-born director James Whale and the discovery of two new classic horror stars, Bela Lugosi and Boris Karloff, to fill the shoes of Lon Chaney who had died suddenly in 1930.

Alongside the horrors was a notable batch of sentimental dramas, the best of them made by John Stahl and including *Back Street* (1932) and *Magnificent Obsession* (1935), both with Irene Dunne; *Only Yesterday* (1933), starred Margaret Sullavan, and *Imitation of Life* (1934) starred Claudette Colbert. In the Fifties, at a time when the age of sentiment seemed past, the old Stahl titles were remade – with Ross Hunter as producer and usually Douglas Sirk as director – to the renewed profit of the company.

From 1930 Carl Laemmle Jr was general manager in charge of production. Despite his successes with *All Quiet* and *King of Jazz* he failed to command the popularity that was

accorded his father, whose own individualistic style was beginning to fall behind the times in an increasingly corporate-minded industry. In 1936, with the company's financial fortunes on the decline, the Laemmles relinquished their control.

The new regime, headed by Charles Cochrane, started out inauspiciously, and *My Man Godfrey* (1936) was the only major success of its first year. Fate still seemed to favour Universal, however; like a gift from heaven came Deanna Durbin, whose option had been dropped by MGM. Durbin helped Universal out of the red with *Three Smart Girls* (1937) and stayed on for seven triumphant years and a series of major musical successes, after which she returned to MGM and the rapid decline of her career.

Cheap 'n' cheerful

In the early Forties comedy was the salvation of the company, with a run of W.C. Fields films and the discovery of the immensely popular Abbott and Costello, lowest of Hollywood's low comics. By now Universal was clearly the most down-market of the major studios. Production was characterized by the double-bill policy and the making of low-budget horror (often with Lon Chaney Jr or Karloff), bargain-counter costume exotics (usually starring Maria Montez, Yvonne de Carlo and Jon Hall), and cheap Westerns shot conveniently on the lot. Sometimes the double-feature stars would be called upon to clash in such films as *Frankenstein Meets the Wolf Man* (1943) and *Abbott and Costello Meet Frankenstein* (1948). At the end of the decade two notable new series were added to the second-feature repertory. One featured Ma and Pa Kettle and their family in a run of films that developed out of *The Egg and I* (1947), Universal's very profitable adaptation of Betty MacDonald's autobiographical novel; the other featured Francis the Talking Mule, the oddest film star to keep a studio solvent.

Even in such cut-price days Universal made the occasional prestige film. Max Ophuls directed *Letter From an Unknown Woman* for them in 1948. Hitchcock contributed *Saboteur* (1942) and *Shadow of a Doubt* (1943); later, as a major stockholder in Universal International, he would release all his films through the company. Other important Universal pictures of the Forties included Lang's *Scarlet Street* (1945), Siodmak's *The Dark Mirror* and *The*

Above: actress Phyllis Brooks drops in on the set of The Bride of Frankenstein *(1935) as James Whale and cameraman John Mescall arrange a close-up of Boris Karloff. Above right: a new logo for the reorganized company. Right: a popular hit of 1953. Below right and bottom:* The Sting *and* Jaws, *two of Universal's colossal hits of the Seventies*

Killers (both 1946) and Jules Dassin's *The Naked City* (1948): the studio's budgeting was by no means unfavourable to the new Hollywood vogue for realistic, contemporary and street-location subjects which were suited to the financial stringencies of the late Forties.

The company had meanwhile gone through various organizational traumas. In 1946 it was merged with International Pictures and became Universal International. The same year the British company Rank had purchased stock that was to be bought up by Decca in 1951. A decade later Decca joined with the Music Corporation of America (MCA) who thereupon assumed control.

Thinking big

With the new threat of television in the Fifties, the days of the little picture and the double feature were numbered. Universal entered into generally more ambitious production and their costume extravaganzas – for which they now possessed a potent new star in Tony Curtis – became increasingly more lavish. The company's flirtation with 3-D movies launched a cycle of science-fiction films. The best of these – *Creature From the Black Lagoon* (1954) and *The Incredible Shrinking Man* (1957) – were directed by Jack Arnold.

Universal continued to thrive on its stars in the late Fifties and the Sixties. A run of well-dressed light comedies were made with Doris Day, Rock Hudson, James Garner and Cary Grant. Audie Murphy was made into a star of modest Westerns. Kirk Douglas became the biggest dramatic star. In the Seventies, Universal International, now associated with the CIC corporative, moved into the era of mega-million movies. The mounting budgets and multiplying grosses of *Airport* (1970), *The Sting* (1973), *Earthquake* (1974), *Jaws* (1975) and *Jaws 2* (1978) seemed a far, far cry from the one-a-week one-reelers Laemmle turned out at IMP, or even from the rustic adventures of Ma and Pa Kettle.   DAVID ROBINSON

Jack Arnold

The Shrinking Man's Director

Despite the American locales, the world created by Jack Arnold is an unearthly place overrun by humanoid reptiles, aliens from outer space, giant spiders and incredible shrinking men

Jack Arnold was a prolific director in the Fifties, making no fewer than 18 features between his debut with *Girls in the Night* in 1953 and the end of the decade. The great majority were made for Universal, a studio whose polished craftsmanship was often unacknowledged at the time (much of its product was released in Britain without benefit of press shows), and of these several were produced by the adventurous Albert Zugsmith, who was also responsible for Douglas Sirk's *Written on the Wind* (1956) and Orson Welles' *Touch of Evil* (1958).

Space craft

Ranging from a lively Western like *The Man From Bitter Ridge* (1955) to the agreeable romantic comedy *The Lady Takes a Flyer* (1957), Arnold took in virtually every genre bar the musical. But it is for a string of science-fiction thrillers, which began with his second movie *It Came From Outer Space* (1953), that his place in the cinema's hall of fame is assured.

Although *It Came From Outer Space* is characteristic of Arnold's work in its narrative economy and its atmospheric use of desert locales, it suffers from a rather anti-climactic plot: the extra-terrestrial visitors who temporarily take over the local inhabitants finally make a peaceful exit with disappointingly little ado. Much more memorable is *Creature From the Black Lagoon* (1954), in which scientists on a South American expedition stir up the eponymous scaly figure from his sub-aquatic abode with alarming results for themselves and the audience. He focuses his particular attention on Kay (Julia Adams), the group's female member, and in a dazzling sequence the underwater camera watches his dark form writhe below her white bathing-suited body as she swims in the lagoon's still waters, an effect at once gracefully balletic and unmistakably sexual. Later he carries her off to his lair in a scene of fairy-tale ghostliness that is reminiscent of *The Phantom of the Opera* (1925).

The gill-man strikes back

The inevitable sequel, *Revenge of the Creature* (1955), has no individual sequence to match this, but overall it is an even better film with a more inventive storyline. By now the Creature

is a captive in a Florida aquarium and it is with him that our sympathies lie. The film builds to a splendid chase climax: the gill-man effects his predictable escape and after causing consternation in a crowded restaurant by bursting in to seize the current object of his desires (played by Lori Nelson), he attempts to make off with her towards the sea.

A similar impetus sustains *Tarantula* (1955). Not content merely with exploiting the pleasurably horrific potential of a spider that – as a result of a botched experiment – grows until it reaches the dimensions of a large building, the movie underpins the grisly spectacle with an edgily suspenseful exposition. The pre-credit sequence, with a gruesomely deformed man suddenly emerging from the barren terrain, and the subsequent first shot of the already enlarged spider rearing up against the glass front of its cage, admirably demonstrates the precision of timing and editing commanded by Arnold's deceptively plain treatment.

The diagrammatic quality of Arnold's style is seen to striking effect in two hard-edged social melodramas he made in 1957. *The Tattered Dress* and *Man in the Shadow* derive a sensationalist rhetoric from their artful combination of black-and-white and CinemaScope. But conversely, by sticking to standard ratio

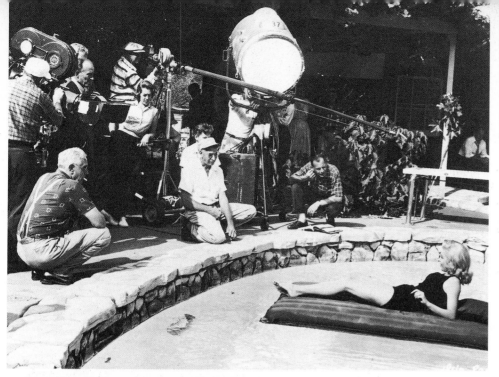

penetrating a 'utopian' housing development rather in the spirit of an alien from outer space.

Arnold's later career has been sporadic and essentially negligible – reflecting the disappearance of the genre-programmer – and his early films are for the most part unsung. But at least *The Incredible Shrinking Man* has achieved acknowledged status, while the grinning rubber features and phallically suggestive cranium of the gill-man from the Black Lagoon have won him a place in the memories of thousands for whom the name of Jack Arnold may mean nothing.   TIM PULLEINE

A FASCINATING ADVENTURE INTO THE UNKNOWN!

Above: Jack Arnold directs The Tattered Dress. *Arnold was born in New Haven, Connecticut in 1916 and, after acting on Broadway and serving in the US air force, began directing features in 1953. Left and far left: Scott Carey (Grant Williams) fends off his assailants in* The Incredible Shrinking Man. *Above right: Ben Chapman as the* Creature From the Black Lagoon. *Right: arachnophobia rears its ugly head in* Tarantula

for possession of a few crumbs of food.

Marred only by a phonily pretentious closing commentary, *The Incredible Shrinking Man* complements its inversion of genre dynamics with a concern for human feelings. Especially touching is the passage early in the hero's reduction when he finds brief solace with a fairground midget, a sequence that might be regarded as an acknowledgment to Tod Browning's *Freaks* (1932).

Monster on the Campus (1958) proved a sadly unworthy next project for Arnold. Feebly derivative of the Wolf Man cycle, the director's only excursion into conventional horror remains stuck at the Z-feature level. Happily, though, *The Space Children* (1958) is quite another matter. Tightly knitted (running only 69 minutes) and graced by Ernest Laszlo's handsomely dark-toned camerawork, Arnold's last science-fiction film brings together most of the major elements of his earlier contributions to the genre. The film deals with a group of youngsters contacted by a 'friendly' alien life-form to prevent an atomic test, treating the children's world with the human sympathy apparent in *The Incredible Shrinking Man*. It also displays Arnold's skill in deploying landscape in his use of the coastal setting, and even revives – to more gripping effect – the peaceful co-existence message of *It Came From Outer Space*.

Interestingly, two comedies by Arnold from this period echo the science-fiction movies. *The Mouse That Roared* (1959) is an attractive if uncertain joke about a pocket-handkerchief, Ruritanian duchy inadvertently becoming a nuclear super-power. *Bachelor in Paradise* (1961) is a genially glossy Bob Hope vehicle with the comedian as a writer disruptively

for his science-fiction movies, Arnold cunningly employed the smaller screen both to compress the action and to arouse his audience's fears of what might lie just beyond the frame.

Diminishing returns

His key sci-fi achievement, *The Incredible Shrinking Man*, was also made in 1957. Scripted by Richard Matheson, this film brilliantly up-ends the premise of *Tarantula* and other sundry mutant movies, notably *Them!* (dir. Gordon Douglas, 1954): now the human protagonist progressively dwindles in size so that his entire environment assumes threateningly monstrous proportions. At the climax, the tiny hero is driven by the family cat out of the doll's house in which he has found refuge and falls into a cellar; here a dripping tap becomes a raging torrent and ultimately – terrifyingly – he must improvise weapons to do battle with a spider

Filmography (films as director)
1950 With These Hands (doc) (+co-prod). **'51** The Challenge (doc) (+co-prod); World Affairs Are Your Affairs (doc). **'53** Girls in the Night (GB: Life After Dark); It Came From Outer Space; The Glass Web. **'54** Creature From the Black Lagoon. **'55** The Man From Bitter Ridge; Revenge of the Creature; Tarantula (+co-sc). **'56** Red Sundown; Outside the Law. **'57** The Incredible Shrinking Man; The Tattered Dress; Man in the Shadow (GB: Pay the Devil); The Lady Takes a Flyer. **'58** Touch of Evil (add. dir. only, uncredited); High School Confidential; The Space Children; Monster on the Campus. **'59** No Name on the Bullet (+co-prod); The Mouse That Roared (GB). **'61** Bachelor in Paradise. **'63** A Global Affair. **'64** The Lively Set. **'68** Hello Down There. **'74** Black Eye. **'75** Sex Play (GB); Boss Nigger (+co-prod) (GB: The Black Bounty Killer); The Swiss Conspiracy (USA-GER).
Arnold also acted in films but there are no reliable listings. During 1946–52 he directed 25 documentaries for the US State Department and private industry, but only three of these films are known.

39

Flash Gordon and the Weenie from Outer Space

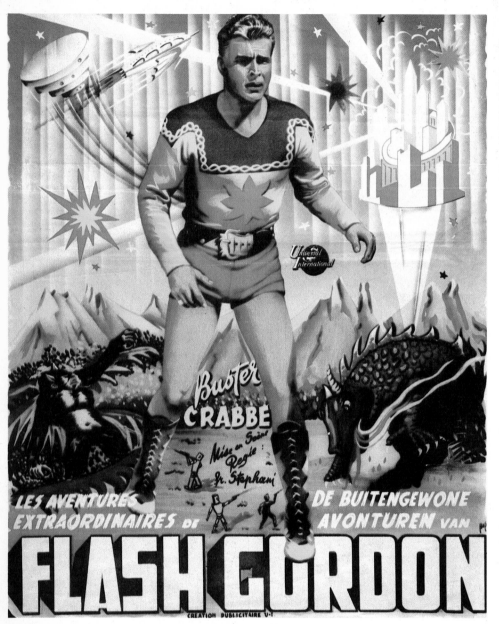

Buster CRABBE

Mise en Scène Régie Fr. Stephani

LES AVENTURES EXTRAORDINAIRES DE DE BUITENGEWONE AVONTUREN VAN

FLASH GORDON

For decades, in movie-houses everywhere, the legend 'To be continued next week' was greeted with cries of disappointment and wild speculation: how could the hero and heroine possibly escape the villain's clutches? When serials moved into the realms of science fiction, the thrills became even more nail-biting, the monsters more monstrous – while the plots exceeded everyone's wildest imaginings . . .

It is the year 1936 and the world is in chaos. There is looting in London, panic in Paris and rioting in Rome. Even New York is nervous. Professor Hensley of the Dorr Observatory looked grim as he said: 'An unknown planet is rushing madly towards the Earth and no human power can stop it!' But among the

frantic messages pouring in from all corners of the globe was one which made the Observatory's chief, Professor Gordon, pause. 'Gentlemen,' he said, 'This message is from my son, Flash. He gave up his polo game and is on his way to join us!'

Here was the human power to stop any-

Above left: Flash Gordon's worldwide popularity is attested by this Belgian poster for the first serial. Top: Flash (Buster Crabbe) with his girl companion Dale Arden (Jean Rogers). Above: Flash's deadly foe Ming the Merciless (Charles B. Middleton)

thing, from an onrushing polo opponent to an onrushing planet. Flash Gordon, Yale graduate, was to become the conqueror of time, space, Ming the Merciless and, ultimately, of the Universe itself – although this last achievement was something of a cheat. At the close of the final chapter of the last serial, *Flash Gordon Conquers the Universe* (1940), Flash's girl companion, Dale Arden, says with a smile: 'Ming called himself the Universe, you

conquered Ming, so Flash Gordon Conquers the Universe!' – thereby justifying the serial's startling title.

Flash Gordon is the ultimate in comic-strip spacemen, (the honour of being the first must go to Buck Rogers, 'born' four years before Flash, in 1929). He is eternal, too, not only living on in TV re-runs, but as the eponemous hero of a brand-new, science-fiction film. Flash Gordon, created by master draughtsman Alex Raymond was brought to the screen in the person of Larry (nickname, Buster; real name, Clarence) Crabbe. Although Crabbe appears to have been born for the part, Universal studios originally wanted Charles Locher (who eventually changed his name to Jon Hall and wooed Maria Montez in a multitude of South Sea Island sagas).

Buster Crabbe (b.1907) stood six foot one inch, weighed 188 pounds, had a 45-inch chest, 32-inch waist, 17-inch neck, 16-inch biceps, 23-inch thighs, 16-inch calves and had swum his way into the free-style championship in the 1932 Olympic Games. The only qualification he lacked was blond hair, but a little bleach and a Marcel Wave soon won him the role. In addition to being the perfect spaceman – he was Flash three times and also Buck Rogers – he became the ideal All-American Saturday hero, playing Tarzan, Billy the Kid and Thunda, King of the Jungle.

Universal's serial, Flash Gordon (1936), made cinema history. Not only was it the first science-fiction space serial ever made, it was also the most expensive, costing $350,000 – more than triple the company's average budget of $125,000. Although it has made more money over the years than any other serial, its director, Frederick Stephani, was never allowed to make another film. Flash Gordon was also the only adaptation from a comic-strip to stick strictly to its story source. Alex Raymond's fine drawings became blueprints for the film's futuristic rocket-ships (built by photographer Jerome Ash) and the other-worldly places and races peculiar to Planet Mongo (designed by the art director Ralph De Lacy).

Every chapter brought some new and dreadful delight: flying Hawkmen and their City in the Sky; submarine Sharkmen and their City beneath the Sea; and hirsute Lionmen and their home in the forests. Flash and his com-

panions were provided with Spaceographs to see with, Gyro-ships and Hydro-cycles to fly, and Orangopoids, Tigrons, Gockos and Octosacs to fight. Fifteen episodes later, when all the excitement was over, there would be only one thing for the studio to do – make a sequel.

Flash Gordon's Trip to Mars (1938) – the very title makes the vast voyage a mere outing for our hero – begins where Flash Gordon left off, although the return journey to Earth has wrought a strange space-change in Dale Arden (played by Jean Rogers). Her blonde tresses have shrunk to a brunette, page-boy bob. Ming the Merciless (played by Charles B. Middleton) was last seen sacrificing himself in the Eternal Flames of the Sacred Palace of the Great God Tao. However he returns unsinged for the new serial, in cahoots with Queen Azura, of Magic and Mars. Hardly have Flash, Dale and Dr Zarkov (the third member of the trio, played by Frank Shannon) landed on Earth than a new world crisis erupts. This time the disasters are caused by a Nitron Ray sucking nitrogen from the atmosphere. Zarkov correctly deduces that Ming is responsible, but incorrectly asserts that the rays are coming from Mongo. The source is discovered to be Mars, and in an instant the trio is up and away,

Left: the cover of the British press book for King of the Rocket Men, *featuring the rocket suit that reappeared in several other serials. Above left: is this the end for the singing cowboy? Gene Autry is menaced by robots in* The Phantom Empire. *Above: Captain America was one of several comic-book heroes to be brought to the screen.*

with comedy relief in the shape of stowaway Happy Hapgood, a reporter from the Dispatch. Played by Donald Kerr, this addition to the cast was a step-down for the serial. Flash Gordon, with its lusty Ming and busty Princess Aura making eyes at Dale and Flash, had been an attempt to upgrade serials to adult audiences. Flash Gordon's Trip to Mars marked the failure of Universal's hopes and a return to the juvenile matinée crowd. But many a young nightmare must have stemmed from the Clay People, hideous things that dissolved in and out of cave walls to the accompaniment of weird music.

In 1938 the USA was panicked by Orson Welles, a young radio director who broadcasted a version of H. G. Wells' novel The War of the Worlds, making it seem as if Martians were indeed attacking the Earth. That year, Universal cashed in on the public furore by releasing Mars Attacks the World, a hastily-pasted feature version of Flash Gordon's Trip to Mars. The resultant financial success prompted the studio to re-edit the first serial into a feature too, and as Rocket Ship (1939) the film helped the company recoup some of its original losses. Later the two features were double-billed with the catch-line, 'They Conquer Worlds and Destroy Planets with Atomic Power', cashing-in on the Bikini bomb.

'As wars and rumours of wars are raging, a new plague has infested the Earth', cries the commentator at the opening of Chapter One of Flash Gordon Conquers the Universe (1940). This is the Purple Death, an electrified dust scattering through space, leaving only a purple spot on the foreheads of its victims. Following the familiar montage of global disasters, Flash,

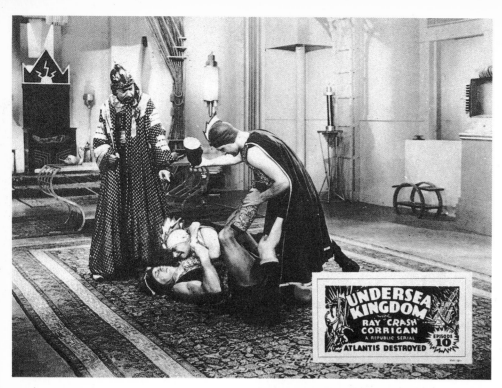

Top: lobby card for Undersea Kingdom.
Right: French poster for superhero – Superman

Dale and Dr Zarkov blast off for Mongo for the third, and final time. Ming, last seen dissolving in his own Disintegration Chamber, is back in action, mysteriously restored. Dale also finds opposition, this time in the form of Queen Fria of Frigia from the frozen North. The chapter titles tell the tale: 'Freezing Torture', 'The Walking Bomb', 'The Destroying Ray', 'Land of the Dead', 'Pool of Peril' and 'The Death Mist'. The final chapter, 'Doom of the Dictator', betrays the period when the serial was made. This spelt the end of Ming the Merciless and Flash, as incarnated by Buster Crabbe who, however, had consolidated his career by playing Buck Rogers in the 1939 serial of that name. Saved from death in a dirigible crash by inhaling Nirvano gas, Buck wakes up in the twenty-fifth century, an ultra-modern Rip Van Winkle. In no time he has formed the standard space serial trio, Wilma Deering (Constance Moore) taking the place of Dale and Dr Huer (C. Montague Shaw) standing in for Dr Zarkov. They then take off for Saturn to save the Zuggs and thwart the evil schemes of Killer Kane (Anthony Ward). Universal also followed the established pattern by cutting the 12-part serial into a feature version, entitled *Planet Outlaws* (1939).

Apart from the hardback reprints of Jules Verne classics, the novels and short stories of H. G. Wells, a couple of comic-strips and the pioneering pulp-magazines of Hugo Gernsback, science fiction hardly existed as a genre before the Forties. Small wonder, then, that movies seldom ventured into that vein. Serials, more than features, flirted with the form, but often only as just another 'weenie'.

'The weenie' meant a plot gimmick, the Poverty Row equivalent of Alfred Hitchcock's 'McGuffin'. Ronald Davidson, a serial writer turned serial producer for Republic, explained in a 1947 interview:

'The most important element of a serial plot is the weenie, that is, the object of all the mayhem. The weenie can be a map, a document, a mine, an oriental scarab with mystic powers, an invention, or a Nazi plot to gain control of Middle-Africa. To justify the number of people done to death during the course of the action, the weenie must have fabulous importance attached to it.'

Science-fiction weenies began in 1932 with *The Airmail Mystery*, in which the Black Hawk shoots his planes into the sky with his Aerial Catapult. Flying serials continued the trend, with the Black Ace's *Mystery Squadron* (1933) bringing down the opposition with back-firing flame-throwers, and *The Phantom of the Air* (1933) who defies Newton's law of gravity with the Contragrav. *Whispering Shadows* (1933) had its villain communicate by transmitting his voice and his silhouette and the following year's *The Vanishing Shadow* featured Onslow Stevens in the title role, wearing a multi-

buttoned cummerbund that rendered him invisible at a touch.

Western serials were livened up with a 'weenie' or two. Tom Mix out-drew a death-ray in *The Miracle Rider* (1935), and Gene Autry made it back to the ranch from the Underground City of Murania (20,000 feet below) in *The Phantom Empire* (1935) just in time to sing 'That Silver-Haired Daddy of Mine'. There was the Flying Wing in *SOS Coast Guard* (1937) and a villain called The Lightning, who killed his victims with thunderbolts, in *The Fighting Devil Dogs* (1938).

In the science-fiction hero stakes the only rival to Flash was Ray 'Crash' Corrigan, who conquered underwater Volkites from Atlantis in *Undersea Kingdom* (1936). However the rise of the comic-book phenomenon, the super-hero, brought new life to the serial during the Forties. *The Adventures of Captain Marvel* (1941) remains unsurpassed in its mix of actor, stunt-man and model to create the illusion of a flying hero. *Spy Smasher* (1942), *Batman* (1943) and *Captain America* (1944) were all super-heroes with science-fiction trimmings. But the second cycle of fully science-fictional serials began in 1945 with Republic's *The Purple Monster Strikes*. Roy Barcroft, the studio's favourite 'heavy', played the vanguard from Mars surveying Earth for an invasion.

Columbia came in on the science-fiction action with three in a row: *Brick Bradford* (1947) goes through Dr Tymak's Crystal Door to fetch vital lunarium from the moon; *Superman* (1948) comes from Krypton to smash the Spider Lady's Reducer Ray; and *Batman and Robin* (1949) return to unmask the Wizard and his Remote Control Machine. All three originally came from comic-books.

Republic struck back with *King of the Rocket Men* (1949), in which Tristram Coffin as King flies in his jet-suit to thwart Vulcan and his Decimator. *The Invisible Monster* (1950) used lightrays and chemically-treated clothing to vanish at will. *Flying Disc Man From Mars* (1951) brought Mota (Gregory Gay) to Earth in a serial that exploited the current flying saucer scare. Columbia returned with a movie serial of the first TV science-fiction series, *Captain Video* (1951). Most important of the film's many 'weenies' was perhaps the unique use of Cinecolor for space sequences.

Republic's *Radar Men From the Moon* (1952) introduced a home-made hero the studio hoped would become their very own Flash Gordon – Commando Cody, Sky Marshal of the Universe (played by George Wallace). He flies to the moon in a rocket-suit (suspiciously similar to King's) and puts paid to Retik the Ruler. *Zombies of the Stratosphere* (1952) put Judd Holdren into a rocket suit. As Larry Martin of the Interplanetary Patrol, he dealt with Marez, Nareb and their robot. Republic loaned Holdren to Columbia to star in *The Lost Planet* (1953) the studio's last science-fiction serial. Virtually every chapter featured a new 'weenie', as the titles tell: 'Trapped by the Axial Propellor', 'Blasted by the Thermic Disintegrator' and 'Snared by the Prysmic Catapult'. Holdren, a Buster Crabbe for the Fifties, returned to Republic for their last serial, in a repeat performance as *Commando Cody* (1953). Its main weenie was rather worn out: it was King's old rocket-suit, yet again. By then serials were worn out too. Their final chapter had been written; they would no longer be 'Continued Next Week'.
                                                   DENIS GIFFORD

Epic entertainment

To win back audiences Hollywood encouraged its technicians to extend the dimensions of the cinema screen, and producers exploited the new technology with bigger-than-life themes

In the face of declining audiences and the threat posed by television, the film industry sought to make the big-screen film as different as possible from the tiny image on the tube in the corner of America's living rooms.

TV in the early Fifties had two clear drawbacks: it was in black and white and the moving pictures it showed were on a small scale. By contrast the cinema offered scope, depth and colour. When the double-bill of Ann Sheridan in *Take Me to Town* and Jeff Chandler in *East of Sumatra* (both 1953) went into release the main line of promotion was:

'Only your cinema can give you an all-Technicolor, 2-picture programme like this!'

Most crucial among these economic measures to win back cinemagoers were the various technical experiments and processes designed to change the shape of the screen to a much wider, panoramic format beyond the reach of television. Cinema returned to the wide-screen experiments of the Twenties. In the Cinerama process, three 35mm cameras were used to shoot a scene and three projectors beamed the final films side by side on a huge curving screen that took up almost all the audience's field of vision. *This Is Cinerama* (1952) was the spectacular launching film for the new process, premiered on September 30, 1952, in New York. This two-hour travelogue also featured stereophonic sound from speakers positioned behind the screen and around the auditorium; sequences like the famous rollercoaster ride seemed frighteningly real. But it was such rapid-motion scenes that came off best in Cinerama, and it did have some distinct disadvantages. The exact matching up of the three images was not always easy to achieve; sometimes the images overlapped and occasionally the colour seemed inconsistent from one image to the next. Cinerama was also a costly system to install and only a few cinemas around the world were converted for it.

A film version of the Broadway musical *Paint Your Wagon* was planned to be shot in Cinerama,

but the production was shelved and the process was most frequently used for travelogues. Eventually most of the movie theatres equipped for Cinerama switched to a single-projector system when the more workable 70mm gauge became available and did the same job of filling the enormous screens.

Late in 1952, 20th Century-Fox decided to take up CinemaScope. This process had been evolved from Henri Chrétien's experiments of the Twenties and Thirties and its advantage in the Fifties was that it provided a means of bringing wide-screen pictures to ordinary cinemas.

Films are always shown in one of several available 'aspect ratios' (the ratio of width to height); the standard or 'Academy' ratio was – and still is – 1.33 : 1 (roughly four units broad for every three units high) but in the early Fifties many so-called panoramic screens had been erected to present films in a broader 1.66 : 1 ratio. It wasn't always fair on the films. George Stevens' *Shane* (1953), for example, was not photographed with the newly fashionable ratio in mind and looked uncomfortable on a panoramic screen with the top and bottom of its images cropped off. CinemaScope, however, was an altogether different ratio (2.55 : 1), and the first film to be screened in this new size was *The Robe* (1953), a biblical epic about the aftermath of the crucifixion. The film was shot by 20th Century-Fox's leading cameraman Leon Shamroy in both a CinemaScope and standard version so that the picture could be given its big-screen spectacular presentations and also released in conventional 16mm prints for use in schools. Like most experimental techniques, CinemaScope was a gamble and the only other studios to attempt it were MGM and Walt Disney, but the public response to *The Robe* convinced the studios that CinemaScope had a future, and by 1954 the demand for big-screen pictures was so great that Warners even halted the shooting of *A Star Is Born* (1954) after three weeks and re-started it in the CinemaScope process.

Above: Phil Karlson's melodramatic thriller was made in VistaVision; the new clarity of definition obtained by this process was advertised in the following terms: '. . . it brings this beautiful girl within reach of [the audience's] arms . . . her full-dimension allure so real, they'll share their emotions with her!' Below: the advertisements for House of Wax *conveyed, imaginatively, the thrill of 3-D cinema. Below left: the most memorable moment from the documentary* This Is Cinerama – *the ride on the rollercoaster*

"The most astounding development in Cinema history since sound"
—DAILY MIRROR

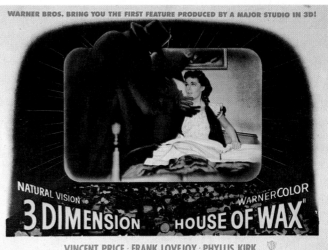

How Natural Vision Functions

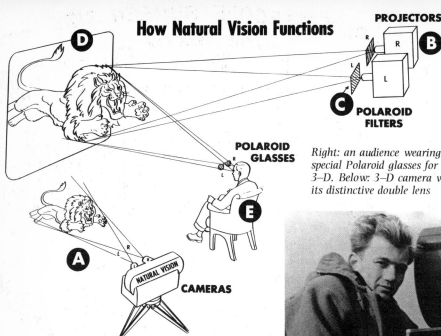

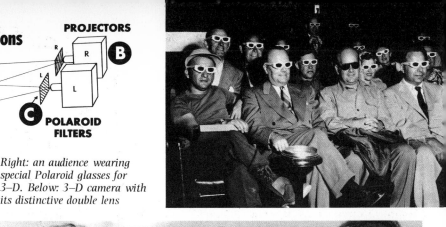

Right: an audience wearing special Polaroid glasses for 3–D. Below: 3–D camera with its distinctive double lens

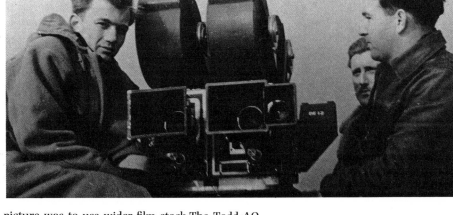

Above: 3-D images are filmed by a special, Natural Vision camera (A) from two different points of view, as they are seen in nature. Each lens, focusing on an object almost as precisely as does the human eye, provides a separate and complete two-dimensional picture. In the cinema two separate pictures from two (conventional) projectors (B) are superimposed on the screen. Right and left images pass through Polaroid light filters (C). The two images are superimposed as one on a reflective screen (D). The images are reflected back to the viewer who is equipped with Polaroid spectacles

Since 20th Century-Fox held the rights to Cinema-Scope and leased its use to other film producers, some studios preferred to adopt the other systems that suddenly appeared on the market. RKO took up SuperScope – first used on the independently made, United Artists release *Vera Cruz* (1954) – and later renamed it RKO-Scope for the studio's own use. Republic opted for a process closely modelled on the French Cinépanoramique system called Naturama. Warners dabbled with their own version called WarnerScope but on the whole they preferred the effects achieved with CinemaScope. Around this time the term 'Scope came into usage to cover all wide-screen processes of differing makes both in the USA and abroad.

The biggest challenge to CinemaScope's dominance of the wide-screen game was VistaVision, a system developed for Paramount which used a larger negative area to achieve better definition of the image. VistaVision films could be shown in a variety of ratios from the old-fashioned 1.33 : 1 to 2 : 1. The usual aspect ratio for VistaVision was 1.85 : 1. Careful composition on the part of the cinematographers ensured that no important detail was cut off at the top and bottom of the image as tended to happen with Academy ratio prints shown in the wide-screen format. *White Christmas* (1954) was the first film to be shot in this process and the principle was quite simple: the negative was made on 70mm film stock and then reduced to 35mm for distribution; the scaling down by half of the image size vastly improved the definition. In the long run, however, VistaVision proved too expensive and fell into disuse. Marlon Brando's visually arresting Western *One-Eyed Jacks* (1961) was perhaps the final demonstration of the process at its best.

It became clear that one way of broadening the

picture was to use wider film stock. The Todd-AO process used 65 mm film along with a special camera (developed by American Optical for the producer Mike Todd) and was chiefly responsible for the visual splendour of *Oklahoma!* (1955) and *Around the World in 80 Days* (1956). Fox came up with CinemaScope 55, a process that depended on the use of 55mm film for shooting, from which would be struck the standard 35mm prints for distribution. Technicolor developed a system called Technirama which involved the use of a 70mm negative for the filming thus providing sharper, better defined images when the 35mm release prints were made from it. *The Big Country* (1958) and *Spartacus* (1960) both owed their exceptional focus and visual clarity to this method.

The same impetus that led to this proliferation of wide-screen systems also encouraged movie technicians to re-investigate the early experiments with 3-D pictures. Once again there was nothing new about the idea of 3-D motion pictures but the notion of making them widely available to the viewing public was a challenge that the rise of television made more acute.

It was an independent film called *Bwana Devil* (1952), shot in Ansco Color and filmed in the new Natural Vision 3-D process, that captured Hollywood's interest in the possibilities of 3-D. *Bwana Devil* promised 'A Lion in Your Lap' and exploited its crude jungle story to good effect by literally throwing everything at the audience.

The big studios quickly took up 3-D, and Warner Brothers enjoyed a huge success with *House of Wax* (1953). In the wake of this hit nearly twenty 3-D features were released in 1953. It must be admitted that 3-D was very effective as a means of enhancing films with spacious settings – the deserts of *Inferno* and *Hondo* (both 1953), the South Seas of *Miss Sadie Thompson* (1953) or the valley over which a cable-car is suspended for the tense climax of *Second Chance* (1953).

All too often, however, 3-D was used as a gimmick. Audiences were assailed by a great variety of objects. Sensational moments of bullets,

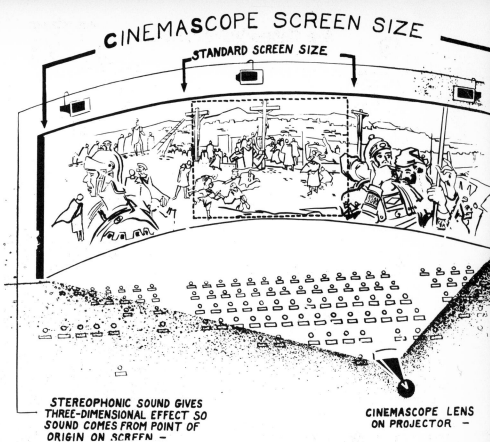

STANDARD SCREEN SIZE

STEREOPHONIC SOUND GIVES
THREE-DIMENSIONAL EFFECT SO
SOUND COMES FROM POINT OF
ORIGIN ON SCREEN –

CINEMASCOPE LENS
ON PROJECTOR –

Below: Cinerama was another attempt to create an impression of three-dimensional reality – but without glasses. Three lenses were used to photograph different sections of the same scene and three separate projectors threw these images onto a 90 foot curved screen. The heart of the illusion lies not so much in the wide expanse of the screen as in its curved shape. The 3-D effect obtained from Cinerama is due to the optical phenomenon of peripheral vision: what we see out of the corners of our eyes is crucial in giving three-dimensional perception. Working from this principle, Fred Waller, Cinerama's inventor, sought to exploit peripheral vision to create in audiences the sensation of being in the middle of the action. Right: CinemaScope was a technical innovation made possible by the introduction of a special anamorphic lens. The word means simply 'changing the shape'. Using this lens on the movie camera, cinematographers could film a scene approximately two and a half times as wide as it was high and the image was then squeezed onto ordinary 35mm negative film. A similar anamorphic lens on the projector swelled the scene out to its original shape. Both Cinerama and CinemaScope aimed to complete the illusion of 'being there' with stereophonic sound. CinemaScope had four tracks (three behind the screen and one for the auditorium) printed on to 35mm film; Cinerama used a separate film just for sound

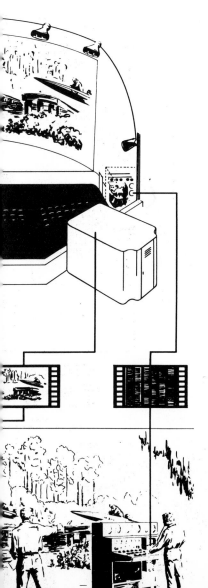

arrows, boulders and bodies coming 'from' the screen frequently distracted viewers from the story-line – the gimmick sometimes became the sole *raison d'être* of the film.

Finally, as well as earning a reputation for being somewhat contrived for the sake of their effects, 3-D films also suffered from the major disadvantage that the audience had to wear special spectacles to see them. Screens had to be specially treated and occasionally the synchronization lapsed between the two projectors operating to give the 3-D image. By the mid-Fifties, audiences were gripped in the excitement of CinemaScope which offered both depth and breadth, and did not require glasses.

ALLEN EYLES

There was little in the technology of wide-screen presentation that had not been perfected in the Twenties, but in the Fifties it was seen as a panacea for the industry's ills

---

It would be wrong to claim that spectacle was a specific creation of Fifties cinema; rather, that during the decade the form had greater reason to indulge its latent tendencies in that direction. The threat from television was naturally a prime motivation in the revival of the genre, but Hollywood had for some years been seeking a way to maintain audiences and support the gigantic structures of the studio system.

Making films bigger, longer and more colourful than ever was a way of providing a complete entertainment in contrast to TV's instant but small-scale attractions. What was required was the technology that would enable film-makers to expand the size of the projected image and to improve sound and colour quality to go with it. Many of the technical innovations of the Fifties had been briefly pioneered in the Twenties, but in view of falling attendances throughout the film trade,

there was now an urgent need to redevelop wide-screen processes and experiment seriously with film of a wider gauge.

The various wide-screen processes that were perfected and used in the Fifties caused directors and cameramen more than a few problems. The new oblong shape imposed its own personality on the screen and the broader space had to be satisfactorily filled. The letter-box shape of CinemaScope was perfect for two-shots, rolling landscapes and casts of thousands but could be less accommodating for single close-ups, intimate moments, or anything of vertical stature.

It was not until the Sixties, when new through-the-lens viewfinders were perfected, that the director could be sure what the final framing would look like in elaborate compositions. In the early days of the application of wide-screen processes, cinemas were reluctant to re-equip for the new system. As a consequence, most audiences saw the films in an ordinary 35mm format. When CinemaScope and the other wide-screen systems began to be more universally appreciated, there was a sudden demand for new visual stylists with a fresh eye for composition.

When 20th Century-Fox released *The Robe*, it was clear that the director, Henry Koster, failed to exploit the potential offered by the 2.55:1 aspect ratio, although Delmer Daves, who directed the concurrently-shot sequel *Demetrius and the Gladiators* (1954), showed greater flexibility and was later to become one of the top artists in the medium of CinemaScope. Fritz Lang's *Moonfleet* (1955) shows how he had surmounted some of the problems of the new screen size by the atmospheric use of light and shadow to break down the screen's rigid rectangular shape.

Other directors found different solutions. Stanley Donen masked off portions of the CinemaScope screen in *It's Always Fair Weather* (1955) and the VistaVision screen in *Funny Face* (1957), so that different scenes would appear on the screen simultaneously. Joshua Logan played with colour filters and hazy iris effects in *South Pacific* (1958). In *Bad*

Day at Black Rock (1955) the director John Sturges used the emptiness of the desert locations to emphasize the social isolation of the stranger (Spencer Tracy), and in *To Catch a Thief* (1955) Hitchcock subtly exploited the new technology by positioning his actors throughout the visual field, and in one shot treating viewers to a visual joke – a huge close-up of a cigarette being stubbed out in a fried egg.

The wide screen was put to a variety of uses, but there was one genre with which it became particularly associated: the epic. Just as silent cinema had sought to present bigger and better spectacle through historical epic films. So the cinema of the Fifties turned to ancient history for inspiration to find subject-matter which would do proper justice to the elaborate filming techniques recently perfected.

The impetus came from Italy where the development of neo-realism gave way to demands for a new, grander look to Italian films. The flamboyance of the historical epic fitted the bill. Alessandro Blasetti's *Fabiola* (1949) was made on a lavish scale and recalled the silent cinema epics of the poet Gabriele D'Annunzio. The film's success was one of many nails in the coffin of neo-realism.

As the Italian cinema developed its native epic genre (which French critics would later term *peplum*), Hollywood companies set up massive productions in Europe and brought large casts and crews to Italy and Spain. Mervyn LeRoy's successful remake of *Quo Vadis* (1951) provided the definitive impetus for a spate of costume pictures.

There was a world of difference between the Italian *peplum* and the Hollywood epic. The first was made quickly and cheaply and the second was shot on a grand scale over a long period with a seemingly limitless budget. *Quo Vadis, Knights of the Round Table* (1953), *Helen of Troy* (1955), *Alexander the Great* (1956), *The Vikings* (1958) and *Ben-Hur* (1959) all exploited European facilities such as the easier tax rates, the relative cheapness of labour and the opportunity to release the once frozen capital that Hollywood companies had amassed in Europe.

At the end of the decade an American producer named Samuel Bronston expanded on these principles by convincing several business cartels, with money tied up in Spain, to invest their capital in a series of historical pictures which he would then sell on a world-wide basis. The first film in this programme was *King of Kings* (1961) which required a financial subsidy from MGM, but Bronston went on to finance *El Cid* (1961), *55 Days at Peking* (1963), *The Fall of the Roman Empire* (1964) and *Circus World* (1964) by pre-selling the distribution rights throughout the world.

With the increased budgets came intensified pressures: these expensive films simply had to

Far left, top: a publicity shot from Helen of Troy attesting to the relationship between screen size and subject matter. Far left: Peter Ustinov as the Emperor Nero in Mervyn LeRoy's Quo Vadis. Far left, below: the building of the pyramids in Howard Hawks' Land of the Pharaohs. Above: a monument to spectacle, design and art direction – the Forum Romanum in The Fall of the Roman Empire Left: Robert Taylor as Vinicius, making his triumphant entry into Rome in Quo Vadis. Below: The slaying of the tiger in the Circus Maximus in Demetrius and the Gladiators; the shot reveals the powerful framing of close-up action in CinemaScope

succeed; production could not be allowed to begin until the sale of distribution rights was well under way. The climactic period of the American historical epic was inaugurated right at the end of the Fifties with the appearance of *Ben-Hur*, William Wyler's triumphant blend of spectacle and psychological drama which will probably never be surpassed.

The first few years of the Sixties were rich in masterpieces which explored different facets of epic form in the cinema: Nicholas Ray's *King of Kings*, Stanley Kubrick's *Spartacus*, Anthony Mann's *El Cid*, Richard Fleischer's *Barabbas* (1962) and, finally, Joseph L. Mankiewicz's *Cleopatra* (1963). Soon, however, social as well as financial pressures were to take their toll on the epic. It was the age of media interest in youth and protest, of moral revaluation and political change beside which the film epic, with all its accumulated grossness of scale and budget, seemed slow and outmoded. And also, quite simply, after a decade of success, the genre needed a rest.

In the pursuit of epic dramatizations, the Hollywood companies plundered the talents of Europe's film industries. Generally the producers opted for a kind of modified realism but occasionally they permitted themselves moments of sheer stylization. Designers such as Veniero Colasanti, John Moore, Mario Chiari, Edward Carfagno, Alexander Golitzen, John de Cuir and André Andrejew provided dramatic settings to the action which often ranked as artworks in their own right: the frontier fort and *Forum Romanum* of *The Fall of the Roman Empire*, the stadium at Antioch in *Ben-Hur*, the Sicilian sulphur mines in *Barabbas*, the temple of Jerusalem in *King of Kings*.

Such handicraft would be nothing, however, without cameramen of great talent to register it. It is often forgotten how much of a debt is owed to such cinematographers as Leon Shamroy, Robert Krasker, Russell Metty and Robert Surtees, as well as the Italians Aldo Tonti and Giuseppe Rotunno, to name a few who did fine work in this field. Equally the emotional effect created by composers of epic music like Miklós Rózsa, Frank Waxman, Alex North and Alfred Newman should never be underestimated in discussion of the epic genre. Their music often supplies that essential accompaniment which both binds and annotates the drama itself. Would *Ben-Hur* possess half its grandeur or emotional undertow, or *King of Kings* its simple majesty, without Rózsa's thematic commentary? Would *The Silver Chalice* (1955) realize its stylized piety without Waxman's finely detailed score, or *Spartacus* its incipient brutality without Alex North's music?

Thematically the historical epic film is dominated by the message of personal and political freedom. In American cinema this notion frequently emerged in the form of Christianity or Zionism triumphant. The

Italian *peplum* was less dogmatically concerned with religion and more inclined to explore areas of (pre-Christian) history in which the Hollywood film-makers showed little interest. The American epics invariably championed a cosy, middle-American life-style and showed an inordinate fascination with the grosser parallels between twentieth-century America and Ancient Rome.

The huge mass of Christian homilies which form the bulk of Hollywood's output are generally dramatized in the form of pious martyrs vs callous Romans, with appropriate Judaic interpolations. Howard Hawks' *Land of the Pharoahs* (1955) – Warner Brothers' response to 20th Century-Fox's CinemaScope showpiece *The Egyptian* (1954) – is interesting for the way in which the central pyramid is personified as the 'hero' of the drama, shaping destinies and delivering its suffering builders from their torment. Both *The Vikings* and *Solomon and Sheba* (1959) make play with their Christian vs pagan themes but the latter film (undoubtedly the better of the two) settles for a glib final conversion of the wicked queen (played by Gina Lollobrigida in a commanding performance of

electrifying sexuality).

When dealing directly with the story of Christ, the epic cycle produced two fascinatingly opposed portraits: *King of Kings* conceals a complex restructuring of the main biblical characters and a specifically Zionist ideology beneath its colourful, Sunday-school appearance, while *The Greatest Story Ever Told* (1965) is structured like a majestic symphony with Christ as the prime mover and central focus in a devout, almost funereal atmosphere.

Curiously, for the greatest works in this genre one must look to those stories in which the central protagonist functions as a mixture of the Christ-figure and pragmatic hero. *Barabbas* evokes *film noir* in its portrait of a man moving towards a destiny only half-perceived and from which he originally appeared to escape. *El Cid* presents an intense portrait of a medieval proto-Christ who is, at the same time, a knight redeemer. Finally, king of them all, is *Ben-Hur* where the protagonist progresses from nobility through oblivion to final redemption. It is a film, that stands as a testament to the entire epic genre.

DEREK ELLEY

Heston's Heroes

From Moses to Michelangelo, Charlton Heston has played some
memorable parts in movie history. But behind the monumental
façade of the epic hero is a man of concern and sensitivity – a
perfectionist of the craft of cinema acting

Charlton Heston, Hollywood's greatest epic hero, is also perhaps Hollywood's most underrated actor. Such critical neglect stems in the main from his close association with epic films – a genre which has been traditionally undervalued by critics who, when reviewing them, all seem to become historical experts more concerned to list factual inaccuracies than to appreciate the visual power and mythic force of the films.

In all Heston's epics, he has been one of their greatest strengths. Towering in height, massive of frame, granite-hard and steel-thewed, Heston immediately elicits such adjectives as 'rugged', 'craggy', 'virile'. He stands tall and solid like one of the buttes in John Ford's beloved Monument Valley or the carven images of American Presidents at Mount Rushmore. His face is not a face of this century. The keen eyes, the strong jaw, the wide mouth, the broken nose, are the features of a medieval warrior-hero; his whole being is a living echo of heroic sagas and *chansons de geste*. It is a fitting appearance for an actor who, with total conviction and considerable skill, has conveyed such qualities as chivalry, duty, honour, courage and faith – the keystones of an age less sophisticated and less cynical than our own, yet undoubtedly more forceful, more direct and in some ways more appealing.

Critics have been deceived by his sheer size into thinking that he cannot be an actor. But he is both actor and a star. He has the presence, the charisma and the luminous quality of a star; but he also has the dedication, the sensitivity and the intelligence of a great actor. His commitment to the acting profession shines through the journals that he kept from 1956 to 1976, and published in 1978 as *The Actor's Life*. These candid and remarkably illuminating journals reveal the man behind the image. He emerges as a devoted and highly principled actor, working hard at his craft, seeking always to improve, driving himself, testing himself, returning regularly to the stage and to his first love – Shakespeare – to maintain his links with the classical theatre. And yet he is not one of those actors who regard the stage as innately superior to film, as his passionate involvement in film-making proves.

A former President of the Screen Actors' Guild and Chairman of the American Film Institute, he has fought for projects he believed

Left: Heston in his award-winning role as Judah Ben-Hur. Below: a rare shot of Heston in tie and jacket, in Dark City, *one of the earliest films he made*

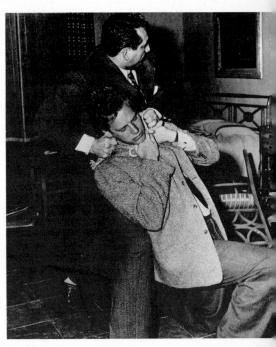

in, devoting years of his life to setting up such films as *The War Lord* (1965). When working on *Major Dundee* (1965) he handed back part of his salary to Columbia to pay for extra shooting which the director wanted and the company did not. More remarkably still, he took comparatively uninteresting roles in *The Big Country* and *Touch of Evil* (both 1958) for the experience of working with their directors, William Wyler and Orson Welles. He has of course had his failures: his bids to extend his range by playing comedy – *The Private War of Major Benson* (1955), *The Pigeon That Took Rome* (1962) – demonstrated conclusively that comedy is not his forte. In another carefully nurtured project he directed and played Mark Antony in a film of Shakespeare's *Antony and Cleopatra* (1972): the result was undistinguished. But always they are honourable failures.

It was both Heston's and Hollywood's good fortune that he was around and at the height of his powers when the industry turned in the Fifties and Sixties to large-scale epics in the hope of winning back audiences who were

being lost to television. Epic films need epic heroes – stars who do not just look the part but who also act the part. No one has equalled Heston in conveying the integrity, the intensity or the mystique of the true epic hero. Those qualities were already apparent to film-maker David Bradley who cast Heston – then only twenty five – as Mark Antony in a 16mm film version of *Julius Caesar*, made in 1949 and shown in 1950.

A television appearance as Mr Rochester in *Jane Eyre* won Heston a film contract with producer Hal Wallis, then releasing through Paramount. He made his professional debut in a tough urban thriller, William Dieterle's *Dark City* (1950), a film which demonstrated how uncomfortable and out of place he looked in a suit and tie. Thereafter Paramount cast him in a series of routine action films such as *Pony Express*, *Arrowhead* (both 1953), *Secret of the Incas* (1954) and *The Far Horizons* (1955); during this period his career marked time. There were, however, two films in this period which hinted at his particular qualities: in Byron Haskin's *The Naked Jungle* (1954) he was perfectly cast as a defiant Amazonian planter battling against an army of soldier ants which threatened to devour his plantation. In Henry Levin's *The President's Lady* (1953) he played the legendary American President, General Andrew Jackson, 'Old Hickory'. Although the film, as its title suggests, was essentially a love story, Heston imbued his Jackson with mythic stature – so much so that he repeated the role in Anthony Quinn's disastrous 1958 remake of Cecil B. DeMille's *The Buccaneer*. Heston was one of the film's few saving graces.

The real breakthrough came when the shrewd old maestro DeMille cast him as Moses

Top left: El Cid does battle with the Moorish enemy. Above left: Heston in another spot of trouble, this time – with Senta Berger – in a scene from Major Dundee. *Above right: Heston, Ava Gardner and David Niven filming* 55 Days at Peking

in *The Ten Commandments* (1956). It was to be DeMille's last film, the triumphant summation of his remarkable career, and showed that he had lost none of his power or cunning in blending spectacle, sex, sadism and religiosity into a box-office blockbuster. Despite the visual power of sequences like the parting of the Red Sea and the destruction of the Golden Calf, the film's centre and focus was the figure of Moses. Heston was magnificent in the part: he transformed himself during its course from noble, commanding warrior-prince into Old Testament prophet – greying, bearded, determined and exuding a genuine apocalyptic splendour. His success in the part led him to become irrevocably associated with epic films.

The list of parts he was offered but which, for one reason or another, he did not accept, includes Darius the Great, Charlemagne, William the Conqueror, Oliver Cromwell, Hernan Cortes and General Custer. Nevertheless it was an epic role – the title part in *Ben-Hur* (1959) – that won him an Academy Award for best actor. William Wyler's film, with its impressive script by uncredited Christopher Fry, concentrates on the dichotomy between the totalitarian power of the Roman Empire and heroic individualism, embodied in an earnest Jewish nobleman, Judah Ben-Hur. The conflict is resolved in one of the cinema's most exciting action sequences: the climactic chariot race in which Ben-Hur bests Messala (Stephen Boyd),

the chief representative of ruthless Roman Imperialism.

In the Sixties Heston went on to star in three of the decade's best epics: Anthony Mann's *El Cid* (1961), Franklin Schaffner's *The War Lord* (1965) and Basil Dearden's *Khartoum* (1966). *El Cid*, the supreme vindication of the epic film, is stunningly handsome in its evocation of the Middle Ages, as seen through the eyes and verses of the troubadours. All noble qualities are epitomized in Rodrigo Diaz de Bivar, the legendary Spanish liberator 'El Cid', and as played by Charlton Heston he was truly 'the best and purest knight of all'. His death and apotheosis are charged with mythopoeic potency.

A Dark Age world of savagery and superstition is the equally powerful setting for *The War Lord* in which Heston plays the stern and formidable Norman war-lord Chrysagon, who abducts a Frisian village girl on her wedding night, only to fall in love with her and later defend her and his bleak, marshland stronghold against ferocious attacks. At the end, mortally wounded, he rides off into the mist, becoming like King Arthur 'the once and future king'.

Khartoum resoundingly demonstrated the subtlety and skill of Heston's art. For in this film he played a totally different sort of epic hero, General Gordon, the Empire's visionary leader who died resisting the forces of the Mahdi at Khartoum. With clipped English accent, monumental serenity of manner and inspirational conviction, Heston became the man who, armed with only a swagger stick, had led the armies of the Emperor of China to victory over the Taiping rebels. His achievement is emphasized by the fact that he com-

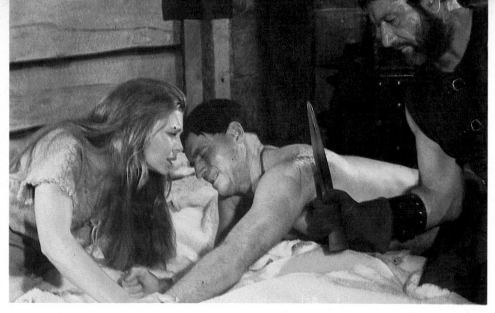

Above: more blood and pain in the medieval melodrama The War Lord. Above right: with Genevieve Bujold in Earthquake, an example of Heston's recent switch from the epic to the more popular disaster movie. Left: strange emotional encounter in Planet of the Apes. Below: a brutal end for the solitary cowboy Will Penny

pletely outplayed Laurence Olivier, whose Mahdi was a caricatured stage-black man, an uneasy mixture of Othello and Al Jolson.

Between these roles he played a US Marine major in a spectacular re-creation of the siege of the European legations in Peking by the Boxer rebels – 55 Days at Peking (1963) – and John the Baptist in George Stevens' commercially disastrous The Greatest Story Ever Told (1965). In Carol Reed's The Agony and the Ecstasy (1965) – a misguided attempt to turn Michelangelo into an epic hero of art – Heston was miscast as the painter who, in reality short, ugly and neurotic, was his antithesis. And the glory was anyway stolen by Rex Harrison who played the engagingly raffish Pope Julius II.

Heston next demonstrated his versatility by lending his heroic stature to two of the Sixties' most notable westerns. Sam Peckinpah's Major Dundee (1965) remains (despite studio cutting) a complex meditation on the nature and identity of the United States, with Heston outstanding as the inflexible Puritan moralist Major Amos Dundee who, while pursuing an Apache war band in Mexico, experiences his own crisis of identity. Heston was equally impressive in a very different part – the rootless, illiterate, middle-aged cowboy in Tom Gries' much-praised Will Penny (1967) – achieving moments of deep pathos in the scenes with the young woman and her son whom Will befriends.

His particular gifts were also an asset to two science-fiction classics. In Franklin Schaffner's allegorical Planet of the Apes (1967) Heston was the marooned astronaut, while in Boris Sagal's underrated The Omega Man (1971) Heston was literally the last man on earth, a titanic Captain America figure waging a lone crusade against zombie mutations.

By the Seventies the vogue for historical epics had passed, and in their place the disaster movie held sway. Heston was an obvious choice to represent the human spirit struggling against cataclysm on land and sea and in the air. As such he fought his way through Earthquake (1974), Skyjacked (1972), Airport 1975 (1974), Gray Lady Down (1978) and Two-Minute Warning (1976). Yet in all these films, in contrast to the historical epics, the emphasis was entirely on the spectacle. Plots were superficial, characterization minimal. However, even if Heston never again dons chain mail or unsheathes his broadsword, his contribution to the epic film has been potent and enormous. The legacy of the man who gave us Moses, Gordon and El Cid will certainly endure.
JEFFREY RICHARDS

Filmography

1941 Peer Gynt (semi-professional; commercial version shown '65). '50 Julius Caesar (semi-professional); Dark City. '51 The Greatest Show on Earth. '52 The Savage; Ruby Gentry. '53 Pony Express; The President's Lady; Arrowhead; Bad for Each Other. '54 The Naked Jungle; Secret of the Incas. '55 The Far Horizons; The Private War of Major Benson; Lucy Gallant. '56 The Ten Commandments; Three Violent People/The Maverick. '58 Touch of Evil; The Big Country; The Buccaneer. '59 The Wreck of the Mary Deare (USA-GB); Ben-Hur. '61 El Cid (USA-IT). '62 The Pigeon That Took Rome. '63 Diamond Head; 55 Days at Peking; The Five Cities of June (narr. only) (short). '65 The Greatest Story Ever Told; Major Dundee; The Agony and the Ecstasy; The War Lord. '66 Khartoum (GB). '67 Planet of the Apes; Will Penny; The Battle Horns (GB: Counterpoint). '69 Number One; Rowan and Martin at the Movies (narr. only) (short); The Heart of Variety (narr. only) (short). '70 Beneath the Planet of the Apes; King: A Filmed Record . . . Montgomery to Memphis (co-narr. only) (doc) (retitling for TV: Martin Luther King); The Festival Game (narr. only) (short); The Hawaiians (GB: Master of the Islands); Julius Caesar (GB). '71 The Omega Man. '72 The Call of the Wild (GB-GER-SP-IT-FR); Antony and Cleopatra (+ dir. + sc.) (SWIT-SP-GB); Skyjacked. '73 Soylent Green; The Three Musketeers: The Queen's Diamonds (GB). '74 Airport 1975; Earthquake. '75 The Four Musketeers: The Revenge of Milady (PAN-SP); Won Ton Ton, the Dog That Saved Hollywood (guest). '76 The Last Hard Men; Midway (GB: Battle of Midway); Two-Minute Warning; America at the Movies (narr. only) (doc). '77 The Prince and the Pauper (PAN) (USA: Crossed Swords). '78 Gray Lady Down. '80 Mountain Men.

METRO-GOLDWYN-MAYER
WILLIAM WYLER'S
PRESENTATION OF

BEN-HUR

Directed by William Wyler, 1959
Prod co: MGM. **prod:** Sam Zimbalist. **sc:** Karl Tunberg from *A Tale of Christ* by General Lew Wallace. **photo:** (Technicolor, Camera 65): Robert L. Surtees. **sp photo eff:** A. Arnold Gillespie, Lee LeBlanc, Rober R. Hoag. **ed:** Ralph E. Winters, John D. Dunning. **art dir:** William A. Horning, Edward Carfagno. **set dir:** Hugh Hunt. **mus:** Miklós Rózsa. **cost:** Elizabeth Haffenden. **sd:** Franklin Milton. **2nd unit dir:** Andrew Marton, Yakima Canutt, Mario Soldati. **2nd unit photo:** Piero Portulupi. **3rd unit dir:** Richard Thorpe. **3rd unit photo:** Harold E. Wellman. **r/t:** 217 mins. World premiere, State Theatre New York, 18 November 1959.
Cast: Charlton Heston (*Judah Ben-Hur*), Stephen Boyd (*Messala*), Haya Harareet (*Esther*), Jack Hawkins (*Quintus Arrius*), Hugh Griffith (*Sheikh Ilderim*), Martha Scott (*Miriam*), Cathy O'Donnell (*Tirzah*), Frank Thring (*Pontius Pilate*), Sam Jaffe (*Simonides*), Finlay Currie (*Balthazar*), Terence Longdon (*Drusus*), George Relph (*Tiberius*), Adi Berber (*Malluch*), Laurence Payne (*Joseph*), André Morell (*Sextus*), Marina Berti (*Flavia*), Claude Heater (*Christ*), John Le Mesurier (*doctor*), Stella Vitelleschi (*Amrah*), Jose Greci (*Mary*), John Horsley (*Spintho*), Richard Coleman (*Metallus*), Duncan Lamont (*Marius*), Ralph Truman (*aide to Tiberius*), Robert Brown (*chief-of-rowers*).

With its current worldwide gross exceeding $80 million and its still unbeaten 11 Academy Awards, *Ben-Hur* is one of the most successful films of all time. It is the Hollywood epic *par excellence*.

Made at Cinecittà Studios in Rome for $15 million, *Ben-Hur* was then the most expensive film ever made. MGM had previously filmed the story in 1925. It was a production beset by difficulties that, owing to its massive cost, failed to show a profit but which was a milestone in cinema history. The 1959 film was a make-or-break venture for MGM and they entrusted it to the fastidious William Wyler, who had worked briefly on the silent version.

If some of the film's spectacle is betrayed by unconvincing model and matte shots, the chariot race (co-directed by Andrew Marton and the ace stuntman Yakima Canutt) is deservedly celebrated as the most thrilling action sequence ever filmed. Early in the film, Ben Hur gives Messala a white horse as a token of their friendship, but from that moment Messala becomes the film's electrifying villain, casting a dark shadow over the whole story. The race is the great symbolic ritual of the narrative as Judah Ben-Hur's white horses run neck-and-neck with Messala's blacks.

It is a tribute to Wyler's narrative skill and to the intense performances by Charlton Heston, as Judah Ben-Hur, and Stephen Boyd, as Messala, that the race does not render the final hour an anti-climax. Despite the towering sets and thronging extras we never lose sight of the human drama. Judah might win the race but, as the dying Messala says, 'the race goes on'. At this point, Judah's victory seems as elusive as ever.

The novel, by General Lew Wallace and first published in 1880, exists within the branch of Victorian fiction which presents the reader with a daunting fresco of characters and sub-plots resolved only by dramatic coincidences. The film's literate and often poetic screenplay — credited to Karl Tunberg, but co-written with the playwright Christopher Fry and the novelist Gore Vidal — eliminates Wallace's padding but retains the Victorian elements of melodrama and divine intervention.

'There are many paths of God, my son', says Balthazar to Judah, 'I hope yours will not be too difficult.' In fact, Judah's path is extremely difficult, involving the moral and physical challenges all classical heroes must endure. Judah's destiny is to become a believer at the Crucifixion and the cross itself becomes a compelling structural motif. Most obviously there is the cross-beam into which Judah and Messala throw their javelins — less obviously there are the three nails in the wall at which Judah prays before the race — and the paths of the characters within each stage of the story repeat the pattern.

After the race Esther snaps to Judah, 'It's as though you have become Messala!' and to underline the point Judah is subsequently seen resisting his destiny by ignoring the Sermon on the Mount, claiming he has 'business with Rome'. The imagery here, with Judah and Jesus occupying the same frame but with an immense distance between them, is epical in the purest sense.

At another point Balthazar mistakes Judah for Jesus and indeed, one can interpret Judah, Messala and Jesus as facets of a single character: Judah's life is saved by Messala, then by Jesus; Judah takes Messala's life and Jesus dies to 'save us all'. In another way the Roman Quintus Arrius and the Wise Man Balthazar are basically the same character, both searching — from pagan and Christian perspectives — for divine guidance and both adopting Judah as their son.

All the characters and episodes are linked in this way and by Wyler's extensive use of water to signify purification. This culminates in the moment when the blood from the cross is gradually dispersed by the rain, heralding a new beginning.

The subtleties of such details are unusual for a film on this scale, as are the varieties of mood and emotion. On the one hand there are sweeping dramatic moments — the race, the prolonged argument between Judah and Messala, the uplifting sequence when Judah is given water by Jesus and later when the scene is reversed on the road to Calvary. On the other hand there are moments of extraordinary warmth and intimacy — the tentative love scene between Esther and Judah, and Balthazar gazing into the night sky ablaze with stars, wondering what became of the child he saw born in Bethlehem. Therefore, even though the spectacular chariot race made *Ben-Hur* famous, it is nonetheless highly valued for a multitude of other reasons.

ADRIAN TURNER

2

3

5

6

8

9

In Jerusalem the newly appointed Roman Tribune Messala meets his childhood friend Judah Ben-Hur, a Jewish aristocrat, and asks his help in eliminating rebellion (1). Judah refuses and his friendship with Messala suddenly ends. When the Roman Governor is injured in a fall after his horse has been spooked by a tile which falls from Judah's roof, Messala declaims Judah as a rebel and imprisons his mother and sister. In chains and dying of thirst, Judah is given water by a carpenter's son (2). Condemned to the galleys (3). Judah saves the life of the Roman Consul Quintus Arrius during a sea battle (4–5). The grateful Quintus Arrius takes Judah to Rome and adopts him as his son (6).

Returning to Jerusalem after seven years, Judah arrives at his old home, now neglected and overgrown, and is reunited with Esther, whom he loves, and her father, steward to the House of Hur. In a chariot race (7) Judah takes revenge on Messala (8) who, on his death-bed (9), tells Judah to look for his mother and sister in the Valley of the Lepers (10). Esther persuades Judah to take them to Jesus of Nazareth. They arrive at his trial. Recognising the Nazarene (11), Judah attends the Crucifixion and returning home he finds his mother and sister cured (12).

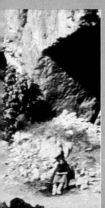

11

12

Left: the familiar outline could only belong to Jacques Tati. Above: as Monsieur Hulot, Tati surveys the aftermath of his helpful intentions while his dazed victims examine themselves for damage in Traffic

Jacques Tati, real name Tatischeff, was born at Le Pecq in France on October 9, 1908. His father, of Russian descent, ran a picture-framing business and when the boy wasn't helping in the shop he was developing a passion for sport. It was in the staging of 'action-replays' for the amusement of his friends that Tati discovered his talent for mimicry. His sporting mimes – in which he would portray the referee, both teams, and the entire crowd – became so accomplished that sport gave way to the music-hall as a prospective career and by his early twenties he was well established as a mime comedian. In pre-war Paris he was in great demand, working with Piaf, finding an ardent fan in Colette, and even achieving some bookings outside France, notably in Berlin.

As early as 1931, Tati experimented with film, creating an extended version of his tennis sketch – later to be expanded further in *Les Vacances de Monsieur Hulot* (1953, *Monsieur Hulot's Holiday*). Written, directed and acted by himself, *Oscar, Champion de Tennis* (1932, Oscar, the Tennis Champion) was of poor technical quality and attracted little attention, but it helped Tati to shape the awkward, amiable figure who was to become François the postman in *Jour de Fête* (1949, Day of the Fair) and

then Hulot. For his second film Tati enlisted the help of two professionals, Charles Barrois and René Clément, to direct him in *On Demande Une Brute* (1934, They Want a Beast); the 'brute' was Tati, a timid husband driven by a series of misunderstandings to pose as a champion in a wrestling match. Then came *Gai Dimanche* (1935, Happy Sunday), directed by Jacques Berr, starring Tati and the clown Rhum. Again the story of a misfit, it showed the brisk deterioration of what was intended as an idyllic picnic being beset by gastronomic, mechanical and rustic upsets, culminating in a stampede. With *Soigne ton Gauche* (1936, Guard Your Left), directed by René Clément, and *Retour à la Terre* (1938, Return to the Land), entirely produced by Tati, further hints of *Jour de Fête* can be spotted in his use of the countryside, of children, and even of a meddling postman. Technically, however, the films were poor and roughly edited.

The war then interrupted Tati's career for six years, but after the French surrender he found himself in Sainte-Sévère-sur-Indre, the village that gave him the setting for *Jour de Fête*. In 1945, Tati started putting all the pieces together – in collaboration with Henri Marquet – and the result was the one-reeler *L'École des Facteurs* (1947, School for Postmen), part-

financed by rather uncharacteristic Tati appearances in two Autant-Lara films, *Sylvie et la Fantôme* (1945, *Sylvie and the Ghost*) and *Le Diable au Corps* (1947, *Devil in the Flesh*). For four years, Tati built up his film, testing different gag sequences on different preview audiences, until in 1949 *Jour de Fête* won the prize for best scenario in Venice and in 1950 the Grand Prix du Cinéma at Cannes.

More of the same was immediately requested by would-be financiers, to the extent that *L'École des Facteurs*, even though only a first draft, was separately promoted and won its own prize in 1949. But Tati was not interested in fresh postman stories; he was preoccupied with what he termed a twentieth-century Everyman, a figure affording him more scope because he would fit – or rather, *not* fit – into a wider range of settings. The filmed result – after financial problems, painstaking preparation, and several years – was *Monsieur Hulot's Holiday*, which became an instant world-wide favourite.

Once again using an authentic background, that of St. Marc-sur-Mer in Brittany, the film satirized the universal holiday-maker and introduced the frightening and endearing character of Hulot, who charged into the peculiarly brittle fabric of seaside society with all the gusto and misapprehension of a three-year-old. Despite his air of desperate improvisation, Hulot's mishaps were meticulously planned before Tati even arrived at the location, and it was another three months before he started shooting. So much comic detail was inserted that at times the film appears not to be about Hulot at all and this, surprisingly, is just what Tati was after. A French interviewer at the time reported:

'Ideally, Tati would like a film of the adventures of Hulot in which Hulot himself did not appear. His presence would be apparent simply from the more or less catastrophic upheavals left in his wake.'

It was not an approach that would find many sympathizers, and Hulot has remained

---

Filmography

1932 Oscar, Champion de Tennis (short) (+sc; +actor). '34 On Demande Une Brute (short) (co-sc +actor only). '35 Gai Dimanche (short) (co-sc +actor only). '36 Soigne ton Gauche (short) (sc. +actor only). '45 Sylvie et le Fantome (USA: Sylvie and the Phantom; GB: Sylvie and the Ghost) (act. only). '47 L'Ecole des Facteurs (short) (+sc; +dial; +act); Le Diable au Corps (USA: The Devil in the Flesh) (act only). '49 Jour de Fête (USA: Day of the Fair) (+co-sc; +co-dial; +act). '53 Les Vacances de Monsieur Hulot (Monsieur Hulot's Holiday) (+co-sc; +co-dial; +act). '58 Mon Oncle (My Uncle) (+co-sc; +co-dial +act) (FR-IT). '68 Playtime (+sc; +act). '70 Trafic (Traffic) (+co-sc; +act) (FR-IT). '74 Parade (+sc; +act) (made for FR TV).

Jacques Tati

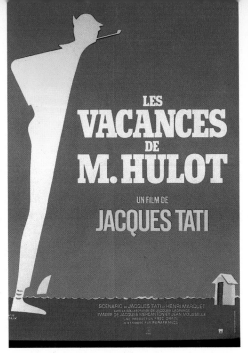

Left and above: the film that established Tati's Hulot character. Below: Hulot regards his sister's new kitchen (left) in Mon Oncle and the modern glass office-blocks of Playtime (right) with equal suspicion

on view in all Tati's subsequent work, He has echoes of many screen clowns, primarily in his embarrassment at the problem of what to do with himself in a world patently ill-suited, not only to his physical awkwardness, but also to his inner remoteness. Hulot works twice as hard as anybody else at the task of integration – the tennis match in *Monsieur Hulot's Holiday* and the garden party in *Mon Oncle* (1958, My Uncle) show him at his most frenzied in the battle to keep up appearances – but a certain jauntiness in the angle of pipe and umbrella, a natty style of hat, and a private choreography of walk in which he seems to choose his own confident road along invisible stepping-stones, imply that secretly he does not care too desperately that the world is hell-bent on progress. He is a gentle anarchist, too polite and affectionate to shake the nonsense out of his contemporaries; if they cannot be contented, at least he can find his own kind of peace in isolation.

In *Mon Oncle* – which appeared after nine months of shooting and a year of cutting and dubbing – Hulot often seems withdrawn, a hermit in his own cosy part of town, although his struggle to be a part of everything continues. Tati explained:

'The film conducts a defence of the individual, I don't like to be regimented, I don't like mechanization. I believe in the old quarter, the tranquil corner, rather than in highways, roads, aerodromes and all the organization in modern life. People aren't at their best with geometrical lines all round them'.

Mon Oncle proceeded to show people *not* at their best in a quietly biased, irresistibly sentimental comparison between the old and the new and the widening gulf between them. Winner of the Special Jury Prize at Cannes in 1958, the film was celebrated by the *Cahiers du Cinéma* critics such as Godard and Truffaut, who were to bring about a stylistic revolution in their films the following year – putting across their own disquiet more forcefully. For all that, however, *Mon Oncle* more clearly defined the views of the 'old-school' such as Renoir and Clair. Hulot the charming recluse was the model for a decade of drop-outs, but his unswerving kindness and imperturbable good manners were an archaic and quixotic armour in the era of computerized dehumanization that called for the rude brutality of Godard's comic-book detective Lemmy Caution to defend such concepts as poetry and love.

When *Playtime* appeared a long time later in 1968, after Tati had spent three years constructing it with a massive £1 million budget, it had nothing to add. An anaemic Hulot wanders around the glass boxes of the modern Paris, an aimless ghost in a procession of repetitive and only mildly amusing incongruities. Like Antonioni, Tati strengthened his anti-urban argument by making the architecture a dominating force, but went a stage further by building his own studio city, spotless and soulless, like a maze enclosing experimental mice. And like the holiday-makers of

Monsieur Hulot's Holiday, the mice are recognizable 'types' – the American tourists, the German salesmen, the little old ladies who need someone to mend a simple electric lamp but find that such expertise is not available in today's sophistication, the fussing married couple, the waiters who never get round to serving anybody. Hulot strikes up a tentative friendship with an American girl and gives her a present to take back home; it is a small bunch of flowers, but they are plastic. Intentional or not, it makes a melancholy symbol for the film as a whole; precise, well-meant, a spectacular piece of craftsmanship but not much of a substitute for reality.

With *Trafic* (1970 Traffic), Tati was on happier ground. Hulot is a driver in a convoy of new cars *en route* from Paris to an international motor show in Amsterdam. More prominent as a character than in *Playtime*, but still a model of detachment, he has come to terms with progress to the extent that he tends to have the solution to such problems as breakdowns, traffic-jams, and car crashes, offering good sense while his contemporaries swarm about in counter-productive distraction. Tati satirizes all the less lethal driving habits, stringing together an amiable line of sight-gags – like a squashed shape under a car-wheel that could be either dead dog or discarded jacket – which have an edge to them that is discreetly blunted to avoid the shedding of blood. Discretion, after all, has always been the essence of Tati's humour, and in the era of the indiscreet we should be grateful that he continues to give us a sporting chance.

PHILIP STRICK

as a magician, who must seduce his audience into accepting the reality of his ventures into the realms of the imagination. In *Le Sang d'un Poète*, all of Cocteau's preoccupations are brought vividly to life, thanks to the cinema's ability to present them in both body and spirit: the immutable barrier that separates a lover from the object of his desire; a mirror that functions as a door offering escape to the beyond; the independent life assumed by a work of art; the deaths an artist must suffer before he can live, and his inevitable martyrdom at the hands of his creation.

The seduction is here, unmistakably, in the charming fantasy with which Cocteau endows such conceits as the living mouth which transfers itself from a drawing to the artist's hand, stubbornly resisting his horrified attempts to erase it. Yet the film remains essentially a hermetic game, with Cocteau content to remain the dilettante who elegantly amuses and puzzles, scenting his hints of mythical profundity with a delicate aroma of perversity. The magic, the mysterious skill whereby an artist makes his audience captive and willing to follow where he leads, was not fully apparent until *La Belle et la Bête* (1945, *Beauty and the Beast*), *Orphée* and *Le Testament d'Orphée* (1959, *Testament of Orpheus*).

Significantly enough, before he eventually returned to film-making after a 15-year gap, Cocteau spent several years of painstaking

Jean Cocteau–Waking Dreams

'I should like people to find my images realistic. If I annoy anyone with my trick shots . . . it's because I want the true irreal that allows all of us to dream the same dream together. This is not the dream of sleep. It's the waking dream, irreal realism, more true than the truth'
Jean Cocteau

Possessed of an enviably diversified talent – as well as an infallible instinct for attracting attention – Jean Cocteau (1889–1963) was a success right from the moment of the publication of his first volumes of verse, *La Lampe d'Aladin* in 1909 and *Le Prince Frivole* in 1910. Gifted with a literary style that could seem either trenchant or precious, and with a knack for line drawing that was limited but uniquely his own, Cocteau proceeded to skip bewilderingly from art form to art form, pouring out an array of poems, novels, plays, essays, films, paintings, ballet and opera libretti, and also designs for posters, tapestries, jewellery, pottery and even neckties.

The title of his second book – 'The Frivolous Prince' – aptly describes the brilliant young man who became the darling of fashionable society during and after World War I, delighting with the daring of his conceits, stimulating with his championing of new forms, scandalizing with his intimations of homosexuality. He was the natural heir to the *fin-de-siècle* aesthete, but busily extended both his image and his talent by becoming tangenitally involved in everything new, from Diaghilev's *Ballets Russes* and the group of composers known as *Les Six* to the Surrealism movement and talking pictures.

This grasshopper image was hardly likely to endear him to the serious-minded. And even in the cinema, where he was first hailed without reservation as a genius, he had earlier been held to be a dilettante frittering away his talent in brilliant pyrotechnics. It is worth remembering, now that Cocteau's reputation is so secure, that his first film, *Le Sang d'un Poète* (1930, *The Blood of a Poet*), used to be disparaged as parlour surrealism by comparison with the genuine article in Buñuel's *L'Age d'Or* (1930, *The Golden Age*); and that when his masterpiece *Orphée* (*Orpheus*) was first shown in Paris in 1950, even the film-buff audience of the Latin Quarter had been conditioned to jeer at Cocteau's supposed affectations.

'I have been accused of jumping from branch to branch', Cocteau once said, 'Well I have – but always in the same tree.' Even a casual glance at his work confirms how constant his preoccupations were. The same themes, memories and images continually recur in different guises, pressed into new associations and revealing new meanings in the long, autobiographical journey into imaginative self-discovery that is formed by his collected works. But it was through the cinema that Cocteau managed to pull all the divergent strands together into a coherent whole.

Film was a perfect medium for the marriage of Cocteau's talents; the 'cinematograph', as he liked to call it, and its marvellous box of tricks was tailor-made for his view of the artist

apprenticeship in which he wrote scripts, acted and served as observer-assistant to other film-makers. His purpose was only partly to absorb the necessary techniques; he was also attempting to discover a structure, a visual and thematic approach, that would enable him to express his private mythologies in terms accessible to the public.

L'Eternel Retour (1943, *Love Eternal*), which he scripted for Jean Delannoy, is usually cited as the most rewarding of these experiments, perhaps because its rather glacial retelling of the Tristan and Isolde legend, characteristically placing the accent on the death wish

The Phantom Baron even heightens this fairy-tale element by juxtaposing it with everyday reality in a manner that was also to become typical of Cocteau's films. In *La Belle et la Bête*, fantasy and reality become so complementary that it is impossible not to believe in the truth of Cocteau's fairy-tale; and in *Orphée*, myth is so firmly rooted in everyday life that Cocteau's poetic exploration of the creative imagination also functions, simultaneously and seamlessly, as a superb *film noir* thriller. TOM MILNE

Opposite page, top left: Cocteau walks the realms of his imagination in Le Testament d'Orphée. *Left and above:* La Belle et la Bête *captured the magic of fairy-tale. Below: the artist's sculpture comes alive in* Le Sang d'un Poète. *Top right: a creature of myth from* Le Testament d'Orphée

(only in death can love remain eternal), echoes the mood and manner Cocteau evolved in such stage plays as *Antigone* and *Renaud et Armide*. Much more interesting, however, is *Le Baron Fantôme* (*The Phantom Baron*), directed by Serge de Poligny in the same year. Cocteau is credited only as dialogue writer, in addition to playing a small role; but the film, despite several lapses, is so quintessentially Cocteau that he either set his stamp on the whole venture, or was radically influenced by the

otherwise obscure de Poligny.

Two of the best sequences in the film are the opening, clearly derived from Murnau's *Nosferatu* (1922), in which a carriage drives through a landscape of mist and blasted trees until the wind begins to howl, a ruined castle looms into view, and the traveller struggles on foot through a garden of fallen tree-trunks and tangled undergrowth; and the even more striking scene in which the sleepwalking hero, like Cesare in *Das Kabinett des Dr Caligari* (1919, *The Cabinet of Dr Caligari*), bears a girl away in his arms through the night, her scarf floating behind her in the moonlight.

The common ground in these sequences, as in much of the rest of the film, is the element of fairy-tale enchantment which Cocteau inherited from the archetypal imagery of the horror film and used in his quest for 'magic'.

Filmography
1925 Jean Cocteau Fait du Cinéma (short). **'30** Le Sang d'un Poète (+sc; +ed; +decor; +voices; +dubbing (all roles but leading actress). **'40** La Comédie du Bonheur (sc. only). **'43** Le Baron Fantôme (dial; +act. only) (GB: The Phantom Baron); L'Eternel Retour (sc. only) (GB: Love Eternal). **'44** La Malibran (act. only); Tennis (+comm; +narr) (short). **'45** La Belle et la Bête (+sc; +dubbing of one actor) (USA/GB: Beauty and the Beast); Les Dames du Bois de Boulogne (dial. only). **'46** L'Amitié Noire (comm; + narr. only) (short). **'47** L'Aigle à Deux Têtes (+sc; +narr) (USA: The Eagle With Two Heads); Ruy Blas (sc. only). **'48** Les Parents Terribles (+sc; +narr) (USA: Intimate Relations); Les Noces de Sable (comm; +narr. only); La Légende de Sainte Ursule (comm; +narr. only) (short) (FR version of IT short: La Leggenda di Sant' Orsola); Venise et Ses Amants (comm; + narr. only) (short) (FR version of IT short: Romantici a Venezia). **'49** Ce Siècle a Cinquante Ans *ep* 1914 (sc. only); Désordre (guest appearance as himself); Jean Cocteau (guest appearance as himself) (short) (DEN); Les Enfants Terribles (co-sc; +dial; +narr; +act; +add. dir, uncredited; +voice only). **'50** Orphée (+sc; +voices) (USA: Orpheus); Coriolan (+sc; +ed; +decor; +act); Goya (comm; +narr. only) (short) (FR version of IT film). **'51** Le Rossignol de l'Empereur de Chine (comm; + narr. only) (FR version of CZ puppet film); Colette (interviewer only) (short). **'52** La Villa Santo-Sospir (+prod; +sc; +ed; +décor; +act) (short); Le Rouge est Mis (comm; +narr. only) (short). **'53** Gustave Doré (introduction only); Cocteau (guest appearance as himself only) (short). **'54** Pantomimes (introduction only) (short); La Porte de l'Enfer (introduction only); Eine Melodie, Vier Maler (guest appearance as himself; +narr. only) (short) (GER). **'55** A l'Aube d'un Monde/A l'Aube d'un Monde Atomique (comm; +narr. only). **'56** 8×8 *ep* Queening of the Pawn (+sc; +act) (FR-USA). **'57** Le Musée Grévin (+act) (short). **'58** Django Reinhardt (introduction only) (short). **'59** Le Testament d'Orphée ou Ne Me Demandez Pas Pourquoi (+sc; +act; +narr) (USA: Testament of Orpheus); Sainte-Blaise-des-Simples (décor only) (short). **'60** La Princesse de Clèves (sc. only). **'62** Anna la Bonne (mus; +lyr. only) (short); Egypte o Egypte (comm; +narr only of *ep* Dans Ce Jardin Stroce). **'64** Thomas l'Imposteur (co-sc. only); Le Désordre a Vingt Ans/Voilà l'Ordre (guest appearance as himself); (included footage from Désordre).

Films de France present

ORPHEUS

AN IMMORTAL THRILLER

written and directed by

Jean Cocteau

*

with **JEAN MARAIS**
FRANÇOIS PÉRIER
MARIA CASARÈS
MARIE DÉA

ORPHEUS (A)

English sub-titles

Directed by Jean Cocteau, 1950
Prod co: André Paulvé/Films du Palais-Royal. **sc:** Jean Cocteau. **photo:** Nicolas Hayer. **art dir:** Jean d'Eaubonne. **mus:** Georges Auric. **sd:** J. Calvet. **cost:** Marcel Escoffier. **prod man:** Emile Darbon. **r/t:** 112 minutes. Released in the USA as *Orpheus*.
Cast: Jean Marais (*Orphée*), Maria Casarès (*The Princess*), Marie Déa (*Eurydice*), François Périer (*Heurtebise*), Juliette Greco (*Aglaonice*), Edouard Dermithe (*Cégeste*), Henri Crémieux (*editor*), Pierre Bertin (*police inspector*), Roger Blin (*poet*), André Carnège, René Worms, Renée Cosima (*judges*), René Lacour (*postman*), Jean-Pierre Melville (*hotel manager*), Maffre (*agent*).

The disarming fact about the fantasy in *Orphée* is its absolutely irrefutable logic. Stand in front of a mirror, and what do you see? Yourself, of course, but in a slightly alien guise, a stranger who might just conceivably have access to another world. Or again, you see the door through which death comes and goes; as Heurtebise explains to the bewildered Orphée: 'Watch yourself all your life in a mirror and you will see death at work, like bees in a hive of glass.'

In front of a café on a quiet square, a literary lion's den where Orphée slightly shamefacedly defends his establishment position, a gleaming Rolls suddenly purrs into view. Out of it steps a woman, elegant and predatory, clad in a white jacket and a black gown. Two motor-cyclists roar by, anonymously muffled in helmets, gauntlets and goggles, leaving a spread-eagled corpse in their wake.

One hardly needs the additional evidence of the strange car journey through the night, pausing at a 'Stygian' level-crossing as the motor-cyclists join the cortège and the landscape is mysteriously transformed (by a sudden switch into negative projection), to recognize that Cocteau has created a perfect modern metaphorical equivalent for the classical mythology of death; here it comes at high speed, brought by 'hell's angels' – a cavalier way to go which trails its own alluring glamour as fearsome, as fascinating and as perverse as the

cold enigmatic Princess herself.

The theme Cocteau orchestrates in *Orphée* is his perennial one: 'A poet must die several times in order to be born.' Orphée dies the first time to affirm his earthly love for his wife; a second time to defend his poetic inspiration (a false inspiration since the poems come from elsewhere, from the exterior rather than from inside the poet himself); and a third, in despairing acknowledgment of the impossibility of his other love in the mirror-world beyond reality.

The astonishing thing about the film is that, even while conducting this intricate metaphysical disquisition, it remains wholly gripping. It is, in fact, immensely *thrilling* in a sense rather lost to the cinema since the days of silent movies. As Orphée watches the Princess and her aides glide through a mirror which becomes instantly impenetrable to his touch, or accompanies Heurtebise in his gliding descent through monumental ruins that mark the limbo between Earth and the Underworld, one is irresistibly reminded of the great, surrealistic serials of Louis Feuillade, in which the real, everyday world is lent a disturbingly unfamiliar quality.

In theory, the rules of the Underworld in *Orphée*, whereby Death comes and goes by mirror, are simple; but in the film, Cocteau keeps a number of surprises up his sleeve. Particularly notable is the marvellous moment when the en-

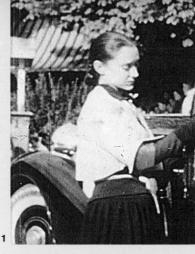

Orphée, a distinguished poet, is fascinated by the appearance, at a literary café, of the enigmatic Princess and her protégé Cégeste (1), whose avant-garde poems are being praised at the expense of his own work. When the drunken Cégeste is run over by two motor-cyclists (2 and 3), the Princess asks Orphée to help put the body in her Rolls. They drive, not to hospital, but to the lady's remote house. Orphée is amazed to see that the same motor-cyclists that killed Cégeste are the Princess' servants.

Orphée later sees the Princess raise Cégeste from the dead; the pair and their attendants then pass through a mirror (4). Orphée tries in vain to follow and falls asleep against the mirror (5). He wakes up lying on the bare ground (6) and is taken home by the Princess' chauffeur, Heurtebise.

Orphée arrives to find his wife, Eurydice, with a police inspector and Aglaonice, who leads a women's group called the Bacchantes (7). He rudely tells them to leave. That night, the figure of the mysterious Princess haunts Orphée's dreams (8).

Heurtebise stays with Eurydice and Orphée, who becomes so fascinated by the strange snatches of poetry emitted by the Rolls' radio that he begins to neglect his wife. Ignoring Heurtebise's warnings that the radio messages offer false inspiration and that Eurydice is in danger, Orphée is heartbroken to learn that she has been killed by the motor-cyclists.

Heurtebise explains that the Princess is one of death's many agents and, in order to help Orphée win back his wife, shows him how to pass through a mirror into the Underworld (9). A tribunal of judges, aware that the Princess killed Eurydice to further her own love for Orphée, decree that Eurydice may return to life provided Orphée never looks at her again. Orphée, still obsessed by the Princess and the poetry from the radio, carelessly breaks

raged Princess, accused by Heurtebise of having killed Orphée's wife because she herself loves him, imperiously shatters the mirror with her fist (instead of observing the prescribed routine of gliding through it wearing rubber gloves), and the sudden metamorphosis of her black robe to dazzling white in **6** simultaneous acknowledgment of Heurtebise's charge.

A common, although minor, critical reservation about the film has often been the banality of the scenes between Orphée and Eurydice at home. Although Cocteau admittedly presents a dismayingly stereotyped view of domesticity (the close-up of a knitted baby shoe which Orphée tramples underfoot, too excited by his discoveries to listen to his wife's 'great news'; the mild comic horseplay as Orphée and Eurydice try to adjust to a home life in which he must not look at her), this banality is an inescapable element of the whole. It is the 'mire' to which the poet must be returned, and which the new vision he has been granted may eventually illuminate. *Orphée* is one of the French cinema's supreme masterpieces, magnificently acted and photographed, and expressing the very quintessence of Cocteau's vision and genius.   TOM MILNE **9**

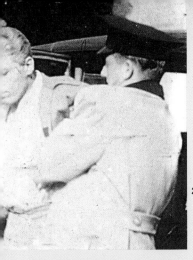

the taboo by glimpsing his wife in the rear-view mirror of the Rolls (10 and 11). He is then killed by a mob led by the Bacchantes (12), who believe that he murdered Cégeste to steal his poems.

Finally the Princess and Heurtebise, who loves Eurydice, are forced to acknowledge that love is impossible for them. They allow Orphée and Eurydice to be reunited (13) and are themselves led away to be punished for falling in love with mortals.

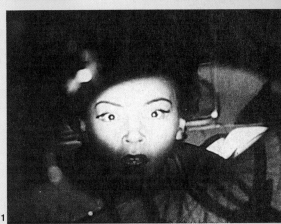

Waiting for Godard

The New Wave of French film-making, spearheaded by Jean-Luc Godard and François Truffaut, was preceded by a period in which cinema consolidated its pre-war reputation for artistic achievement

In commercial terms, French cinema in the Fifties was the healthiest in Europe. Production was maintained at a steady and relatively high rate in comparison with other major film-making countries outside of the USA. Although the market was restricted to domestic and French-speaking territories, (thereby limiting the amount of money French films could earn), careful budgeting on the part of producers along with an efficient and well-established star system and regular attendance figures guaranteed reasonable profit margins.

It was only towards the end of the decade that the threat of television made itself felt; this new distraction, together with the burgeoning French obsession with cars, holidays and other leisure pursuits, would cause annual attendances between 1957 and 1966 to plummet from 411 million to 232 million. In consequence, some 4000 cinemas closed their doors for the last time.

In the meantime, however, French audiences appeared well pleased with their national cinema. The staple diet was Hollywood-influenced thrillers, 'naughty' sex comedies and period pieces, along with perennial vehicles designed for such local superstars as Jean Gabin, Fernandel and Martine Carol. More significantly the cinema had, almost since its inception, enjoyed intellectual respectability in France and was soon to become a positive passion among educated young people. In this way it was possible for a so-called 'art film', like Robert Bresson's *Un Condamné à Mort S'Est Echappé* (1956, *A Man Escaped*), to chalk up excellent returns at the box-office.

This respectability was encouraged by unusually energetic government measures to aid the industry at its frequent moments of crisis. In the immediate post-war period, the number of domestically made films had declined to the point where numerous cinemas risked closure through lack of product. This situation was aggravated by the quota system (instituted long before World War II) that limited the importation of dubbed American films to 120 a year. In 1946 a pact known as the Blum-Byrnes Agreement was signed between France and the USA under the terms of which the quota was lifted and replaced by one regulating the number of French films that cinemas were compelled to screen. The authorities settled on a figure of 37 per cent, even though French film production could have easily exceeded such a quota.

Those sectors of the industry engaged in distribution and exploitation benefited enormously from the Blum-Byrnes Agreement and flooded the market with dubbed Hollywood films. The effect on the production side of the business, however, was disastrous. After concerted protests from the industry and the press, the Agreement was revoked in 1949; the domestic quota was revised upwards and the level of imported American films re-established at 120. Furthermore, a surtax was levied on cinemas and from it a fund was set up to help finance the industry. This proved a major boost to production until the system was changed again in 1959.

Artistically, however, the picture was less sanguine. Viewed with hindsight, the Fifties appears as an interim period, a generally flat plateau sandwiched between the glories of pre-war cinema (and the isolated miracles effected under the Occupation) and the irresistible ascension of the *nouvelle vague* in the early Sixties.

Many of the film-makers who had dominated the Thirties – Jacques Feyder, Julien Duvivier, René Clair, Jean Renoir – were only now returning to France from self-imposed exile. Although the last three (Feyder died in 1948) were to continue working with semi-regularity all through the Fifties, only the youthfully inquisitive Renoir really knew how to adapt to changing conditions and evolving techniques.

The pre-war style of 'poetic realism' lingered on in post-war films like *Les Portes de la Nuit* (1946, *Gates of the Night*) but after the dream-like *Juliette,*

Above: in Juliette, ou la Clé des Songes *Gérard Philipe plays a young prisoner who dreams of a mysterious land where his ideal love, Juliette (Suzanne Cloutier), is engaged to the evil but debonair Bluebeard (Jean-Roger Caussimon). Below: Gérard Philipe as Modigliani in* Montparnasse 19, *a biopic about the celebrated French painter who succumbed to drink in the last years of his life*

Top: Edouard et Caroline, *though virtually plotless, was a memorable study of young married life in middle-class Parisian society. Above: poster from one of André Cayatte's social problem films*

ou la Clé des Songes (1950, Juliette, or the Key to Dreams), Marcel Carné, who together with his scenarist Jacques Prévert had been the architect of this style, found himself driven into a career of crass commercialism.

For the three most notable mainstream directors who had come to prominence during the Occupation – Jacques Becker, Henri-Georges Clouzot and René Clément – the Fifties saw the consolidation of their talents. If Becker, the most original, is largely forgotten today, it is doubtless due to the slightly disconcerting diversity of his work, almost all of it in a minor key. He was a modest creator, unconcerned with uttering grand statements and it was this modesty which endeared him to some of the younger directors such as François Truffaut, later in the decade.

Becker's work is marked by a meticulous, though never oppressive, sense of detail and a precise rendering of time and place, whether in the register of intimate comedy-drama like Edouard et Caroline (1951), the thriller Touchez Pas au Grisbi (1954, Honour Among Thieves), the 'biopic' Montparnasse 19 (1958, The Lovers of Montparnasse) in which Gérard Philipe played the painter Modigliani, or the prison-escape movie Le Trou (1960, The Hole). In a period when French cinema was balefully devoid of human warmth, it was especially refreshing to encounter Becker's characterizations and the bemused affection which he contrived to extend, even to the most minor of characters.

Becker died in 1960 at the age of 54. If he left behind no undisputed masterpiece, he will perhaps be most fondly remembered for Casque d'Or (1952, Golden Marie), a tragic love-story set in turn-of-the-century Paris and enshrining a magnificent performance by Simone Signoret.

Clouzot's position could hardly be more diametrically opposed to that of Becker. His reputation for absolute rigour and perfectionism was often more applicable to his notoriously finicky shooting methods than to the results he achieved on the screen. Clouzot's is a cinema shot through with blackness verging on nihilism. Manon (1949), his version of the Abbé Prévost's novel Manon Lescaut, updated to the twilight, post-war world of black-marketeers and clandestine refugee ships bound for Palestine, has at its centre what must be the least sympathetic pair of young lovers in cinema history.

The work which established Clouzot internationally, Le Salaire de la Peur (1953, Wages of Fear) concerned four dead-enders paid to transport a cargo of nitro-glycerine over the bumpy, deeply rutted roads of South America, and ended with the violent deaths of all four.

Except for Le Mystère Picasso (1956, The Picasso Mystery), an utterly fascinating and intelligently straightforward study of the artist in the throes of creation, Clouzot never regained the heights of his artistic achievement, although Les Diaboliques (1955, The Fiends) was a huge commercial success both in France and abroad. Les Espions (1957, The Spies) was a confused and pretentious spy thriller, obviously intended to be Kafkaesque and even more obviously failing. La Vérité (1960, The Truth), a court-room drama, revealed the growing nouvelle vague influence in its choice of theme (the amorality of modern youth) and star (Brigitte Bardot), but was otherwise stamped with Clouzot's own stolid if efficient technique. After this box-office triumph his career went into decline until his death in 1977.

Clément, who had served his apprenticeship as Jean Cocteau's assistant on La Belle et la Bête (1945, Beauty and the Beast) and made one of the rare French films with any claims to neo-realism, La Bataille du Rail (1946, The Battle of the Railway Workers), was the quintessential craftsman, cru-

cially dependent on his scripts and not noticeably animated by a passion to explore the boundaries of his chosen medium. Clément's greatest success was Jeux Interdits (1952, Forbidden Games) which dealt with the secret universe created by two small children in wartime. His subsequent career included a British film, Knave of Hearts (1954), an Ealing-like comedy set in London; Gervaise (1956), the obligatory adaptation from a classic novel with Maria Schell as the heroine of Zola's tale of alcoholism in nineteenth-century France; and La Diga Sul Pacifico (1958, The Sea Wall), a turgid international co-production based on a novel by Marguerite Duras.

Among Clément's more interesting work is Plein Soleil (1959, Blazing Sun), an adaptation of one of Patricia Highsmith's Ripley thrillers. Its fluid, versatile camerawork by the cinematographer Henri Decaë (later to become a major stylist in the nouvelle vague), the predominantly young and attractive cast (including Alain Delon, Maurice Ronet and Marie Laforet) and a clearly perceptible influence from Hitchcock, further underlines the inroads which the young directors were making into mainstream cinema.

To these names should be added that of Claude Autant-Lara who started as a set-designer with the painter Fernand Léger and the architect Mallet-Stevens on Marcel L'Herbier's silent film L'Inhumaine (1924, Futurism). From the lending-library of literary adaptations which comprise Autant-Lara's post-war work (ranging from Stendhal, Dumas and Dostoevsky, to Feydeau, Colette and Simenon) we might single out La Traversée de Paris (1956, A Pig Across Paris), a black comedy about two men involved in the black-market meat trade. Though marred by a complacent reliance on studio sets and lighting, when the material cried out for location shooting, the film is distinguished by a quite subtle modulation from comedy to tragedy and the cold, not to say, beady eye cast by the director on his two hapless protagonists.

From the point of view of subject matter, French cinema was very tightly controlled during this period. Government aid was withheld from any film seeking to reflect the contemporary political reality of the country, plagued in these years by two colonial wars – in Indo-China and Algeria. Indeed the only French film by a major director treating, even indirectly, the Algerian war was Jean-Luc Godard's Le Petit Soldat (1960, The Little Soldier), and that was banned from exhibition for three years.

The prevailing political climate may explain the critical favour then enjoyed by André Cayatte, a barrister turned film-maker. In four widely discussed films: Justice Est Faite (1950, Let Justice Be Done), Nous Sommes Tous des Assassins (1952, Are We All Murderers?), Avant le Déluge (1954, Before the Flood) and Le Dossier Noir (1955, The Black Pamphlet) Cayatte and his scenarist Charles Spaak tackled a variety of social and legal problems such as euthanasia, capital punishment and juvenile delinquency. The films are, however, very flatly shot: André Cayatte's penchant for the basic shot/reaction-shot set-up ideally suited the dramatic confrontations in which his films traded. Dry and schematic, they frequently made recourse to loaded arguments and special pleading. The issues are developed in terms of right versus wrong, sympathies are engaged according to the charismatic qualities of the actors playing the roles, the condemned man whose fate hangs in the balance invariably turns out to be innocent, and so on.

These were the directors most violently attacked by a group of up-and-coming critics (François Truffaut, Jean-Luc Godard, Eric Rohmer) who wrote in Cahiers du Cinéma and who, as directors

Above: the poster from Godard's Breathless *(1960) aptly reflects the fragmentary, modernist style of the film itself. Below: the director Henri-Georges Clouzot and the starlet Brigitte Bardot relaxing on the set of* La Vérité

themselves, were to revitalize French cinema towards the end of the decade. A celebrated polemical piece by Truffaut entitled 'Concerning a Certain Tendency in French Cinema' was a St Valentine's Day Massacre of what he derisively referred to as 'le cinéma de papa'.

Only a handful of film-makers survived the massacre. Renoir was one, and in the Fifties he completed a trio of what might loosely be termed 'musical comedies'. *Le Carrosse d'Or* (1952, *The Golden Coach*) was a bitter-sweet meditation on the interrelation of theatre and life centred on a Commedia dell'arte troupe touring in eighteenth-century Peru; *French Cancan* (1955) emerged as a lovingly detailed homage to La Belle Epoque, which his father (the impressionist painter, Auguste) had immortalized. *Eléna et les Hommes* (1956, *Paris Does Strange Things*) took the form of a witty 'spoken operetta' about General Boulanger's attempted *coup d'état* in the 1880's.

In his haughtily austere manner, Robert Bresson continued his lonely pursuit of cinematic Grace in *Le Journal d'un Curé de Campagne* (1951, *Diary of a Country Priest*), tracing the career of a priest from his arrival in the village of Ambricourt through his sufferings to his death from cancer. In *Un Condamné à Mort S'Est Echappé* the same severe, single-minded approach to character was evident in the account of a condemned man's escape from prison. *Pickpocket* (1959) was set in the bustling, crowded streets of Paris, but once again the central character's inner life was Bresson's subject.

The supreme stylist of the period – and the cinema's equivalent of the novelist Marcel Proust – was the Viennese-born Max Ophuls. His long, intricately plotted tracking and dolly shots in *Le Plaisir* (1952, Pleasure) and in *Madame de . . .* (1953) embellished these fine adaptations from Maupassant and Louise de Vilmorin respectively. Ophuls' masterpiece, *Lola Montès* (1955), an account of the nineteenth-century courtesan told within the framework of a circus-ring setting, was hacked to pieces by its producers but virulently defended by the young critics: Truffaut compared the humiliation of Martine Carol's Lola to that of Joan of Arc at the stake.

With only two features to his credit in the Fifties, Jacques Tati laid claim to being the most original creator of comedies France had ever produced. *Les Vacances de Monsieur Hulot* (1953, *Monsieur Hulot's Holiday*) portrayed the accident-prone Hulot character on vacation in a normally quiet seaside town. The sequel, *Mon Oncle* (1958, *My Uncle*), showed the same character attempting to cope with the gadgetry of modern living at the home of his brother-in-law Arpel.

Finally, although Jean Cocteau made only two films in the decade – *Orphée* (1950, *Orpheus*) and *Le Testament d'Orphée* (1959, *Testament of Orpheus*) – the spidery watermark of his signature could be traced through the whole decade and even more visibly in the one that followed.

These great artists, always considerably more than regents waiting for the young princes of the *nouvelle vague* to come of age, kept French cinema alive until François Truffaut's *Les Quatre Cents Coups* (*The Four Hundred Blows*) and Alain Resnais' *Hiroshima Mon Amour* (Hiroshima My Love) created the now historic *succès de scandale* at the 1959 Cannes Film Festival.

Indeed the rigid structure of the industry had already been dented by the work of a few younger directors, notably Roger Vadim, whose Bardot vehicles have often been confused with *nouvelle vague* cinema but were rather the frothy foam on its crest, and Jean-Pierre Melville. But it was in the field of short films that the first tangible signs of aesthetic renewal emerged. Shorts were generously subsidized by the state and provided an exceptionally fruitful training ground for apprentice directors.

Georges Franju, who was subsequently to pursue his career in feature films, made his reputation with a series of shorts which transformed the mundane format of 'information films' into cooly poetic indictments of injustice. *Le Sang des Bêtes* (1949, Beasts' Blood), a documentary on abbatoirs, made an unforgettable impression by the surreal juxtaposition of its placidly banal treatment and narration and the elemental horror of its imagery.

Franju's *Hôtel des Invalides* (1952, The Invalides Museum) took as its subject the French war museum whose trophies, memorials and weaponry it catalogued to hauntingly evocative effect. Other themes subjected by Franju to similar demystification were salmon breeding, stray dogs, and the cathedral of Notre Dame. At the end of the Fifties, Franju completed his second feature film *Les Yeux Sans Visage* (1959, *Eyes Without a Face*), a horror movie about a surgeon who 'steals' young girls' faces to graft onto that of his badly disfigured daughter. To put it fancifully, it was just what one imagines Cocteau's nightmares to be like.

Alain Resnais also started with short films, which were graced by a painterly sense of composition and a musical sense of editing. His first were studies of artists and their work and included Gauguin, Van Gogh, Picasso's *Guernica*, and African sculpture and statuary. His masterpiece in the short film was *Nuit et Brouillard* (1955, *Night and Fog*) in which touristy colour film of the concentration camps in 1955 was juxtaposed with newsreel and Nazi 'home movie' footage of the camps in operation, thus producing a document of great emotional power. In his following film, *Toute la Mémoire du Monde* (1957, The Whole Memory of the World), Resnais depicted the labyrinthine French national library as a concentration camp where books were incarcerated.

A more literary approach to film-making was evident in *Le Rideau Cramoisi* (1953, *The Crimson Curtain*) by the former critic Alexandre Astruc. A somewhat academic director, Astruc was of greater significance to film history as the author of an influential essay 'Le Caméra Stylo' (the movie camera as pen), in which he argued persuasively that films should be composed by their 'authors' in the same way that novels are—that the camera, in short, was the director's pen. It was this article together with the iconoclastic writings of the *Cahiers du Cinéma* critics and the theories of André Bazin that championed the work of those half dozen maverick French film-makers and prepared the way for the infinitely more bracing decade to come.

GILBERT ADAIR

Sweat, lust and dreams

The Italian popular cinema of the Fifties ranged from the lust of *Bitter Rice* by way of the blood-soaked fantasies of pirate films to the belly-laughs of Totò's comedy series

The years 1951–60 were the most exciting ever for Italian film-makers; they were the years of a remarkable and sustained dominance of European film culture by a group of writers and directors whose work astonished the world. Rossellini, Visconti, Fellini, De Sica, Antonioni and the unjustly neglected Pietro Germi destroyed the complacent image of the Italian cinema which had flourished under Mussolini. Their mastery of the medium was immediate, their talent acknowledged both at home and abroad, and their output prolific.

The neo-realist films of Rossellini and others had made immediate impact on critics and film-makers everywhere, and their influence on all Italian directors of the Fifties, excepting the historical genres, was considerable – especially in the matters of choice of subject and locations. The major effect of neo-realism on Italian cinema had been to broaden the scope of the industry, and to admit to its preoccupations the activities of the lower strata of Italian society. These were the influences which shaped the professional activities of many directors and writers thereafter.

The outstanding visual feature of neo-realism was the rawness of the image. The plots were simple or melodramatic, the dialogue functional or contrived, only some of the actors non-professionals. All the directors and writers whose work was initially neo-realist in style became full and confident users of the professional studios and equipment as they became available. The look of early neo-realism therefore was largely determined by economic constraints. The interest in the social and personal problems of real people – partly a reaction against the glossy fantasies of the Italian fascist cinema – was certainly sincere; but no Italian director in 1945 could afford to make *Quo Vadis* anyway.

By 1952, films such as Renato Castellani's *Sotto il Sole di Roma* (1948, Under the Roman Sun) and *Due Solde di Speranza* (1952, *Two Pennyworth of Hope*), Luciano Emmer's *Domenica d'Agosto* (1950, *Sunday in August*) and also Pietro Germi's work had led to the coining of a new phrase to describe a branching-out from neo-realism to *neorealismo rosa*, or realism through rose-tinted spectacles.

The films of Pietro Germi, whatever their ostensible backgrounds, were invariably preoccupied with questions of personal honour and commitment to codes of behaviour. Although he had never been to Sicily before making *In Nome della Legge* (1949, *In the Name of the Law*), he frequently returned to the island, with its brooding ambience of fearful independence, its tribal suspicions and its perverse moralities. Marcello Mastroianni's restlessly comic wife-murderer in *Divorzio all' Italiana* (1961, *Divorce – Italian Style*) is a prisoner of the same society as Sarò Urzi's honest carabiniere of *In the Name of the Law* and the tragic heroine of *Sedotta e Abandonata* (1964, *Seduced and Abandoned*), a Sicilian girl (Stefania Sandrelli) whose life is ruined because of the rigid code of honour which prevails in the mafioso-riddled island.

The protagonists of *Il Ferroviere* (1956, *Man of Iron*) and *L'Uomo di Paglia* (1958, *Man of Straw*) are faced with problems of choice, of betrayal of family or social obligations. In each case the strong paterfamilias is ultimately destroyed by the pressure of doubt or renunciation of previously accepted codes of behaviour. Even in the frothy costume comedy of *La Presidentessa* (1953, The Lady President), the plot involves the age-old double standard of wife and mistress and 'never the twain shall meet'. In *Un Maledetto Imbroglio* (1959, *A Sordid Affair*), the police investigator's constantly renewed touchstone of reality amid the deceit and violence of his daily routine is the camaraderie and mutual trust of his colleagues.

Artists like Germi, Rossellini, Visconti and the later neo-realists did not work in isolation but the masterpieces of great directors are rarely the first choice of the cinema-going public. Most of these film-makers were recognized by Italians as their finest directors and writers, but the comedies and melodramas of Mario Monicelli, Dino Risi and Raffaello Matarazzo were usually better attended.

The largest studios, at Cinecittà, had resumed production in 1947, with a programme of five films. In the ten years from 1950, total Italian film production rose to an average of 140 films per year. Box-office admissions reached 819 million in 1955, compared with 662 million in 1950 and 745 million

Below left: Pietro Germi, as the adulterous Man of Straw, *breaks with his girl (Franca Bettoja), who then commits suicide, forcing him to confess to his wife. Below: Gina Lollobrigida in King Vidor's lavish epic,* Solomon and Sheba *(1959). Bottom: Anna Maria Pierangeli (also known as Pier Angeli) is menaced by Robert Alda, Alan's dad, in Steno's* I Moschettieri del Mare *(1962, The Musketeers of the Sea)*

Top left: a French poster for the third of the Don Camillo series, Don Camillo e l'Onorevole Peppone *(1955), distributed in Britain as* Don Camillo's Last Round. *Top right: in* La Nave delle Donne Maledette *(1953, Women's Prison Ship), Mai Britt loves and suffers as an innocent convict whose cousin (Kerima) plots against her. Above: Gina Lollobrigida and Vittorio De Sica became an immensely popular team in the 'Bread, Love and . . .' films. Right: Totò plays the tutor in safe-cracking to an incompetent gang led by Vittorio Gassman in* Persons Unknown, *a prize-winner at the Locarno Film Festival in 1959*

in 1960 (falling to 319 million in 1978).

Much of the production activity reflected the peculiar and perennial preoccupation with the *peplum* and historical adventure film. The direct Hollywood involvement, from *Quo Vadis* (1951), directed by Mervyn LeRoy, through to *Ulisse* (1954, *Ulysses*), *Attila Flagello di Dio* (1965, *Attila the Hun*) and Robert Wise's *Helen of Troy* (1955), complemented and encouraged local initiatives.

Although more public and critical attention has been paid to the historical-mythological *peplum* films, the cape-and-sword melodramas were not entirely devoid of interest. They lacked the budgets and the lightness of touch of their Hollywood cousins, but often their disturbing mixture of juvenile plot development and blatant sadism was exemplary of a recurrent theme in Italian popular culture. Two films directed by Mario Soldati and starring Mai Britt, a would-be Garbo who never reached the heights, are clear examples: *Jolanda, la Figlia del Corsaro Nero* (1952, Yolanda, Daughter of the Black Pirate) and its simultaneously shot sequel, *I Tre Corsari* (1953, The Three Pirates). Bloody revenge, flogging, transvestism and torture embellish the threadbare plots of these swashbuckling

Sex and violence, preferably combined, were a sure-fire formula for commercial success

melodramas. The later so-called 'spaghetti' Westerns and increasingly perverse comic books, or *fumetti*, of the late Sixties and the Seventies amply illustrate developments of these themes.

Film series, in Italy as elsewhere, usually degenerated in quality as each succeeding film reworked the material of the original. Occasionally, a subsequent film in a series could equal the first. Both Julien Duvivier's *Il Piccolo Mondo di Don Camillo* (1952, *The Little World of Don Camillo*) and his *Il Ritorno di Don Camillo* (1953, *The Return of Don Camillo*) were exceedingly funny and faithful to Giovanni Guareschi's tales of unholy discord between the wily priest (Fernandel) and the communist mayor, Peppone (Gino Cervi), of a small village in the Po Valley. Later Don Camillo films, however, increasingly caricatured the pair, becoming unfunnier in the process, and failed to repeat the international success of the originals.

The 'Bread, Love and . . .' films, which also had wide distribution abroad, began with two directed by Luigi Comencini, *Pane, Amore e Fantasia* (1954, *Bread, Love and Dreams*) and *Pane, Amore e Gelosia* (1954, *Bread, Love and Jealousy*), both featuring Vittorio De Sica and Gina Lollobrigida at their most appealing. But it was the third in the series, Dino Risi's *Pane, Amore e . . .* (1955, *Scandal in Sorrento*) which achieved the greatest critical and public success.

The Totò films were the most enduring series: low-budget comedies which were rarely exported but were churned out by the dozen from 1948 to 1964. Totò (Antonio de Curtis Gagliardi Ducas Comnuno di Bisanzio) was a phenomenon. Between 1951 and 1960 he appeared in 48 films, most of which carried his name in the title and were opportunistically linked to some current film success or public event. In spirit they were a throwback to the Mack Sennett/Ben Turpin satires of the Twenties. The titles told all, and the quality of the material was rarely equal to the star's considerable talents: *Totò le Moko, Totò Sceicco* (Totò the Sheik) and *Totò Tarzan* (all 1950); *Totò Terzo Uomo* (1951, Totò the Third Man); *Totò al'Inferno* (1955, Totò in Hell); *Totò nella*

Luna (1958, *Totò on the Moon*) and so on. Totò was beloved by the crowds in the same way the British adore their comedians, with great tolerance of weak material. An admixture of Max Linder, Keaton and Chaplin, he combined lower class gentility with sly anti-authoritarianism, presented with an economical inventiveness of gesture and ingenious facial manipulation.

His Pulcinello face and slightly demonic dapperness were seen to brilliant effect in Mario Monicelli's superb caper-movie satire, *I Soliti Ignoti* (1958, *Persons Unknown*). He played an elder statesman of safe-cracking, tutoring a gang of resolutely incompetent thieves in the finer arts of larceny. While Totò's contribution was masterly, the whole film was a triumph of ensemble playing. Vittorio Gassman and Marcello Mastroianni were particularly effective.

Gassman never equalled the lightness of touch and comic sureness that he showed in the Monicelli and Risi films. Prior to *Persons Unknown* he had been known as a rather heavy dramatic actor, particulary in his Hollywood films of the early Fifties. After his success as the decidedly unintelligent would-be mastermind in that film, he largely concentrated on comedy. The results were variable, and he tended to ham. Nevertheless, he became a great favourite with the public, and in later years he expanded his range with considerable success.

Marcello Mastroianni took longer to gain the high regard his performances deserved. Constantly in demand, he served a steady apprenticeship, from his debut in Riccardo Freda's *I Miserabili* (1948, *Les Misérables*) and by 1960 had appeared in some fifty films. He had always seemed deliberately to avoid an easy choice of roles, and although his greatest successes came in the Sixties he had already made *Cronache di Poveri Amanti* (1954, *Chronicles of Poor Lovers*) for Lizzani and Visconti's *Le Notti Bianche* (1957, *White Nights*) when *Persons Unknown* and Monicelli's *La Grande Guerra* (1959, *The Great War*) confirmed him as one of the country's outstanding comic actors. He varied his performances and subjects as much as possible, and at the end of the Fifties was heading for the international stardom which came with *La Dolce Vita* (1959, *The Sweet Life*), Bolognini's *Il Bell'Antonio* (1960, *Handsome Antonio*), Antonioni's *La Notte* (1961, *The Night*) and *Divorce – Italian Style*.

Italian stars shone most nights in as many film appearances as health and strength would permit

Italians were very loyal to their stars, who rewarded them by appearing in as many films each year as their doctors would allow. Ugo Tognazzi, whose comic appeal remained resolutely local during 30 years of effort, starred in 12 films in 1959 alone, while the incredible Vittorio De Sica – in between directing six features of his own – appeared in 65 films between 1951 and 1960.

Alberto Sordi is a magnificent screen actor, and of late has turned to directing with some success. His recent work has renewed the respect of those who must have become wearied by the succession of Sixties and Seventies comedies and light dramas which atrophied the image of the star of Fellini's *Lo Sceicco Bianco* (1952, *The White Sheik*) and *I Vitelloni* (1953, *The Spivs*) and of Rosi's *I Magliari* (1959, *The Swindlers*). These three films alone, with their subtle change-ringing of the same basic character gave some indication of the flexibility and depth of his screen persona. The dangerous gangster of *I*

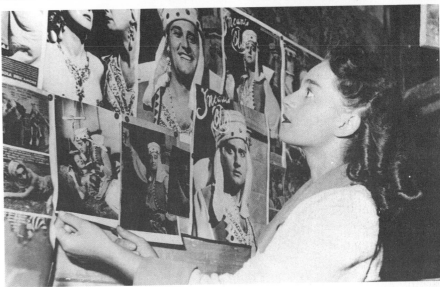

Top: Marcello Mastroianni has established himself since the Fifties as the versatile and ever-reliable star of many films, including La Notte, *the second of Antonioni's 'trilogy'. Above: Brunella Bovo, as a star-struck girl, feasts her eyes on images of her hero.* The White Sheik, *played by Alberto Sordi. Left: knee-deep in the Vercelli marshes of northern Italy, Silvana Mangano became a star in* Bitter Rice, *which managed to be both neo-realist and yet very popular at home and abroad*

Above: Francesco Rosi's Salvatore Giuliano *reconstructs the life and death of the notorious Sicilian bandit, mysteriously killed in 1950. Right: an unusual publicity shot of Sophia Loren in* Due Notti con Cleopatra *(1953, Two Nights With Cleopatra), in which she plays a dual role, as Cleopatra and her look-alike maid who rescues her lover from execution after he has spent one night each with the false and the real Cleopatra. Below:* Amore in Città *(1953, Love in the City) was the first and only edition of a magazine film,* Lo Spettatore *(The Spectator). Carlo Lizzani's episode,* L'Amore Che Si Paga, *(Bought Love), examined prostitution in Rome*

Magliari is recognisably brother under the skin to the vainglorious photo-comic hero of *The White Sheik.*

Few Italian actresses of this period were esteemed by overseas critics, although the world's press took keen interest in the physical attributes of many Italian leading ladies. Giulietta Masina and Anna Magnani were respected and admired for the consistent intensity and brilliance of their performances; but Silvana Mangano's effective work in De Santis' *Riso Amaro* (1948, *Bitter Rice*) was overshadowed by the publicity attendant on her physical presence: the famous thighs-in-the-paddy-fields shot boosted the film's earnings but adversely affected her career as a dramatic actress for many years.

Gina Lollobrigida and Sophia Loren were both international cleavage celebrities well in advance of their acceptance as fine actresses. Each of them survived this early publicity and subsequent Hollywood careers in banal material to earn overdue recognition of their genuine talent.

Film production companies in Italy rarely specialized in particular genres, and individual producers were far more adventurous than their British and American counterparts. Carlo Ponti and Dino De Laurentiis formed Ponti-De Laurentiis Productions in 1950, and in the seven years they were together they worked on projects as diverse as Totò films, Rossellini's *Europa '51* (1951), *Jolanda, La Figlia del Corsaro Nero, Le Notti di Cabiria* (1957, *Nights of Cabiria*), Germi's *Man of Iron* and epic Hollywood co-productions such as King Vidor's *War and Peace* (1956).

Carlo Ponti's earlier involvements had included neo-realist films by Germi, Alberto Lattuada and Luigi Zampa; and after the break-up of Ponti-De Laurentiis he continued with great success to produce a wide variety of films, often starring his wife, Sophia Loren. De Laurentiis was the more ambitious of the duo. After a number of unremarkable low-budget features, he had achieved great success with *Bitter Rice*, and worked steadily to increase his international affiliations. Today the De Laurentiis organization is the largest in Europe.

Old and new producers responded to the excitement of the booming Fifties. Angelo Rizzoli started in films in 1934, but had been inactive for many years when, in 1950, he produced Rossellini's *Francesco, Giullare di Dio (Flowers of St. Francis)*. For the rest of the decade he was very active indeed, often setting up French co-productions, including René Clair's *Les Belles de Nuit* (1952, *Beauties of the Night*) and *Les Grandes Manoeuvres* (1955, *The Grand Maneuver*) as well as the first two Don Camillo films. He entered the Sixties on a high note with Fellini's *La Dolce Vita*.

Franco Cristaldi was only 30 when he produced his first three films in 1954. His early films were routine romantic dramas but did reasonably well at the box-office. Following greater success with Steno's *Mio Figlio Nerone* (1956, *Nero's Weekend*), starring Alberto Sordi and Vittorio De Sica, he showed himself willing to take chances by producing Visconti's *White Nights*. He backed Francesco Rosi's first two features as director, *La Sfida* (1958, *Defiance*) and *I Magliari*, and was later to finance the same director's politically sensitive examination of the myth of the Sicilian bandit, *Salvatore Giuliano* (1961). He also produced the two best Italian comedies in *Persons Unknown* and *Divorce – Italian Style*.

The Fifties were years of enthusiasm and manic energy; geniuses and hacks rubbed shoulders in a crowded, jostling film factory. An industry which had been virtually wiped out in 1944 was back and booming.
BARRY EDSON

Arrivederci, Roma!

As the Italian cinema became more and more commercial in the Fifties and Sixties, it produced a galaxy of glamorous actors and actresses whose natural charms inevitably attracted the Hollywood studios, eager to 'internationalize' their films. Some stayed at home but most obeyed the lure of world-wide stardom – only to return to consolidate their fame in Europe

Above left: space-age chic for an apprehensive Silvana Mangano in Le Streghe *(1967, The Witches). Top: Valentina Cortesa in Fellini's* Giulietta degli Spiriti *(1965, Juliet of the Spirits). Above: Cortesa as Rica, with Richard Conte as Nick, in her American debut,* Thieves' Highway, *a thriller about trucking and racketeers*

It is easy to think of the post-war Italian cinema as dominated by the masters of neo-realism, but nothing could be further from the commercial truth. In those days Rome was busily establishing itself as a Hollywood on the Tiber. Stars were at a premium as films of every kind came off the assembly lines: routine vehicles for comedians like Totò and pin-up girls like Silvana Pampanini; traditional genre exercises including Ancient-world spectaculars, sentimental comedies and biopics; and productions which cross-bred the neo-realist impulse with the more sure-fire formulas of sex and violence.

Silvana Mangano

Perhaps the most renowned example of the latter strain was *Riso Amaro* (1948, *Bitter Rice*), a striking melodrama directed by Giuseppe De Santis, which exposed simultaneously the conditions of workers in the Vercelli marshes and the scantily clad assets of Silvana Mangano.

The film made the former beauty queen Mangano (b.1930) world-famous, and her marriage in 1949 to its producer, Dino De Laurentiis, consolidated her position. She remained a top box-office attraction throughout the Fifties, equally at home in spectaculars like *Ulisse* (1954, *Ulysses*) or intimate modern

subjects such as De Sica's *L'Oro di Napoli* (1954, *Gold of Naples*). She also starred in many of De Laurentiis' blockbuster co-productions, memorably drawn to the bright lights in René Clément's *La Diga sul Pacifico* (1957, *The Sea Wall*), and more conventionally in the Biblical epic *Barabbas* (1962).

A 'grande dame' astonishingly unmarked by the passing years, she has bestowed an elegant presence on some of the most distinguished of recent Italian films, appearing in four movies for Pasolini and three for Visconti, perhaps most famously as the mother in the latter's *Morte a Venezia* (1971, *Death in Venice*).

Valentina Cortesa

Whereas Mangano stuck to home ground, many of her top-line Italian contemporaries did not. Hollywood had never been reticent about recruiting foreign talent. With the domestic audience declining in the Fifties, there was all the more incentive to boost the overseas appeal of American movies. Notable among those who made the trip to California is Valentina Cortese (b.1924), who appeared in *Il Bravo di Venezia* (The Brave of Venice), the first of her several routine Italian films, in 1941, and then in 1949 starred in the British-made *The Glass Mountain* (renowned for its soupy

theme music). The following year – her name changed to Cortesa – she brought an unaccustomed sensuality to the American screen as a truck-driver's mistress in Jules Dassin's *Thieves' Highway* (1949).

She made a few other US films, including the 1951 thriller *The House on Telegraph Hill*, in which she was murderously pursued by the villain played by Richard Basehart (in real life their relationship was somewhat happier – they got married). She then concentrated her career mainly in Europe. One of her most memorable later roles was as the increasingly distraught actress in Truffaut's *La Nuit Américaine* (1973, *Day for Night*).

Alida Valli

Alida Valli (b.1921) was signed up by David Selznick in 1946, but her only memorable American role was as the dissembling murderess in Hitchcock's *The Paradine Case* (1947). Her triumph came in Britain in *The Third Man* (1949), playing the adoring mistress of the racketeer Harry Lime. In one of the most famous closing shots in film history she walks with expressionless contempt past the man (Joseph Cotten) who has been Lime's nemesis.

Valli later brought faultless hieratic style to the tragic heroine of Visconti's *Senso* (1954, *The*

67

Left: Gina Lollobrigida as soprano Lina Cavalieri in La Donna più Bella del Mondo *(1955, Beautiful But Dangerous). Above left: as Sheba in King Vidor's* Solomon and Sheba. *Above: Alida Valli as Maddalena Paradine, the nymphomaniac murderess in Hitchcock's* The Paradine Case

Wanton Countess), and admirable restraint to one of the most chilling of all horror movies, Franju's *Les Yeux Sans Visage* (1959, *Eyes Without a Face*). Her striking authority remained intact in two films for Bertolucci, *La Strategia del Ragno* (1970, *The Spider's Stratagem*) and *La Luna* (1979).

Gina Lollobrigida

If she was hardly the equal of these players as an actress, there is no doubt that Gina Lollobrigida (b.1927) was Italy's most celebrated screen export in the Fifties. La Lollo, as the headline-writers dubbed her, had figured bustily in many Italian movies – and rather more demurely in René Clair's *Les Belles de Nuit* (1952, *Beauties of the Night*). She especially clicked with audiences as the enthusiastic rustic heroine of *Pane, Amore e Fantasia* (1954, *Bread, Love and Dreams*). In her first major American movie, *Trapeze* (1956), she carried over something of her gypsy appeal, and in more statuesque guise she brought a suitably voluptuous glitter to *Solomon and Sheba* (1959). Later, however, feeble melodramas like *Go Naked in the World* (1961) and weak comedies like *Strange Bedfellows* (1964) did little to strengthen her appeal.

It was reassuring, though, to find her glamour undimmed in the more favourable circumstances of *Un Bellissimo Novembre* (1969, *That Splendid November*), as the older woman with whom a teenage boy becomes all too understandably besotted.

Sophia Loren

In fact, by the late Fifties La Lollo had been overtaken in the international popularity stakes by the compatriot who had been her main rival at home earlier in the decade, and by any reckoning was Italy's most famous film star export: Sophia Loren. Her early career followed a familiar course: impoverished childhood, beauty contests, bit parts in movies. She

through the Fifties, but was mainly relegated to colourless, routine parts. She regained some of the raw-nerved appeal of *Teresa* when she played the wife of fighter Rocky Graziano (Paul Newman) in *Somebody Up There Likes Me* (1956), and was very lively as the trapeze-artist heroine of the Danny Kaye comedy *Merry Andrew* (1958).

Elsa Martinelli

On the whole, the strongest contender for the Lollobrigida mantle of earthy appeal was Elsa Martinelli. Italian-born (in 1932), she was discovered by Kirk Douglas, who launched her career when he gave her the part of an Indian girl in *The Indian Fighter* (1955). She lent a ragamuffin sexuality to the British *Manuela* (1957) and was chosen by Howard Hawks as the leading lady of *Hatari!* (1962), in which she contrived to hold her own with both John Wayne and a group of baby elephants. Unfortunately though, stereotyped roles in films like *Rampage* (1963) and *Maroc 7* (1967) did little to capitalize on her assets.

Left: Sophia Loren in Man of La Mancha *(1972). Below: portrait of Elsa Martinelli for* Rampage *in which, as in* Hatari!, *she provided the love-interest for big-game hunters. Bottom: an early glamour shot of Pier Angeli (left) and with Paul Newman in* Somebody Up There Likes Me *(right)*

then became the protégée of producer Carlo Ponti – they later married – and after starring in several mainly routine Italian films, including *Attila Flagello di Dio* (1955; *Attila the Hun*) and *Pane, Amore e . . .* (1955, *Scandal in Sorrento*), she was launched into worldwide stardom.

Her first English-language movies, like *The Pride and the Passion* (1957), mainly served to show off her striking appearance, usually in the guise of a conventional spitfire. But soon she emerged as much more: an actress of notable range and subtlety in such varied roles as the embittered widow of a gangster in *The Black Orchid* (1958), or a rich man's mistress falling in love with a naive GI in *That Kind of*

Woman (1959). Since 1960 she has worked wholly in Europe, though often in English-speaking movies of indifferent quality. But in *C'era una Volta* (1967, *Cinderella – Italian Style*) she blithely recaptured her early *élan*, and in *Una Giornata Particolare* (1977, *A Special Day*) she showed that she has remained an actress to be reckoned with.

Pier Angeli

Other Italian actresses moved smoothly to Hollywood. Pier Angeli (1932–1971) was signed up by MGM after only a handful of local roles to play the GI bride in Fred Zinnemann's *Teresa* (1951). She stayed on in the USA – briefly married to singer Vic Damone –

Claudia Cardinale

An actress in the La Lollo mould was Claudia Cardinale (b.1939), protégée and later wife of the prominent producer Franco Cristaldi, who seemed set to become a major star. After appearances in Visconti's *Rocco e i Suoi Fratelli* (1960, *Rocco and His Brothers*) and Fellini's *Otto e Mezzo* (1963, *8½*), she starred in a string of prestigious American movies, among them *The Pink Panther* (1963), *Circus World* (1964) and *The Professionals* (1966). But although she was given better parts than Lollobrigida, Cardinale never really made a great impact.

Vittorio Gassman

Several of Italy's post-war male stars made the journey to Hollywood, generally with less desirable results. Vittorio Gassman (b.1922) – Mangano's co-star in *Bitter Rice* – went to MGM in the early Fifties, but found himself restricted to programmers; he played, for instance, a convict on the run who escapes to his native Louisiana swamp country in *Cry of the Hunted* (1953). After the break-up of his mar-

riage to Shelley Winters (with whom he starred in *Mambo*, 1954), Gassman returned to Italy. He went on to establish himself as a comic actor of wide range in such films as *I Soliti Ignoti* (1958, *Persons Unknown*) and *La Grande Guerra* (1959, *The Great War*). He remained successful, and recently made a happy return to American films as the shady father of the groom in Robert Altman's *A Wedding* (1978).

Rossano Brazzi

Rossano Brazzi (b.1916) fared – at least commercially – rather better as a Hollywood leading man than Gassman, though he tended to be typecast as an off-the-peg Latin lover,

Top left: Claudia Cardinale in The Hell With Heroes *(1968), and (top) in* C'era una Volta il West *(1968,* Once Upon a Time in the West*). Left: Vittorio Gassman, on right, with Alberto Sordi in the World War I drama,* The Great War. *Below: Rossano Brazzi, reflecting on Mitzi Gaynor in* South Pacific *(left) and (right) in an Italian publicity shot*

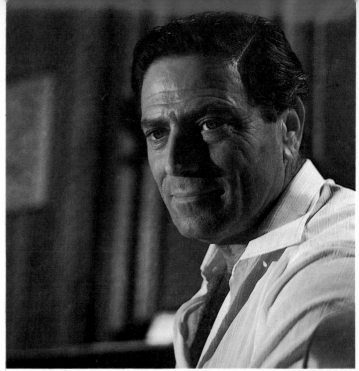

providing romantic adventure for Katharine Hepburn in *Summer Madness* (1955) and for June Allyson in *Interlude* (1957). But he appeared over-reticent amid the musical numbers of *South Pacific* (1958), and for the action movie *Legend of the Lost* (1957) he was relegated to the status of a neurotic, egghead villain. In later years Brazzi randomly starred in South American productions and appeared in supporting roles in such films as *The Great Waltz* (1972).

Raf Vallone

The career of Raf Vallone (b.1920) branched out more gradually. He made films in France – co-starring with Simone Signoret in Marcel Carné's version of *Thérèse Raquin* (1953) – Germany and Spain then, back in Italy, was the male lead in De Sica's *La Ciociara* (1961, *Two Women*). Only later did he venture into a major English-speaking role, as the fatally flawed longshoreman in *Vu du Pont* (1961, *A View From the Bridge*), which was adapted from Arthur Miller's play. Since then he has

had a steady run of character roles in American as well as European films (if not always distinguished ones), including that of Jean Harlow's stepfather in *Harlow* (1965) and the Mexican rebel in *Cannon for Cordoba* (1970).

Nazzari: Salvatori: Eastwood

As veteran Italian male stars like Amedo Nazzari (b.1907) began to mellow into character roles – he is probably best recalled as the film actor in Fellini's *Le Notti di Cabiria* (1957, *Nights of Cabiria*) – occasional younger players would come to replace them. Notable among them was Renato Salvatori (b.1933). He first made his mark in teenage comedies like *Poveri ma Belli* (1957, *Girl in a Bikini*), riding around on a scooter in vest and jeans, and made a startlingly successful transition to heavy drama as the boxer who turns to crime in Visconti's *Rocco and His Brothers*. The husband of French actress Annie Girardot, he later played featured roles in such films as *Z* (1969).

By the end of the Fifties, as the Italian cinema sought to boost its fortunes with a

deluge of cut-price spectaculars, musclemen like Steve Reeves and Gordon Scott and fading American second-string performers like Guy Madison and Cameron Mitchell came flooding into Rome to wield hatchets and spears. A few years later the Italian Western emerged and – in the series of films initiated by Sergio Leone's *Per un Pugno di Dollari* (1964, *Fistful of Dollars*) – made an international star of Clint Eastwood, a previously unknown television actor. Eastwood duly returned to the USA as a box-office champion. The journey from neo-realism to makeshift macho may have looked like a long one – but in a roundabout way the Italian film industry was upholding its status as an exporter of talent to the world. TIM PULLEINE

Top left: Raf Vallone in Il Cammino della Speranza *(1950,* Road to Hope*) and (top) in a later studio portrait. Below left: the boxer (Renato Salvatori) stabs the woman he loves (Annie Girardot) in* Rocco and His Brothers. *Below: Amedo Nazzari and Mangano in* Il Brigante Musolino *(1950,* Fugitive*)*

fellini's cinema

With unrivalled flair and panache, Fellini blazons his obsessions, fears and fantasies across the screen. A parade of unforgettable images of beauty, degradation, sensuality and corruption succeed each other in his films, defying critical cries of self-indulgence and decadence with their exuberance

Fellini was born in 1920 in Rimini on the Adriatic coast. He worked in Florence and Rome as a cartoonist before being hired by various film studios as a re-write and gag man, exercising his talents on approximately fifty features until the Germans closed down Italian film production in 1943. After the liberation, Fellini opened and ran a series of joke shops. His first break in cinema came when the director Roberto Rossellini asked him to help write the script of *Roma, Città Aperta* (1945, *Rome, Open City*).

Fellini's first film as a director was *Luci del Varieta* (1950, *Lights of Variety*), which initiated his association with the scriptwriters Tullio Pinelli and Ennio Flaiano. With *I Vitelloni* (1953, *The Spivs*) he first began to show signs of

the autobiographical preoccupations which predominated in his films until *Giulietta degli Spiriti* (1965, *Juliet of the Spirits*). The film is also interesting in that it hints at the cynical and despairing representations of male sexuality that featured in his later work, culminating in *Il Casanova di Federico Fellini* (1976, *Casanova*).

However it was with the international success of his fourth film, *La Strada* (1954, *The Road*) that Fellini staked his claim for serious critical attention. The film stars Fellini's wife, Giulietta Masina as Gelsomina, a simple girl who is bought by Zampano (Anthony Quinn) as his assistant in his travelling strong-man act. Zampano is a brutish man with no more than basic animal appetites and no apparent capacity for human feeling, least of all love. *La*

Strada is basically concerned with Gelsomina's uncomprehending love for Zampano, her ultimate abandonment and death, followed by his gradual recognition of his loss of and need for her. The film is crucial to Fellini's avowed sense of man needing to be more than a creature of lust, and of women as his potential redeemer. In addition, the role of Gelsomina crystallized Masina's image in Fellini's films as one of vulnerability, sensitivity and purity.

Fellini's next two films, *Il Bidone* (1955, *The Swindlers*) and *Le Notti di Cabiria* (1957, *Nights of Cabiria*) maintained critical and public interest in his work. The basic tension that informs *Il Bidone* is between a world of basic drives and ugliness and its alternative, the world of beauty and the spirit – again symbolized by women. The central character is a petty con man (Broderick Crawford), whose spiritual awakening is brought about by his realization that he has failed his daughter. His last con trick, carried out against a peasant family, is successful but he fails in his attempts to convince his criminal associates that he was incapable of seeing it through; they attack him and leave him to die, having found the ill-gotten money (which would have enabled his daughter to remain at school) in his shoe.

Le Notti di Cabiria (on which Bob Fosse based *Sweet Charity*, 1969) stars Giulietta Masina as a prostitute. Although she is twice robbed by her lovers, her simplicity and basic innocence give her the moral strength to carry on.

It was with *La Dolce Vita* (1959, The Sweet Life) that Fellini once again took the world by storm. The film is concerned with the descent of Marcello, a journalist (Marcello Mastroianni) into a modern Roman world of idleness, debauchery and *ennui*. Its depiction of people alienated from themselves and each other and lacking any sense of purpose in their lives invited comparisons with the films of Michelangelo Antonioni, Fellini's contemporary. However the similarity ends there, since whereas Antonioni has increasingly banished all extraneous detail from his work, leaving only its bare, existential bones, *La Dolce Vita*'s extravagant and unrestrained imagery represents Fellini's first jump into the deep waters of his visual imagination.

Fellini's next two films were to put the seal on his reputation as a 'personal' and 'autobiographical' film-maker. *Otto e Mezzo* (1963, *8½*) deals with the artistic crisis of a film director, Guido (Marcello Mastroianni) who is also having problems with his wife (Anouk Aimée) and an affair with a young woman. It is set in a spa, where Guido has gone to stave off a nervous breakdown and to complete a script for a film about an escape into space by the survivors of World War III. He is constantly besieged by the producer and other personnel connected with the picture and gradually comes to recognize that he must make a personal film which confronts his own anxieties and compromises. This time Fellini produced a film of extraordinary spectacle in which reality and fantasy merge and divide with masterly fluency. The subject-matter strongly suggested that Fellini had made an autobiographical film. He himself admitted:

'I realize that *8½* is such a shameless and brazen confession, that it is futile to try and make people forget that it is about my own life. But I try to make a film that pleases me, first of all, and then the public. In *8½* the boundary line between what I did for myself and what I

created for the public is very subtle.' To complicate the issue, he has also been quoted as saying that, '8½ is not so autobiographical as it would seem'.

His next film, *Juliet of the Spirits*, immediately raised the assumption that it was based on his marriage with Masina. Fellini both supported such a reading – 'It was born as a film about Giulietta and for Giulietta' – and denied it – 'But everything the artist does is somehow about himself. The woman Giulietta is not *precisely* my wife, the marriage is not *precisely* my marriage'. What is certainly true is that it continued Fellini's increasing predilection for extravagant, exaggerated and surreal imagery which can so easily be read in symbolic and not least, in this film, Freudian and Jungian terms. Certainly, too, the character of Giulietta remains constant to Fellini's theme of women as essentially healthy in spiritual terms. Where Marcello in *La Dolce Vita* succumbs totally to the alienation of modern, urban man, Giulietta, faced with a personal crisis centred around her home, realizes that life has no meaning without personal or moral codes. The last shot of her in sunshine on the open road outside her house is, it might be suggested, an indication of her having achieved a sense of the direction in which her life should go.

Fellini's next two major films, *Fellini Satyricon* (1969) and *Fellini's Roma* (1972), show a change of emphasis and direction away from the autobiographical elements of his previous work. Despite being full of visual spectacle, they are more cerebral in theme. As Fellini said about *Fellini Satyricon*:

'. . . the audience must fight as never before their preconception about movies having to tell them a story with a start, a development, an end: preconceptions about historical pictures: preconceptions about myself . . .'

Its subversive effects are precisely encapsulated in another of Fellini's statements:

'I've tried first of all to eliminate what is generally called history. That is to say, really the idea that the ancient world "actually" existed. Thus the atmosphere is not historical but that of a dream world.'

Based on Petronius' text, the film is quite clearly the director's vision of Roman society

before Christ. In the amoral world of the film, the sole drive that animates society is sexual fulfilment; its totem is the hermaphrodite. The range of bizarre characters that inhabit it are embodiments of sensual appetite, at times beautiful in their joyful, unashamed sense of themselves.

In addition to attacking the concept of historical truth and disdaining traditional narrative methods, *Fellini Satyricon* is the director's most gargantuan, ironic, and absurd film in visual terms. Unfortunately the film tends to be a 'hit or miss' affair, depending solely on the extent that the audience permits itself to be involved in Fellini's imaginative and surrealist creations.

Amarcord (1973), dialect for 'I remember', is a similarly complex film: on the one hand it is a very personal work, re-creating a Rimini of the Thirties with a boy, who can be interpreted as a young Fellini, as the main character; on the other, it can be regarded as a valid historical exercise along the lines of *Fellini Satyricon*, since the only opposition which the individual can

Far left: the hermaphrodite and its elderly help-mates in Fellini's Satyricon. *Above left: Marcello Mastroianni as the neurotic film director in* 8½. *Above: Sandra Milo in* Juliet of the Spirits. *Below: prostitutes in a scene from Fellini's* Roma

offer to the institutional, and thus dominant, form of history *is* the personal.

Casanova brings to its ultimate conclusion the preoccupation which had informed very nearly all Fellini's films – directly in *I Vitelloni*, *La Strada*, and *La Dolce Vita* and indirectly in his other films – male sexuality. The film offers a particularly bleak view of it as Casanova journeys through the bodies of women, going nowhere. The visual imagery is extravagant but stringently allied to the theme of the sexual anxieties upon which male identity is constructed. It is utilized with a degree of irony which produces a confrontation with the myth of Casanova and the cultural associations the name possesses for Western society.

was the one consistent contributor until his death in 1979.) Too little account is taken of this coincidence by critics writing about Fellini's work, who refer glibly to his genius without asking themselves whether his films are not rather the fruits of a corporative effort by Fellini and his team.

Fellini's greatest strength is not simply his extraordinarily vivid visual imagination, but his phenomenal cinematic mastery. One can revel in his imagery – surreal, ironic, comic as it may be; wonder at the freakish characters with which he fills his films (he interviews thousands of non-professionals to get the right look, usually dubbing another's voice to get that right too); ponder over his thematic preoccupations; identify his specifically Italian love-hate relationships with the Church and its members; analyse his symbolic and metaphoric use of the sea, roads, clowns and circuses; but over-riding all these is the fact that he has a control of the film-making process which has probably never been surpassed. To that extent his claims as an artist have yet to be challenged.

SHEILA WHITAKER

When Fellini extended his personal vision to explore the ideological constructs of human nature and society – instead of producing films bathed in a rosy glow of romantic humanism – he was deserted by most critics. Those commentators that praised his earlier work, hailing him as an artistic genius, were clearly confused by the overtly satirical and ironical turn of his later films.

A contributory factor to this change in style in the mid-Sixties must have been Fellini's break with his former collaborators. Tullio Pinelli and Ennio Flaiano co-scripted all Fellini's features until *Juliet of the Spirits* in 1965; since then he has worked mainly with Bernadino Zapponi and Brunello Rondi. The editor Ruggiero Mastroianni, who began his association with Fellini on *Juliet of the Spirits*, has since worked on all his films. The photographer Ottello Martini shot all of Fellini's films until *Boccaccio 70* (1962), whereupon Giuseppe Rotunno took over. (The composer Nino Rota

Above: the musicians play on amid chaos in Prova d'Orchestra *(1978, Orchestra Rehearsal). Below: the self-advertisement of the clergy, modelling the latest lines in ecclesiastical wear, in this scene from Fellini's* Roma

Filmography
1939 Lo Vedi Come Sei . . . Lo Vedi Come Sei? (co-sc. only). '40 Non Me Lo Dire! (co-sc. only); Il Pirata Sono Io! (co-sc. only). '43 Quarta Pagina (co-sc. only); Shi L'ha Visto? (co-sc. only); L'Ultima Carrozzella (co-sc. only). '45 Roma, Città Aperta (co-sc. only) (USA: Rome, Open City; GB: Open City). '46 Paisà (co-sc. only) (USA/GB: Paisan). '47 Il Delitto di Giovanni Episcopo (co-sc. only) (USA/GB: Flesh Will Surrender); La Fumeria d'Oppio/Ritorna Za-la-Mort (co-sc. only); L'Ebreo Errante (co-sc. only); Senza Pietà (USA/GB: Without Pity). '48 L'Amore *ep* Il Miracolo (co-sc; + actor only) (GB: The Miracle); La Città Dolente (co-sc. only). '49 In Nome delle Legge (co-sc. only) (GB: In the Name of the Law); Il Multino del Po (co-sc. only). '50 Francesco, Guillare di Dio (co-sc. only) (USA/GB: Flowers of St Francis); Il Cammino della Speranza (co-sc. only) (GB: The Road to Hope); Persiane Chiuse (co-sc. only) (USA/GB: Behind Closed Shutters); Luci del Varieta (co-dir; + co-sc; + co-prod. only) (USA/GB: Lights of Variety/Variety Lights). '51 Cameriera della Presenza Offresi (co-sc. only); La Città si Difende (co-sc. only) (USA: Four Ways Out); Europa '51 (uncredited co-sc. only). '52 Lo Sceicco Bianco (+co-sc) (USA/GB: The White Sheik); Il Brigante di Tacca del Lupo (co-sc. only). '53 I Vitelloni (+co-sc) (USA/GB: The Spivs/The Wastrels/The Young and the Passionate); Amore in Città *ep* Agenzia Matrimoniale (+co-sc). '54 La Strada (+co-sc). '55 Il Bidone (+co-sc) (GB: The Swindlers). '57 Le Notti de Cabiria (+co-sc) (IT-FR) (USA/GB: Nights of Cabiria); Fortunella (co-sc. only) (IT-FR). '59 La Dolce Vita (+co-sc). '62 Boccaccio 70 *ep* Le Tentazioni del Dottor Antonio (+co-sc). '63 Otto e Mezzo (+co-sc) (IT-FR) (USA/GB: 8½). '65 Giulietta degli Spiriti (+co-sc) (USA/GB: Juliet of the Spirits). '68 Histoires Extraordinaires/Tre Passi del Delirio *ep* Il ne Faut pas Parler Sa Tête Contre le Diable (+co-sc) (IT-FR) (USA/GB: Tales of Mystery *ep* Toby Dammit). '69 Fellini Satyricon (+co-sc; +des); Fellini: a Director's Notebook (+co-sc; +actor) (USA)*. '70 I Clowns (+co-sc; + actor)*; Alex in Wonderland (actor only) (USA). '72 Fellini's Roma (+co-sc; +act). 73 Amarcord (+co-sc). 74 C'Eravamo Tanto Amati (actor only). '76 Il Casanova di Federico Fellini (+co-sc; +co-des) (USA/GB: Casanova/Fellini's Casanova). '78 Prova d'Orchestra (+co-sc) (IT-MONACO) (USA/GB: Orchestra Rehearsal)*. '79 La Città delle Donne (USA/GB: City of Women).
* shot as TV film but shown in cinemas.

Teen dreams

Suddenly, in the mid-Fifties, there were teenagers everywhere, dancing to rock'n'roll music and dating at the drive-ins; up on the screen, the teenage hero acted out a generation's fantasies

The Fifties was that era when the cinema really discovered 'problems' – specifically problems of youth. Spurred on by newspaper headlines, film-makers proceeded first to present, then to exploit and, by default, investigate the 'teen problem'. This process required that the movies assimilate contemporary events and attitudes, so that every fad and fetish of society served as raw material – grist to the mills of mythology.

The Fifties also saw the full integration of popular music into an evolving youth culture. It was a culture of full-blooded consumerism. In the public mind, the adjective 'teenage' referred to leisure, pleasure and conspicuous consumption. The teenagers' new music, rock'n'roll, symbolized a world of youth, caught up momentarily in hedonism and unrelated to adult interests. Rock'n'roll also brought with it a host of concepts and images that fired the public's ideas of youth: delinquency, adolescent gangs, motorcycle worship, ballroom-dance halls, jazz clubs, Melody Bars, Teddy Boys and similar phenomena.

Parents feared that the uncouth jungle music meant an end to the civilized order as they knew it. Of course, they were to be proved wrong as rock'n'roll became big business and, later, show business. Through its stars and principals, however, early rock'n'roll was aggressive in providing ideas of style that were exclusively teenage.

The young had always worshipped idols: Frank Sinatra, Johnny Ray, sports heroes and film stars. But now they had idols whose backgrounds, ages and interests they perceived as similar to their own. They sensed a whole culture of their own with a codified set of values clearly different from those of older generations. Participating in such a culture seemed a fitting rebellion against unreasonable, or merely conventional, ideas of how things should be experienced.

A commitment to enjoyment and consumer culture was in itself a statement against seriousness, drabness, 'adult' duties and responsibilities. And those professionals who dealt with the young (doctors, teachers, clergymen and social workers) feared what they interpreted as the absence of any public or community spirit on the part of the teenagers. The result of this anxiety was the image of a 'teenage jungle' as depicted by the media. A 1957 paperback called *The Teenage Jungle* gives an adequate description:

'Here is a frightful indictment of youthful crime and vice in the USA. It shows how the violent and sex-crazed teenage cult exists in a living nightmare of ruthlessness and depravity. These are the ordinary kids you read about every day of your life – ordinary, that is, until they shoot a store-keeper, assault a girl, torture a bum or wind up dead in a ditch.'

The aggressive manner, in which teenagers identified with one another, and the singularity and exclusivity of the teenage cult, quickly became bracketed with deviancy and delinquency in the view of the scandal-hungry media. The teenagers'

deliberate gestures of individuality, therefore, were interpreted as stances of defiance, aimed at their elders.

But in opposition to this view of the teenager there was the image of the pre-packaged teenager ready to be served up on the screen, in paperbacks and record stores. And the sentiments of the ordinary teenager in the Fifties were still very much a part of their period. The rhythms on the radio might have quickened but the emotional texture of the time had not. Like their parents, most middle-class teenagers were trusting and optimistic. What this meant in terms of the way they were represented in cinema was that film musicals incorporating rock'n'roll – rather like the music itself – often carried absurdly romantic lyrics and the 'teenpix', as the genre became known, often lumbered under abysmally stilted plots in an effort to reconcile new energies with traditional ideals.

The motion picture – which might appear to be a series of typical teenage happenings, but which was always framed, directed and marketed by adults – provided the mechanism for resolving the problems of being a teenager. Anticipation of everything that was new gave way to acceptance of things as they were. And, in the movies, acceptance meant happy endings. The teenager's naive crusade for abstracts like justice, freedom or individual dignity, could be portrayed and simultaneously merged with the comforts of the middle-class goal – conformity. If young people could be assimilated in this way they could be tacitly absolved from questioning the *status quo*.

Some of the musical films which evolved to cash in on rock'n'roll reflected this trend in their form as much as in content. They drew directly on the proscenium-arch tradition of the American musical which, by nature of its rigid division between stage and audience, could be described as a theatre of

Top: Tom Ewell and Jayne Mansfield in The Girl Can't Help It. *Frank Tashlin's garish but good-natured send-up of the rock'n'roll scene revolved around the dumb blonde's bid for rock stardom; despite the third-hand plot and older-generation stars, the film had more anarchic energy than all its imitators – and it had a line-up that included Fats Domino and Little Richard. Above: the inspiration for teen dreams and for most rock'n'roll movies was the hit single, though some – like Ricky Valance's 'Tell Laura I Love Her' – dealt in tragedies that many mainstream rock movies preferred to avoid*

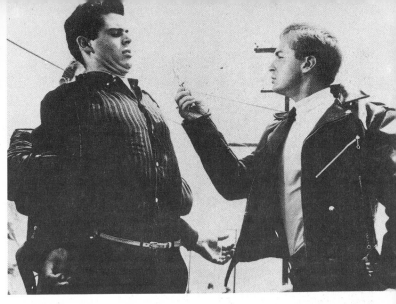

Top right: the flash of steel in the 'teenage jungle'; Bob Turnbull threatens Gary Clarke in Dragstrip Riot, *which climaxed in a war between youth gangs. Top: similar, real-life battles were waged on the streets of New York; this news photo shows kids wearing protective body-shields. Centre: Sandra Dee in the title role of* Gidget, *every teenager's dream date. Above: Anne Neyland and Steve Terrell as teenage lovers in* Motorcycle Gang

acceptance. Films as diverse as *Where the Boys Are* (1960), *West Side Story* (1961) and the early Elvis Presley epics all assume that the new, younger audience will automatically accept the old conventions and will swallow the hotted-up version of the so-called big production number – Hollywood's unwitting celebration of mindlessness.

The thrill of the star-vehicle musical remained undeniable: proof that the star could be fitted into an ordinary social perspective and could be sold at the box-office as a commodity to America's consumer class. The advent of the teenage idols of the Fifties – James Dean, Elvis, Sandra Dee – heralded youth's yearning to see the rite of stardom enacted over and over again. He or she symbolized the individual's rise not to riches – as might have been the case for the idols of the previous generation – but to popularity, social mobility and that state of absolute self-knowledge characterized by the adjective 'cool'.

Stardom was always double-edged. As well as confirming the collective aspirations of teenhood, stars also became part of an elite which put a distance between them and their fans and dramatized the worshipper's isolation and sneaking sense of unworthiness. The star was doomed to become an individual, isolated from his or her society.

Teenage idolatry had its origins in the pre-rock'n'roll era when jazz clubs, coffee bars and motorcycle gangs acted as a focus for the emerging teenage sensibility. In 1953, Marlon Brando appeared as Johnny, leader of the motor-bike gang the Black Rebels in *The Wild One.*

Two years later, *The Blackboard Jungle* (1955) featured Glenn Ford as a vocational schoolteacher trying to 'get through' to his New York City charges. The kids refer to him as 'Daddy-O' – one of the earliest commercial usages of the teenagers' 'heptalk' – and in the same year youth confronted adult incomprehension in *Rebel Without a Cause.*

The first big burst of rock films came in 1956 with *Rock Around the Clock*, directed by Sam Katzman and starring Bill Haley and the Comets. Katzman was to become a prolific producer of 'teenpix' none of which ever lost money. In 1961, less than a month after Chubby Checker hit the top of the record charts with 'The Twist', Katzman opened his movie *Twist Around the Clock* (1961) which starred Dion and The Marcels. Before the craze faded, he also managed to churn out *Don't Knock the Twist* (1962), featuring Chubby Checker again, this time with The Dovells and Gene Chandler.

Speed was of the essence in the manipulation of the 'teen market'. *Don't Knock the Rock* (1956) a sequel to *Rock Around the Clock*, was on the screen the same year as its predecessor. So was Frank

Tashlin's trail-blazing *The Girl Can't Help It* (1956) in which Fats Domino, Little Richard, Eddie Cochran and Nino Tempo lend support to a plot that revolved around Jayne Mansfield's attempts to become a singer.

Then, at the height of his celebrity, Elvis Presley made the classic *Jailhouse Rock* (1957), in which he played a good-kid-gone-wrong in a rags-to-riches saga. Here was real rock drama as Elvis, rehearsing in a recording studio, spontaneously decides to cut an upbeat number for a change. Another teenage idol was immortalized on screen in *The James Dean Story* (1957), co-directed by George W. George and Robert Altman. This posthumous documentary flopped at the box-office but Altman's other film of 1957, *The Delinquents*, had strong 'teen appeal' in its archetypal tale of a troubled teenager, his loving, but disapproving parents, a gang of local hoods, and a forbidden party on the edge of town. Like the voice-over narration of *The James Dean Story,* the disclaimers which frame *The Delinquents* have a familiar 'preaching' quality. Speaking about *The Delinquents* from the perspective of the Seventies Altman claimed:

'The violence was aimless, the result of restlessness and a feeling of "Let's just go in there and mess around".'

The film offered the same existential view of directionless youth as *Rebel Without a Cause*. In the notorious 'chicken-run' sequence, Jim asks Buzz 'Why do we do this then?' and Buzz replies 'You've gotta do something now, don't you?'

Towards the end of the decade, the wilder side of youth's aimlessness was being commercially cultivated by studios like American International Pictures. Two producers, Samuel Z. Arkoff and James H. Nicholson, had founded AIP with the aim of mounting 'teen appeal' packages which would portray American youth as decent rather than delinquent. The closely knit, family-style unit of directors, producers, writers and actors enabled AIP to minimize costs and production time on films. These movies were shot for next to nothing but their production costs were always equalled or surpassed by the amount poured into their promotion and for this reason they became known as 'exploitation movies'.

Of the many AIP producers and directors, the most brilliant was Roger Corman who produced for AIP *The Fast and the Furious* (1954), a road-racing epic with plenty of heptalk. Corman's most important youth movie of the period was, however, made for Allied Artists. Entitled *Teenage Doll* (1957), it was a moody picture with a well-paced plot and sympathy for teenage alienation. On a rainy street one night, the Black Widows (a girl gang) are cornered

'I couldn't stop. I swerved to the right,
I'll never forget the sound that night,
The cryin' tires, the bustin' glass,
The painful scream that I heard last.'
Death meant never having to grow up, never having to accept adult realities and values.

There was, of course, a lighter side to romance. In *Summer Love* (1958), starring Jill St John and Rod McKuen, the Daley Combo make a guest appearance at a summer camp with their hit song 'To Know You Is to Love You'. The same formula also lingered on in similar blends of rock and romance like *Juvenile Jungle* and *Let's Rock* (both 1958).

Eventually television supplied the movies with fresh teenage idols: Ed 'Kookie' Byrnes appeared in Sam Katzman's dreadful *Life Begins at 17* (1958). Cliff Richard was the British hipster in *Expresso Bongo* and the music business continued to supply stars for films like *Go Johnny Go* (both 1959) which starred Richie Valens, Eddie Cochran, The Cadillacs, The Flamingoes and Chuck Berry. The appearance, in 1959, of *Gidget* announced the arrival of the 'teen queen' – Sandra Dee.

By the end of the decade, serious considerations of teenage problems gave way to a tidal wave of beach and beat movies. *College Confidential* (dir. Albert S. Zugsmith, 1960) presented Mamie Van Doren as 'the student body', only this time the

by the police; most of them flee, but a few walk rebelliously into the glare of the squad cars' headlights. The mood of the scene perfectly matches the mean and moody spirit of the Shangri-Las' hit singles like 'Leader of the Pack'.

Similarly aggressive in tone were AIP's *Dragstrip Girl* and *Motorcycle Gang* (both 1957) which both featured the teen–parent conflicts, heroines torn between bad boyfriends and good boyfriends, plenty of hep jargon and high-speed motorbiking.

Katzman did not rule the teenage movie market alone: with *High School Confidential* (1958), Albert S. Zugsmith whipped up his own brand of hysteria. The film was notable for the introduction of the dope issue and the teenage star Mamie Van Doren. Zugsmith coined some 'jive talk' especially for the occasion and added plenty of scenes with hot-rod automobiles just for good measure. Soon 'reefer madness' became a hot theme in movies. In *The Cool and the Crazy* (1958) a kid who has served time in a state institution sells some dope to his classmates and even kills 'Eddie the Pusher' before himself succumbing and dying in a flaming car wreck in the middle of the desert.

Tragedies were becoming the very stuff of the teenage movie. AIP's *Dragstrip Riot* (1959) culminated in a free-for-all between two warring gangs of fast-living youths. In the record charts, the hit song 'Tom Dooley' (by the Kingston Brothers) raised the morbid death song to a teenage art form but the phenomenon was to be attacked by the clergy and parent-teacher groups as depraved and corrupt. The first morbid death songs dealt with the demise of actual contemporary heroes such as Johnny Ace and Buddy Holly. Truly great 'death discs' managed to pack all the trauma of teenage life into one metaphor – the big break-up. The songs had titles like 'Endless Sleep' and 'Teen Angel' and they were consciously up-to-date. Death came as a result of a stock-car race, or a rash dip in the river, or a joy ride in a borrowed car.

The victims always perished unexpectedly, accidentally and innocently. But, like their counterparts in the movies, they often made rash decisions. In 'Leader of the Pack' one falls in love with a boy whose love is more solid than his moped; 'I Want My Baby Back' proves how all the teenage casualties suffer horribly:

emphasis was equally on her professor, the well-known comedian Steve Allen. *Date Bait* (1960), a cheap and colourful 'exploitation' movie gave filmgoers a 'good' young couple who want to marry but get no help from their folks or her dope-crazy ex-boyfriend.

The trend towards wholesomeness continued with *Because They're Young* (1960), where the TV actor Dick Clark plays an ex-football star turned teacher, battling with youth problems in a high school in the style of *The Blackboard Jungle*. Finally, a film like *Where the Boys Are* (1959) demonstrates where the Fifties teenager had ended up. He or she was no longer a threat to civilized life, however many hi-jinks they might perpetrate. At the beginning of the Sixties, the movies saw the teenager as an energetic creature in need of advice and guidance, but meaning no real harm to society.

CYNTHIA ROSE

Above left: even the British promotion for the 'exploitation' double bill of Motorcycle Gang *and* Reform School Girl *(1957) pulled no punches, proving that sex and violence made movies marketable to teenage filmgoers too. Top: Ray Danton and Mamie Van Doren in* The Beat Generation *(1959). Above: Elvis Presley in the stylish but traditionally choreographed title number of* Jailhouse Rock *(1957), an early example of the tendency to cast rock'n'roll stars as maltreated and misunderstood*

JAMES DEAN NATALIE WOOD SAL MINEO

in Warner Bros.

"REBEL WITHOUT A CAUSE"

CINEMASCOPE
AND WARNERCOLOR

...and they both come from 'good' families!

Directed by Nicholas Ray, 1955
Prod co: Warner Bros. **prod:** David Weisbart. **sc:** Stewart Stern, Irving Shulman, from a story by Nicholas Ray. **photo:** Ernest Haller. **ed:** William Zeigler. **art dir:** Malcolm Bart. **mus dir:** Leonard Rosenman. **r/t:** 111 minutes.
Cast: James Dean (*Jim*), Natalie Wood (*Judy*), Jim Backus (*Jim's father*), Ann Doran (*Jim's mother*), Rochelle Hudson (*Judy's mother*), William Hopper (*Judy's father*), Sal Mineo (*Plato*), Corey Allen (*Buzz*), Dennis Hopper (*Goon*), Edward Platt (*Ray*), Steffi Sidney (*Mil*), Marietta Canty (*maid*), Ian Wolfe (*lecturer*), Frank Mazzola (*Crunch*).

When *Rebel Without a Cause* was premiered in Britain, in January 1956, the British critics considered it well-made, but some reviewers sustained severe moral outrage. *The Spectator* said:

'Its solemnity is rather irritating, seeing that a few good spanks would settle a lot of its problems.'

The *Daily Sketch* critic praised Nicholas Ray's direction but warned: 'That kind of brilliance in this kind of picture can be dangerous.'

Rebel Without a Cause is, of course, a 'problem picture' in the honourable Warner's tradition and can trace its ancestry back through the Dead End Kids' movies and *Angels With Dirty Faces* (1938) to the founding principles of 'social conscience' drama. In the wake of location-shot thrillers like *Gun Crazy* (1949) and alongside con-temporary 'teenpix' – B movies like *Five Against the House* (1955) – *Rebel Without a Cause* looks even more like the 'realist' romance it is. But Nicholas Ray and screenwriter Stewart Stern made determined efforts to accommodate a documentary feel within the parameters of the high-gloss, A-feature production values required at Warners.

Ray and Stern spent weeks interviewing youth leaders and juvenile officers. They sat in on juvenile court sessions and spoke with criminologists including one who had been the chief psychiatrist at the Nuremberg trials. They did their homework.

The scenario, as Eric Rohmer observed in the French magazine of film theory *Cahiers du Cinéma* in 1955, falls neatly into the five acts of classical tragedy: exposition, with the conflict between the parents and the children clearly stated; act two, in which Jim befriends Plato and is taunted by Buzz; act three, which includes the 'chicken run' with its fatal climax; act four, where Jim and Judy enjoy a transitory peace and share their love with Plato; and the final tragic act whose full impact is engraved on Jim's anguished face. As befits Aristotle's rules, the action is all but contained within 24 hours.

With that kind of narrative compression, the film could have emerged as hysterical melodrama, but even in the emotionally climactic scene of the domestic quarrel, the audience is never allowed to assume a dispassionate, 'objective' perspective. 'We are all involved!' as Jim exclaims. Ray's direction is in control: his camera spins upright out of a brilliant inverted shot from Jim's viewpoint. He then forces the action of the argument across the room and back against the stairs for greater dramatic effect and intercuts low-angle, high-angle and obliquely distorted shots to disrupt the perspective that the viewer normally considers his or her privilege. It is a bravura piece of direction in a film whose *mise-en-scène* is elsewhere distinguished by set-pieces, like the 'chicken run' and the final planetarium scenes – both of which are staged under the artificial, theatrical lighting of a circle of car headlamps.

The real director of *Rebel Without a Cause*, however, may be James Dean, in the sense that the film critic David Thomson describes him 'redirecting the picture by virtue of sheer presence'. If the complex experience of reading a film can be premised on the *look* constantly exchanged between the viewer and the on-screen protagonists, then *direction* may be construed as the control and orientation of that look. The unique qualities of James Dean as an actor, especially in the intuitive relationship he shared with Nicholas Ray, permit the 'lingering' of the look (Dean's characteristic pauses) and provoke the disorientation of the look (his restlessness in the CinemaScope frame). In short, Dean tells us where to look and what to notice.

In the scene where Jim meets Judy outside her house at night, we anticipate the confirmation of the love between them and, therefore, might expect a progression from individual close-ups, to two-shot, to embrace. Instead, shooting in medium close-up, Ray shows Jim, agitated, lolling or rolling over, dominating the central and left areas of the vast CinemaScope image; while Judy remains almost motionless right of frame. The framing, like everything else in the film, privileges Dean, confirming his dominance and suggesting that Ray was taking advantage of this opportunity to play Dean as his *alter ego* and extend the art of directing through performance so that Dean can be seen as acting out Ray's romantic fantasy. To quote David Thomson again:

'Arguably only Nicholas Ray could have given Dean a part that guessed at the looming alienation in America.'

Dean and Ray were two loners from Middle America, down there in the comfortable (studio-set) sub-urban homes, who fled to the wide-open spaces of a mansion in the hills and an observatory that showed moving pictures of the heavens.

MARTYN AUTY

2

3

5

6

7

8

9

Jim, the adolescent son of middle-class parents recently moved to California, is run in for drunkeness by the police (1). He sobers up and has a sympathetic hearing from the juvenile-offenders officer (2).

The following day, Jim's first day at his new high school, he meets Judy and her gang of rowdy friends. In the course of a school visit to the local planetarium, Jim becomes friendly with Plato, an unbalanced, orphaned kid seeking affection. Outside the planetarium Jim is taunted into a fight with Buzz (3), the leader of the pack and Judy's boyfriend. They agree to meet later that evening for a 'chicken run' – an endurance test in which each will drive an old car to the cliff edge and leap clear at the last possible moment.

Seeking, but failing to get, advice from his father, Jim joins Buzz at the rendezvous (4). They line up (5), Judy signals the start of the race and the cars head for the cliff-edge. Buzz's sleeve catches in the doorhandle causing him to go over the edge with the car. Jim consoles Judy and drives her home.

Jim feels he must go to the police but his parents object: a violent quarrel ensues (6). However, Jim goes to the police station and is seen by Buzz's gang-mates (7). They swear to get even with him.

Picking up Judy on the way, Jim drives to a large deserted house in the hills where they are joined by Plato (8). Jim and Judy declare their love (9). Buzz's gang follow them there and beat up Plato who nevertheless manages to shoot one of them. The police arrive and chase Plato to the planetarium.

Jim finally persuades the frightened Plato to give himself up but, at the crucial moment, shots are fired from the police cordon and Plato falls down. An anguished Jim zips up the jacket on his friend's body and escorts Judy from the scene.

Right: setting up the final scene in which Plato is lured from the planetarium to his death

James Dean was killed in a car crash on a Californian highway in the late afternoon of September 30, 1955, a fact that warranted little attention at the time. But within a couple of weeks, following the release of Dean's second major film, *Rebel Without a Cause*, he had become an idol for every *angst*-ridden teenager in America – and to this day remains the ultimate symbol of adolescent pain and rebellion born of despair

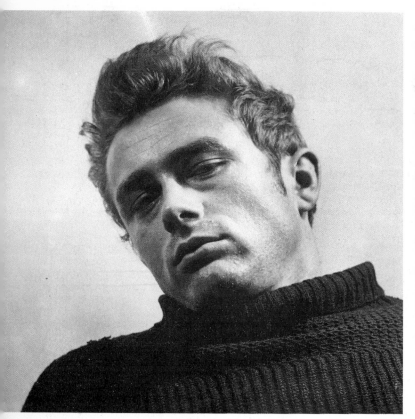

Films sometimes speak with an intimacy that makes us forget everything but the people on screen. However inspired the construction, photographed presence is the viewer's dream, so urgent and personal that involuntary cries or movements may overtake us in the dark. It is as if the ghost up there had made love to us, *us* alone, in an act of divining, penetrating kindness. And if the ghost looks out into the darkness with the guarded knowingness of James Dean, then our being ravished is a ceremony in which reality and fiction are blurred by the enigma of a star's existence. The greatest stars know that nothing can make them as memorable as heartfelt hesitation. It is a way of commanding the threshold of the screen, not just working in the film like an actor.

People still think of him as vulnerable, but James Dean was the most dominating movie star since Garbo. Of course, Valentino's funeral and death cult were greater than Dean's, but 25 years after the silent star's death, his acting style had been eclipsed by Brando, Clift and Garfield. Dean died over 25 years ago, yet his style prevails, albeit with softer, less deadly exponents. No young actor today is as sinister as Dean was. No-one has his stealth, or seems as capable of redirecting a picture by virtue of sheer presence.

Rather than subscribe to the old myth that a movie was a story being told, Dean knew that it was a fantasy that had to be lodged in the soul of the audience. Story was less relevant than the chance that imagery might fulfil emotional hope. Dean could speak, weep or cry out, to be sure, but he was most himself as a watchful, waiting actor. And because the films waited for him, the delay suggested a magical knowledge in Dean that was sensitive but frightening.

Like Garbo, he had a pessimistic vision of the world, and no amount of company could ease it. Indeed, cheerful groups and getting on well with life were the fabrications that most amused him. When he came to Hollywood for *East of Eden* (dir. Elia Kazan, 1955), Dean broke through all the bland hype of studio releases with this bleak admission of masquerade:

'A neurotic person has the necessity to express himself and my neuroticism manifests itself in the dramatic. Why do most actors act? To express the fantasies in which they have involved themselves.'

It is possible to measure Dean's brief glory, and the slow bruise of his legend, sociologically. He came along between the Beats and rock'n'roll. The generation that would slouch in his path included not just Paul Newman, Dennis Hopper and Steve McQueen, but Elvis, Dylan and every rock star. Dean found the clothes and gestures of young performance:

Above left: 'the resentful hair, the deep eyes floating in lonesomeness, the bitter beat look, the scorn on the lip' – words from a poem by John Dos Passos that admirably capture the James Dean image. Below: Dean as the glowering Cal Trask with Julie Harris and Raymond Massey in East of Eden

James Dean
The grace of loneliness

Shots from Robert Altman's documentary The James Dean Story *(1957): Dean on 52nd Street while staying in New York (above); Jimmy, age nine, shortly after going to live with his aunt and uncle (top right); in the centre of the front row of the Fairmount High School baseball team (below right)*

but, before that, he authorized the acting out of teenage problems. He marks the very first self-conscious younger generation. This was not just the potency of a new audience, but the commercialization of lonely hostility to the establishment. Dean negotiated the transition from Andy Hardy growing into his allotted place in the American Dream, to rock's intransigence, surly hipsterism and the wholesale denial of American values.

When Warners advertised *Rebel Without a Cause* (1955), they believed they had been lucky enough to catch the slipstream of a phenomenon known as juvenile delinquency. But Dean's radicalism was an existential disenchantment anticipating the squalor of Viet-

nam, network TV, assassinations, plastic ecology and American self-doubt. *Rebel* was not simply a film about high school: after all, the age of the actors was closer to 24. The picture had more to do with its director Nicholas Ray's pioneering discontent with America – as vivid, rueful and self-destructive as the director himself, who had found an actor so attuned to that atmosphere that Ray must have marvelled at the lucid enactment of his own anguish:

'The conflict between giving himself and fear of giving in to his own feelings . . . a vulnerability so deeply embedded that one is instantly moved, almost disturbed by it. Since infancy he had engaged in this struggle between impulsive violence and a grand defiance.'

That is Ray talking about the actor, but actually identifying himself, and indicating that the director who would do no major work for the last 16 years of his life, but wandered in a haze of outcast vitality and brooding self-pity, was yet another whose life was affected by James Dean. And Ray was possibly more vulnerable than Dean, who never bothered to conceal a furtive alienation from others, a kind of calculation that indicated a future career as a director and a producer.

Dean's life had the requisite elements of tragedy that biographers would pick over. But we cannot know if he was ever as disturbed as they would be. He was born in Indiana in 1931 and moved to Los Angeles as a young child. His mother died there when he was nine. Dean went back to the farmlands of Indiana to live with an aunt and uncle, during which time he saw little of his father. After ten years he

returned to California in search of an acting school. That was in 1949, in six years Dean would be dead. His work was so lyrical that there is no plausible way of tracing it to unhappiness. The legend quickly smothered facts. It alleged he was morose *and* appealing, that he searched for a mother substitute, loved the sweet Pier Angeli, slept with anyone available, was drawn to homosexual encounters, practised self-abuse, and so on and so on until the wreckage of a Porsche Spyder embodied the tangle of possibilities.

As if to solve his own confusion, he was determined to be an actor. Acting, and the moments of lying, are the only times our minds are set. Every character he played on screen is brimming with that pretence. They are all dreamers, hiding behind shifty materialists. It is as if he knew there was a darkness somewhere, as awesome as the planetarium in *Rebel*, and that if he looked into it, then he would be resolved, happy and unhappy, evil and benign, seeing and being seen. He wanted us, like a ghost in search of a house to haunt.

With scant training he had made a name for himself on Broadway and in live television drama. In 1954 he won a Tony Award as the Arab boy in *The Immoralist*, a play adapted from Gide's novel. On television, he had so entranced directors with his improvisations that the irritation of such co-stars as Mary Astor and Paul Lukas was overruled and they were told to let Jimmy do it his way. They were prototype parent figures, rebuked by his insight and required to stand to attention while his muse climbed. Dean was a jazz actor who could solo at will from the set chords, never repeating himself. He could reduce Raymond Massey, Natalie Wood or Elizabeth Taylor to rhythm sections anxious to support the rapture with which he occupied the moment. It is acting that dares boredom and breakdown and threatens such things as text and production with perilous delays, new lines and inspirational bits of business. It came just before

cinéma-vérité, and it makes all that actuality look banal and hollow. Dean had stylized the real more than anyone before or since.

It got him into trouble on the stage and it impeded his last film, *Giant* (1956). But he was lucky to have Nicholas Ray and Elia Kazan as his first directors, because they both needed him and were both lifted by the occasion. Kazan had exactly the training and disposition to understand Dean's sulky method. More important, Dean's improvisation freed the pent-up but often schematic emotionalism in Kazan. The film of *East of Eden* is a staggering glorification of the immature distress of adolescence. Kazan dropped 90 per cent of the Steinbeck novel and refashioned the last part as his own psycho-drama. He made it the mirror of a personal rebellion against his own father. The fantasy revealed on the screen is that of parenthood brought down to the level of adolescent wishful recrimination. In terms of box-office history, *East of Eden* is the first teenage weepie, never questioning the central figure's tantrum at being neglected or misunderstood. Cal Trask is a tyrant of feelings, an *enfant terrible* actor in a household of characters, demanding a father's love, aiming to buy it and confronting an envied stooge brother with their mother's shocking existence. Cal may not be Cain, but he has a taste for self-serving melodrama that rivals Citizen Kane's. But because of Kazan's complicity, so Dean's performance confounds reason or maturity. In its form, *East of Eden* is one of the most uncompromisingly romantic American films. In letting the teenage yearning soar uncorrected, it becomes a testament to vibrant infantilism, with the hero and the heroine left to play house and the father reduced to the status of a doll.

Dean is supposedly playing a 20-year-old, but Cal could be as old as Dracula. Vampirism is explicit in extreme stardom – and it is spelled

out in the action of Kazan's film as every other character succumbs to Cal's view of the world. Dean preys upon the others and upon the audience. As the camera indulges his pauses, so it flatters his authority. *East of Eden* is a disconcertingly languid film because Kazan has relinquished his own decisiveness to Dean's rhapsody upon hurt feelings. Cinema-Scope seemed hallowed because it allowed more space for Dean's nervy prowling.

Rebel did the same, from Dean's foetal pose before the credits to his spread-eagled agony as he tells the police he had removed the bullets from Plato's gun. Ray's film seemed contemporary, but Dean crooned Wagner in the precinct station and surveyed Natalie Wood like a dissipated Hamlet contemplating a drugstore Ophelia. Dean seems so much more aware than parents, police, teachers or other kids. He could be a traveller from the past or from one of those remote planets he watches in the ominous theatre of space. He knows a level of feeling that this Californian society is numb to, and it confers on him the pain and privilege of a poet, or a director.

Jim Backus, the actor who played Dean's father in *Rebel*, told *Variety*, 'This is the first time in the history of motion pictures that a 24-year-old boy, with only one movie to his credit, was practically the co-director.' Years after *Giant*, director George Stevens regretted that he had not given Dean more license. In particular, there is a scene where Jett Rink comes to a party at the Reata ranch and accepts a drink. Dean wanted Jett to use his own flask so that he would be beholden to no-one. Such a ploy was characteristic of Dean, too: he wanted to usurp his directors, and he had his eyes set on making his own films.

But on *Giant*, a solemn and respectable director could only see that the solid Texan family was better behaved than the oil-trash kid who becomes a tycoon. Whenever Dean

Above: Dean with Nicholas Ray; they planned to work together again after discovering great creative rapport while making Rebel Without a Cause. *Below: 'Racing is the only time I feel whole' – James Dean in his first Porsche at a race meeting early in 1955, and with destiny in his hands*

has a scene on his own – pacing his land or splashing in the oil – his ability to reach us physically, and to idealize solitude, bring the film to life. He makes a more committed effort to ageing than either Rock Hudson or Elizabeth Taylor, and his performance lets us see something not appreciated by Stevens: that the nobody who becomes a lord of Texas is more interesting and just as American as the self-satisfied Benedicts.

When Dean died, François Truffaut recognized that his acting had not been psychological or focused on the text. It was a delicate escape, set in the manner of naturalism, from raw being into a butterfly performance. It seems to be made up on the spur of his moment and our dream. That immediacy was what enlisted us in the transformation. For it was an assertion of make-believe such as we must make whenever we watch a movie personage at once so real and so phantom. Truffaut compared Dean with Chaplin – there was the same facade of downcast failure turning into glittering control and perfection:

'Something else is at work, a poetic game that lends authority to every liberty – even encourages it. Acting right or wrong has no meaning when we talk about Dean, because we expect a surprise a minute from him . . . With James Dean everything is grace, in every sense of the word . . . He isn't better than everybody else; he does *something else*, the opposite; he protects his glamour from the beginning to the end of each film.'

DAVID THOMSON

Filmography
1951 Fixed Bayonets; Sailor Beware. '52 Has Anybody Seen My Gal? '55 East of Eden; Rebel Without a Cause. '56 Giant.

A little light relief

As the Fifties progressed, the movies showed American life becoming more secure, cosy and domestic. Hollywood comedies endorsed the image

The Fifties may have been the decade which began with the Cold War and ended with the Campaign for Nuclear Disarmament, but it was also the era of Jayne Mansfield, the hula-hoop craze and rock'n'roll. Just as in the Thirties people found relief from the external worries of the Depression and the rise of fascism in the elegant abstractions of Astaire-Rogers musicals and in screwball comedies, so in the Fifties the dark clouds had to have a silver lining of some kind.

In the magical sanctuary of the cinema you could have been forgiven for supposing that the most important issue in the world was whether Doris Day would succeed, despite all the fairly gentlemanly stratagems of her leading men, in preserving her virginity until wedding bells at the final fade-out. The star system was still functioning unshakably, or so it seemed, and it was hard to tell, watching Marilyn Monroe's progress from a one-gag scene in The Marx Brothers' *Love Happy* (1949) to superstardom in *Gentlemen Prefer Blondes* (1953), that we were seeing the last act of the star-making machine which had been so carefully built up over the years in the Hollywood dream factory.

In the Fifties nearly all the great stars of the talkies were still alive and working. It was only at the end of the decade, with the deaths, in rapid succession, of Humphrey Bogart, Tyrone Power, Errol Flynn, Clark Gable and Gary Cooper, that filmgoers realized how frail and mortal the gods of the screen were.

For the moment, however, the worst menace was the new toy, television. Film-makers – real film-makers who made movies exclusively for cinemas – could still afford to wax satirical about television, or simply dismiss it as beneath notice. Likewise, movie stars steered clear – with one or two spectacular exceptions. Lucille Ball, for instance, who had been a star of fairly modest stature around Hollywood for a decade or so, but then went on to television in a family situation-comedy series, *I Love Lucy*, with her real-life husband Desi Arnaz, instantly found fame and success far greater than anything she had ever dreamed of in the movies. When she went back to the cinema, it was on her own terms, as a visiting celebrity. This she did most notably in *The Long Long Trailer* (1953), in which Vincente Minnelli gave polish and sparkle to what was basically an extended *I Love Lucy* episode, and *The Facts of Life* (1960), in which she co-starred with Bob Hope, in a comic variation on *Brief Encounter* (1945).

Bob Hope was rather a different matter. He was a veteran from the Thirties and had been big in films throughout the Forties. He entered the Fifties with his star lustre more or less intact. Like Lucy, he did not shun television – or indeed anything which would keep him busy and before the public. But his films of the Fifties came to seem more and more like sequels to his earlier successes such as *Son of Paleface* and *Road to Bali* (both 1952), or films in which his special gift for quick-fire, stand-up comedian gags was less suited to the more relaxed comic style of Hollywood in the Fifties. With the solitary

exceptions of *That Certain Feeling* (1956) and *The Facts of Life*, he seemed to have difficulty playing a character instead of merely playing Bob Hope. Even in such lightweight biographies as *The Seven Little Foys* (1955) and *Beau James* (1957), the ostensible subjects (the vaudevillian Eddie Foy and the famous Mayor of New York, Jimmy Walker) were fed through Hope's gag machine to come out disconcertingly more like the usual screen Hope than anyone else.

Things fared better for the other important survivor from wartime comedy, Danny Kaye. After the lavish musical biography, *Hans Christian Anderson* (1952), he separated from Sam Goldwyn, the producer who had made him what he was. But Kaye managed to keep his own brand of zany, frenetic comedy going in films like *Knock on Wood* (1954), *The Court Jester* (1956) – perhaps the best of all his films – and *Merry Andrew* (1958). He even did surprisingly well, when he succumbed to the alleged ambition of all comics to play Hamlet, by taking the straight role in *Me and the Colonel* (1958) and leaving most of the comedy to Curt Jurgens. But then, love him or hate him, Danny Kaye was always in a class of his own and likely to be less affected than most by changing fashions in comedy.

It was characteristic of the Fifties that Danny Kaye could peacefully co-exist with the biggest new challengers in comedy, Dean Martin and Jerry Lewis. They were to the Fifties what Laurel and Hardy had been to the Thirties and Abbott and Costello to the Forties. Martin and Lewis somehow brought to perfection a sort of lowest common denominator in comedy, and so built their popularity up from a solid base of mass appreciation on the part of unsophisticated audiences. In the case of Laurel and Hardy, the duo eventually became the idols of the intelligentsia as well as the idiots' delight and the same thing happened to Martin and Lewis as a result of their critical acclaim in France. But Anglo-Saxon film critics of the Fifties, when they were not moralizing about the overstressed sexuality of Elvis Presley and the dangers of his effect on the young, were quite likely to be tut-tutting about Jerry Lewis' spastic humour and claiming that his moronic screen persona made cruel fun of the afflicted.

Despite such admonitions, the films Martin and Lewis made together between *My Friend Irma* (1949) and *Hollywood or Bust* (1956) were among the most reliable box-office champions of their day, and after the team split up each individually went on to become a major star in his own right.

Comedy in the Fifties tended to be pretty unsophisticated as, for example, in the endless encounters between Donald O'Connor and Francis the Talking Mule. But even glossy comedy had a heart of pure candy-floss. This was certainly true of the comedies and lightweight dramas to which Doris Day graduated when she gave up musicals towards the end of the decade. Though some of them, like *Pillow Talk* (1959) and *That Touch of Mink* (1962), might seem to feature mildly risqué situations, it

Top: Bob Hope and a cast of juveniles in The Seven Little Foys, *a comedy about a father who raises his seven children as vaudeville performers. Above: Bob Hope and Jimmy 'Schnozzle' Durante do a soft-shoe shuffle in* Beau James *the story of a man who becomes mayor of New York but is compromised by his love for an actress*

84

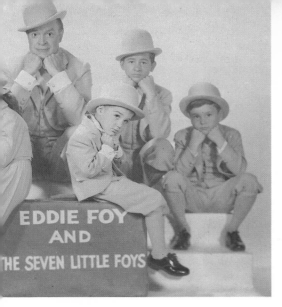

EDDIE FOY
AND
THE SEVEN LITTLE FOYS

was from the outset a foregone conclusion that the heroine's virtue, faintly endangered though it may have been, was going to remain impregnable. Besides, audiences could comfort themselves with the knowledge that Miss Day, now nearing forty, seemed old enough to look after herself – hence the famous comment 'I knew Doris Day before she was a virgin'. The rather jolly, absurd thrillers like *Julie* (1956) and *Midnight Lace* (1960) similarly eschewed any real sense of menace, especially when, as with the latter film, drenched in soapy colour thanks to the production values unique to Ross Hunter's Universal-International house style.

Not all comedy during the Fifties was quite so toothless. There was a little cycle all on its own which harked back in a fresh way to the splendours of the Thirties. In collaboration with the husband-and-wife team Garson Kanin and Ruth Gordon (who worked as writers, either separately or together), George Cukor made a series of sparklingly witty and sometimes surprisingly tender comedies with Spencer Tracy and Katharine Hepburn and a distinctive new discovery – the zany comedienne Judy Holliday.

The three-way partnership between Tracy, Hepburn and Holliday began with *Adam's Rib* (1949), a battle between rival lawyers who just happen to be married to each other. Tracy and Hepburn were then teamed (without Judy Holliday) as athlete and trainer in *Pat and Mike* (1952). Tracy then played the unwilling father of *The Actress* (1953) and Judy Holliday portrayed several variations of her lovable kooky character who turns out to be somehow wiser than the rationalists around her in *Born Yesterday* (1950), *The Marrying Kind* (1952) and *It Should Happen to You* (1954). Indeed Judy Holliday made a career from such roles throughout the decade, with other writers and directors, in films like *Phffft* (1954), *The Solid Gold Cadillac*, *Full of Life* (both 1956) and the last Minnelli musical made at MGM, *Bells Are Ringing* (1960).

What these films have in common with the less sophisticated variety during the Fifties is that they are all star vehicles, and take their tone and pace very largely from the established screen personality of the star or stars in question. Spencer Tracy and Katharine Hepburn, for example, extended their sparring screen partnership in *The Desk Set* (1957). They also preserved their individual, slightly spiky personalities which had made and kept them famous by exploiting these comic personae outside of the celebrated partnership. Tracy appeared alone in *Father of the Bride* (1950) and its sequel *Father's Little Dividend* (1951), while Hepburn starred with Bob Hope in a pale imitation of *Ninotchka* (1939) called *The Iron Petticoat* (1956).

And the newest stars were not forgotten. Once Marilyn Monroe had arrived as a superstar in Hawks' gloriously garish musical *Gentlemen Prefer Blondes*, her energies were most happily channelled into comedy rather than drama, and in Billy Wilder she found a director who knew how to display her qualities to perfection. *The Seven Year Itch* (1955) and *Some Like It Hot* (1959) captured unforgettably – and hilariously – her innocent sexuality and her air of being the totally unconscious *agent provocateur* of all the male preenings, palpitations and jockeyings for position which went on around her.

With *Sabrina* (1954) and *Love in the Afternoon* (1957) Billy Wilder also created ideal vehicles for the very different charms of another brand-new star, Audrey Hepburn, and made the definitive transition from his image as a hard-hitting scourge of the world's follies to that of Hollywood's most brilliant comedy director, a role he was to revel in throughout the Sixties.

Not that he had so much competition. By the end of the Fifties, his were just about the only comedies not suffering from terminal softening of the brain. The musical too, which entered the decade at some kind of peak, left it a faded, overblown remnant. In 1949 Gene Kelly and Stanley Donen had made their debut as directors with *On the Town*, which boldly took its singing and dancing stars out on the streets of New York and blended song, dance and drama more inextricably than ever before into one unquestionable whole. It was the cue for a series of triumphs. In 1951 Kelly worked with Minnelli on *An American in Paris*, and in 1952 Kelly and Donen were back together again for *Singin' in the Rain*, which remains for many the finest flower of the genre. But it had ample competition for the title, notably from Minnelli's 1953 offering *The Band Wagon*. Judy Garland achieved some sort of apotheosis in *A Star is Born* (1954) but great musical stars were few and far between in the Fifties. Gene Kelly danced in films like *Invitation to the Dance* (1956), *Brigadoon* (1954), *It's Always Fair Weather* (1955), his final collaboration with Donen, and *Les Girls* (1957), which included Cole Porter's last original score for the screen.

More astonishing still, Fred Astaire, who had announced his definitive retirement in 1946, considering himself too old at 47 to go on dancing, reversed his decision and continued to dance and delight right through the decade.

The high points of the Fifties for him were *The Band Wagon* and *Silk Stockings* (1957), in both of which he partnered the statuesque Cyd Charisse. There were also two May-September matings, first with the elfin Leslie Caron in *Daddy Long Legs* (1954) and then with the ineffable Audrey Hepburn in *Funny Face* (1957).

Most of the musical partnerships of the Forties and early Fifties broke up towards the end of the decade. Stanley Donen went on to direct two more musicals at Warners, *The Pajama Game* (1957) and *Damn Yankees* (1958) before transferring his allegiance to dramatic films too. Gene Kelly went on to direct non-musical films too. Many of the musicals that were made in the latter half of the Fifties were safe, faithful transcriptions of recent Broadway successes: *Oklahoma!* (1955), *The King and I* (1956) and *South Pacific* (1958). Original creations for the screen like *Seven Brides for Seven Brothers* (1954) and *Gigi* (1958) were, by and large, considered too risky in a Hollywood reeling at the onslaught television had made on its public. Never mind the quality, look at the size, might be the motto of Hollywood in the Sixties, and in comedy and the musical the small, sophisticated pleasures which lit up so much of the Fifties had been brushed aside for ever.   JOHN RUSSELL TAYLOR

Above: Bob Hope and Lucille Ball in The Facts of Life, *a wry comedy about a couple who spend an illicit weekend together away from their respective spouses and confront the familiar domestic situations once again. Top: Bob Fosse and Gwen Verdon in the smash-hit musical* Damn Yankees *– yet another Fifties film that revolved around a marriage break-up*

Minnelli's Web of Dreams

His musicals are magical, his melodramas are memorable and his style is stunning. Vincente Minnelli uses colour, costumes and settings to create films that bring to life people's emotions and fantasies

Above left: Vincente Minnelli and his screen triumphs. Left: in Gigi, *Hermione Gingold and Isobel Jeans play two sisters, one-time Parisian courtesans. Below: the disturbed villain (Robert Taylor) of* Undercurrent *with his wife (Katharine Hepburn)*

Vincente Minnelli is one of the screen's great stylists. Everybody has always agreed about that although they have not always meant the same thing by it. In his early years as a film director critics applauded the tastefulness of his style, whereas from the mid-Fifties he was put forward as a Hollywood director who used style consistently and coherently to embody and enrich the content of the film. In recent years, critics have focused their attention on the 'excessive' quality of his films, the way his style goes 'over the top' on occasions. These different views of how Minnelli's films work in terms of style do not reflect changes in his work so much as changes in critical opinion, and there is a fair degree of truth in each approach.

Minnelli was born (in 1913) into a vaudeville family and his pre-Hollywood career was in the theatre. He began by designing sets and costumes for Broadway shows in the Thirties and was associated with the developments in musical theatre at that time: the sophistication

Above: Minnelli's fascination with art provided the incentive for Lust for Life with Kirk Douglas as Vincent Van Gogh. Left: the two lovers, Emma (Jennifer Jones) and Rodolphe (Louis Jourdan) in Minnelli's historical drama, Madame Bovary

and 'cleverness' of revue, with its allusions to modern art, fashion and intellectual trends; the attempts to integrate the musical numbers with the story in musical comedy, and to deal with more serious topics than the perennial, light-hearted treatment of boy-meets-girl. It is not surprising that when Arthur Freed set up his innovatory musicals unit at MGM, he should have wanted Minnelli for it.

Minnelli had already had experience of Hollywood, as a producer at Paramount, but it had been an unhappy liaison. He said later that the studio 'weren't willing to support the kind of musicals I wanted to do', and he quickly got out. Freed, however, was interested in making that kind of musical – and MGM had the money to make them. At MGM, Minnelli, backed by Freed, produced a series of musicals that were in many ways innovatory. They integrated the numbers more fully with the plot – most notably in his third feature, Meet Me in St Louis (1944), where the songs seem to arise naturally out of the lives of the characters. They explored a sophisticated range of subject-matter – the subconscious in Yolanda and the Thief (1945), modern art in An American in Paris (1951), the world of the courtesan in

Gigi (1958). They incorporated the clever wit of Broadway, like the send-up of swashbuckling heroics in The Pirate (1948), and they were well in line with trends in fashions and interior decorations. Above all, they experimented with the musical possibilities of the technology of film itself – rhythmic editing, dancing camera movement, the harmonic use of colour.

Meet Me in St Louis was the first film that Minnelli made with Judy Garland, whom he married in 1945. His association with her not only produced Liza in December 1946, but also some of the best work of either of them. Apart from another full-length musical, The Pirate, and sequences in Ziegfeld Follies and Till the Clouds Roll By (both 1946), they also made a non-musical together, The Clock (1945), about a GI who meets, falls in love with and marries a secretary all in the space of two days. This lovely film is rather like a boy-meets-girl musical without songs.

That a director of musicals should become a director of melodramas is not so remarkable since melodrama means, originally, drama with music. In melodrama, the happy numbers of the musical are replaced by searing climaxes, often set to insistently plangent music. Besides, there are dark elements in Minnelli's musicals, despite their apparent froth and jollity, that would find fuller expression in melodrama.

Undercurrents

All his melodramas explore and expose obsessive, frustrated, traumatic aspects of human experience, in a wide variety of situations. The standard setting of the Hollywood melodrama is the middle-class family in small-town America. Several of Minnelli's melodramas are in this mould – Undercurrent (1946), Some Came Running (1958), Home from the Hill (1959). They explore the tensions of family life – power and dependence between parents and children, rivalry between siblings, conflicts between the sexes. Many of these tensions are also shown to lie behind the relationships in

other, non-family, groups, such as the film-making community in Hollywood (The Bad and the Beautiful, 1952) or Italy's Cinecitta (Two Weeks in Another Town, 1962), a psychiatric clinic (The Cobweb, 1955) or a boys' college (Tea and Sympathy, 1956).

Minnelli's musicals have received so much acclaim that it is often forgotten that he has made almost as many comedies. Starting with Father of the Bride (1950), these all dealt with aspects of family life and the battle of the sexes: Father's Little Dividend (1951), a sequel to Father of the Bride, The Long, Long, Trailer (1953), with Lucille Ball and Desi Arnaz, Designing Woman (1957) and The Reluctant Debutante (1958). In 1963 he made what might be considered to be his finest comedy, The Courtship of Eddie's Father, about a young boy's efforts to find his widowed father a wife.

Until 1964, Minnelli worked exclusively and apparently perfectly happily for MGM. Unlike other directors, he does not seem to have found MGM's wealthy but conservative house style a restriction – indeed, it gave him the money to experiment, as in the use of colour in his story of Van Gogh, Lust for Life (1956). In 1964, he made a comedy, Goodbye Charlie, for 20th Century-Fox. None of his later films, though all working in his usual genres and containing many of the characteristic features of his work, have been very successful, commercially or critically. Goodbye Charlie was followed by the Richard Burton–Elizabeth Taylor vehicle, The Sandpiper (1965), and two musicals with the top singing stars of contemporary cinema: On a Clear Day You Can See Forever (1970) with Barbra Streisand, and A Matter of Time (1976) with his own daughter Liza.

Certain thematic consistencies can be seen in Minnelli's work. The one most often cited is the idea of the pursuit of a dream – all his characters have a fantasy ideal that they wish to pursue. The ideal is more deeply felt, more important to them, than the everyday world in which they must live. The films address the problem of how to come to terms with the vivid urgency of the ideal against the drab necessity of living in the ordinary world. The films appear to have happy endings, in which either the ideal is realized or the character is reconciled to everyday life – yet these endings are only apparently happy. The keenness of the longing for the ideal lingers in the mind, leaving a dark undertow to even the most

Above: fashion designer (Lauren Bacall) and writer (Gregory Peck) with friends (Dolores Gray, Tom Helmore) in Designing Woman. *Above right: Eddie (Ronny Howard) disapproves of his father (Glenn Ford) and his date (Dina Merrill) in* The Courtship of Eddie's Father. *Below right: director (Kirk Douglas) and the star (George Hamilton) in* Two Weeks in Another Town

glittering of his musicals. It is as if the effort of imagination required to see that reconciliation between the ideal and the everyday eludes Minnelli, and more often than not he makes only a mere token gesture towards the solution.

A most ingenious paradox
Related to this theme is a concern with illusion and reality. Minnelli's films are, in many ways, a play on the elusive nature of illusion and the difficulty of knowing whether anything at all is, in the end, 'real'. This theme is clearest when the film's background is artistic creation – theatre, film-making or painting. Minnelli is not concerned to expose the falsity of the illusions that art spins, but rather he takes a delight in the paradoxes that ensue if you try to think through the relations between art/illusion and reality. In *The Pirate*, Judy Garland states, 'I know there is a dream world and a real world, and I shan't confuse them' – but the film is really all about confusing them. In *Madame Bovary* (1949), starring Jennifer Jones and Louis Jourdan, it is never clear whether Emma's relationship with the handsome Rodolphe is a genuine, if trivial affair or a case of romance for her and sex for him. In *The Bad and the Beautiful*, the film-producer (Kirk Douglas), gets the best from his star (Lana Turner), by tricking her into believing he loves her: by eliciting her love in return, he gets her to express the 'true' feeling of love on the screen, leaving the audience in total confusion about what real feeling is and is not. In *On a Clear Day You Can See Forever*, in which the heroine (Barbra Streisand) remembers a previous existence under hypnosis, Minnelli never reveals whether her memories are real, or products of her fertile imagination, or fantasies put to her by the hypnotist (Yves Montand). Always the question of illusion, of what is and what is not real, remains unanswered, perhaps unanswerable.

A third concern arises from this, namely the nature of sex roles. Throughout Minnelli's work there is an awareness that the roles of women and men are not natural but social, that they are, in a sense, illusions. Sometimes this emerges in parodies of the extremes of masculinity (Gene Kelly in *The Pirate*) and femininity (Dolores Gray in *Kismet*, 1955; Kay Kendall in *The Reluctant Debutante*). Sometimes it becomes the subject-matter of the film. In terms of masculinity, the films focus upon manhood as something that has to be achieved and perhaps is not worth achieving when so high a price has to be paid for it in terms of sensitivity (*Tea and Sympathy*) and even human life (*Home From the Hill*). In terms of femininity, the films often pose a set of irreconcilable, stereotypical female roles that the male character has to choose from – the virgin or the whore in *Some Came Running*, the dumb blonde, the rich bitch or the girl next door in *The Courtship of Eddie's Father*. Whatever the man's choice, he will have less than a whole person – but then, aside, notably, from his work with Judy Garland, women as whole people are few in Minnelli's films. Alongside this interest in the artificial polarities of the sex roles, there is also a liking for characters who do not fit, who are in between – the 'feminine' young men of *Tea and Sympathy* (John Kerr), *Home from the Hill* and *Two Weeks in Another Town* (both George Hamilton) or his use of wittily independent women stars such as Garland, Lucille Ball, Lauren Bacall and Judy Holliday.

Lovely to look at
In the Forties and early Fifties, critics emphasized Minnelli's concern with taste and beauty, his feeling for *haute couture* (like the fashion show he directed in *Lovely to Look At*, 1952) and smart interior decoration. In some ways, this is to take Minnelli at his own estimation of himself. In his book of memoirs, *I Remember It Well*, it seems that what Minnelli himself rates most highly in his work is its good taste, and especially as this is approximated to the high art of painting. The look of many of his films is deliberately related to famous painters – the American realist, Thomas Eakins, in *Meet Me in St Louis*, Van Gogh in *Lust for Life* and a whole roster of turn-of-the-century French artists (including Dufy, Renoir, Toulouse-Lautrec and Douanier Rousseau) in the ballet sequence that ends *An American in Paris*. Yet this concern with taste, beauty and art has also been a stick to beat Minnelli with – it is seen as trivial, mere prettification by some, as pretentiousness and snobbism by others.

The critics of the mid-Fifties onwards, however, especially those associated with the British magazine *Movie*, saw the question of Minnelli's style differently. For them, Minnelli used camera movement, colour, editing, costume, sets and the rest to express the meanings he wanted to convey – the style was the meaning. *Home From the Hill* illustrates this. The film revolves around a conflict between a man (Robert Mitchum) and his wife (Eleanor Parker). The husband's den in the film is painted a deep, blood red all over and is furnished in a 'masculine' way, with leather armchairs, rifles and hunting trophies. The rest of the house is the woman's domain – it is decorated in off-white, with chintzy patterns and in upper-class good taste; she wears pastel

colours that blend in with the setting. The house is thus divided dramatically between the male and female parts, as is the family itself. The use of colour, however, goes beyond this, through the way it relates to a blood symbolism that runs through the film. He is associated with blood, with hunting, with death, whereas she is aloof from this, cold and bloodless. Their son (George Hamilton) has to choose between these two sets of values and life-styles. The blood connection goes further still, to subconscious associations of blood – and fear – with maleness and femaleness. Thus Mitchum's room is engorged with blood, as an erect penis, whereas Parker's domain is drained of blood as in menstruation.

Visual dynamite

This final level of interpretation fits in with a quality of psychic torment that runs through Minnelli's work. For the most part this remains buried beneath the chic and the crafted story-telling – but every so often there is an eruption of anguish and hysteria, and this too is expressed, above all, in style. It's as if there is an excess of frustrated emotion and desire that can finally no longer be contained, and when it bursts out it is in the form of delirious camera movement, explosions of light and colour, deafening music and rapid editing. Examples include the film star's careering car ride in *The Bad and the Beautiful*, when she realizes that the producer does not really love her; the boar chase in *Home From the Hill*, echoed at the end of the film when the son pursues his father's murderer along the same path; and the climax of *Some Came Running*, set amidst the gaudy moving lights, swirling crowds and pounding music of a fair ground, where the intended murderer of Dave Hirsh (Frank Sinatra) pursues him, violently silhouetted by neon light that seems to explode onto the screen. At these points, a raw delirium tears apart the tasteful surface and organic connectedness of the rest of the film – Minnelli goes right over the top, with results that are exhilarating and shattering. It is in the interplay of these three different, and in some ways contradictory, uses of style and the way that they relate to the themes of dreams, illusions and role-playing, that the fascination of Minnelli's films lies.

RICHARD DYER

Above: a lonely master's wife (Deborah Kerr) offers Tea and Sympathy *to a misunderstood schoolboy (John Kerr). Below: contrasting sets from* Home From the Hill – *husband (Robert Mitchum) and wife (Eleanor Parker) in his den (left) and wife and son (George Hamilton) in her domain (right). Bottom: an exotic dream sequence from* On a Clear Day You Can See Forever *with Barbra Streisand*

Filmography
1942 Panama Hattie (some scenes only, uncredited). '43 Cabin in the Sky; I Dood It (GB: By Hook or By Crook); Thousands Cheer (some scenes only, uncredited). '44 Meet Me in St Louis. '45 The Clock (GB: Under the Clock); Yolanda and the Thief. '46 Ziegfeld Follies (some scenes only); Undercurrent; Till the Clouds Roll By (some scenes only, uncredited). '48 The Pirate. '49 Madame Bovary. '50 Father of the Bride. '51 An American in Paris; Father's Little Dividend. '52 Lovely to Look At (some scenes only, uncredited); The Bad and the Beautiful. '53 The Story of Three Loves (episode: Mademoiselle); The Band Wagon; The Long, Long Trailer. '54 Brigadoon. '55 The Cobweb; Kismet. '56 Lust for Life; Tea and Sympathy. '57 Designing Woman; The Seventh Sin (add dir. uncredited). '58 Gigi; The Reluctant Debutante; Some Came Running. '59 Home From the Hill. '60 Bells are Ringing. '62 The Four Horsemen of the Apocalypse; Two Weeks in Another Town. '63 The Courtship of Eddie's Father. '64 Goodbye Charlie. '65 The Sandpiper. '70 On a Clear Day You Can See Forever. '76 A Matter of Time (USA-IT).

A DELUGE OF *Delight* – SPLASHED WITH SONG HITS!

METRO-GOLDWYN-MAYER *presents*

Singin' in the Rain

IN COLOUR BY *TECHNICOLOR*®

Starring

GENE KELLY • Donald O'CONNOR

Debbie REYNOLDS • CyD CHARISSE

1

If there is one image which sums up the MGM musical, it is this: Gene Kelly, walking home in euphoric mood, is caught in a particularly heavy fall of Californian dew. But does he care? No, not a bit of it. On along the empty street, past the glamorous shop windows he dances, twirling under a water spout, tap-dancing in the gutter, finally stamping around with child-like delight and abandon in a giant puddle which covers half the road. When a mystified and vaguely hostile policeman comes up to find out just what is going on, Kelly has a simple answer: 'Just singin', and dancin', in the rain.'

The convention of the musical as a never-never land, where normal rules of life were for the moment suspended and invisible orchestras would accompany ordinary people as they expressed their ordinary emotions in an extraordinary way, found its complete justification in the integrated musicals of producer Arthur Freed. *Singin' in the Rain* is the finest hour of this school of film-making. It does, it is true, contain elements of the old 'putting on a show' musical formula (or in this case a film), but hardly any of its numbers are tied down to a stuffily rational context. Even the ambitious 'Broadway Melody' sequence is presented as a fantasy in the minds of its creators which they are trying to put over to their reluctant boss – and which he stubbornly fails to visualize.

In *Singin' in the Rain*, as in all the best musicals, the characters' behaviour has its own logic: song and dance are kept in reserve for the moments of irrepressible high spirits, passionate romance and the like, those moments when we might all feel like bursting into song or whirling away into dance if only we knew how, if only we were not worried what passers-by might think, if only we had the MGM orchestra and chorus to hand.

The title number is the climax of the film, but it is also the simplest. At the other end of the scale is the big 'Broadway Melody' number, which

Above right: a publicity shot of the film's opening scene

tells a show-business rags-to-riches story in miniature with a multiplicity of sets, costumes and extras. As a sizzling addition to the proceedings, Cyd Charisse features as the hero's dream woman.

The film's story manages to comprehend both these extremes. The script by Betty Comden and Adolph Green (both of whom had already worked with directors Gene Kelly and Stanley Donen on their first great success, *On the Town*, 1949) is probably the funniest and sharpest ever invented for a film musical. The image that it offers of Hollywood at the coming of sound has the ring of truth, for all its comic exaggeration. Who can forget the picture of the nitwit silent-movie queen Lina Lamont wrestling with round vowels as she bleats 'I caaan't stan'm' in response to her voice coach's patient tuition? Or the opening sequence in which her opposite number, romantic idol Don Lockwood reminisces for the listening public about his rise to the top, with 'dignity, dignity, always dignity', while the scenes of dancing for pennies and tatty burlesque which flash before us belie every word he says? Or the unstoppable *élan* with which Don and his two fellow conspirators, once they hit on the perfect solution to their dilemma (make the disastrous costume movie into a musical), burst into 'Good Morning' and gyrate and tap all over Don's beautiful, baronial, Hollywood home?

However, it is invidious to pick out any single treasure in *Singin' in the Rain* without mentioning all the rest. None of its stars were ever shown to better advantage and the formidable MGM machine never worked more smoothly or to greater effect, down to the last detail of design and orchestration. What ever happened to the Hollywood musical in later years, *Singin' in the Rain* survives as irrefutable testimony to the wonderful way they were. JOHN RUSSELL TAYLOR

2

3

6

7

10

90

Directed by Gene Kelly and Stanley Donen, 1952
Prod co: MGM. prod: Arthur Freed. sc: Betty Comden, Adolph Green. photo: Harold Rosson. col: Technicolor. ed: Adrienne Fazan. art dir: Cedric Gibbons, Randall Duell. mus dir: Lennie Hayton. mus: Nacio Herb Brown. lyr: Arthur Freed. r/t: 103 minutes.
Cast: Gene Kelly (*Don Lockwood*), Donald O'Connor (*Cosmo Brown*), Debbie Reynolds (*Kathy Selden*), Jean Hagen (*Lina Lamont*), Millard Mitchell (*R. F. Simpson*), Rita Moreno (*Zelda Zanders*), Douglas Fowley (*Roscoe Dexter*), Cyd Charisse (*dancer*), Madge Blake (*Dora Bailey*), King Donovan (*Rod*), Kathleen Freeman (*Phoebe Dinsmore*), Bobby Watson (*diction coach*), Tommy Farrell (*Sid Phillips*).

Hollywood, 1927. Don Lockwood and Lina Lamont, famous stars of the silent screen, arrive at the premiere of their latest romantic swashbuckler (1). Don entertains the radio public with a conveniently laundered account of his rise from vaudeville (2) to stardom opposite Lina. On his way to a party after the film, Don is mobbed by fans and seeks refuge in the car of an aspiring actress, Kathy Selden (3). She piques Don by making 'superior' remarks about the movie business.

At the party, where Don's producer, R. F. Simpson, demonstrates talking pictures (4), a huge cake is brought in. Out of it pops none other than Kathy herself. Don makes fun of her; she throws a pie at him, hitting Lina by mistake, and vanishes.

Don looks in vain for Kathy, but his friend, Cosmo Brown, cheers him up with a song about the entertainer's lot (5).

Following the tremendous success of *The Jazz Singer*, Simpson orders the instant conversion of Don and Lina's new film, *The Duelling Cavalier*, to sound. Don has no real trouble with this, but Lina's squeaky Brooklyn accent and inability to speak into the microphone drive the director to distraction (6). While making the movie, Don encounters Kathy, who has a bit part in a musical being made at the studio; he makes his peace with her and declares his love (7). On the way home, Don sings and dances with joy during a cloudburst (8).

The premiere of *The Duelling Cavalier* is a hilarious disaster. That night, Don, Kathy and Cosmo come up with the idea that matters can be retrieved if the film is quickly turned into a musical and Lina's voice replaced by Kathy's (9). Don and Cosmo tell Simpson their adventurous plans, which concern the story of a young dancer's success on Broadway (10) and his involvement with an exotic nightclub queen (11). Simpson does not share the boys' enthusiasm but agrees to make *The Duelling Cavalier* into a musical.

Lina discovers that her voice has been dubbed by Kathy, whom she jealously regards as the breaker of her (non-existent) romance with Don. By a clause in her contract she seems able to confine Kathy to being for ever her voice in films. But when Lina decides to 'sing' following the triumphant premiere of the revamped movie, Don and Cosmo reveal to the audience that Lina's vocal talents really belong to Kathy. Kathy becomes a star in her own right, and she and Don live happily ever after (12).

4

5

8

9

12

91

bestselling army novel, *From Here to Eternity*.

His performance was a revelation. In a film crammed with impressive acting by such as Montgomery Clift and Burt Lancaster, Sinatra's playing of the loyal, reckless Maggio, doomed to meet his end at the hands of Ernest Borgnine's memorably sadistic 'Fatso' Judson, effortlessly held its own. It won him an Oscar for Best Supporting Actor and revitalized his career. As a singer, too, Sinatra's reputation was about to be greatly enhanced: his collaboration with the arranger-conductor Nelson Riddle led to several classic LPs in the mid-Fifties, the most famous of all being *Songs for Swingin' Lovers*.

Yet in the wake of his triumph as Maggio, it was towards the cinema that much of Sinatra's professional energy was now directed. Between *From Here to Eternity* and the end of the decade, he starred in 15 movies, with guest appearances in a couple more. Indeed it would not be stretching a point to suggest that the character of Maggio helped to formulate his career in a more specific sense.

From his musical comedies of the Forties no very discernible performing identity had emerged beyond a bashful charm that could be

Ol' Blue Eyes

Ditched by record companies, dropped by Hollywood and even dumped by his agents, Frank Sinatra was fast becoming the entertainment industry's leading forgotten man of the early Fifties. A single film role took him right back where he belonged – at the top

In the middle years of the Forties, Frank Sinatra (b. 1915) reigned supreme over Tin Pan Alley. The one-time vocalist with the Tommy Dorsey Band was 'The Voice', besieged at every appearance by hordes of teenage fans in scenes of hysteria unsurpassed until the days of Beatlemania some twenty years later.

Inevitably, Hollywood beckoned. In 1943 RKO had given him his first starring role, *Higher and Higher* – a lightweight comedy in which he nominally played himself. He not only croons his way through a score that includes 'This Is a Lovely Way to Spend an Evening' but also handles dialogue with some charm and assurance. These qualities were confirmed by the following year's *Step Lively* and the more lavish *Anchors Aweigh* (1945), Sinatra's first feature for MGM. He remained at the studio to make several more films.

However, by the end of the decade – astonishing as the prospect might have seemed a short while before – Sinatra's star appeared to be waning. As the ballads with which he was associated were supplanted by a more upbeat form of pop, his record sales – and consequently his Hollywood standing – declined. In addition, press allegations that he had gangland connections harmed his image.

Sinatra did, of course, figure in that first great milestone of the post-war movie musical *On the Town* (1949), but only as one of a team. It was Gene Kelly who took top billing, and while Kelly became an instant jewel in MGM's crown, Sinatra was subsequently reduced to

appearing in programmers at RKO and Universal, then to finding himself, at least in the studios' eyes, unemployable.

Luck be a lady

Sinatra's winning streak seemed to have run out, but he still had an ace in the hole. By dint of perseverance and offering to work for next to nothing, he managed to persuade Columbia to cast him in the wholly straight role of Private Maggio in the 1953 movie of James Jones'

Top: a boyish air of studied casualness not quite masking the tautness of a man under pressure was the key quality of Sinatra's movie persona. Right: Sinatra with Anne Jeffreys in Step Lively. *Below: though pictured smiling, his marriage with Ava Gardner was anything but harmonious*

Above: nightclub singer Danny (Sinatra) rehearses with his pianist friend Mike Ryan (Alex Nicol) in Meet Danny Wilson. *Above right: Private Maggio (Sinatra) and the bullying Sergeant Judson (Ernest Borgnine) confront each other in* From Here to Eternity

variously inflected to wistful or wisecracking ends. However, with hindsight, Sinatra's appearance in *Meet Danny Wilson* (1951), a melodrama in which he plays a bumptious singer caught up with nightclub crooks, had hinted at the disaffection and hidden *angst* that would be the main features of his Maggio. This role stamped him as an 'outsider', giving rise to several 'dark' roles during the Fifties.

Suddenly (1954), a tight, small-scale thriller, has Sinatra as a hit-man hired to assassinate the US President; in *Johnny Concho* (1956), his first Western, he plays a boastful coward who hides behind his brother's reputation; and in Otto Preminger's *The Man With the Golden Arm* (1956), he played a tortured drug addict, finally undergoing an agonizing 'cold turkey' withdrawal cure.

Two films that were closer, in a sense, to Sinatra the man were *Young at Heart* (1954) and *The Joker Is Wild* (1957). In the first he plays a cynical, dejected songwriter, at one point shown slumped at the piano, hat on head and cigarette in mouth. In the second, a somewhat maudlin account of the fall and rise of comedian Joe E. Lewis, his path is strewn by gangsters, alcohol and unhappy love affairs;

the film may almost be seen as a fantasy on Sinatra's own life.

A guy and dolls
There was, of course, a lighter side to Sinatra in the Fifties, represented by well-upholstered comedies and musicals. Yet his roles in these can be regarded as 'sunny-side-up' variations on the loner figure of the 'dark' films; there had, after all, been a strain of comedy in his Maggio.

Thus in *The Tender Trap* (1955) he plays a breezy, philandering, Broadway promoter finally domesticated by a young actress (Debbie Reynolds); as Nathan Detroit, proprietor of the 'oldest-established permanent floating crap game in New York' in *Guys and Dolls* (1955), he is prepared to go to desperate lengths to leave his inamorata waiting at the altar; and in *High Society* (1956) where he memorably serenades Grace Kelly with 'You're Sensational', he is an acidulous newspaperman cocking a snook at Long Island wealth. The air of raffishness he sought to cultivate was nicely encapsulated by the honky-tonk pianist he plays in his guest-star appearance in *Around the World in 80 Days* (1956), and by the unscrupulous entertainer whose cynicism is ultimately melted by an adoring chorine (Kim Novak) in *Pal Joey* (1957), which featured the show-stopping number 'The Lady Is a Tramp'. He was able to round off the decade with two wholly assured portrayals in quite different registers, the vulnerable, embittered novelist of Vincente

Above: Sergeants Three (1962) was one of several films Sinatra made with fellow 'Clan' members Dean Martin (left), Peter Lawford and Sammy Davis Jr. Below left: publicity shot for The Man With the Golden Arm *featuring Kim Novak. Below: Sinatra, Shirley Maclaine and Maurice Chevalier in* Can Can

Minnelli's *Some Came Running* (1958) and the go-getting hotelier of Frank Capra's under-valued *A Hole in the Head* (1959).

Who wants to be a millionaire?

By the beginning of the Sixties, Sinatra had become a corporate power to be reckoned with in the entertainment industry. His renewed popularity as a singer was largely undimmed and many of his movies – especially those in which he surrounded himself with fellow-members (Dean Martin and Sammy Davis Jr among them) of his much-touted 'Clan' – fared more than respectably at the box-office, although their artistic level was well below his previous work.

The thriller *The Manchurian Candidate* (1962) allowed him to recover elements of the old *angst*, but it was something of an isolated out-post in a desert of dud comedies and caper movies. Almost as if sensing the need for a change of tack, Sinatra made a solitary foray into direction with *None But the Brave* (1965), confining himself to a cameo role in this pacifist but somehow redundant war movie.

His appearance in a more jingoistic war film, *Von Ryan's Express* (1965), represented something of a return to hard-bitten loner form, though – rather revealingly – the loneliness here is that of an unpopular commanding officer. Another film that showed Sinatra returning to 'safe' ground was *Tony Rome* (1967). His portrayal of the laconic Florida private eye contained some nostalgic echoes of his Fifties comedy roles.

Between this film and its inferior sequel, *Lady in Cement* came *The Detective* (both 1968), which features Sinatra's last worthwhile screen performance. His portrayal of a dogged, increasingly disillusioned cop, struggling to hold on to his liberal beliefs, has sufficient edge to provide the centre of a genuinely serious if ultimately rather evasive film. This would have made a fitting farewell to the cinema, but in the event Sinatra went on to make *Lady in Cement* and, much worse, the loutish, witless, spoof Western *Dirty Dingus Magee* (1970). Though it may be claimed that Sinatra's most essential achievement has been as a singer and that his key legacy to the world is on vinyl, his celluloid bequest will not be readily over-looked: Dingus Magee may be happily forgotten, but Maggio lives on.   TIM PULLEINE

Below: Sinatra takes a tumble as private eye Tony Rome. Bottom: Colonel Ryan (Sinatra) briefs a group of escaping prisoners-of-war (including Trevor Howard, right) in Von Ryan's Express. *Bottom left: a conference during production of* Dirty Dingus Magee

Filmography

1935 Major Bowes' Amateur Theatre of the Air (short). **'41** Las Vegas Nights/The Gay City (short). **'42** Ship Ahoy! (short). **'43** Reveille With Beverly; Higher and Higher. **'44** Step Lively; Road to Victory (guest appearance as himself) (short). **'45** Anchors Aweigh; The House I Live In (short); The All Star Bond Rally (short); Special Christmas Trailer (short) . **'46** Till the Clouds Roll By (guest appearance as himself). **'47** It Happened in Brooklyn. **'48** The Miracle of the Bells; Lucky Strike Salesman's Movie 48-A (short); Words and Music (guest appearance as himself); The Kissing Bandit. **'49** Take Me Out to the Ball Game (GB: Everybody's Cheering); On the Town. **'51** Double Dynamite; Meet Danny Wilson. **'53** From Here to Eternity. **'54** Suddenly; Young at Heart. **'55** Not As a Stranger; The Tender Trap; Guys and Dolls. **'56** The Man With the Golden Arm; Meet Me in Las Vegas (GB: Viva Las Vegas!) (guest appearance as himself); Johnny Concho; High Society; Around the World in 80 Days (guest). **'57** The Pride and the Passion; The Joker Is Wild; Pal Joey. **'58** Kings Go Forth; Some Came Running. **'59** A Hole in the Head; Never So Few; Invitation to Monte Carlo (short). **'60** Can Can; Ocean's Eleven; Pepe (guest appearance as himself). **'61** The Devil at 4 O'Clock. **'62** Sergeants Three; The Road to Hong Kong (uncredited guest appearance) (USA-GB); The Manchurian Candidate; Sinatra in Israel (short). **'63** The List of Adrian Messenger (guest); Come Blow Your Horn. **'64** Robin and the Seven Hoods (+prod). **'65** None But the Brave (+exec. prod;+dir); Will Rogers' Hospital Trailer (+narr) (short); Von Ryan's Express; Marriage on the Rocks (+exec. prod). **'66** The Oscar (guest appearance as himself); Cast a Giant Shadow; Assault on a Queen. **'67** Tony Rome. **'68** The Detective; Lady in Cement. **'70** Dirty Dingus Magee. **'74** That's Entertainment! (co-narr. only).

War and anti-war

Cinema in the Fifties continued to be preoccupied with World War II and its aftermath, but attitudes to war were changing and films began to expose the underbelly of heroism

During the Sixties the cinema began to be discussed in terms of genres – collections of films which exhibit common themes, plots and formal characteristics. At that time serious critical writing dealt almost exclusively with the Western, the gangster movie and the horror movie. Although various picture books purporting to deal with the war movie appeared, it was curiously absent from writing about genre. Insofar as war films were seriously written about at all, it was in the context of studies on film authorship – the classic case being Sam Fuller through whose films the metaphor and imagery of war run irrespective of their generic base – and in relation to discussions of wider topics such as violence in the American cinema.

The main reason for this apparent critical oversight was that war movies constituted, or were included within, the terrain over which an earlier issue had been debated in the late Fifties and early Sixties. Taking its impulse from events outside cinema, the question of how war was portrayed on the screen became dominant. Some of the compass points of this debate as it occurred in Britain were the Campaign for Nuclear Disarmanent, the radical journal *Peace News*, and the film criticism characterized by journals like *Sight and Sound*. Broadly speaking, the humanist approach of such groups was focused on questions of peace and war, and was introduced into the school curriculum by teachers influenced by this ethos.

The central question of this debate was certainly not concerned with the operations of cinema in its own right, although some astute critics displayed sensitivity to cinematic form in passing. The issue was not even political; it was essentially *ethical*. In terms of the arguments of the time, the main question to be asked of any film was whether it was a 'pro-war' or 'anti-war' film. Although it arose in the Fifties, the discussion ranged over the whole history of the war movie.

Hand in hand with it went the unspoken but equally important question of so-called 'commercial cinema' versus 'art cinema'. There was a distinct tendency for the critics participating in this

debate to favour the latter over the former and to see Europe and Asia as the site of 'art cinema' and Hollywood as the site of 'commercial cinema'. Not surprisingly, non-Hollywood films tended to be regarded as 'anti-war' and therefore good. Among these were: Luigi Zampa's *Vivere in Pace* (1947, To Live in Peace), a satirical farce about wartime Italy; René Clément's *Jeux Interdits* (1952, *Forbidden Games*), an allegory of the war from the perspective of two children; Rossellini's *Il Generale Della Rovere* (1959, General Della Rovere), and two films by Alain Resnais – the concentration-camp documentary *Nuit et Brouillard* (1955, *Night and Fog*) and the complex love story with flashbacks to the war *Hiroshima Mon Amour* (1959, Hiroshima My Love). On the other hand films such as Tay Garnett's *Bataan* (1943), Raoul Walsh's *Objective, Burma!* (1945) and *The Naked and the Dead* (1958), and

Above: the meticulous re-staging of Dunkirk – *the greatest evacuation in European military history – was taken to be a fitting celebration of how Britain had snatched a victory from the jaws of defeat in 1940. In its twin stories of a young corporal (John Mills) and a non-combatant civilian (Richard Attenborough), the film raised some moral questions about duty but resolved them in a flurry of patriotic activity. Below: teenage boys, drafted into the German army to defend a bridge of no strategic value, fight against an American tank unit in* The Bridge

Above: Jack Palance rallying his men with a heroic gesture in Robert Aldrich's otherwise anti-heroic movie Attack! *which sought to expose cowardice and corruption among American Army officers. Below: Japanese soldiers leave their dead comrade in the rain-soaked jungle of the Philippines in* Fires on the Plain. *Below right:* Cockleshell Heroes *depicted a kind of Dunkirk operation in reverse as marines raided Bordeaux harbour in a fleet of flimsy canoes to plant limpet mines*

Robert Montgomery's *The Gallant Hours* (1960) were seen as 'pro-war' and therefore judged to be bad films.

There was a third body of films – for example *La Grande Illusion* (1937, *The Great Illusion*), *Paths of Glory* and *The Bridge on the River Kwai* (both 1957) – which did not fit neatly into either camp. These films questioned moral absolutes and generated some argument as to whether they respectively celebrated male cameraderie, criticized pig-headed leadership, or wallowed in the spectacle of destruction; but essentially everyone seemed to have a good idea which films 'glorified' (a favourite term of the time) war and which did not.

Accepting then that the war movie has always been a cover for a simplistic kind of moralizing film criticism and a crude anti-Hollywood prejudice, it is possible to arrive at a description of the classical war or (more accurately) combat movie of the Forties, of the way it was developed in the Fifties and of the different interpretations of war offered by different cultures in the Fifties.

Whether its origins were American, British or Soviet, the classic combat movie tended to be characterized by the following features: the inclusion of several scenes in which large-scale combat is presented; a focus in the narrative on the platoon as the central group, with half a dozen figures pre-eminent within it; concentration on a single or small series of specifically military engagements (the attack on a hill, a farmhouse, a bridge); the absence of any critique of the war *per se* – although

individual soldiers may have problems of fear or breakdown; and the almost total absence of the enemy except as a faceless amorphous, opposing force – something 'foreign' that we are not permitted to 'know' in the film.

These features were common to the combat films of all the participant nations which were producing films during World War II. In the altered moral and political climate of the Fifties and in the light of the very different experience of war shared by the various participants, film-makers were able to shape their subjects around an established framework.

Any number of films might serve as illustrations. In Britain *Cockleshell Heroes* and *The Dam Busters* (both 1955), dealing respectively with the attacks on blockade-running German ships and the strategy for knocking out vital industrial water supplies, celebrated heroic achievements in the field of conflict. For the USA, *The Young Lions* (1958), an account of US Army campaigns in Europe, and *The Steel Helmet* (1951), an expedition behind enemy lines in the Korean war, were similar tributes to successful military actions. Films which dealt with defeat – like Joseph H. Lewis' *Retreat Hell!* (1952), set in Korea, and the British film *Dunkirk* (1958) – were rare in Fifties cinema and though the latter film chronicles the military evacuation of the port of Dunkirk, the film construes the action as a victory for the ostensibly British quality of strength and adversity.

It is not unusual, however, for the Fifties war

movies of Germany or Japan to be about defeat. Bernhard Wicki's *Die Brücke* (1959, *The Bridge*), which concerns the calling up of 16-year-old boys to guard a strategically important bridge during the last days of World War II, was widely praised outside its native Germany for its 'anti-war' sentiments. Two Japanese films, *Biruma No Tategoto* (1956, *The Burmese Harp*) and *Nobi* (1959, *Fires on the Plain*) extended the sense of atonement that was at least partly responsible for the acclaim heaped upon these particular war movies by critics in the 'victorious' nations. *The Burmese Harp*, through its tale of a wounded Japanese soldier who becomes a Buddhist monk and dedicates his life to burying the war dead, and *Fires on the Plain*, with its account of a starving soldier reduced to cannibalism, both fitted the humanist interpretation of war movies insofar as they offered the possibilities for salvaging human values at the point where they are most imperilled.

The overwhelming optimism which characterized the films of all the participant nations made during the war does, however, begin to crack in the war movies of the Fifties, though in ways peculiar to

---

Heroism in war was much favoured in British and American films but elsewhere the image of war was decidedly more ambivalent

---

the culture in which they were made. Thus, while the commitment to victorious action remained strong in British and American films, the themes of suffering and divisiveness are not completely ignored.

This undermining of the confidence and complacency so long characteristic of the war film is intriguingly revealed in Robert Aldrich's *Attack!* (1956) in which the commanding officer (Eddie Albert) loses his authority as a result of his own fear and is supplanted and subsequently shot by an officer from his own company (Jack Palance). In the British film *The Bridge on the River Kwai* class conflicts conspire to lower the morale between officers and men in a Japanese prisoner-of-war camp.

Gradually notions of physical breakdown and psychosis became more common. Lewis Milestone's *Halls of Montezuma* (1950) analyses group neurosis and combat fatigue through the character of a

company commander (Richard Widmark) with a narcotic addiction. Similarly, *The Caine Mutiny* (1954) challenged the authority of an inefficient commanding officer and, in its court-martial scene, raised vital questions about military conduct.

Certain of the contradictions which were papered over in Forties war movies began to be exposed in the Fifties. The ambiguous role of American blacks serving in the US armed forces while engaged in their own struggle was broached in *Home of the Brave* (1949), while *Go For Broke* (1951) focused on the treatment of American-born Japanese who had been drafted into the army. Under the guidance of their commanding officer (Van Johnson), a platoon of these men is put through basic training and each distinguishes himself in action in Italy. Towards the end of the Fifties the changing politics of international alliances exerted an influence over the way the movies told the history of the war, and by the time *The Guns of Navarone* (1961) was released, important distinctions were being made between Germans and Nazis in the film's narrative.

This process took a different form in the USSR. In the change from the monolithic, Stalin-inspired war films, for example *The Fall of Berlin* (1949) and *Battle of Stalingrad* (1950), to the more humanist films, like *The Cranes Are Flying* (1958) and *Ballad of a Soldier* (1960), which were made after Khruschchev's 'liberalizing' speech at the 20th Soviet Congress in 1956, notions such as fear, doubt and betrayal were conceded as existing in battle. Ultimately, however, the humanist rhetoric of these

Above left: two comrades (Alexei Batalov and Vasily Merkuryev) return from the front in Mikhail Kalatozov's The Cranes Are Flying, *a humanistic account of relationships in wartime that contrasted sharply with war films from the Stalin era like* The Fall of Berlin (above) *where mass victory rather than personal tragedy was the issue at stake. Below:* Sands of Iwo Jima (1949) *was in many ways the prototype of the Fifties American war film; literally flag-waving and inevitably 'action-packed', the film commemorated 'The Marines' Greatest Hour'*

THE MARINES' GREATEST HOUR

A GREAT HUMAN STORY ...MAKES A MIGHTY MOTION PICTURE

SANDS OF IWO JIMA

JOHN WAYNE

JOHN AGAR · ADELE MARA · FORREST TUCKER

WALLY CASSELL·JAMES BROWN·RICHARD WEBB·ARTHUR FRANZ·JULIE BISHOP·JAMES HOLDEN·PETER COE·RICHARD JAECKEL

Above: Polish prisoners-of-war in German custody in Eroica, *a downbeat prison-camp film in which the possibility of escape is presented as a distinctly bleak prospect. Above right:* The Colditz Story *offered a quite different perspective on the situation of prisoners-of-war; here the CO (John Mills) leads a typically British group of captives in an escape bid that is planned under the very noses of their German gaolers. Below:* Hiroshima, *a newsreel compilation of the A-bomb blast and its aftermath that had considerable impact both in Japan and abroad in the late Fifties*

new war films created no better understanding of political structures than the authoritarian rhetoric of the earlier ones.

The best way of comparing the experience of the war to different cultures may lie in the contrasting of two films which deal with substantially the same situation – that of prisoners-of-war. *The Colditz Story* (1955), a British film, and *Eroica* (1957), a Polish film, were made within two years of each other. The tone of the British film is jocular; incarceration, and the process of escaping are seen as a game and the Germans are portrayed as buffoons, and honour and patriotism are values which the film implicitly accepts. However, in the episode of *Eroica* set in the prison camp, the tone is extremely bleak. It is not that the German captors are portrayed as oppressive, they are scarcely seen. The bleakness lies in the presentation of the Polish officers. Only one officer is believed to have escaped from the camp and he is used by the others as the figure who has redeemed the honour of the officer caste. In fact, dying from consumption, he is hiding in the roof of one of the huts.

That the same experience can be handled so differently in two films from different cultures partly relates to the actual experience of war in Britain and Poland respectively. Aerial bombardment and austerity, while hardly pleasant, pale to insignificance against occupation, deportations, executions and seven million dead. Moreover, the ethos in

which *Eroica* was made – that is, post-revolutionary Poland – was much more conducive to criticism of the officer caste than Fifties Britain.

The growing preoccupation with the threat of nuclear war found its way into the cinema, not exclusively but most appropriately in the films of two countries who were the protagonists of the holocaust in World War II – Japan and the USA. Characteristically, in the American cinema it took the form of speculation about the aftermath of a nuclear attack but with a curious reticence about the actual physical effects. *The World, the Flesh and the Devil* (dir. Ranald MacDougall, 1959) concerned three survivors from the holocaust who end the movie by espousing the principles of the United Nations, and *On the Beach* (dir. Stanley Kramer, 1960), a solemn account of the last days of the world after an atomic war, were both restrained in their treatment when compared, for example, to the explicitness of the British film *The War Game* (dir. Peter Watkins, 1965).

The range of responses in the Japanese cinema was wider. It took in fatalistic reconstructions of the holocaust such as *Hiroshima* (1955) which presented the event as tragedy rather than atrocity, but it also extended to constructive documentaries and stories of individual human suffering. The long-term effects of radiation were to blame for the problems featured in Imai's *Jun-ai Monogatari* (1957, *A Story of Pure Love*) and Kurosawa's *Ikomono No Kiroku* (1955, *Record of a Living Being*). Finally, in a fascinating variation of the theme, the kind of terror attendant upon nuclear attack was acted out in a cycle of monster pictures which began with *Gojira* (1954, *Godzilla*) and attributed the birth and appearance of such creatures to the after-effects of nuclear fall-out.

In conclusion, it is useful to recall that, certainly in the case of Britain, responses to the war films of the Fifties were shaped not only by the political climate of the times but by the politics of film exhibition and distribution. While most of the British and American war movies reached the screens of popular cinemas – and, therefore, mass audiences – the war films of continental Europe and Japan reached only the screens of the 'art house' cinemas and even then the choice of which war films were deemed worthy of presentation was conditioned by the old, humanist arguments of whether the films were 'art' or 'entertainment'. To understand fully what actually happened to the war movie in the Fifties requires that we first strip away the layers of outmoded criticism and privileged reputation in which war movies have traditionally been wrapped.
                                                    COLIN McARTHUR

Eastern promise

The appearance of a handful of Japanese films in the West during the early Fifties heralded
a world-wide interest in Japanese cinema and testified to its richness and variety

For two centuries, Japan chose to isolate itself from the rest of the world. Then, in 1894, the American Commodore Perry sailed into Tokyo Bay and 're-discovered' the Japanese islands. Yet nothing was known about Japanese cinema in the West for almost another century. The difference was that whereas Perry had come upon a country that appeared technologically backward, the West encountered a cinema that was, on the evidence of the films that began to be shown in the Fifties, every bit as advanced as its own.

By and large Western recognition and appreciation of Japanese films can be said to have dated from the appearance of key movies at the Venice and Cannes Film Festivals. Akira Kurosawa's *Rashomon* (1950) won the Golden Lion at Venice in 1951 and the same honour was bestowed upon four films by Kenji Mizoguchi in the succeeding years. The films were: *Saikaku Ichidai Onna* (1952, *The Life of Oharu*), *Ugetsu Monogatari* (1953, *Tales of the Pale and Silvery Moon After the Rain*), *Sansho Dayu* (1954, *Sansho the Bailiff*) and *Yokihi* (1955, *The Empress Yang Kwei-Fei*). By the time that Teinosuke Kinugasa's *Jigokumon* (1953, *Gate of Hell*) was awarded the Cannes Film Festival's Golden Palm, Japanese cinema had clearly become a cultural force to be reckoned with.

Why did it take so long for the West to acknowledge the depth and sophistication of a national cinema that had already been undergoing

steady developments for half a century? Part of the answer lies in the geographical and cultural insularity of the country itself – a tendency that was most pronounced during the late Thirties and in the course of World War II. This compounded the attitude that there was little to interest Westerners in Japanese culture anyway. One recent Western commentator on Japanese cinema, the critic Noël Burch, has argued that the 'golden age' of Japanese film was precisely the period when the country was

most closed to outside influences and therefore able to pursue its own concerns in relative isolation from the cultural values of Hollywood and Europe.

This raises yet another reason for the long-term remoteness of Japanese cinema: what might be called an alternative set of traditions and conventions – not only in film-making *per se*, but also in some of the facets and habits of filmgoing and film appreciation. Foremost among these is a tradition that can be traced back to the singular figure of the *benshi*, the narrator whose lengthy explanations, interpretations and dramatic inflections accompanied most silent film screenings.

Essentially a popular star in his own right, the *benshi* was often more interesting than the movie he was called upon to 'explain' and he could sometimes rival the top film actors in his billing and salary. From the beginning the *benshi* reflected the Japanese passion for understanding things in detail and it is significant that one of his roles in the early days was to explain the mechanisms of film projection. Apart from assuming the voices of male and female characters alike and furnishing supplementary information on whatever the audience was watching, the *benshi* would frequently embroider the plot with fancies and inventions of his own. He also helped to restrict and ritualize certain film conventions through his story-telling, reducing the unfamiliar (eg Hollywood Westerns) to terms and character names that would standardize the narrative and make it more familiar.

There are several continuing traditions in

Above left and left: an untypical example of the jidai-geki *historical genre,* Rashomon *was initially assumed in the West to be characteristic of the inscrutable Orient, with its complex tale of a probable rape and an unsolved killing – the bandit, the wife and the husband himself all claim to have stabbed the husband. Even the comparatively innocent woodcutter may have stolen the husband's valuable dagger. Toshiro Mifune (the bandit) and Machiko Kyo (the wife) for long remained the Japanese actor and actress best known in the West*

Top left: Repast is a shomin-geki (lower-middle-class life) film, starring Ken Uehara and Setsuko Hara as an unhappily married couple. Top right: Machiko Kyo and Masayuki Mori in The Empress Yang Kwei-Fei, *Mizoguchi's first colour film, the tragic story of a Chinese emperor and his favourite concubine.*
Above: Naruse's Ukigimo (1955, Floating Clouds) starred Hideko Takamine in the sad tale of a young girl wronged by a married man (Masayuki Mori). The film was produced by the Toho Company, whose familiar logo is seen here (right)

Japanese cinema that can be interestingly related back to the *benshi*, even though the actual profession died after sound came in around the mid-Thirties. For one thing, the impulse to explain everything and leave little or no room for ambiguity can be connected to the more contemporary Japanese practice of labelling and footnoting certain details in foreign films in the form of explanatory subtitles. More generally, the continuing restriction of most commercial Japanese features to a few very well-established genres (and in many instances, well-known plots) may not be unrelated to the former presence of the *benshi* whose 'commentary' could assume a certain familiarity with the stories being played out on the screen.

Returning to Kurosawa's *Rashomon*, it is interesting to note that the film was not regarded as 'typically Japanese' by critics back home in Japan. In the film four contradictory versions of the same incident – the violent encounter of a bandit (Toshiro Mifune) with a married couple (Masayuki Mori and Machiko Kyo) in a forest – are related to us via flashbacks from the perspective of the three participants (one of them the murdered samurai husband, the woman herself, the bandit) and a passing woodcutter. The unconventional narrative structure was in many respects as challenging to Japanese audiences as it was to European and American ones. It is even reported that a few wary domestic cinema managers took the anachronistic step of hiring retired *benshi* to speak during the film and drop certain hints about its meaning, to set troubled minds at rest.

Set in the early part of the remote Heian era, *Rashomon* is only the second film by Kurosawa that strictly qualifies as a period drama, or *jidai-geki*. The historical settings and exotic 'foreignness' of Japanese cinema made it most attractive to Western audiences and it might be argued that all five of Mizoguchi's prize-winning masterpieces of the mid-Fifties were made with at least one eye trained on the international market.

The Life of Oharu chronicles the decline of a beautiful court lady in seventeenth-century Japan, while *Ugetsu Monogatari* takes as its setting a much earlier period of Japanese history. The two Mizoguchi films from 1954 *Sansho Dayu* (*Sansho the Bailiff*) and *Chikamatsu Monogatari* (*The Crucified Lovers*) are set in the eleventh and seventeenth centuries respectively and demonstrate the power of the feudal system. Kinugasa's *Gate of Hell* also used

Japan's feudal past as a setting for its tale of the conflict between passion and duty.

According to his scriptwriter Yoda Yoshikata, Mizoguchi's decision to make *The Life of Oharu* may have been motivated by the foreign demand for Japanese period films as well as by sheer competitiveness. After all, Kurosawa, a relative newcomer at 40, had walked away with the Golden Lion at Venice, while Mizoguchi, 15 years older, had already been making films for 30 years. The vogue for *jidai-geki* films constituted a revival of a genre which had been popular during the silent era especially in the hands of directors like Masahiro Makino and Daisuke Ito. What is significant about Mizoguchi's work of the Fifties is the way in which he combines the social concerns implicit in the Japanese tradition of *keiko-eiga* ('tendency films') and *shakai-mono* (social-problem pictures) with an expertise in the historical genre of *jidai-geki*. Hence, *The Life of Oharu* works as a potent feminist protest of great contemporary interest despite or even because of its period setting.

Gate of Hell was a progressive film for Japan, winning an Academy Award for Best Foreign Film in the USA on account of its extraordinary use of colour. Daiei, the studio that produced the film, sent two Japanese technicians to Hollywood for three years to study colour processing and to make tests. These efforts were amply rewarded in the rich palette of orange-reds, blues and other striking colours achieved in the final film. Shot in Eastman Colour by the cameraman Kohei Hasegawa and starring Kazuo Hasegawa (two solid professionals who had worked with Kinugasa since their days

together at the Shochiku studios in the early Thirties), *Gate of Hell* was the big international success that the studio boss Masachi Nagata had hoped for and the critics paid generous compliments to the colour quality.

Before World War II, period dramas comprised almost half of the total film production in Japan. Then, after the war, owing to the guidelines laid down by the American occupation forces, attempts were made to discourage *jidai-geki* films in view of their feudal backgrounds and anti-democratic tendencies. During the period of the Occupation *gendai-geki* (films about contemporary life) comprised roughly two-thirds of Japanese film production. A number of distinct genres developed within this category that dealt with family roles and questions of social class.

Rumpen-mono are films about the lumpen proletariat and can be traced back to a film called *Ningenku* (1923, *Human Suffering*), directed by Kensaku Suzuki for the Nikkatsu Studios whose house style became closely identified with the *rumpen-mono*, rather as Warner Brothers became associated with Hollywood social protest during the Thirties. *Ningenku* was reputedly the first Japanese production to incorporate exterior night-time shooting to heighten its essential 'realism'. Other touchstones of the genre include Mizoguchi's *Shikamo Karera Wa Yuku* (1931, *And Yet They Go*) a film about the miserable life of Tokyo prostitutes, Ozu's *Tokyo No Yado* (1935, *An Inn in Tokyo*), the story of a vagrant father and his two sons who find

Above left: Isuzu Yamada, in theatrical makeup as the Lady Macbeth character, stares at the imaginary blood on her hands in Throne of Blood. *Above: the dutiful but reluctant son carries his mother, in accordance with village custom, to die on the mountain-top in* The Ballad of the Narayama. *Below: the climactic battle in Kurosawa's* Shichinin No Samurai *(1954, Seven Samurai), in which the samurai and villagers defeat the bandits. The Magnificent Seven (1960) was the remake*

Above: many of Mizoguchi's films (including his last one The Street of Shame) concerned the lives of prostitutes. In The Life Of Oharu, based on a story by the 17th-century writer Saikaku, the court lady who declines into common prostitution is played by Kinuyo Tanaka. Top right: an example of tsuma-mono, Sounds From the Mountains starred Setsuko Hara as a mistreated wife who has an abortion, while her husband (Ken Uehara) fathers an illegitimate child. Above right: Keisuke Kinoshita (born 1912) began directing films in 1943 and made over forty films in the next twenty-five years before turning mainly to television production

companionship with an equally poor widow, and Kaneto Shindo's Dobu (1954, Gutter), which also dealt with low-life in an embittered portrait of the Tokyo slums.

The more mainstream genre of shomin-geki, on the other hand, depicts lower middle-class life. At its most sophisticated stages of development, this genre was a starting point for the films of Ozu, Heinosuke Gosho and Mikio Naruse. It seems that the shomin-geki was more or less launched by a silent comedy about a country girl and a baseball player. The film was Yasujiro Shimazu's Chichi (1924, Father) and with hindsight it can be seen as the forerunner of such outstanding films as Gosho's Mura No Hanayome (1928, The Village Bride), which is concerned with the small-mindedness of life in a rural village.

Ozu's unforgetable silent film Umarete Wa Mita Keredo (1932, I Was Born, But . . .) also exemplifies the shomin-geki style through its depiction of family life. In the film a suburban middle-class father loses the respect of his sons through his toadying behaviour towards his boss. Mizoguchi's Naniwa Ereji (1936, Naniwa Elegy) shows sexual exploitation of a telephone operator by her boss and was banned by government censors after 1940 for its so-called decadent tendencies. Finally, Mikio Naruse's Meshi (1951, Repast) develops the genre in a Fifties context with its story of the gradual break-up of a childless couple who live in the suburbs of Osaka.

The most prominent genres based on familial roles are undoubtedly the haha-mono and the tsuma-mono – 'mother films' and 'wife films' respectively. Both of these categories could be considered as sub-

divisions of kachusha-mono. Named after the heroine of Tolstoy's late novel Resurrection, these films feature self-sacrificing women. In the haha-mono mothers suffer and sacrifice everything for their children. The best-known actress who specialized in such parts was Yuko Mochizuki, who appeared in such films as Keisuke Kinoshita's semi-documentary Nihon No Higeki (1953, A Japanese Tragedy) and Tadashi Imai's Kome (1957, People of the Rice Fields). Other striking examples of the haha-mono films include Naruse's Okasan (1952, Mother) which is based on a schoolgirl's composition and told from the viewpoint of the widow's eldest daughter, and Yuzo Kawashima's Ai No Nimotsu (1956, Bundle of Love).

For the most part, the tsuma-mono is a post-war phenomenon and is best exemplified by Ozu's Kaze No Naka No Mendori (1948, A Hen in the Wind), a film about a wife becoming a prostitute in order to pay for her child's hospital bills while waiting for her husband to be demobilized. A genre that gained in popularity around the same time as the haha-mono was going into decline, tsuma-mono became associated in the public mind with the roles of the actress Setsuko Hara in such movies as Naruse's Yama No Oto (1954, Sounds From the Mountains) and Ozu's celebrated domestic tragedy Tokyo Monogatari (1953, Tokyo Story).

Just as the benshi was a figure whose origins could be seen in the commentators of traditional Japanese drama, other elements in Japanese cinema can be traced back to certain literary and theatrical forms. The medium who speaks for the dead samurai husband in Rashomon, for instance, is

102

essentially a figure from the classical, lyric Noh theatre (a dramatic form played out on a bare stage by male actors using carefully restrained and measured gestures). Kurosawa's remarkable version of Shakespeare's *Macbeth*, *Kumonosu-Jo* (1957, *Throne of Blood*), which is said to have been a favourite film of T. S. Eliot, utilizes other Noh elements for the strange makeup style of Lady Macbeth and the background music. In general, however, the influence of Noh theatre on cinema has been somewhat minimal. Kabuki theatre, on the other hand, has furnished a certain number of *jidai-geki* (including the sub-category known as the *chambara*, or sword-fight films) with numerous themes and plots. Most notable of these is the story of the *Loyal 47 Ronin* of which many film versions have been made. On a more experimental level the cinematic uses of Kabuki theatre in Kinoshita's *Narayamabushi-Ko* (1958, *The Ballad of the Narayama*) are quite explicit. His sets drop or slide out of the frame when they are no longer required; the lighting is dimmed at the end of certain sequences in deliberate imitation of Kabuki stage techniques. The best-known development of Kabuki influence is, however, Kon Ichikawa's *Yukinojo Henge* (1963, *An Actor's Revenge*) in which Kazuo Hasegawa plays the same double role (small-time gangster and Kabuki actor of female roles) that he had played in Kinugasa's 1935 version of the same story.

The influences of Japanese literature on the cinema are traceable through the *kodon* and *naniwa-bushi* forms of oral story-telling in which audiences are usually very familiar with the basic plots. There are also direct correlations between cinema and the uses of visual metaphor in the poetic form and discipline of *haiku*, the classical verse form of Japan. Adaptations of novels into films extend to *junbungaku* ('serious' literature) as well as more popular works of fiction such as the pulp thriller and newspaper serials.

Writing about an extended visit to Japan a few years ago, the *avant-garde* composer Karlheinz Stockhausen remarked on the relative slowness *and* alacrity of Japanese ceremonial events, in comparison with Western forms. It is an observation that goes a long way towards explaining yet

Above left: in Gate of Hell, *Kazuo Hasegawa plays a warrior whose overwhelming and essentially unreciprocated passion for a married woman leads to disaster. Above centre: another example of shomin-geki is Ozu's Ochazuke No Aji (1952, The Flavour of Green Tea Over Rice), in which Shin Saburi and Michiyo Kogure play a middle-aged childless couple whose marriage is nearly wrecked by her contempt for him. Left: A* Japanese Tragedy *was a haha-mono (mother film), typical in starring Yuko Mochizuki as the widowed and ultimately suicidal mother of ungrateful children, but unusual in that it included newsreel footage intercut with the fictional story to provide a general context for the story of a few individuals*

another facet of a foreign cinema that we continue to experience as exotic today. When one thinks of the rapidity of the action and the movements of the camera in a Kurosawa samurai film or the placid stillness of a location or a family grouping in a film by Ozu, one begins to get some sense of the broad range of experiences that is broached and assumed by a popular cinema that the Western world has only just begun to learn about.

JONATHAN ROSENBAUM

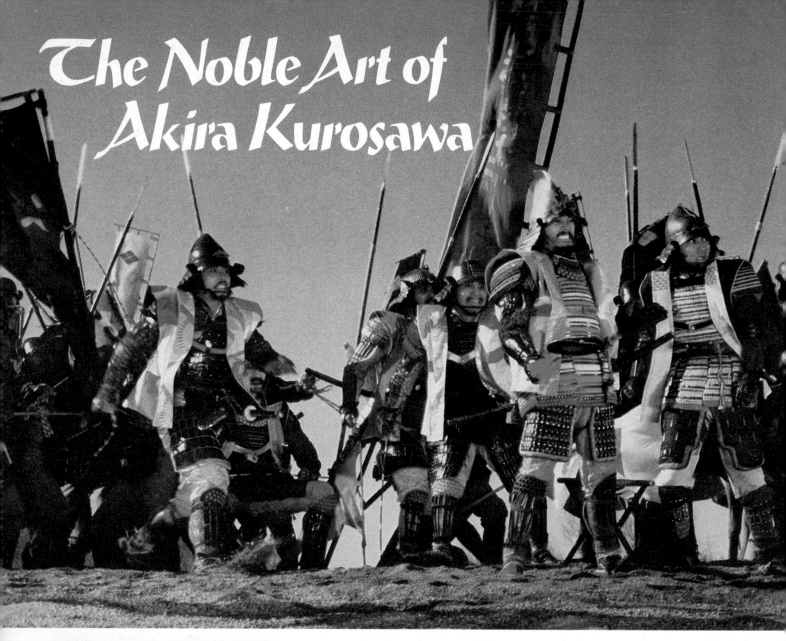

The Noble Art of Akira Kurosawa

The films of Kurosawa first opened Western eyes to the imaginative power and beauty of Japanese cinema. Best known for his enthralling, epic studies of the samurai warrior, he has also investigated modern themes, displaying a deep compassion for the human condition

The impact of Akira Kurosawa's *Rashomon* (1950) on the 1951 Venice Film Festival was nothing short of shattering, and only the Japanese were surprised when it won the Golden Lion. Daiei, the company that produced the film, had been reluctant to submit it, certain that it would meet with incomprehension, even ridicule. But *Rashomon* triumphed and opened Western eyes to other great names of Japanese cinema such as Mizoguchi, Ozu, Gosho and Ichikawa; it seems incredible that an industry which had had its beginnings at the turn of the twentieth century should have remained until then virtually unknown in the West.

Japanese critics had never rated *Rashomon* highly, declaring that it lacked the social

commitment of Kurosawa's earlier films and ignoring its basic theme of the subjective nature of truth. It deals with four separate accounts of a rape and murder. A samurai and his wife are travelling through a bandit's territory. A gust of wind blows the lady's veil aside revealing her beauty to the bandit who is inflamed at the sight. He rapes the lady and murders the samurai, a coward who abjectly begs to be spared. Or does he? The samurai's own version of the event, told through a medium in the courtroom where the case is investigated, claims that he killed himself according to the samurai code, unable to live with dishonour. The bandit's version insists that the lady was compliant; she, of course denies this. The complications mount, compounded by a fourth witness, a woodcutter, who tells his version to a priest as they shelter under the rain-lashed, ruined Rashomon Gate, a symbol of the demoralized, anarchic nature of Japan in the eighth century.

Above: a poor thief (Tatsuya Nakadai), posing as his clan's chief, leads his men in battle in Kagemusha. *Left: Akira Kurosawa on location during the making of that film*

Above: Sugata Sanshiro *(1943, Judo Saga). Kurosawa's first feature. Above right: a violent scene from the gangland drama* Drunken Angel. *Above, far right: poster for* Living. *Below right: a dishonoured woman (Machiko Kyo) asks her husband (Masayuko Mori) to kill her in* Rashomon. *Below: Denjiro Okochi in* They Who Tread on the Tiger's Tail

Many key aspects of Kurosawa's genius emerge from *Rashomon*: his masterly control of a complex narrative; his direction of his actors; and the film's dazzling use of light and shade. No one could forget the bandit's race through the glinting forest, or the rape scene when the camera makes a 360° revolution around the tree tops to suggest an orgasm (a device that was subsequently much imitated). It was abundantly clear that henceforward Kurosawa must be numbered among the world's truly great film-makers.

Kurosawa was born in Tokyo in 1910. He initially wished to become a painter, but decided that his talents did not lie in that area. He became instead the assistant to the director Kajiro Yamamoto (also collaborating on his scripts) before becoming a director in his own right. The acclaim won by *Rashomon* afforded Western access to Kurosawa's earlier work, in particular *Toro-no-o* (1945, *They Who Tread on the Tiger's Tail*). Though much less successful in the West than *Rashomon*, this film was a fascinating, hour-long version of a Noh play. It was not released until eight years after its completion because the American occupying authorities condidered it too feudalistic – a doubtful judgement, as a character inserted by Kurosawa and played by a famous comedian, Kenichi Enomoto, makes mock of the traditional values ritualistically observed by the rest of the cast.

Another key early work was *Yoidore Tenshi* (1948, *Drunken Angel*), a great success in Japan and Kurosawa's first film with Toshiro Mifune, who was to become the director's favourite actor. This tale of a tubercular ex-gangster (Mifune) whose spiritual redemption is fought for by a doctor working in the slums, clearly prefigures Kurosawa's later studies of close relationships between two men.

It is certain that the foreign success of *Rashomon* gave Kurosawa greater artistic freedom; the immediate result of this was *Ikiru* (1952, *Living*), which must rank among his finest works. The main character is a late middle-aged bureaucrat (superbly played by Takashi Shimura) who learns that he is suffering from terminal cancer; this causes him to take stock of his life, which he realizes has been sterile and empty. He overhears a conversation which brings home to him that his family cares only for his money; he also discovers that in his professional life he has been little more than a cog in the bureaucratic wheel. When he happens upon a filed, ignored request from slum-dwellers for a patch of wasteland to be turned into a children's playground, he determines to bring this to fulfilment as a belated justification for his life. He dies, a lone figure, on a swing in the playground he has helped to create. In his last months he had forged a pleasurable relationship with a young girl from his office; this he foregoes, sacrificing everything to what becomes an obsession. The film's message is that one cannot afford to leave this life unfulfilled or with bitter misgivings – a belief implicit in Zen and Indian Buddhism.

The latter half of *Living* deals with the old man's funeral rites. His office associates, his son and daughter-in-law and the suppliants for the playground gather together to appraise his life. Only one speaks of him with any genuine sympathy or understanding, while credit for the playground goes to everyone except its real instigator.

Two years later, Kurosawa made his greatest world success, *Shichinin No Samurai* (1954, *Seven Samurai*). He has always claimed that John Ford was one of his inspirations and *Seven Samurai* does have affinities with the Western. Each of the samurai is impeccably characterized, and Mifune as a jokey braggart,

a would-be samurai and a hanger-on to the sternly dedicated band of warriors, reveals an unsuspected gift for comedy. The underlying moral of the film is that only in unity lies strength. The peasants who employ the samurai to deliver them from oppression are saved but at the end of the titanic struggle, a samurai observes: 'We have won but we have lost', indicating that they, unlike the peasants, are rootless, migratory, lost in time, heading for extinction.

In 1957 Kurosawa filmed two adaptations from foreign sources: *Kumonosu-Jo* (*Throne of Blood*), based on Shakespeare's *Macbeth*, and *Donzoko* (*The Lower Depths*), from Gorky's play. In *Throne of Blood*, for the first and only time, the director allowed Mifune to be overshadowed: splendid though Mifune is, it is the subtle, deadly performance by Isuzu Yamada as his wife that haunts the imagination. As she glides through the sleeping castle directing their murderous activities with only the sinister swish-swish of her kimono on the soundtrack she becomes the very incarnation of evil.

For *The Lower Depths* Kurosawa employed a new multi-camera technique. He rehearsed his cast and crew for six weeks with full makeup.

Above: Yuzo Kayama and Toshiro Mifune in Red Beard. *Right: poster for* Throne of Blood, *starring Mifune and Isuzu Yamada. Below: Mifune as a samurai warrior in the action-packed adventure* The Hidden Fortress

costumes and lighting. The result was an unusually closely-knit acting ensemble which perfectly served this series of vignettes set in the latter days of the Tokugara period of Japanese history (1601–1868). Death loses its sting when life is hardly worth living and yet the strange little dance executed by the band of wretched characters at a final drinking party is buoyant until news of another suicide is brought. A character looks straight into the camera and remarks: 'What a pity! Just when the party was getting going.' And thus, curtly, unsentimentally (and true to the spirit of Gorky's play) the film ends. There are no star roles, but once more Mifune and Yamada are outstanding, the former as a thief, the latter as a fiendish virago of a landlady.

Having plumbed the depths of human depravity, treachery and greed in *Throne of Blood* and *The Lower Depths*, Kurosawa made three period films over the next five years which dealt with the less lethal, even the comic aspects of evil. The first was *Kakushi Toride No San Akunin* (1958, *The Hidden Fortress*), a kind of action-packed fairy-tale. The other two were *Yojimbo* (1961) and *Tsubaki Sanjuro* (1961, *Sanjuro*). All three starred Mifune, his formidable presence and athletic prowess still undiminished. Underlying the comic approach to the traditional violence however, was a thread of something akin to desperation; a suggestion that the human condition was so irretrievably base that the only thing to do was to poke fun at it.

Yojimbo ridiculed feudal values, while in *Sanjuro*, Mifune (as a samurai) makes a group of young apprentice samurai aware that real life cannot be encompassed by their rigid codes of honour and traditional obligations. There is also in these two films an element of what one might call today 'high camp', as exemplified in the scene from *Sanjuro* where messages are transmitted to fellow-fighters by an arrangement of lotus flowers drifting down a stream through enemy lines.

In *Akahige* (1965, *Red Beard*) Kurosawa plunged once again into deeper waters. The film traces the growth of a strong emotional relationship between Red Beard, a doctor (Mifune) and his young disciple (Yuzo Kayama). The doctor convinces the young man that only by dedicating himself wholly to the service of the needy can his life become meaningful. Yet the final implications have a bleak edge. In *Living* Kurosawa hinted that even a last-minute bid to redeem an egotistical life could bring spiritual salvation and a serene acceptance of death. *Red Beard* implies that although the old feudalistic concepts are patently valueless, no other, more humane doctrines have been evolved to take their place. Therefore people live in a state of flux, if not desperation. Although this beautiful film is once more set in late-Tokugara Japan, it is evident that the film's forebodings have their reference to the social evils of today.

By the early Seventies Kurosawa's career had hit the doldrums. In 1970 he made his first colour film *Dodesukaden* (*Dodeskaden*) the title of which is onomatopoeic, evoking the sound of a train running along the tracks. It dealt with low life in a large city and is a stylized variant on *The Lower Depths*. A proposal that he would co-direct the American account of the Japanese attack on Pearl Harbor, *Tora! Tora! Tora!* (1970) aborted in disagreeable circumstances. In addition, the Japanese film industry

was at a low ebb; finance for anything but routine subjects was well-nigh impossible to find. These factors may well have contributed to the depression that led him to attempt suicide. Happily Kurosawa rallied and found new inspiration in the USSR.

The Soviet-sponsored story he embarked on, *Dersu Uzala* (1975), is set in the nineteenth century and once more explores a relationship between two men, this time from vastly different cultural backgrounds, that changes both their lives. The eponymous hero is a hunter whose life is inextricably linked with his surroundings; he is at one with nature. Dersu is hired by Arseniev, the leader of an expedition to survey the wastes of Siberia. The guide reveals the ways of nature to the party; Arseniev thus discovers through Dersu the true meaning of life. When Dersu's eyesight begins to fail, diminishing his hunting prowess, Arseniev takes him back to live with his family in Moscow – an environment in which Dersu is pitifully out of place. Dersu decides to return to his beloved wilderness, but is killed on the outskirts of the city by a thief who covets the gun that Arseniev had given Dersu to help him survive in the wild.

True purity of spirit, the film attests, can only be attained in the world today by those who have remained outside the mainstream of modern life and who remain close to nature. Kurosawa worked mainly with Russian technicians on this project, the chief exception being a Japanese cameraman, Asakadzu Nakai, with a rare talent for capturing the beauty of the desolate landscapes.

When Kurosawa succeeded in setting up *Kagemusha* (1980, Shadow Warrior) ten years had elapsed since he had worked in his own country. The directors Francis Ford Coppola and George Lucas helped to persuade 20th Century-Fox to invest in the production. Set in the latter part of the sixteenth century, the film concerns a poor thief who is spared on account of his resemblance to a powerful warlord. When this leader is wounded in battle and dies, the thief is ordered to impersonate him to keep the warlord's clan together and keep its enemies at bay. He grows more and more accustomed to the role of clan leader, but is exposed when he is unable to ride the warlord's horse. Thrown out, he watches helplessly as his clan is overwhelmed by enemy forces.

Above: Yoshitaki Zushi as the young hero of Dodeskaden, *a vivid portrait of life in the slums. Below: a close relationship develops between Dersu (Maksim Munzuk) and Arseniev (Yuri Solomin) as they cope with life in the wilderness in* Dersu Uzala

Kagemusha, budgeted at $6.5 million was the most expensive Japanese film ever made. At the Cannes Film Festival in 1980, where the film shared the Grand Prix with Bob Fosse's *All That Jazz* (1979), some critics found the battle scenes magnificent but protracted. This was not surprising as, in the rush to make the film available for the Festival, Kurosawa had left himself no time to trim these scenes as he had envisaged. For years he has favoured a multi-camera technique of shooting which, while ensuring the spontaneity that he feels may become lost in repeated takes, naturally calls for a longer period than usual in the cutting room.

To meet and talk with Kurosawa (even through an interpreter) is an experience not easily forgotten. An unusually tall man, especially for a Japanese, his manner is unvaryingly smiling and gentle. It is hard to reconcile this benign image with the desperately passionate humanist or the past-master of violent action scenes that emerges from his work. In his case, still waters run exceptionally deep.   DEREK PROUSE

Filmography
1943 Sugata Sanshiro (+sc) (USA/GB: Judo Saga). '44 Ichiban Utsukushiku (+sc) (USA: The Most Beautiful). '45 Zoku Sugata Sanshiro (+sc) (USA/GB: Judo Saga, Part II); Tora-no-o/Tora no o o Fumu Otokotachi (+sc) (USA; The Men Who Tread on the Tiger's Tail; GB: They Who Tread on the Tiger's Tail). '46 Asu O Tsukuru Hitobito (co-dir. only) (USA: Those Who Make Tomorrow); Waga Seishun Ni Kui Nashi (+co-sc) (USA/GB: No Regrets for Our Youth). '47 Subarashiki Nichiyobi (+co-sc) (USA: One Wonderful Sunday; GB: Wonderful Sunday). '48 Yoidore Tenshi (+co-sc) (USA/GB: Drunken Angel). '49 Shizukanaru Ketto (+co-sc) (USA/GB: The Quiet Duel); Nora Inu (+co-sc) (USA: Stray Dog). '50 Skyandaru (+co-sc) (USA: Scandal); Rashomon (+co-sc). '51 Hakuchi (+co-sc) (USA/GB: The Idiot). '52 Ikiru (+co-sc) (USA/GB: Living). '54 Shichinin No Samurai (+co-sc) (USA/GB: Seven Samurai). '55 Ikimono No Kiroku (+co-sc) (USA: I Live in Fear). '57 Kumonosu-Jo (+co-sc) (USA/GB: Throne of Blood); Donzoko (+co-sc) (USA/GB: The Lower Depths). '58 Kakushi Toride No San Akunin (+co-sc) (USA/GB: The Hidden Fortress). '60 Warui Yatsu Hodo Yoku Nemuru (+co-sc) (USA: The Bad Sleep Well). '61 Yojimbo (+co-sc); Tsubaki Sanjuro (+co-sc) (USA/GB: Sanjuro). '63 Tengoku To Jigoku (+co-sc) (USA/GB: High and Low). '65 Akahige (+co-sc) (USA/GB: Red Beard). '70 Dodesukaden (+co-sc) (USA: Dodeskaden). '75 Dersu Uzala (+sc) (USSR-JAP). '80 Kagemusha (+co-sc).

Un film
d'AKIRO KUROSAWA

Directed by Akira Kurosawa, 1954
Prod co: Toho. **prod:** Shojiro Motoki. **sc:** Shinobu Hashimoto, Hideo Oguni, Akira Kurosawa. **photo:** Asakazu Nakai. **art dir:** So Matsuyama. **fencing dir:** Yoshio Sugino. **archery dir:** Tenori Kaneko, Shigeru Endo. **mus:** Fumio Hayasaka. **sd:** Fumio Yanoguchi. **r/t:** 160 minutes. Japanese title: *Shichinin No Samurai*. Released in GB/USA as *Seven Samurai*.
Cast: Takashi Shimura (*Kambei*), Toshiro Mifune (*Kikuchiyo*), Yoshio Inaba (*Gorobei*), Seiji Miyaguchi (*Kyuzo*), Minoru Chiaki (*Heihachi*), Daisuke Kato (*Shichiroji*), Ko Kimura (*Katsushiro*), Kamatari Fujiwara (*Manzo*), Kuninori Kodo (*Gisaku*), Bokuzen Hidari (*Yohei*), Yoshio Kosugi (*Mosuke*), Yoshio Tsuchiya (*Rikichi*), Keiji Sakakida (*Gosaku*), Keiko Tsushima (*Shino*), Toranosuke Ogawa (*grandfather*), Yu Akitsu (*husband*), Noriko Sengoku (*wife*), Gen Shimizu (*masterless samurai*), Jun Tatari (*coolie*), Atsushi Watanabe (*vendor*), Sojin Kamiyama (*minstrel*), Kichijiro Ueda, Shimpei Takagi, Akira Tani (*bandits*).

Akira Kurosawa has always been the most problematic of the major Japanese directors. Having made the first real breakthrough for Japanese cinema in the West with *Rashomon* (1950), he continued to enjoy a commercial success that was (and still is) denied to Kenji Mizoguchi and Yasujiro Ozu. There were ample reasons for this, not least the clear accessibility of Kurosawa's work, (where the influence of John Ford's Westerns is unmistakable), the source material which is often familiar (Shakespeare, Dostoyevsky, Gorky), and the distinctly cosmopolitan sensibility of his films.

The problem was highlighted when *Shichinin No Samurai* (*Seven Samurai*) became a worldwide hit in 1954. Although Kurosawa cannot be said to have been critically misjudged, the lingering suspicion that he was indulging in un-Japanese activities in order to court Western favour seemed to be confirmed by the ease with which *Seven Samurai* took to being remade as a Hollywood Western, *The Magnificent Seven* (1960). There was also the question of the techniques used in the film.

Claiming with some justification that Mizoguchi's historical epics were magnificent *except* for their battle scenes (usually either elided or dismissed in a handful of tableaux) Kurosawa planned to redress the balance in filming the carnage and confusion of the battles in *Seven Samurai*. To give the audience the feeling that they were present in the past, watching something that was actually happening rather than represented, he therefore pioneered the use of multiple cameras (filming scenes from several angles so as to be able to select the most vivid take of any given moment), and of the telephoto lens (giving the illusion that the action is much closer to camera than it actually is).

He also made systematic use of jump-cuts in editing to speed up the action (a character is asked a question in one location; his reply comes in another, with a different scene already under way) six years before Jean-Luc Godard 'revolutionized' cinema by doing the same thing in *A Bout de Souffle* (1960, *Breathless*). The result is a film in perpetual motion, moving to and fro with such concentrated intensity that the threat of violence remains inescapably present until it explodes in the final sequence.

All these techniques are, of course, commonplace now, especially on television. At the time, they

seemed innovatory to Western audiences especially when compaired with other Japanese films, where the images seemed to be highly stylized, adopting a pictorial formalism derived from Japanese painting. Attempting to seize action on the wing, uncertain in advance which of his cameras would actually capture it, Kurosawa naturally could not compose for the frame with the precision and care expended upon every image by Ozu or Mizoguchi. But to conclude from this that Kurosawa is un-Japanese is false. The formalism of much Japanese art is based on suspended movement: freeze any frame of *Seven Samurai*, and you have the makings of a Hokusai woodcut.

Similarly, although the film seems as clear as any standard Western, it enshrines a number of subtle ambiguities. When the village emissaries first see Kambei, for instance, they watch in amazement as, prior to posing as a priest to trap the homicidal thief, he has his head shaved. In Japanese custom, this means that a samurai is either disgraced, or about to leave the world to become a priest. Building on this enigma, since Kambei is clearly bent on following neither course, Kurosawa proceeds to show how he is in fact following both. As a samurai, in

3

7

108

effect a hired killer in the lawless society of the times, Kambei *is* disgraced already; and through the wisdom and charity he displays on behalf of the villagers he *becomes* in effect a priest.

In one of the nicest ironies of the film (teaching a social lesson which *The Magnificent Seven* omits entirely), it is the halfwit Kikuchiyo, the 'innocent', who reveals this truth to Kambei. When the seven samurai first arrive, the villagers vanish in terror only to come flocking back for protection when a bandit attack is threatened. Just as the outraged Kikuchiyo succeeds in shaming the villagers for their illogicality, the samurai take umbrage after discovering a hidden store of weapons indicating that the villagers have been killing and robbing wandering samurai.

'One who has never been hunted wouldn't understand,' says Kambei, explaining the viewpoint of the unhappy, unemployed samurai, wandering and weary, an easy prey to the very people they had once kept firmly in order.

'Do you think farmers are angels?' the angry Kikuchiyo replies, ending his long, impassioned tirade with irrefutable logic:

'They're mean, stupid and murderous. But then, who made them such beasts? You samurai did it . . .'
TOM MILNE

It is late sixteenth-century Japan. In the troubled times following civil war, the farmers are terrorized by bandits (1) making regular raids on their harvests. Encouraged by their elders the inhabitants of one village (2) at last decide to follow the example of another which reputedly hired samurai to fight for them.

Watching one samurai deal expertly with a homicidal thief who is holding a child hostage, the emissaries from the village are encouraged by learning that, masterless and hungry, the samurai accepted a payment of two rice balls. Unable to offer money, they nevertheless manage to hire the samurai, Kambei, when he realizes the sacrifices entailed in their proposal to pay three meals a day.

Aided by Katsushiro, an admiring young disciple, Kambei recruits individually (3) four more unattached samurai – Shichiroji, Gorobei, Heihachi and Kyuzo – who accept the terms out of a mixture of pride, hunger and respect for Kambei. Followed by Kikuchiyo, a half-crazy braggart who refuses to take no for an answer (4), the six are escorted to the village. There Kikuchiyo, himself a farmer's son, is instrumental in establishing a mutual trust between the villagers and the samurai they have learned to fear.

Defences are prepared, the villagers are trained. Katsushiro, meanwhile, has struck up a friendship with one of the village girls (5). When three bandit scouts are killed (6) before they can tell the bandits about the new defences, their horses are used by Gorobei, Kyuzo and Kikuchiyo in a successful raid on the bandit hideout, though Gorobei is killed. The bandits finally attack (7) and are wiped out under Kambei's expert leadership in a long and bloody battle (8, 9), in which many villagers are killed. Of the samurai, only Kambei, Shichiroji and Katsushiro survive the bloodshed.

Already forgotten by the farmers, who are back at work in the fields (10), the samurai prepare to leave; but Katsushiro, having fallen in love with a farmer's daughter, decides to remain in the village.

1

2

4

5

6

8

9

10

Satyajit Ray-Visions of India

More than any other director, Satyajit Ray has articulated and interpreted the Indian way of life. His films explore the forces that govern and quicken the hearts and minds of his people and form a rich and varied contribution to world cinema

Satyajit Ray is universally regarded as India's foremost film-maker, in addition to being a notable artist, journalist, composer and novelist. His background and middle-class orientation are the two most important factors behind his talent for perceiving the reality around him and rendering it with simplicity. He comes from an extremely gifted family. His father (who died when Ray was three) was a writer and artist, while Ray's grandfather was a prominent author of children's books. Ray paid homage to his grandfather by basing two films, *Goopy Gyne Bagha Byne* (1968, *The Adventures of Goopy and Bagha*) and *Hirok Rajar Deshe* (1980, *The Kingdom of Diamonds*) on one of his novels. In addition, Ray's mother had a tremendous influence on his life; he tried to capture this relationship in *Aparajito* (1956, *The Unvanquished*) in his depiction of the adolescent Apu and his mother Sarbojaya.

After gaining a degree in science and economics at Calcutta University, Ray joined Shantiniketan, an educational institution founded by the Nobel Prize-winning author Rabindranath Tagore. The main emphasis in Shantiniketan (the name literally means 'house of peace') is to bring pupils close to nature and offer them freedom to create in tranquil surroundings. Ray's experience there helped to make him keenly aware of the value of form,

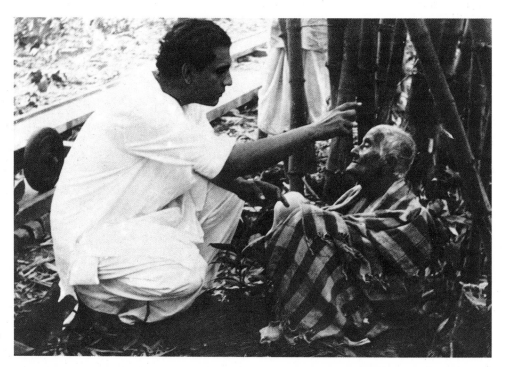

rhythm and movement.

Sometime before he left Shantiniketan in 1942, Ray had come across the film theories of Rudolf Arnheim and Paul Rotha. These writers made Ray aware of cinema as an art form, and he resolved to become a film-maker. In order to train himself (there were no film schools in India at that time), Ray invented his own way of writing screenplays. Whenever it was announced that a Bengali film based on a famous Bengali literary work had begun shooting, Ray would write his own treatment. When that film was released, he would compare his treatment with the finished work.

Top left: Aparna Das Gupta as Pagli, the wayward young bride of Samapti, *the final part of* Teen Kanya. *Top: Ray sets up a shot for* The Chess Players. *Above: Ray with the actress Chunibala Devi, who at the age of 80 agreed to take part in* Pather Panchali

In 1948, while Ray was working as a commercial artist for an advertising company, he and his friends formed the Calcutta Film Society. This gave him a chance to view many of the world's finest films and to meet various celebrities, in particular Jean Renoir. Renoir came to India in 1950 to make *The River* (1951)

and was to be an early influence on Ray's work.

Ray became increasingly determined to make a film himself and decided to adapt for the screen a novel by Bibhutibhushan Bandapaddhaya called *Pather Panchali* (which Ray had been asked to illustrate some years earlier). Ray did not want to lose the security of his job, so he became a part-time film-maker, devoting Sundays and holidays to shooting *Pather Panchali*. He pawned his wife's jewellery and sold his precious books and records in order to buy raw stock and hire a camera.

Ray would have been unable to afford to finish the film without the help of a friend of his mother-in-law, who persuaded the Bengali government to provide financial assistance. *Pather Panchali* (*Song of the Little Road*), completed in 1955, was shown at the Cannes Film Festival the following year and won worldwide acclaim. Its success resulted in Ray receiving many offers to make films abroad; yet, though he speaks excellent English, he has said that he feels incapable of making films in any language other than his own, Bengali.

An exception to his standard practice was *Shatranj Ke Khilari* (1977, *The Chess Players*), which he made in Hindi-Urdu. The film is based on a short story by the most prominent Hindi author, Munshi Premchand, and concerns two chess players who are so obsessed with their game that they are totally unaware of the important political developments taking shape around them. Ray interwove Premchand's story with details of the annexation of the state of Oudh by the British in 1856, a major factor behind the Indian Mutiny of the following year. Ray commented:

'Though the story and the history could be kept separate, since they were linked both thematically and temporally, the film ended up as one piece about the annexation. This was one of the most peaceful historical events – not a single shot was fired and Wajid Ali Shah, the last king of Awadh [Oudh], who was more interested in various art forms than battles, gave up his throne without any recourse to action.'

This film was a big challenge to Ray because the language used in that period was a very ornate, highly Persianized Urdu, replete with difficult idioms. It was necessary to keep the flavour of the period without making the language incomprehensible to his audience. In addition, there had to be a difference between the language spoken in Wajid Ali Shah's court and the more everyday speech used by the chess-playing Nawabs (noblemen) and their acquaintances. At that time, too, the women used a different style of Urdu, which had certain peculiar idioms and forms of address; then there were the house servants and the village boy of the closing scenes who spoke the dialect used in the villages around Lucknow.

Shama Zaidi, who assisted Ray on his Urdu script, recalled:

'In his Bengali films, he makes almost no changes in the dialogues once he has written them but in this film he kept making minor changes – sometimes just before the shooting started. Even the English portions were rewritten in this manner.'

Ray employed the best professional actors available in *The Chess Players*. Probably because he was working in a new language and because it was an historical film, he preferred to work with actors and actresses with whose work he was already familiar. He has said that in Bengali he is able to work with inexperienced actors because he can instruct them about each gesture and intonation by demonstrating what he wants; not being as fluent in Hindu, he could only direct the actors of *The Chess Players* by suggestion.

Indian politics are glimpsed in Ray's films though he does not make direct political comments in his work. In *Jana Aranya* (1975, *The Middle-Man*), Somnath Bannerjee (Pradip Mukherjee) walks through the Calcutta streets, past walls painted with the slogans of the Naxilites (an extremist wing of the Indian Communist Party which had started a futile terrorist campaign in an attempt to abolish the

Above: Apu (Soumitra Chatterjee) teaches Aparna (Sharmila Tagore) to read in The World of Apu *(1959). Below: Soumitra Chatterjee and Madhabi Mukherjee in* Charulata

bourgeoisie and economic disparities). Ray's camera pans over these walls with Pradip in the foreground.

Pratidwandi (1970, *The Adversary*) was close to the political climate of India in the late Sixties. But here, Ray concentrates on the pursuit of security (the perennial problem of an Indian youth) undertaken by the hero, Siddhartha; the uncompromising political activism of Siddhartha's brother is kept in the background. In *Ashani Sanket* (1973, *Distant Thunder*) a man-made famine (brought about by the requisition of food for military requirements), leads to the death of five million people. Only the events leading up to the calamity are shown. The film's last, lingering shot of starving villagers makes no comments but raises questions about the human values and priorities of civilization. These themes are also explored in *Seemabadha* (1971, *Company Limited*), in which a young married couple struggles to adjust to the competitive business ethics of the Western capitalist system.

Ray spoke of his predominantly humanist concerns in an interview about *Hirok Rajar Deshe* (*The Kingdom of Diamonds*):

'I hope . . . *Hirok Rajar Deshe* makes my commitment to moral values clear to all. In this picture, I am telling a story which may be a continuation of the characters in *Goopy Gyne Bagha Byne*. There is a King Dictator and a crazy scientist who has invented a brain-washing machine – he has abolished education and only discipline and obedience are being fed into people's brains. The revolt is led by the school teacher with Goopy's and Bagha's help, so that the people are freed at last from the tyranny of the King Dictator and the mad scientist.'

'The moral values to which I am committed will be clear in this film. There are haves and have-nots, there is good and bad. My films and I are all for the have-nots and the good . . .'.

Speaking of the issues raised in some of his other films, Ray said:

'*Devi* (1960, *The Goddess*) was against superstition and dogmatism. *Jalsaghar* (1958, *The Music Room*) tried to show the inevitability of the old being replaced by a new (not necessarily better) system. But my commitment is not to a particular political system because it may begin as good but become bad because of the personalities of its leaders. I am certainly not interested in power politics.'

The portrayal of women in Ray's work differs from film to film; sometimes they are one step ahead of men and sometimes they are subservient to them. In *The Goddess*, Dayamoyee (Sharmila Tagore), deified as the result of a vision seen by her father-in-law,

Above: a young wife (Shabana Azmi) tries to convince her husband (Sanjeev Kumar) that there is more to life than chess in The Chess Players. *Below: a scene from* The Adventures of Goopy and Bagha

eventually rebels against being an object of worship. In *Kanchenjunga* (1962) Ray's first film about contemporary society, the women assert themselves and their independence in a so-called man's world. In *Mahanagar* (1963, *The Big City*), Arati Majumdar (Madhabi Mukherji) not only fights against the conventions of making women home-bound but also becomes the financial supporter of her family.

Ray has strong feelings about children. He has not only made four films for children, but has also created much of his fiction and illustrative work for the young. He was a champion of The Year of the Child in 1979, and headed the jury of the Bombay International Film Festival for Children.

The references to children in Ray's 'adult' movies are at times indulgent. In *Samapti* (*The Conclusion*), the final episode of *Teen Kanya* (1961, *Two Daughters*), the tomboyish Pagli, constantly plays with her pet squirrel even when she is married and expected to behave in a responsible manner. Later, when she has acquired a measure of worldly wisdom, having separated from her husband, a young friend brings the dead squirrel to her. She tells him to cremate it; its death symbolizes the death of her childhood.

Ray uses the term 'artless simplicity' to describe his style. Though he has made a number of films in colour, he believes that colour can never be realistic as it has a tendency to make things look attractive whatever the context. Ray operates the camera himself and leaves the technical aspects of shooting to his cameraman – a post usually held by Subrata Mitra. Ray knows how much to take in a shot and where to cut while he is filming, although he is open to improvisations by the actors which might add extra depth to the finished film. The dialogue tends to be strictly functional, though in *Charulata* (1964, *The Lonely Wife*), which he considers his best

film, he resorted to dialogue in order to probe the psychology of his characters.

Despite his popularity in the West, Ray remains adamant in his determination to retain his national identity:

'My first audience is India. It is not true that I make Indian films for the West. Sometimes they find my works too simple and innocuous.'

The world of Satyajit Ray's films is India in miniature, with all its paradoxes and baffling complexities.   RAKESH MATHUR

Filmography

1955 Pather Panchali (+sc) (USA: Song of the Little Road). **'56** Aparajito (+sc) (USA/GB: The Unvanquished). **'57** Paras Pather (+sc) (USA/GB: The Philosopher's Stone). **'58** Jalsaghar (+sc) (USA/GB: The Music Room). **'59** Apur Sansar (+sc) (USA/GB: The World of Apu). **'60** Devi (+sc) (USA/GB: The Goddess). **'61** Rabindranath Tagore (+sc; +comm) (doc); Teen Kanya (+sc; +mus) (USA/GB: Two Daughters; one *ep* was cut from the original print). **'62** Kanchenjunga (+sc; +mus); Abhijan (+sc; +mus) (USA: Expedition). **'63** Mahanagar (+sc; +mus) (USA/GB: The Big City). **'64** Charulata (+sc; +mus) (USA: The Lonely Wife). **'65** Two (+sc; +mus) (short); Shakespeare Wallah (mus. only); Kapurush-o-Mahapurush (+sc; +mus) (USA: The Coward and the Saint; GB: The Coward and the Holy Man). **'66** Nayak (+sc; +mus) (USA/GB: The Hero). **'67** Chiriakhana (+sc; +mus). **'68** Goopy Gyne Bagha Byne (+sc; +mus) (USA/GB: The Adventures of Goopy and Bagha). **'69** Aranyer Din-Ratri (+sc; +mus) (USA/GB: Days and Nights in the Forest). **'70** Pratidwandi (+sc; +mus) (USA/GB: The Adversary). **'71** Seemabadha (+sc; +mus) (USA/GB: Company Limited); Sikkim (+sc; +mus) (doc). **'73** Ashani Sanket (+sc; +mus) (USA/GB: Distant Thunder); The Inner Eye (+sc) (short). **'75** Sonar Kella (+sc; +mus) (USA/GB: The Golden Fortress); Jana Aranya (+sc; +mus) (USA: The Masses' Music; GB: The Middle-Man). **'77** Shatranj Ke Khilari (+sc; +mus) (USA/GB: The Chess Players) (made in Urdu and English language versions); Bala (+sc; +mus) (short). **'79** Joi Babs Felunath (+sc; +mus) (USA/GB: The Elephant God). **'80** Hirok Rajar Deshe (+sc; +mus) (GB: The Kingdom of Diamonds).

Scandinavian screen

The cinemas of Sweden, Finland, Denmark and Norway share certain common preoccupations arising from ethnic, cultural and even geographical similarities

The fifteen years between 1925 and 1940 are usually dismissed by critics as a Dark Age in the history of Swedish cinema. Films were turned out with prolific haste, but success at the box-office, rather than quality, was the touchstone. Domestic comedies ruled the roost, and few directors attempted to use the cinema for artistic-purposes. One of those who did, Alf Sjöberg, was unpopular with the Swedish studios after the film he co-directed, *Den Starkaste* (1929, *The Strongest*), a tale of seal-hunters in the Greenland Sea, had evinced an authenticity and uncontrived dramatic force not seen since the great days of Sjöström and Stiller. Sjöberg could not embark on another project until 1939, and devoted his creative energies to the theatre instead.

One director, however, did pursue a competent career throughout the entire period, and on even into the Sixties. Gustaf Molander had started as an actor in Stockholm in 1911, and worked as a screenwriter on such early Swedish classics as *Terje Vigen* (1917). His first significant film as a director was *En Natt* (1931, One Night), a drama involving two brothers who join different sides at the outbreak of the Finnish revolution. Sound and lighting were particularly sophisticated. In *Intermezzo* (1936), Molander yielded somewhat to the prevailing mood of the time, telling an intense and melancholy love story against the backdrop of European cities and resorts. The film introduced Ingrid Bergman to the outside world (she later remade the film in Hollywood), and her performance as the young piano teacher entranced by a famous (but married) violinist has a freshness and spontaneity that challenge the *kitsch* of the period.

Six years later, Molander made a laudable screen version of the novel by Vilhelm Moberg, *Rid i Natt!* (1942, *Ride Tonight!*). Set during the aftermath of the Thirty Years War, *Rid i Natt!* denounced the feudal dominance exercised over the common folk by a group of robber barons in Sweden. Both Moberg and Molander stressed the parallels with Nazi Germany and the war that was threatening to engulf even traditionally neutral Sweden.

The Occupation of Norway formed the background to Molander's *Det Brinner en Eld* (1943, There Burned a Flame) and *Ordet* (1943, The Word). The latter film was based on a play by the Danish writer Kaj Munk, who was shot by the Nazis a few years later.

The turning point in the fortunes of the Swedish cinema occurred in 1942 when Carl Anders Dymling was appointed head of Svensk Filmindustri, the country's largest film company.

One of Dymling's first acts was to name Victor Sjöström, then over sixty, as production supervisor. Now at last talent was able to assert itself. Sjöberg was soon to the fore with *Himlaspelet* (1942, *Road to Heaven*), a morality play by Rune Lindström and *Hets* (1944, *Frenzy*), based on an original screenplay by the young Ingmar Bergman, and introducing a bright new star, Mai Zetterling. For the next decade, Bergman and Sjöberg would be the guiding lights of Swedish film, although Sjöberg was the senior by

nearly fifteen years.

The Swedish cinema of the Forties was marked by a kind of undeveloped guilt in the face of the war in Europe. Sweden's neutrality worried the intellectuals and artists of the period, especially when both Denmark and Norway were overrun by the Nazis. This mood of foreboding emerged in the visual style of many films, in which the characters seem oppressed by their environment and menaced by a fate beyond their comprehension.

Molander's *Kvinna Utan Ansikte* (1947, *The Woman Without a Face*) scripted by Bergman, showed the world in a cruel light as a young man strays from his marriage into a doomed liaison. *Frånskild* (1951, *Divorced*), again directed by Molander and written by Bergman, contained a moving performance by Inga Tidblad as the deserted wife for whom the lure of suicide is strong.

Top: the celebrated Swedish stage actor Gösta Ekman and Ingrid Bergman in a tender love scene from Molander's Intermezzo. *The Hollywood remake was directed by Gregory Ratoff for David O. Selznick with Leslie Howard as the violinist. Above: Erik Hell, as the hangman, confronts Oskar Ljung, as the dispossessed peasant whom he will later murder, in Molander's anti-German period piece.* Ride Tonight!

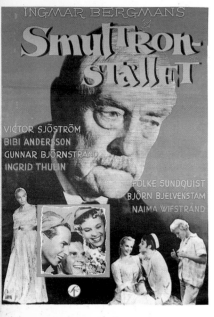

Top: Rune Lindström as the peasant whose dead fiancée is eventually restored to him, and Anders Henrikson as God's representative, in Road to Heaven. Top right: in Hets the young lover discovers his sadistic teacher (Stig Järrel) hiding outside the room of his dead girlfriend (Mai Zetterling). Above: Wild Strawberries (1957), with Victor Sjöström, as an embittered old doctor who relives ancient memories; Bibi Andersson portrays his first love and a modern girl. Centre right: Ulla Jacobsson as the doomed country girl who 'only danced one summer' in One Summer of Happiness, considered rather shocking because of a lakeside love scene and a glimpse of bare breasts. Right: Matti Kassila's Harvest Month was a Finnish attack on alcoholism, in the story of a drunken lock-keeper torn between two women; a sub-plot of young love relieves the gloom

Arne Sucksdorff was, meanwhile, following his personal line of exploration through film. His ethnographic and animal documentaries remain classics of their genre; they are specifically Swedish in their preoccupation with the passage of the seasons and in their meticulous technique. His most acclaimed achievement is the feature *Det Stora Äventyret* (1953, *The Great Adventure*), but *En Sommarsaga* (1941, *A Summer Tale*), *Trut!* (1944, *The Gull*), *Gryning* (1944, *Dawn*), *Människor i Stad* (1947, *People of the City*) and *En Kluven Värld* (1948, *A Divided World*) are all worthy of note.

Bergman's reputation, even in Sweden, would not reach the heights until the mid-Fifties. Sjöberg, with masterpieces like *Bara en Mor* (1949. *Only a Mother*) and *Fröken Julie* (1951, *Miss Julie*), was regarded as pre-eminent in his field and for a short period between 1951 and 1955 it appeared as though Arne Mattsson would equal his accomplishment. Mattsson was much influenced by the work of Hitchcock and Ford and yet drew on the inspiration of Sjöström in his depiction of bucolic life in Sweden. *Hon Dansade en Sommar* (1951, *One Summer of Happiness*) provoked controversy when it was released. Its story of young love in the countryside was nothing new, but its frankness of expression certainly was – at least in one brief scene beside a lake. *One Summer of Happiness*, however, was by no means the best of Mattsson's films. *Kärlekenns Bröd* (1953, *The Bread of Love*) unfolded in the snowbound forests of Finland during the Russo-Finnish war of 1939, and focused with relentless accuracy on the behaviour of a small

patrol of men trapped in a minefield by their Soviet enemy. Mattsson, deploying an elaborate time structure (the film consisted of interlocking flashbacks) with the most elegant of camera movements, built up a psychological suspense that would become the hallmark of his finest work.

Mattsson's *Salka Valka* (1954) was drawn from a novel by the Icelandic author Halldór Laxness. It recounted how a mother and her young daughter come to a fishing community and survive on a combination of wits and energy. Salka grows up into a shrewd businesswoman but her love for Arnaldur, the leader of the fishermen's unionist movement, lies at the core of her existence. The landscape in *Salka Valka* is shown and used to perfection; man lives almost in defiance of nature as he did in the classic films of Victor Sjöström.

Mattsson's last film of real note was *Hemsöborna* (1955, People of Hemsö), based on the novel by August Strindberg about a tiny island in the Stockholm archipelago.

Comedy was a genre much appreciated in Sweden of the Thirties and Forties. The huge avuncular figure of Edvard Persson lurched through a number of farces, often breaking into song in the manner of George Formby. Persson celebrated the traditions and habits of Sweden's southernmost province, Scania. Nils Poppe, known to foreign audiences for his appearance as Jof in Bergman's *Det Sjunde Inseglet* (1957, The Seventh Seal), created a Chaplinesque figure in such comedies as *Pengar* (1946, Money) and *Soldat Bom* (1948, Private Bom).

Hampe Faustman was the most committed of his generation of directors, with an open sympathy for the Soviet Union. An ardent admirer of Mark Donskoy in particular, he expressed himself with passionate rigour, seeking to view his proletarian characters from angles that would make their conditions meaningful to film audiences. *När Ängarna Blommar* (1946, When Meadows Bloom) was a protest against the conditions of Swedish farm labourers, while *Främmande Hamn* (1948, Foreign Harbour) adopted a powerful stand against fascism in its story of sailors refusing to unload clandestine shipments of arms in a Polish port in 1938.

Many of Sweden's film-makers have been fine actors in their own right. Sjöström, for instance, and Anders Henrikson, who made the Strindberg adaptation *Giftas* (1956, Married Life). Hasse Ekman, a handsome juvenile lead, was the son of the great actor Gösta Ekman, who had starred in certain films of the Thirties (his best role being that of the violinist in *Intermezzo*). Hasse Ekman soon took to film-making himself, and his audacious visual compositions were reminiscent of Orson Welles.

Ombyte av Tåg (1943, Changing Trains) concerned the chance meeting at a railway station of two people who become lovers. *Excellensen* (1944, His Excellency) described an ailing poet's refusal to succumb to torture in a conflict between liberty and dictatorship. Ekman's *Flicka och Hyacinter* (1950, Girl with Hyacinths) was an anatomy of woman's suicide after she has been treated with malice and insensitivity by the men in her life.

DAY OF WRATH
A DRAMA OF FEAR AND SUPERSTITION IN THE 17th CENTURY
A CARL DREYER FILM

Top: De Røde Enge. *co-directed by a Danish actress, Bodil Ipsen, starred Lisbeth Movin, better remembered as the lovely young witch in* Day of Wrath. *Above: another woman, Astrid Henning-Jensen, directed her six-year-old son in a short fantasy,* Palle Alene i Verden, *about a boy who dreams he is in a world without other people, where he can do as he pleases, but is glad to wake up when he feels lonely*

Apart from Ingmar Bergman, whose work attracted world-wide acclaim but failed to break box-office records in his own country, none of the established directors made significant progress. After 1955 no worthwhile film reflected the true state of life in Sweden at the time. Escapism was once again the order of the day.

As the Fifties drew to a close, conditions in the domestic industry worsened and the Swedish cinema would be saved only by the foundation in 1963 of the Swedish Film Institute, which encouraged a new generation of film-makers, among them Bo Widerberg, Vilgot Sjöman and Jan Troell to pursue their distinctive careers in the cinema.

Film is, and always has been, a cottage industry in Finland. To achieve success a feature must attract nearly half a million filmgoers to the box-office – and the country's population is a mere 4.7 million, spread over 130,000 square miles.

During the Thirties and Forties, between 15 and 25 features were completed annually. Feather-light comedies, literary adaptations and rural romances were commonplace. Risto Orko and T.J. Särkkä were the leading personalities in this middle period.

Orko's gift for effervescent farce in an upper-class milieu was shown to good effect in *Siltalan Pehtoori* (1934, The Steward of Siltala), while his rousing sense of melodrama was at its best in a flamboyant war film – set in 1916, with Finnish soldiers returning from Germany after fighting for the Kaiser – entitled *Jääkärin Morsian* (1938, The Infantryman's Bride). Särkkä's picaresque *Kulkurin Valssi* (1941, The Vagabond's Waltz) is one of the few Finnish films to have been seen by more than one million spectators in its own land.

Nyrki Tapiovaara, who was killed at the age of 28 behind Russian lines just before the end of the Winter War, has acquired a posthumous reputation on the strength of just five features. *Varastettu Kuolema* (1938, Stolen Death) is the most intriguing and imaginative of them, and takes place in the grey, dubious years at the start of the century when 'activists' were engaged in an underground campaign to thwart the expansionist designs of Tsarist Russia.

War has frequently been the inspiration for imposing films from Finland. None more so than *Tuntematon Sotilas* (1955, The Unknown Soldier) directed by Edvin Laine from the famous novel by Väino Linna. It captured the peculiar blend of joviality and bitterness that characterizes the Finnish people's attitude towards the Soviet Union, and the wars of attrition that have engaged both nations.

During the Fifties other names came forward for consideration in the history of Finnish film: Erik Blomberg, for his searing and visually exhilarating saga *Valkoinen Peura* (1952, The White Reindeer); Matti Kassila for *Sininen Viikko* (1954, Blue Week) which described, in an idiom very similar to that of Bergman, a clandestine affair between a young man and a married woman during the summer holidays. Kassila was also highly regarded for *Elokuu* (1956, Harvest Month) which attacked the evils of alcoholism in a rural environment. The film was based on a novel by F. E. Sillanpää, one of Finland's greatest writers.

Denmark has produced a single great director – Carl Theodor Dreyer who was born in 1889, just ten years after Victor Sjöström. His career spanned almost six decades and yet his work never caught the public imagination in the way that Bergman's did. His greatest film of this central period was *Vredens Dag* (1943, Day of Wrath), a grim and haunting study of man's inhumanity to man in the face of witchcraft. Danes suffering under the Nazi occupation could perhaps see more in this film than was apparent to the casual viewer. *Ordet* (1955, The Word) was a remake of Molander's 1943 film from Kaj Munk's play. Dreyer's version is less naturalistic than Molander's and ends on an almost mystical note with the awakening from the dead of the younger Inger, rising from her coffin in the ghostly light of a bare white room at the farm where she lives.

A husband-and-wife team of outstanding talent in Denmark were Astrid and Bjarne Henning-Jensen, who between 1940 and 1960 made some twenty films. Their collaboration was particularly fruitful in respect of the films they made on childhood and adolescence. *Palle Alene i Verden* (1949, Palle Alone in the World) and *Paw* (1960, Paw – Boy of Two Worlds) were among the most rewarding of their works. Denmark scored a surprise victory at the first Cannes Film Festival in 1946 with *De Røde Enge* (1945, The Red Earth) dealing with the wartime Resistance movement.

Norway, like Finland, lacks a film tradition, although the government has long been involved in the industry and maintained a greater influence over film-making than is common in other Scandinavian countries. The nation's first film studio was built at Jar, in the Oslo suburbs in 1936, but the Kristiania Film Company had been producing features on a steady scale for a decade or so prior to this. Tancred Ibsen, who had worked in Hollywood for MGM, returned to Norway to earn fame as the director of *Den Stora Barnedåben* (1931, The Great Baptism), which was Norway's first talkie. Lief Sinding's *Fantegutten* (1932) was the first Norwegian screen musical. Rasmus Breistein was active throughout the period with films like the seafaring adventure *Jumfru Trofast* (1921, Miss Faithful), and romances such as *Liv* (1934, Life) and *Gullfjellet* (1941, The Golden Mountain). Sinding elected to work under the Germans as director of the Norwegian Film Industry, and for a long while after the war he was unable to practice his craft owing to this collaboration. In the wake of the liberation, Arne Skouen emerged as one of the promising Norwegian directors on the strength of his feature film debut, *Gategutter* (1949, Street Children), adapted from his own screenplay.

PETER COWIE

The Intimate Dramas of Ingmar Bergman

'What matters most in life is being able to contact another human being.' This remark by Ingmar Bergman explains his devotion to cinema, perhaps the most powerful means of communication. It also crystallizes the plight of his characters in their bitter struggles for understanding and love

Above: in this scene from Persona, *Alma (Bibi Andersson, left), nurse to a neurotic actress, Elizabet (Liv Ullmann) dreams that her charge has come to her room*

Since the mid-Forties, Ernst Ingmar Bergman has been making feature films at an average rate of one a year. If sheer output were the sole criterion, he would fully have earned his celebrity status alongside such prolific grand masters of celluloid as Hitchcock, Ford, Buñuel and Renoir.

Uniquely, however, Bergman's work reflects no apparent interest in commercial success, no urge to appeal to a wider audience. When Hollywood names have been thrust upon him as part of the production price – Elliott Gould in *Beröringen* (1971, *The Touch*) for example, or David Carradine and James Whitmore in *Das Schlangenei* (1977, *The Serpent's Egg*) – they have been absorbed almost without trace into Bergman's world. It is as though throughout his career he has been making one continuous film, personal and autobiographical, a diary of dreams, damnations and desires.

Such introspection is seldom accessible or entertaining to anyone but its author, but Bergman's genius has been to render from privacy a miraculously public text. His sense of

the dramatic, his command of his players, his mesmeric story-telling, all have been combined to display for us an anguish in which we can all share, an anguish resulting from the special complexities of survival in contemporary Western society. No other film-maker has so obsessively, so intelligently or so openly analysed what it has been like to live on this planet since World War II.

Bergman was born on 14 July, 1918 in the Swedish university city of Uppsala where, as he has since recalled, a number of influences came to bear upon him so vividly that they have recurred throughout his work. The bells of Uppsala Cathedral, the heavy furniture in his grandmother's flat which 'in my fantasy, conversed in a never-ending whisper', the nursery blind which, when lowered, somehow unleashed a horde of menacing shadows – these recollection continue to echo in Bergman's mind. Fifty years later, for example, they are combined to create the hallucinatory atmosphere of *Ansikte mot Ansikte* (1975, *Face to Face*), in which a woman (Liv Ullmann), visit-

ing her grandparents, sleeps fitfully among the shadows, cries and whispers of her nursery room. More crucially, *Face to Face* also restages a particular trauma from Bergman's childhood, the severe punishment administered on occasion by his father: the boy would be locked in a cupboard containing, it was asserted, a creature that would bite off his toes. Not surprisingly, the characters in Bergman's films have often been subjected to confinement, sudden outbursts of violence, and almost casual torture.

According to Bergman, his parents were 'sealed in iron casks of duty', his mother running a meticulous household for his father, a Lutheran pastor who was chaplain to the Royal Swedish court. The severity of this upbringing, leading to an inevitable conflict between love and rejection, between faith and doubt, richly and fortuitously provided for Bergman what were to be both the message and the method of his career. He remembered:

'If one is born and brought up in a vicarage one gets an early picture of behind-the-scenes of life and death. Father performed funerals, marriages, baptisms, gave advice and prepared sermons. The devil was an early acquaintance

117

behind it, that we are both victims and instigators, but in the era of the television newsreel it is not an easy truth to share.

'I have worked it out that if I see a film which has a running time of one hour, I sit through 27 minutes of complete darkness. When I show a film I am guilty of deceit. I am using an apparatus which is constructed to take advantage of a certain human weakness, an apparatus with which I can sway my audience in a highly emotional manner – to laugh, scream with fright, smile, believe in fairy stories, become indignant, be shocked, be charmed, be carried away or perhaps yawn with boredom. Thus I am either an imposter or, in the case where the audience is willing to be taken in, a conjurer.'

Bergman's harsh opinion of himself and his work, again a legacy from his Lutheran upbringing, finds illustration in the perpetual doubts and confusions of his chosen characters. Best conveyed by the haggard features of Max Von Sydow, the burden of guilt has also been carried in recent films by Erland Josephson; its opposite, the burden of cold, absolute certainty, has been borne most often in Bergman's work by Gunnar Björnstrand.

Above: the girls of the remand home in Hamnstad *(1948,* Port of Call), *a Bergman film that dealt with social as well as personal issues. Right: Harriet Andersson and Åke Grönburg as a pair of ill-matched lovers in* Sawdust and Tinsel

and in the child's mind there was the need to personify him. This was how the magic lantern came in. It consisted of a little metal box with a carbide lamp (I can still remember the smell of the hot metal) and coloured glass slides – Red Riding Hood and the Wolf and all the others. And the Wolf was the devil, without horns but with a tail and a gaping red mouth, strangely real but yet inapprehensible, a picture of wickedness and temptation on the flowered wall of the nursery.'

Presented with a toy projector when he was ten, Bergman's fascination with images grew:

'This little rickety cinematograph was my first conjuring set. It was strange. The toy was simply a mechanical one and there were always the same little men doing the same thing. I have often wondered what fascinated me so about it, and what still does in exactly the same way. It will suddenly come over me in the studio or in the dimness of the cutting room, as I look at the little frame in front of me, the film running through my fingers . . .'

The spell cast both by the cinematic gadget and by the experiences it could produce is integral to Bergman's work; repeatedly his characters have paused in their remorse to gaze at unexpected dramas, microcosms of their own plight, flickering before them. In *Fängelse* (1949, *Prison*), Birger Malmsten and Doris Svedlund find an old projector in the attic and watch a fragment of silent slapstick directed by Bergman in the style of Méliès and featuring, as Méliès' comedies so often did, a demonic visitation. In *Summarlek* (1951, *Summer Interlude*), another doomed couple watches, during their brief idyll, an animated film. In *Ansiktet* (1958, *The Face*), a tormented illusionist and a dying actor contemplate images thrown by a smoking magic lantern, even mingling with them at one point. And in *Persona* (1966), which briefly resurrects the

silent film from *Prison*, the whole artifice of film itself is analysed, from the flaring carbons providing illumination to the fragile sprocketholes, until it finally falls apart in the despairing director's hands.

In later films, the small screen has logically become that of the television set, although other images confronting Bergman's spectators include enlarged photographs, in *En Passion* (1969, *A Passion*), slides, in *Herbstsonate* (1978, *Autumn Sonata*), and even, in *Vargtimmen* (1968, *Hour of the Wolf*), a tiny model theatre with magically living performers. But the charm has gone, and when his characters stare at the light-shows today it is not to lose themselves but horrifyingly to find something they would prefer to have avoided. In *The Serpent's Egg*, the whirring projector shows stages in the decline and collapse of victims of Nazi experiments with drugs – terrible and violent episodes that are studied with urbane pride by the scientist responsible. Bergman is once again repeating his point that we are all in front of the projector as well as

The key film in the confrontation between conjurer and analyst is *The Face*, in which Von Sydow plays a melancholy travelling showman who may or may not have genuine magical powers and is dissected by the merciless Björnstrand, scalpel in hand. The film came hard on the heels of the two masterpieces, *Det Sjunde Inseglet* (1957, *The Seventh Seal*) and *Smultronstället* (1957, *Wild Strawberries*), which had suddenly established Bergman's international reputation, and it was seen as an ironic comment on the many critics who sought to interpret Bergman's signs and meanings with excessive zeal.

Since *The Face* there have been a number of harrassed illusionists in Bergman's films: the painter in *Hour of the Wolf*, the violinist in *Skammen* (1968, *Shame*), the forger in *A Passion* – all played by Von Sydow. All have been savaged by their environment, their ultimate fate uncertain; in the case of *A Passion*, the central figure is actually pulled apart by the celluloid itself, processed so that his shape is no more than a mass of colour dots on the screen.

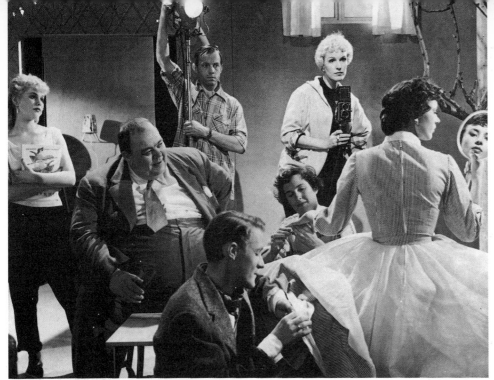

It is an ending which reaffirms Bergman's apology; he is using deceit to portray deception, yet the inexplicable magic remains.

The question of the artist's place in society is one of Bergman's most familiar themes. It can be traced from the broken-hearted ballet-dancer in *Summer Interlude* to the unemployed tightrope-walker in *The Serpent's Egg*, with some particularly emphatic outbursts represented by *För att inte Tala om Alla Dessa Kvinnor* (1964, *Now About These Women*) and *Riten* (1969, *The Rite*). In such films as *Persona* (dealing with a silent stage actress), and *The Shame* (musicians) and *Autumn Sonata* (concert pianist), the art-in-society debate can, however, be seen as part of a more general discussion about the predicament of the average human being in a collapsing environment. Again *The Face* provides a reference point, in the despairing words of the actor:

'I have prayed one prayer in my life: use me. Make use of me. But the Lord never understood how strong and devoted a servant I would have been, so I went unused . . .'

The sense of helplessness refers back to the film by which Bergman is perhaps best known, *The Seventh Seal*, and forward to perhaps his most disregarded film, *Nattvardsgästerna* (1962, *Winter Light*), and again it is linked with his childhood. The search for God – or some acceptable equivalent – haunted the Bergman career up to the point at which, with the trilogy of *Såsom i en Spegel* (1961, *Through a Glass, Darkly*), *Winter Light* and *Tystnaden* (1963, *The Silence*), he appeared to exorcise it. If God insisted on remaining silent, to pursue Him was at worst to risk insanity (Harriet Andersson in *Through a Glass, Darkly* claims to see God as a giant spider) and at best futile (the priest in *Winter Light* is unable to deflect one of his parishoners from suicide). Although hints of both can be found in the later films, particularly in *Viskningar och Rop* (1972, *Cries and Whispers*), with its central character on the brink of death, and in the despondent priest in *The Serpent's Egg*, from *The Silence* onwards Bergman begins to favour a different kind of comfort.

Left: inner suffering in a tranquil setting is conveyed by this close-up of Ingrid Thulin in Winter Light. *Above left: Björnstrand and Max Von Sydow in* The Face. *Above: the demonic inhabitants of the castle as they appear to the artist in* Hour of the Wolf

At the time he escaped from the parental tyranny in 1937, to study literature and art at the University of Stockholm, the only panacea he could find for the pain of agnosticism was the theatre. His first public success was with a stage production of *Macbeth* in 1940, and for two years he was assistant director at the Royal Dramatic Theatre, writing and producing plays. Although Svensk Filmindustri tempted him into screen play-writing in 1942, and them into film direction, Bergman's theatrical work has continued ever since, in startling parallel to his cinema career. His earliest films demonstrated more of a theatrical energy than a cinematic awarness, but by 1947 this had begun to take shape. *Musik i Mörker* (1947, *Night Is My Future*), although written by somebody else, clearly anticipates Bergman's later work not only in its cast (which includes Birger Malmsten, Naima Wifstrand and Gunnar Björnstrand) but also in such assertions as 'Pain and suffering are part of God's design'. With his first original piece for the

screen, *Prison*, his agnostic irony was at its most poisonous: 'Life is only a cruel, meaningless journey from birth to death', stated the film, illustrating its theme with the wrist-slashed suicide of a defeated girl. The Devil rules the world, churches are his allies and God is his own invention.

Fortunately the darkness begins to lift almost immediately, and by the time of *Summer Interlude*, a fine, delicate, complex elegy of a film, Bergman's affection for overstatement has been tempered with subtlety. For the ballet-dancer, the stage is the only compensation for the lover she has lost after one perfect (and very Swedish) summer, but in the course of the film she shows signs of being resurrected from beneath the mask of greasepaint. Himself divorced in 1950, Bergman seemed able to study the processes of love and marriage with a more varied perspective from this point onwards – affectionately in *Sommaren Med Monika* (1953, *Summer With Monika*), sensitively in *Gycklarnas Afton* (1953,

Sawdust and Tinsel), humorously in *En Lektion i Kärlek* (1954, *A Lesson in Love*) and with elegant and memorable irony in *Sommarnattens Leende* (1955, *Smiles of a Summer Night*), which marks the end of the cycle.

The Seventh Seal and *Wild Strawberries* were two journeys through the wasteland that led Bergman's restlessness to a temporary haven. In both films, the only certainty is death, in both the only compensation is the family unit, in both the only unknown is God's ultimate purpose, if any. In *The Seventh Seal*, the knight, trying to discover something of value in the plague-swept country he is about to leave, realizes that the clown's family, eating wild strawberries in the afternoon sun, has found the only available peace of mind. In *Wild Strawberries*, the aged professor, pursuing a solution to his 'death-in-life' problem on a pilgrimage through the territory he knew as a young man, discovers in the evocation of the family birthday party and in the memory of his parents beside a lake in summer the love that slipped so long ago out of his own marriage and left it empty. Marriage alone is hell; marriage as a trinity (with definite holy connections) is salvation.

Bergman was unable to see it quite so simply in his later films in which, more realistically and more courageously, he was prepared to tackle more elusive matters. The signpost was *The Silence*, with its despairing illumination of the obstacles confronting *any* kind of communication between generations, between sexes or between nations. The political events of the Sixties and Seventies increasingly touched upon in his work even it was centred on his island home of Fårö, have seemed to support his argument – culminating in his own flight from the Swedish tax authorities into a cathartic exile. But in *Cries and Whispers*, *Scener ur ett Äktenskap* (1973, *Scenes From a*

Marriage), *Face to Face* and (if perhaps less convincingly) *Autumn Sonata*, he has found the same small crust of comfort. The priest expresses it in *The Serpent's Egg*:

'We live far away from God, so far away that no doubt He doesn't hear us when we pray to Him for help. So we must help each other. We must give each other the forgiveness that a remote God denies us.'

Bergman has not, of course, prepared us for too sympathetic a hearing to the words of his clergymen, but it is intriguing that this viewpoint is consistent with Bergman's own enthusiasm for his work – an enthusiasm which serves also to explain it:

'There is something about the work itself that you get very dependent upon. You are part of a group. If you are a relatively inhibited, shy and timid person like me who has difficulty establishing deeper relations, it's wonderful to live in the collective world of film-making. I think it's an outgrowth of an enormous need for contact. I have a need to influence other people, to touch other people both physically and mentally, to communicate with them.

Below left: Elliott Gould in The Touch, *Bergman's first English-language film. Above: though* Cries and Whispers *was set in the late 19th century, Bergman avoided period 'prettiness', using colour symbolically to suggest the characters' troubled states of mind. Right: Liv Ullmann in a nightmare sequence from* Face to Face, *in which she is terrified by the apparition of her dead grandmother*

Movies, of course, are a fantastic medium through which to touch other human beings, to reach them, to either annoy them or make them happy, to make them sad or to get them to think. To get them started, emotionally. That's probably the truest, deepest reason why I continue to make films.' PHILIP STRICK

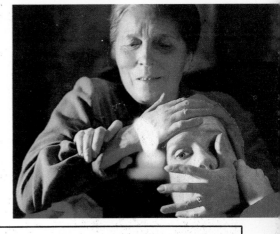

Filmography
1944 Hets (sc; + ass. dir. only) (USA: Torment; GB: Frenzy). **'46** Kris (+ sc) (USA/GB: Crisis); Det Regnar på Vår Kärlek (+ co-sc) (USA: It Rains on Our Love; GB: The Man With an Umbrella). **'47** Kvinna Utan Ansikte (sc. only) (USA/GB: The Woman Without a Face); Skepp till Indialand (+ sc) (USA: The Land of Desire/A Ship to India; GB: Frustration); Musik i Mörker (USA/GB: Night Is My Future). **'48** Hamnstad (+ sc) (USA/GB: Port of Call); Eva (co-sc. only). **'49** Fängelse (+ sc) (USA: Prison/The Devil's Wanton); Törst (USA: Three Strange Loves; GB: Thirst). **'50** Till Glädje (+ sc) (USA/GB: To Joy); Sånt Händer inte Här (USA: This Can't Happen Here; GB: High Tension). **'51** Summarlek (+ co-sc) (USA: Illicit Interlude; GB: Summer Interlude); Frånskild (co-sc. only) (USA/GB: Divorced). **'52** Kvinnors Väntan (+ sc) (USA: Secrets of Woman; GB: Waiting Women). **'53** Sommaren Med Monika (+ co-sc) (USA: Monika; GB: Summer With Monika); Gycklarnas Afton (+ sc) (USA: The Naked Light; GB: Sawdust and Tinsel). **'54** En Lektion i Kärlek (+ sc) (USA/GB: A Lesson in Love). **'55** Kvinnodröm (+ sc) (USA: Dreams; GB: Journey Into Autumn); Sommarnattens Leende (+ sc) (USA/GB: Smiles of a Summer Night). **'56** Sista Paret Ut (co-sc. only) (USA: The Last Couple; GB: Last Pair Out). **'57** Det Sjunde Inseglet (+ sc) (USA/GB: The Seventh Seal); Smultronstället (+ sc) (USA/GB: Wild Strawberries). **'58** Nära Livet (+ co-sc) (USA: Brink of Life; GB: So Close to Life); Ansiktet (+ sc) (USA: The Magician; GB: The Face). **'60** Jungfrukällan (+ sc) (USA/GB: The Virgin Spring); Djänlens Öga (+ sc) (USA/GB: The Devil's Eye). **'61** Såsom i en Spegel (+ sc) (USA/GB: Through a Glass, Darkly); Lustgården (co-sc. only under pseudonym) (USA: The Pleasure Garden). **'62** Nattvardsgästerna (+ sc) (USA/GB: Winter Light). **'63** Tystnaden (+ sc) (USA/GB: The Silence). **'64** För att inte Tala om Alla Dessa Kvinnor (+ co-sc. under pseudonym) (USA: All These Women; GB: Now About These Women). **'66** Persona (+ sc). **'67** Stimulantia *ep* Daniel (+ sc; + photo). **'68** Vargtimmen (+ sc) (USA/GB: Hour of the Wolf); Skammen (+ sc) (USA: The Shame; GB: Shame). **'69** Riten/Ritorna (+ sc) (USA: The Ritual; GB: The Rite) (shot as TV film but shown in cinemas); En Passion (+ sc) (USA: The Passion of Anna; GB: A Passion) (GB retitling for TV: LI82 – A Passion). **'70** Fårödokument (+ sc) (doc) (USA/GB: The Färö Document. **'71** Beröringen (+ sc) (USA-SWED) (USA/GB: The Touch). **'72** Viskningar och Rop (+ sc) (USA/GB: Cries and Whispers). **'73** Scener ur ett Äktenskap (+ sc) (USA/GB: Scenes From a Marriage)*; Trollflötjen (+ sc) (USA/GB: The Magic Flute). **'75** Ansikte mot Ansikte (+ sc; + co-prod) (USA/GB: Face to Face)*. **'77** Das Schlangenei (+ sc) (GER-USA) (USA/GB: The Serpent's Egg); Paradistorg (prod. only) (USA/GB: Summer Paradise). **'78** Herbstsonate (+ sc, uncredited) (GER) (USA/GB: Autumn Sonata). **'80** From the Marionettes (GER).

* *adapted from TV series*

INGMAR BERGMANS

Det sjunde inseglet

1

The Seventh Seal

2

Directed by Ingmar Bergman, 1957
Prod co: Svensk Filmindustri. **sc:** Ingmar Bergman, from his play *Trämaln-ing.* **photo:** Gunnar Fischer. **ed:** Lennart Wallén. **art dir:** P. A. Lundgren. **cost:** Manne Lindholm. **mus:** Erik Nordgren. **ass dir:** Lennart Olsson. **prod man:** Allan Ekelund. **r/t:** 95 minutes. Released in the USA as *The Seventh Seal.*
Cast: Max Von Sydow (*Antonius Block*), Gunnar Björnstrand (*Jöns*), Bengt Ekerot (*Death*), Nils Poppe (*Jof*), Bibi Andersson (*Mia*), Åke Fridell (*Plog*), Inga Gill (*Lisa*), Maud Hansson (*girl-witch*), Inga Landgré (*Block's wife*), Gunnel Lindblom (*mute girl*), Bertil Anderberg (*Raval*), Anders Ek (*monk*), Gunnar Olsson (*painter*), Erik Strandmark (*Skat*), Bengt-Åke Bengtsson (*merchant*), Ulf Johansson (*leader of the soldiers*), Lars Lind (*young monk*), Gudrun Brost (*woman in the tavern*).

7

3

4

8

9

The Seventh Seal was a radio and stage play entitled 'Wood Painting' before becoming the film that finally established Bergman's world-wide reputation. The title of the play refers to religious paintings in medieval churches, showing the Dance of Death, the plague and the sufferings of sinners; the film's title is taken from Block's wife's Bible reading, Revelation/Apocalypse 8:1-2, 7-8, just before Death enters the Knight's castle.

The story, though gripping and suspenseful, is less memorable than the series of great set-pieces that make up most of the film: a knight plays chess with Death in order to prolong his life; victims of the Black Death foam at the mouth or lie dead, a humble juggler/actor named Jof (Joseph), whose wife is Mia (Mary), sees a vision of the Holy Mother and Child; wretched sinners flagellate themselves and each other, while a mad monk preaches a venomous sermon to a crowd; a girl-witch is tortured and burned alive; a lecherous actor, having played dead to save himself from an angry husband, watches help-lessly as Death saws through the bough on which he is sitting; and a group of people from every level of society rise courteously from table to acknowledge that Death has entered the hall.

Despite the grimness of the subject-matter, there is consider-able humour in its treatment, wheth-er dry, as in the squire's cynical remarks, charming, as in those parts featuring the gentle Jof and Mia, or broad, when the low-life triangle of Plog, his wife and the rascally Skat appear. Death himself is not without a sense of humour as when he sneaks up on Skat in his tree.

The evocation of medieval life has a vivid tactile reality rare in historical films that is enhanced rather than limited by the black-and-white photography of Gunnar Fischer. This quality of everyday reality is particularly necessary in a film that is on the edge of allegory and rich in symbolism, most not-ably the chess game that recurs throughout the film until Jof and Mia's temporary escape from Death. They and their baby survive as symbols of regeneration in a world of both physical and moral decay.

Critical assessments of The Sev-enth Seal have been divided. Peter Cowie has dubbed the film 'the richest expression of Bergman's genius', while Robin Wood has claimed that it is 'unsatisfying', a 'public' film, lacking 'inner necess-ity', and that the medieval frame-work makes 'the thematic concerns somewhat remote and schematic'. However Bergman takes pains to present his characters as fully rounded human beings, while the events of the film dramatize time-less (and thus modern) dilemmas, such as the problem of good and evil, the evanescence of life and the meaning of love as conditioned by death.

Bergman's finest films, such as Nattvardsgästerna (1962, Winter Light) and Persona (1966) are not always his most 'perfect' nor his most obviously autobiographical. In The Seventh Seal he achieved a rare balance of forces that places it among his most beautiful and long-lasting films.
DAN MILLAR

A knight, Antonius Block, and his squire, Jöns, have returned from the Crusades and are journeying homeward. Block encounters Death, who claims him for his own. Block challenges Death to a game of chess in order to gain time; Death agrees (1).

The country is beset with plague; disease and desolation are everywhere. Jöns accidentally asks the way from a corpse (2). Block is tortured by doubt concerning the existence of God, brought on by His seeming indifference to human suffering. He confesses to a priest who is Death in disguise (3), and unwittingly reveals the moves he will make which would have won the chess game. Block and Jöns see a girl-witch in the stocks being punished for having had sexual relations with the Devil.

The pair next encounter an ex-priest, Raval, stealing a bracelet from a plague victim. Jöns rescues a mute girl from him and she goes with them. The trio then come across a troupe of entertainers, whose performance (4) is cut short by a religious procession (5). Block meets the family of players (Jof, Mia and their baby) and shares their meal of wild strawberries and milk (6). He invites them to travel with the others to his castle to escape the plague. For the first time Block is content, but Death pays him another visit (7).

The blacksmith Plog joins them; his wife has been seduced by the actor Skat, one of the circus players. They all set off for the castle. Skat returns with Plog's wife but is killed by Death. The company re-encounter the girl-witch about to be burned at the stake.

Jof sees Block playing chess with Death and flees with his family. The rest of the company arrive at the castle and are greeted by Block's wife, (8). At the table they look up (9) to see that Death has come for them (10). Jof, Mia and their child, having escaped from Death, continue their journey (11).

5

6

10

11

Andrzej Wajda

As Poland recovered from the horrors of World War II, Wajda's films strove to construct some hope for the future from the wreckage of the past. This director has continued to explore Polish society with a personal vision that has often been at odds with the political climate of Eastern Europe

Films from the Ashes

At various points in history, particular national cinemas (and thus particular film-makers) move to the centre of critical attention. This happened to Polish cinema in the Fifties with the work of Andrzej Wajda being construed as of special interest and as essentially Polish.

At the political level, Poland became prominent in 1956 with the so-called Polish October, where – unlike in Hungary – the Stalinist apparatus was bloodlessly dismantled. The 'Polish road to socialism' involved a considerable degree of national autonomy which was to make itself felt in many areas of Polish life. For instance, both the subject-matter of Polish films and the organization of the film industry were to benefit from this development. The awarding of a prize at Cannes in 1957 to Wajda's second feature film *Kanał* (1957, *They Loved Life*) rendered Wajda's work and, by extension, Polish cinema highly fashionable in the West.

To a large extent, therefore, the films of Wajda and other Polish directors were removed from their national context and interpreted in terms congenial to critics in other countries. This was unfortunate, for one of the keys to understanding Wajda's work is an awareness of the tradition of Polish Romanticism, of the extent to which Wajda surrenders to its bleaker aspects, and the extent to which he tries to transcend it. With the exception of England, Romanticism in the other countries of Europe was very closely bound up with movements for national self-determination. Where these were thwarted or diverted, the national Romanticism took on a decidedly regressive and unwholesome quality. Thus the denial of full nationhood to Poland from the

eighteenth to the twentieth century created a tradition in its art of doomed foreboding, of heroic martyrdom in the nationalist struggle, and a sometimes delirious cultivation of style and elegance.

Andrzej Wajda was born in 1926 and, as the son of a serving cavalry officer, would have been particularly exposed to this tradition. On the other hand, he came to maturity during World War II, served briefly in one of the Resistance groups, and received his higher

education in post-revolutionary Poland, the ideology of which was adamantly opposed to all the things the Polish Romantic tradition stood for.

The tension between the two ideologies is very evident in Wajda's first feature film, his

Above left: victims of Nazi oppression hide in the sewers in Kanał. *Below: Serge Moulin as a Jewish Resistance fighter in* Samson (1961), *an updated version of the bible story*

Left: sailors lie dying of malaria in Smuga Cienia *(1976,* The Shadow Line). *Above left: an inmate of a concentration camp hangs a crucifix on the wire in* Landscape After Battle. *Above: a young consumptive (Daniel Olbrychski), with only weeks to live, frolics with a girl in* The Birch Wood

Filmography
1950 Keidy ty Śpisz (short) (+sc) (USA/GB: While You Are Asleep); Zy Chopiec (short) (+sc) (USA/GB: The Evil Boy). **'51** Ceramika Iłżecka (short) (+sc) (USA/GB: The Pottery of Hża/Iłża Ceramics). **'53** Trzy Opowieści (sc. only) (USA/GB: Three Stories); Piątka z Ulicy Barskiej (ass. dir. only) (USA/GB: Five Boys From Barska Street). **'55** Pokolenie (USA/GB: A Generation/ Light in the Darkness); Idę ku Słońcu (doc) (+sc) (USA/GB: I Go Towards the Sun). **'57** Kanal (USA: They Loved Life). **'58** Popiol i Diament (+co-sc) (USA/GB: Ashes and Diamonds). **'59** Lotna (+co-sc). **'60** Niewinni Czarodzieje (USA/GB: Innocent Sorcerers). **'61** Samson (+co-sc). **'62** Sibirska Ledi Magbet (YUG) (USA: Fury Is a Woman; GB: Siberian Lady Macbeth/Lady Macbeth of Mtsenk); L'Amour à Vingt Ans *ep* Warsaw (FR/IT-JAP-POL). **'65** Popioły (USA/GB: Ashes). **'67**

diploma film at the State Film School in Lodz, *Pokolenie* (1955, *A Generation*). Its theme of the growth to personal and political maturity of a young working-class layabout was a common one in socialist realist art since the Thirties. It is an extremely good film at every level and one can easily understand its wide appeal to politically committed critics in the West: its obviously socio political theme; its assured handling of the resources of cinema; the superb playing of its actors; and its obvious 'poetry' and unashamed simplicity of feeling. But perhaps it is more interesting in its contradictions, the central of which is its veering between socialist realism, rational, progressive, optimistic, on the one hand, and on the other, Polish Romanticism, regressive and pessimistic.

This opposition is clearest between the two central figures in the film, Stach (Tadeusz Lomnicki) and Jasio (Tadeusz Janczar). 'If the film's 'head' is with Stach in his movement towards maturity and enrolment in the Communist Resistance group, its 'heart' is assuredly with Jasio. The death of Jasio provides one of the great set-pieces of the film. Fleeing from the Germans, Jasio retreats up a spiral staircase, emptying his gun at his pursuers. Reaching the top, he opens a wooden door to find his way

barred by a locked grill (this image of confinement recurs in Wajda's later work, most notably in *Kanał*). He climbs onto the bannister, balances himself precariously, then commits suicide by hurling himself into the well of the staircase. The care with which this scene is mounted and its emotional force in the film as a whole suggests that Wajda had invested a lot of himself in it.

The scale of Wajda's second film *Kanał*, is much more ambitious and marks a significant advance in his handling of the medium. It features a large number of characters and relationships and has a bolder *mise-en-scène* – for example, the very lengthy opening tracking shot within which the members of the military unit are introduced. At the same time, however, the commentary over this shot – 'Look at these men and women. We are going to watch them die' – indicates the extent to which the film will surrender to the atavistic Romanticism which is held in balance in *A Generation*. Because it was made in 1957, *Kanał* could take a much more sympathetic view of the nationalist underground army than could *A Generation*, one of the weaknesses of which is the parodic view it takes of that group. Paradoxically, however, the liberalizing of the

political climate in Poland cleared the way for Wajda to indulge all his Romantic predispositions. Nevertheless, despite its Romantic excesses (recurrent images of doomed, young people dying heroically for Poland in the sewers of Warsaw), *Kanał* is a film of undeniable power. *Popiół i Diament* (1958, *Ashes and Diamonds*) is generally considered to be Wajda's most considerable work. In it he explicitly brings into collision the two traditions which shaped his artistic growth. The film is set during the last day of World War II and the first day of peace. Its central figures are two young nationalist underground fighters who are on a mission to kill a visiting Communist leader. By mistake they kill two workers, and then hang around the visiting leader's hotel until the younger of the two gets a chance to kill the old man. He is himself subsequently killed.

A bare outline gives little indication of the complexity of *Ashes and Diamonds*, of how it weaves together its complex narrative, bringing the large cast of characters into relationship with each other so that a complete cross-section of Polish society is presented – communist and non-communist, aristocrat and worker, old bourgeois and new party bureau-

often considered to surpass the English versions by Laurence Olivier and Peter Brook.

Other classic adaptations were Josif Heifitz's version of Chekhov's *Lady With a Little Dog* (1959); Ivan Pyriev's *The Idiot* (1958), after Dostoyevsky; and Sergei Yutkevitch's *Othello* (1955) and *The Bath House* (1962), from Mayakovsky's famous satirical comedy.

Yulia Soltntseva, the widow of the great director, Dovzhenko, brought to the screen several of his unfilmed scenarios, including *Poem of the Sea* (1958) and *The Flaming Years* (1961); unfortunately their quality did not make up much for the destruction, years before, of Dovzhenko's career by Stalin's personal hostility. Mikhail Romm, who was the first to present an adulatory image of Stalin on the screen in *Lenin in October* (1937), became one of the fiercest post-Stalin reformers of the Soviet cinema, to which he contributed such important films as *Nine Days of One Year* (1961), concerning the work and love problems of nuclear physicists.

The hopes of Soviet film-makers during the late Fifties remained mostly unfulfilled. The liberalization under Khrushchev did not go far enough to allow for truly personal expression, really individual styles or subjective approaches. It soon became all too clear that the bulk of mainstream production would have to continue serving the purposes of state propaganda and indoctrination of the masses, although in a more sophisticated and subtle way than before.

The most important reaction against the Stalinist and Cold War years, and against socialist realism, occurred in Poland, which had been struggling against Russian domination for centuries. The first breakthrough was by the veteran Aleksander Ford, with *Piątka z Ulicy Barskiej* (1953, *Five Boys From Barska Street*), about the rehabilitation of a group of young delinquents; the film was stylistically influenced by the French cinema of the period. Ford's later and better-known *Krzyzacy* (1960, *Knights of the Teutonic Order*), which commemorated the fourteenth-century battle of Grünwald, was a colourful patriotic epic, made primarily to appeal to the nationalism of Polish audiences, but with an eye on the popular international market.

But three younger directors, Andrzej Munk, who died prematurely at 40, Andrzej Wajda and Jerzy Kawalerowicz, were mainly responsible for creating the 'Polish school'. They were concerned with analysing, criticizing and, quite often, de-romanticizing Polish history, particularly the recent war years.

Andrzej Munk, in his memorable *Człowiek na Torze* (1956, *Man on the Track*), told of a simple engine-driver who is attacked and persecuted because he is old and resistant to change. He becomes a hero, however, when he perishes on the tracks while preventing a train crash. Poland was in a state of political crisis, with public demonstrations and a change of government; and the film became

symbolic of the tragic years that preceded its production. It also introduced the subjective perception of a disintegrating world of reality, which would have been impossible in the Stalinist cinema, since it emphasized the viewpoint of the individual.

Until his accidental death in 1961, Munk continued his examination of the Polish past: *Eroica* (1957) was a two-episode feature film consisting of a comedy set in wartime Warsaw and an ironic tragedy in a prisoner-of-war camp; and *Zezowate Szczęście* (1960, *Bad Luck*) was a satirical portrait of a dedicated but unsuccessful follower of political fashion, who is always out of step with the march of time. His last film was the unfinished *Pasażerka* (1961, *Passenger*) completed and released in 1963, about two women, a prisoner and a guard, in a concentration camp. With his deep and almost grotesque sense of irony and contradiction, Munk was convinced that thorough demystification of the past liberated both society and individuals.

Since *Pokolenie* (1955, *A Generation*), Andrzej Wajda has established himself progressively as one of the world's leading film-makers. He dominated the Polish film scene; his films provoked a succession of conflicts, among critics, officials and audiences. But he always managed to preserve his own artistic integrity and to create a consistently personal body of work.

Wajda completed a war 'trilogy' with his second and third films, *Kanał* (1957) and *Popiół i Diament*

Above: Sergei Bondarchuk adopts a war-orphan in Destiny of a Man. *Below left: Alexei Batalov is a wrongly accused man cleared by his workmates in Heifitz's* The Rumiantsev Case *(1955). Below: Tatiana Samoilova mourns her lover, killed at the front line, in* The Cranes Are Flying, *Kalatozov's wartime romance*

talents – Polanski is best known for *Rosemary's Baby* (1968) and *Chinatown* (1974), Skolimowski for *Deep End* (1970). The two most brilliant Polish animators of the Fifties, Jan Lenica and Walerian Borowczyk, also left their native country for the West.

Czechoslovakia after World War II inherited a long cinematic tradition and intact production facilities, including the Barrandov Studios in Prague. Yet it did not emerge into the mainstream of post-Stalinist film-making as quickly as Poland, and not as impressively until the Sixties. The 'first thaw' around 1956 brought renewed life to such established directors as Jiří Weiss and Jiří Krejčik but belonged mainly to the younger Zbyněk Brynych, formerly Weiss's assistant, whose first film was *Žižkovská Romance* (1958, A Local Romance), and Vojtěch Jasný, whose poetic, four-episode film, *Touha* (1958, Desire), was the most radical denial of the restrictive philosophy and aesthetics of the preceding years. Jan Kadár had collaborated

---

The revival of Eastern European cinema led to a reassessment of wartime experiences and new hopes for the future, expressed in love stories and social dramas

---

(1958, *Ashes and Diamonds*). In the 'trilogy' he dealt with the years of Nazi occupation and the resistance. His style was a blistering mixture of the deeply romantic and the elaborately symbolic. His combination of vivid realism with expressionistic vision was too rich and contradictory for some Polish critics. He reopened the nation's still unhealed wounds, capturing the hopelessness of the 'moments of truth' at which people seem to perceive truth clearly but are unable to act effectively.

Jerzy Kawalerowicz made an early impression with such films as *Celuloza* (1954, A Night of Remembrance) and *Pod Gwiazda Frygijska* (1954, Under the Phrygian Star), about the growth of a young peasant's consciousness. But he is mostly remembered for an artistically successful version of the 'Devils of Loudun' story, *Matka Joanna od Aniołów* (1961, *Mother Joan of the Angels*). In his hands the story became an aesthetically beautiful metaphor for intolerance and dogmatism – the destroyers of both inquisitors and victims.

Despite occasional later successes, and Wajda's continuing struggle for his artistic identity and relevance to the changing times, in general the Polish school died as quickly as it had emerged. It was repressed in the 'restoration of order' which, in the early Sixties, succeeded the agitated and relatively liberal post-Stalin years. The best of a later generation, such as Roman Polanski and Jerzy Skolimowski, mostly went abroad to develop their

with Elmar Klos since 1952; but their four features of the Fifties were little-known abroad compared with their Academy Award-winning *Obchod na Korze* (1965, *A Shop on the High Street*).

Shortly after the 'first thaw' had been brought to a halt in the late Fifties, a deep economic and political crisis undermined the repressive cultural policy of the establishment and provided an unexpected degree of freedom for Czechoslovak art and culture in the Sixties. Similarly, the fresh revival of the Hungarian cinema after the crushing of the Revolution in 1956 did not come until seven or eight years later. In Yugoslavia, film-making had to start again from scratch after World War II and, slowly developing over the years into an original culture, did not achieve a period of great blossoming until the end of the Sixties.

East Germany built up its post-war film industry on the ruins of the Nazi-controlled Ufa company. In the early years of the new Defa company, there was a brief revival of early German expressionist and realist trends to challenge the tradition, still predominant as in the Nazi period, of film as an instrument of propaganda and indoctrination. Though the ideology was now communist, the same strict surveillance as before rapidly prevailed, even over simple love-stories and films for children. Film in East Germany, uniquely in Eastern Europe, has never allowed for the emergence of individual styles, a subjective approach to reality or untamed

Top: The battle of Grünwald in Aleksander Ford's Knights of the Teutonic Order. *Above: Grigori Kozintsev filming on location. Below: Ya Savina as the* Lady With a Little Dog, *based on Chekhov's story. Below right: Alexei Batalov as the son in Donskoy's version (1956) of Gorky's* Mother

Above: Five Boys From Barska Street *catch a would-be saboteur under a new highway. Above right: Izolda Izvitskaya played the Red Army sharpshooter whose lover was the 41st victim of her skill in Chukhrai's remake of the silent film classic,* The Forty-First *(1956) Below: Edward Dziewonski dodges a faithless wife and German tanks as a resistance fighter during the September 1944 Warsaw uprising in* Eroica. *Below right: in* Na Malkya Ostrov, *prisoners attempt to escape after the abortive left-wing Bulgarian rising of 1923*

and ironic laughter.

The major exception, Konrad Wolf, son of a leading German anti-fascist writer, spent his child-hood in Moscow and returned to Germany with the Soviet army in 1945. Because of his model personal history and the strength of his talent, Wolf alone was able to create in the years since 1955 an individual body of work, rarely sinking into the lower depths of Defa-type conformism. The best of his early films included *Lissy* (1957) and *Sterne* (1959, *Stars*; a co-production with Bulgaria), both set in the Nazi era. *Stars* was a tragic love-story, which attacked anti-Semitism, and became an international prize-winner.

The twin Cinderellas of the East European cinema have been Romania and Bulgaria. After 1945 they had to start building up industrial facilities for film-making and also to learn basic crafts. Romania's first international impact was with the animated films of Ion Popescu-Gopo, prize-winners in the Fifties. But the outstanding talents (who doubled as theatre directors), such as Liviu Ciulei and espe-cially Lucian Pintilie, did not emerge until the Sixties and have since been exiled and confined to working in the theatre. Otherwise almost nothing of interest came out of the technically well-equipped Bucharest studios.

In Bulgaria, by contrast, the lesson of modern film-making was learned rather well, despite per-iodical crackdowns on nonconformist directors and consequent lack of continuity in their careers. The first internationally important film was Rangel Vulchanov's *Na Malkya Ostrov* (1958, On the Little Island) and Vulchanov also worked on Wolf's *Stars*. Under the influence of the 'Polish school' and the French *nouvelle vague*, he did much to pull the Bulgarian cinema out of its provincialism. Bulgaria's biggest international success was to come in the Sixties with Vulo Radev's *Kradetsat na Praskovi* (1964, *The Peach Thief*), a doomed romantic story of love across national barriers during World War I.
ANTONIN LIEHM

Method in their acting

Influenced by new ideas developed by Stanislavsky in Russia, American movie actors began to develop a style of performance that would capture the truth of human experience more directly

Melodrama was the predominant form of popular dramatic theatre when, after 1900, the cinema discovered dramatic narrative. So melodrama provided both a source of film material and a style of presentation. Actors in movies often came from the popular theatre; but even the classic theatre of Europe relied on the elaborate gestures and exaggerated mannerisms which were the hallmark of melodrama. The so-called 'signal acting' could interpret anything from Shakespeare to music-hall songs. It also fitted the requirements of early narrative cinema. When cameras did not move and the actors could not be heard, emphatic gestures and mannerisms expressed the profound emotions – shock, fear, jealousy, anger, love – which were the meat of popular silent film dramas.

With the coming of sound, film borrowed more parasitically from theatre. Successful plays, writers, directors and actors all crossed the continent to Hollywood. But many performers were completely changed by the experience as the techniques of stage and screen acting began to diverge rapidly: for example, James Cagney was transformed from song-and-dance man to weaselly gangster.

During the Thirties, America had the largest and richest entertainment industry in the world, and was also a cultural melting pot. It was open to the influence of traditions from the countries supplying it with immigrants. American theatre and cinema attracted directors, actors and writers from all over the world so that the performing arts mirrored a multitude of diverse cultural trends. The most significant was a general notion that art should reflect real life.

The growth of education, the political upheavals between the wars and the mass media as instantaneous news transmitters all impelled drama towards social awareness and didacticism. The development of psychology and sociology challenged traditional ideas about character and the depiction of human relationships. Where the performing arts had once sought to provide entertainment or spiritual enlightenment, they now aimed at relevance to the real world and authenticity of representation. The goal of such art was to be found, as before, in a quest for 'truth.' But the artist's idea of truth, and how it was to be discovered, did change.

In cinema, the first change was in the development of 'technological' realism. Sophisticated editing techniques, better film stock and lighting, more sensitive and mobile cameras and sound equipment freed the movie actor from the need to signal each emotion, reaction or plot development with an emphatic gesture or an exaggerated intonation. A close-up, a pan, a judicious piece of editing or the *mise-en-scène* in a deep-focus shot did much of the work the actor had once performed. Action or plot may not have been truer to life, but the development of film language made the director less reliant on actors' techniques.

On the other hand, audiences became more vividly aware of individual actors: they could see them from all angles and a wide range of apparent

distances; they heard them whisper or shout. The star-system ensured that the voices of many leading actors would be distinctive, in the manner of Cagney, James Stewart, Cary Grant or Bette Davis. All this made actors, especially stars, seem curiously familiar: the role then became an extension of the actor's persona, convincing because of the actor's apparent 'reality' and naturalness, however unlikely the plot and script.

So screen-actors ran the gamut of artistic extremes. Sometimes they dominated their films by a magnified presence and individual persona; sometimes they merely served as the passive instrument of a particularly subtle or brilliant director. Hitchcock's aphorism, 'Actors should be treated like cattle', reminds us how the director can elicit resonant performances by manipulating the screen personas of good actors like Grant, Stewart and

Above: a breathtaking scene from The Little Witness *(c.1900) by a pioneer of the 'Brighton school', George Albert Smith, shot in his Hove studio. Note the stagy posed gestures, the painted backdrop and the influence of theatrical melodrama. Below: Michael Chekhov plays the Jewish father-in-law of a pretty Irish-American girl (Joanne Dru) in Edward A. Sutherland's 1946 remake of* Abie's Irish Rose. *Chekhov, an exponent of Stanislavsky's teachings in America, is probably best remembered as the old psychiatrist in Hitchcock's* Spellbound *(1945)*

Henry Fonda. Sometimes a director and a star worked together to create a believable synthesis of actor and role. George Cukor's direction of Judy Garland in *A Star Is Born* (1954) is commonly cited as an example, although there are many others. It should be noted that these collaborations are memorable only because the two extremes are so much more common.

The 'realism' of the narrative cinema during Hollywood's 'golden age' was largely an illusion created by new techniques and an elaborate publicity machine. In other areas of film, reality was approached with much more reverence. The documentary movement experimented with the use of non-professional actors in drama-documentaries based on the work or social life of real communities. This sort of social realism was a natural, if not entirely logical, extension of the search for authenticity and relevance. In one sense, it merely confirms the idea of the cinema as a director's rather than an actor's medium; but, blended with the visual sense of a Bresson or of a post-war neo-realist director like Rossellini, it has often given a hard edge to subject-matter that might otherwise have been trite, sentimental or at best vacuously beautiful. Nonetheless, the use of non-professional actors is still seen (notably on television) as one means to portray an authentic social reality which traditional narrative film-making has tended to ignore or distort.

The American stage began to experiment with another means towards achieving less stylized performances during the Thirties; eventually much of the modern cinema felt its influence. In 1912, the Russian actor and drama theorist, Constantin Stanislavsky, set up the First Studio at the Moscow Art Theatre to develop and teach a radical new approach to acting. His early experience coincided with the growth of realism in the Russian theatre, exemplified by Anton Chekhov and Maxim Gorky. Stanislavsky had worked with both playwrights, who represented the two poles of the realist theatre, psychological realism (Chekhov) and social realism (Gorky).

Stanislavsky placed the actor at the centre of dramatic creativity. In his elaborate system, involving deep imaginative study of the psychologies of characters, the actor was almost required to become the role. His actors lived communally so that they could rehearse and improvise freely. Stanislavsky tried to systematize, through arduous exercises, the ability of great actors to convince an audience in their roles. The aim was an authenticity which transcended mere mimicry.

Interestingly, this approach converged with mainstream Hollywood acting. In the Method, actors become identified with characters; in Hollywood, the role dissolved into the actor's persona. In the Fifties, Lee Strasberg, who was one of Stanislavsky's most influential American disciples, defended the so-called 'Method' which he and his colleagues had based on Stanislavsky's system. He argued that stars like Gary Cooper, John Wayne and Spencer Tracy were, in effect, Method actors, since they 'try to be themselves and do and say what is consonant with their own characters'. For Strasberg, it did not seem to matter much from which direction came the sense of watching a 'real' person on the stage, whether the actor became the character or the character conformed to the actor.

Several of Stanislavsky's students moved to America between 1917 and 1939. Maria Ouspenskaya and Richard Boleslavsky helped persuade Strasberg, Stella Adler and Harold Clurman to set up the Group Theatre, founded 1931. This combined Stanislavskian techniques of psychological realism with a belief in theatre's social mission. Actors who graduated from the Group Theatre to Hollywood included Elia Kazan, Lee J. Cobb, John Garfield and Franchot Tone. Michael Chekhov, Anton's nephew, came to live in America in 1939; his studio theatre productions featured, among others, Yul Brynner and Hurd Hatfield. Moving to Hollywood, he taught and also acted, for example in

---

Actors lived, loved and worked together in an all-out effort to bring the characters they played to vivid breathing life

---

Hitchcock's *Spellbound* (1945), until his death in 1955.

Before 1945, the impact of Stanislavskian techniques in Hollywood was minimal. The very newness of Stanislavsky's ideas and the conflicting interpretations of them seemed alien and difficult. All exponents of Stanislavsky's system in America agreed in opposing the commercial establishments of Broadway and Hollywood. Besides, Hollywood's self-image at first militated against new acting techniques. While the boom lasted, the film industry had no need of radical ideas, or of the intimacy and versatility of the Stanislavsky-trained actor. Such actors, in their screen assignments, usually ended up as character actors or, worse still, caricature actors.

The post-war period brought changes. Labour disputes and anti-trust legislation upset the industry. Audiences shrank, more so with the growing popularity of television. A protectionist European film industry bit further into Hollywood's profits, while the anti-communist witch-hunts instigated by the House Un-American Activities Committee (HUAC) brought a chaos of unemployment, guilt, recrimination and betrayal. Efforts to pull Hollywood out of its doldrums included low-budget productions using new talent and relying on the documentary-type realism so successful in Europe. Their ingredients preferably were a good script, a small cast, small sets or lots of location work and a small theme eschewing grandiose ideas. Contemporary social life and psychological drama were perfect subjects, and the theatre provided suitable raw material.

In 1947, Elia Kazan, an actor turned stage and screen director, with Cheryl Crawford and Robert Lewis, formed the Actors' Studio in New York (Lewis left shortly and was replaced in the teaching trio by Lee Strasberg). The Actors' Studio was mainly an advanced study centre for experienced

Above: George Cukor, the director, with Judy Garland on the set of A Star Is Born *(1954). Cukor said that Garland had never before played a serious role with highly charged emotional scenes. She brought much of her own personality to the part. Below: Jack Garfein's* The Strange One *(1957) was based on Calder Willingham's novel and play about a Southern military academy,* End as a Man. *Most of the cast, which included Ben Gazzara, George Peppard, James Olson, Pat Hingle, Larry Gates and Julie Wilson, seen here in rehearsal, were Actors' Studio members and had played in the stage version*

actors. The techniques of improvisation, 'affective memory' and character building practised at the Studio were by Stanislavsky out of the Group Theatre, although Michael Chekhov in Hollywood and Stella Adler in New York had developed divergent interpretations, stressing imagination over immersion in the character's being. The Studio called its training a 'Method' out of deference for the irreplaceable role Stanislavsky's own practice played in the development of his theories. Despite the dissent of other Stanislavskian disciples, a new orthodoxy grew up as the so-called 'Method school' of acting.

Theoretically, there was no Method acting as such – only a flexible and informal rehearsal process aimed at psychological realism. In practice, through association with particular actors, writers and directors, the Method became identified with a brooding intensity suggestive of dark neurotic emotions. Marlon Brando typified the Method hero – surly, dishevelled and contemptuous of established values. His appearance in Kazan's 1951 film of Tennessee Williams' play, *A Streetcar Named Desire*, provided the perfect image of the Method. Hollywood loved it. It was scandalous, sexy, raw and compelling. It fitted the doom-laden, youth-centred mood of the time. Above all, it was economical to produce.

Kazan's professional stock went up when he testified before HUAC the following year, recanting his youthful Communist Party beliefs and naming names. He nurtured Brando's rebellious image and gave employment to several Actors' Studio members. The Studio soon became the hub of a new creative movement, involving a whole generation of actors: James Dean, Paul Newman, Geraldine Page, Carroll Baker, Eli Wallach, Rod Steiger, Eva Marie Saint, Ben Gazzara, Marilyn Monroe and Jane Fonda, among others.

During a time of Hollywood crisis, the stage seemed to reassert its originality and seniority. But Hollywood's version of the Method had eventually little to do with Stanislavsky's bold experiments. The unambiguous radical ambition of the defunct Group Theatre vanished. The Actors' Studio, on the ascendant, dropped any pretensions to social realism and busied itself in a crude but politically uncontroversial psychologizing. Hollywood continued to condemn the youthful rebelliousness, violence and amorality of its new heroes and themes while profiting greatly from a string of films portraying them. The *Wild One* (1953), *On the Waterfront* (1954), *East of Eden*, *The Blackboard Jungle*, *Rebel Without a Cause*, (all three 1955). *Baby Doll* (1956) and a number of the films of Williams' plays all followed *Streetcar* into the territory of moral uncertainty, sexual promiscuity and brutal violence. The films were influenced by neo-realism, and the performances invariably resonated against their settings and period. But the authenticity for which the Method had striven now conveyed only a subjective mood rather than a social reality.

The confusion between actor and role became total with the success of Method-trained actors like Brando and Dean. Both role and actor dissolved, leaving nothing but a hollow symbolism of the inarticulate pain and anger which characterized the Fifties. Brando merged into Dean who merged into Newman . . . and so on. Their success kept alive a tradition of liberalism in Hollywood and a few of these actors went on to better performances in better films. Others declined, once again, into character parts or self-caricatures. Hollywood in the Fifties could not provide the Method with a fertile soil for growth. Curiously, the tension between theatricality and cinematic technique magnified the presence of leading players so that, against a background in which social issues were replaced by moral issues, their efforts to convey a psychological reality gave every impression of melodramatic acting.

GARY HERMAN

Left and above: two versions of Tennessee Williams' A Streetcar Named Desire, with Marlon Brando and both directed by Elia Kazan. In the 1947 stage production, Jessica Tandy played Blanche Dubois; Vivien Leigh took the part in the 1951 film. Rather than 'opening up' the play, Kazan decided that the film should adhere closely to the text and atmosphere of the theatre production. Below: Lee Strasberg made one of his rare screen appearances in Francis Ford Coppola's The Godfather, Part II (1974), based on Mario Puzo's novel about the Mafia. Strasberg played a top-ranking gangster and is seen here with Al Pacino, who had the role of the young godfather, Michael Corleone

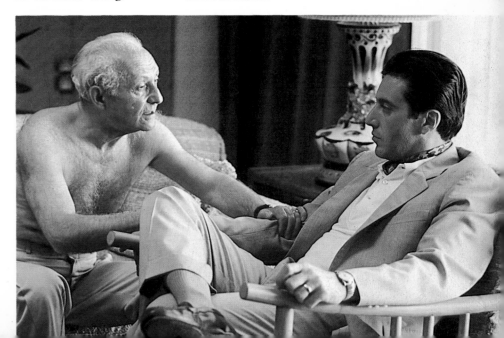

A Rebel Named Brando

When Marlon Brando went to Hollywood his challenging style of acting became the controversial symbol of new hopes for American culture. Since the Fifties, he has brought to the screen a range of memorable characters – from Stanley Kowalski to Superman's father

Nowadays, one approaches a performance by Marlon Brando with a certain trepidation. Will he have bothered to learn his lines, or will he, as is his recent want, pin bits and pieces of the script to the set, so that the problem of memorization will not, as he claims, interfere with the process of creation? Will he be merely overweight, or will he be completely grossed out – as he was in *Apocalypse Now* (1979)? Will he focus his full concentration on the role, or will he content himself with what amounts to self-parody?

It seemed for a short time in the early Seventies, after *The Godfather* (1972) and *Ultimo Tango a Parigi* (1972, *Last Tango in Paris*), that he had not merely returned to form, but attained a new one – an ability to literally act his age – and that such tense questions might finally be rendered moot. Ah, foolish optimism! How could we have forgotten that the very basis of his screen character, the source of its fascination, lies in his childishly erratic, entirely anarchical nature. Brando would not be Brando if you could count on him. From the beginning we have attended his work not in search of seamless technical perfection, but as we do a thrill act at a carnival. We go to see him dive down into the depths of himself, to see if he will surface with some new pearls of existential awareness or a heap of rusting mannerism or, more likely, a

couple of the former mixed with a lot of the latter. If you cannot stand the sometimes instantaneous alternations between exasperation and exhilaration which he thus induces, then you have no business at a Brando film – which is, of course, a position many have adopted.

About the deepest sources of his wild ways one can only speculate. But about one of the matters that has driven him crazy, right from the start of his career, there can be no doubt. That is his unsought position as a hero of a special modern sort, a *cultural* hero, burdened with the large, if ill-defined, hopes of at least two generations for the renewal of American acting, and through it, of the American theatre, American films, perhaps even of American culture. It was not a role he sought! It was, indeed, a role he fought. And yet, somehow, it settled upon him.

Brando's Method

Brando, a high-school dropout, came more or less accidentally to acting, and he enjoyed an early success in it before developing a sense of vocation. He was thus forced to confront the personal and public demands of his profession without an aesthetic or a sense of cultural tradition. This gap was filled by the 'Method', that American variation on Stanislavky's theories, which was very much in the air in

New York when Brando was breaking into the theatre. Emerging from small parts into the unforgettable glory of his Stanley in *A Streetcar Named Desire*, he was seen as the personification of 'Method' principles (though, in truth, he had passed only briefly through its cathedral, the Actors' Studio). And since his own instinctive method – a search through memory for psychological truth, a rejection of classic manner and technique, squared with the 'Method', ('You have to upset yourself! Unless you do you cannot act'), the role of leader in a generational revolt was imposed upon him. American provincialism was to be shaken off; English acting standards would no longer go unchallenged.

Many in the older generation were appalled, but if you were young and cared about the mystery of acting, then Brando's singularity – there really never had been anyone quite like him – exercised a powerful symbolic hold on your imgination. Indeed, some part of you became his forever. And when he went out to Hollywood, hope mingled with fear over what would result. Would he revolutionize the place, or succumb to it. In the event, he remained . . . himself. That is to say, volatile and difficult, brilliant and indifferent. But there was no gainsaying the impact of his work in those first films, which were widely variable in their overall quality: the crippled war veteran in *The Men* (1950), the brutal Stanley Kowalski in *A Streetcar Named Desire* (1951), the Mexican revolutionary in *Viva Zapata!* (1952), the motorbike rebel in *The Wild One* (1953) and the ex-boxer in *On the Waterfront* (1954) – in these pictures he gave us moments which had never been seen on the screen before. For young

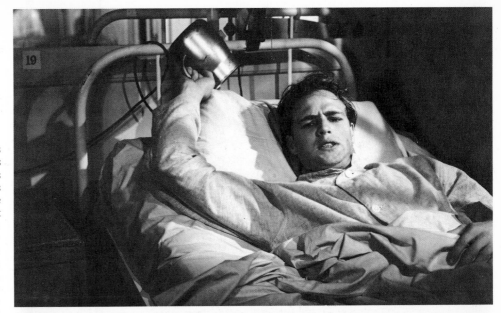

Opposite page: one of the exciting aspects of Marlon Brando's acting is his ability to transform his whole presence into the character he is portraying – from Stanley Kowalski in A Streetcar Named Desire *(far left) to the Mafia chief in* The Godfather *(left). Right: for* The Men, *he spent some weeks in a wheelchair learning how it feels to be a paraplegic. It was his first chance to try Method acting on the screen*

people his sullen, inarticulate rebelliousness won them to him forever. Even when he was playing brutes and dummies you sensed his vulnerability, his tentativeness, and, even, his underlying sweetness and sense of comedy. He was the first movie star who showed, right there on the screen, the truth behind the image – the insecurity and the nagging, peculiarly American fear that acting may not be suitable work for a grown-up heterosexual male. He was exploring what no-one else had explored.

In his first great role, that of Stanley Kowalski in *A Streetcar Named Desire*, people identified Brando with the image he played. Few heard him when he said:

'Kowalski was always right, and never afraid . . . He never wondered, he never doubted. His ego was very secure. And he had that kind of brutal aggressiveness I hate . . . I'm afraid of it. I detest the character.'

Stanley was crass, calculating and materialist – a type who was a factor in every aspect of American life in this century. The power of Brando's performance derives from his hatred and fear of the character, though manifestly there is something of Brando's own egotism and rudeness in Stanley too.

Winds of change

Brando found Hollywood – a town always full of Kowalskis – in a state of transition. The reliable mass market was slipping away to television; the factory system, ruled by a handful of industry 'pioneers', was losing its sovereignty to stars and directors who were, with the help of powerful agencies, creating their own packages. Brando had a long-term contract with Fox, but he fought the studio constantly and, unlike the older generation of stars, had the option to make independent films, so he could not be disciplined by suspensions or blacklisting. In addition he did not dress like a star, could not be coerced into interviews or publicity gimmicks he found demeaning. 'The only thing an actor owes his public is not to bore them' he declared.

The men who ruled Hollywood, quite rightly, distrusted Brando. They might talk about his manner and style (or lack of it) but deep down, they knew he was on to them, was parodying them on the screen. Still, through *On the Waterfront* an uneasy truce was maintained between Brando and Hollywood, if only because until that picture was finished – and they rewarded him with an Oscar – he stuck close to the type they had decided was correct for him and which was easily saleable – brooding, capable of brutality, yet gropingly sensitive and rebelious. Indeed, Terry Malloy, the ex-boxer, betrayed by his brother in *On the Waterfront*, seemed to many at the time a painfully accurate projection of Brando's own mood. When he says 'I could have been a contender . . . instead of a bum', some took this as an admission that the great roles were not for him. Others saw it as a generational

Above: Brando brought new depth – and an English accent – to Fletcher Christian, the officer who confronts Captain Bligh (Trevor Howard) in Mutiny on the Bounty. *Left: One Eyed Jacks shows up the images of male strength and violence used in Westerns*

lament, a declaration of betrayal not merely by an institution, but by the whole society in which humane, liberal values now seemed inadequate to a monstrously complex age.

Nevertheless, he won an Academy Award for *On the Waterfront* and continued to maintain himself as his contemporaries hoped he would – an inner-directed man in an other-directed world. There was, however, one big change in him. He no longer wanted to play roles that were projections of himself or even of his earlier image. In Terry Malloy he had achieved a kind of apotheosis; he now wanted to prove he could submerge self in characters. He undertook a staggering variety of roles from 1954 onwards: a Damon Runyon gambler in *Guys and Dolls* (1955); Napoleon in *Desiree* (1954); Sakini, the Japanese interpreter in *The Teahouse of the August Moon* (1956); the Southern soldier fighting his own racial prejudice in *Sayonara* (1957); the German soldier undergoing self-induced de-Nazification in *The Young Lions* (1958); the vengeful good-bad man in *One Eyed Jacks* (1961) and Fletcher Christian in *Mutiny on the Bounty* (1962).

Some of these pictures were successful at the box-office; some were not. There was a steady muttering about his waste of himself in subjects that, for the most part, were drawn from the less exalted ranges of popular fiction. In fact, he was playing a higher risk game than the critics knew, for his price was now something like a million dollars a picture in return for which he was supposed, by his presence, to guarantee a profit. What other actor would have risked that status in roles which were deliberately off-type and which caused him to use weird makeups and strange accents?

Gillo Pontecorvo, who directed him in *Queimada!* (1969, *Burn!*), declared, 'I never saw an actor before who was so afraid of the camera.' His hatred of publicity, his desire to hide-out in roles was based, in part, on simple shyness. Moreover, the kind of acting he was now doing demanded less of him emotionally, if more of him technically. As he said:

'There comes a time in one's life when you don't want to do it anymore. You know a scene is coming where you'll have to cry and scream and all those things, and it's always bothering you, always eating away at you . . . and you just can't walk through it . . . it would be disrespectful not to try to do your best.'

So he settled for imitations of life, which was not only easy for him, but fun. Acting at this level, he has been heard to say, is 'a perfectly reasonable way to make your living. You're not stealing money, and you're entertaining people'.

Other pressures came from the financial expectations of the industry. Directing *One Eyed Jacks*, he went way over budget, perhaps because he thought directing was a way of making an artistic statement without exposing so much of himself. The result was a lovely and violent film but still, to most people, just another Western.

Mutiny on 'Mutiny'
He might have escaped that set-back unscathed had he not followed it with *Mutiny on the Bounty*. There was a certain logic in the casting – Brando, the famous rebel, playing Fletcher Christian, the famous rebel. The trouble was that Brando insisted on playing Christian, not as a he-man of principle, as Clark Gable had, but as a foppish idler, with homosexual overtones, a character whose previously dormant sense of class difference, the basis of order in the British navy, turns torpid under Tahiti's tropical skies. It was not at all what the producers had in mind for a multi-million-dollar film on which MGM was depending for survival.

They claimed it was Brando's temperament that cost them an extra $10 million, but he was, in fact, taking the rap for all kinds of mismanagement, which included sending cast and crew off to shoot in the rainy season without a finished script in hand. Of course, Brando was angry and of course he turned as mutinous as Christian himself had.

What got lost in the resulting controversy was the fact that Brando's Christian was one of his finest sustained performances, a daring attempt to blend the humorous with the heroic, a projection of a modern, ironic sensibility backward into history. There was no-

thing cool or held back in this characterization; Brando took it right up to the hot edge of farce. If he was out of key with the rest of the players and the square-rigged plot, he actually did what a star is supposed to do, hold our interest in a big dumb remake – while risking comparison with the remembered performance of a beloved actor in a beloved role.

After *Mutiny on the Bounty*, came the deluge – poor parts, not a few of which he walked out on. In some of these films one can see the germ of the idea that attracted Brando: the chance to confront comedy directly in *Bedtime Story* (1964) and *A Countess From Hong Kong* (1967); the opportunity to make social comments he considered worthy in *The Ugly American* (1963), *The Chase* (1966) and *Queimada!*; even roles that matched his gift, despite their flawed context, notably that of the repressed homosexual army officer in *Reflections in a Golden Eye* (1967).

There are in these films isolated moments where Brando shines through. There is the scene in *Sayonara*, for example, when he confesses to his commanding general (and would-be father-in-law) that he is throwing

Top: in The Chase, *Bubber Reeves (Robert Redford) is arrested by the sheriff (Brando) but is shot – like Lee Harvey Oswald – before he can be tried. Directed by Arthur Penn, The* Chase *is a highly political film of bigotry and violence in the Deep South. Above: Brando plays a disillusioned English adventurer in* Queimada! *– a film about slavery and the colonization of the Caribbean*

over his fiancée for a Japanese girl. He conveys his anguish over this decision by picking up a cushion and concentrating on it the entire time they talk – a perfectly observed banal gesture. In *Reflections in a Golden Eye*, there is the scene when he thinks Robert Forster is coming to pay a homosexual call on him and he absurdly pats down his hair and smiles vainly to himself. Then there is *The Nightcomers* (1971) in which he hides out behind an Irish brogue and spends a lot of time indulging a bondage fetish with the governess, when, in the midst of it, he tells the children a long tall story and suddenly he's alive and playful and inventive, giving himself pleasure and making us share in it.

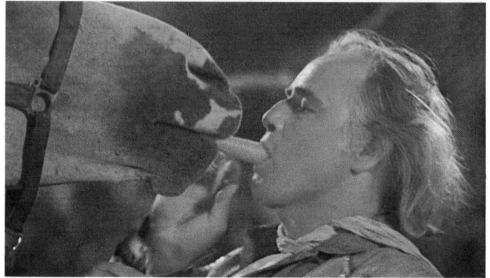

Left: light relief from Brando and Maria Schneider as the couple who share a frenentic sexual relationship in Last Tango In Paris. Below left: in The Missouri Breaks (1976), Brando is a lawman – a typical John Wayne character – who, in this scene, shares a carrot with his horse before declaring his undying love for her. Above: the deranged Major Kurtz from Apocalypse Now

nities. There is also in him something of the youthful, public Brando – self-romanticizing, self-pitying, yet self-satirizing too. All Brando's character Paul does in the film is have a restorative affair with a much younger woman. In the last sequences he is restored to a handsomeness that can be termed nothing less than beauty, a vitality, even a romantic energy, that is both miraculous and moving.

In the brilliant monologue at his dead wife's bier, perhaps the single greatest aria of his career, it all comes together, talent and technique, to express the violent ambivalence of his relationship with not merely this woman, but with himself and the world at large.

It was Brando's art, not director Bertolucci's, that made the highly melodramatic ending – in which, for no good reason, the star must die – a triumph. Brando removes the sting of death by the simple act of removing his chewing gum from his mouth and placing it neatly under the railing of the terrace where he takes his final fall – the tiny, perfect bit of actor's business, neatly undercutting the director's strain for a big finish.

Perhaps only a young director, cognizant of what Brando has meant to his generation, a director who self-consiously stripped from his work all intellectual and artistic traditions other than that of the cinema, could give his age's great *movie* actor this unprecedented opportunity for self-portraiture.

RICHARD SCHICKEL

Filmography
1950 The Men. '51 A Streetcar Named Desire. '52 Viva Zapata! '53 Julius Caesar; The Wild One. '54 On the Waterfront; Desiree. '55 Guys and Dolls. '56 The Teahouse of the August Moon. '57 Sayonara. '58 The Young Lions. '60 The Fugitive Kind. '61 One Eyed Jacks (+prod; +dir). '62 Mutiny on the Bounty. '63 The Ugly American. '64 Bedtime Story. '65 Morituri (GB: The Saboteur – Code Name 'Morituri'). '66 The Chase; The Appaloosa (GB: Southwest to Sonora). '67 A Countess From Hong Kong (GB); Reflections in a Golden Eye. '68 Candy (USA-FR-IT); The Night of the Following Day. '69 Queimada! (USA: Burn!) (IT-FR). '71 The Nightcomers (GB). '72 The Godfather; Ultimo Tango a Parigi (USA/GB: Last Tango in Paris) (IT-FR). '76 The Missouri Breaks. '78 Superman, the Movie (GB). '79 Apocalypse Now. '80 The Formula.

But it was *The Godfather* that provided the long-awaited proof that he could still do most of it as an actor. He went after the part; even submitted to the indignity of a test. The result was a sustained characterization that depended for its success on more than a raspy voice and a clever old man's makeup. There were in his very movements, the hints of mortality that men in their forties begin to feel no matter how youthfully they maintain their spirits. His manner epitomized all the old men of power who had leaned across their desks to bend the young actor to their will – their wile and strength sheathed in reasonableness, commands presented in the guise of offers it *is*

hard to refuse. It was the culmination of his second career as a character man.

What one really wondered, though, was whether he had it in him to go all the way down the well again, come out from behind the masks and show again the primitiveness and power of his youth. That, quite simply, is what he did in *Last Tango in Paris*. Brando was playing physically what he is psychologically, an expatriate from his native land. Moreover, he was playing a man passing through the 'male menopause'. Yet in his sexual brutality there is something of Stanley Kowalski, and, like Terry Malloy, he is a one-time boxer, vulnerable in his mourning for lost opportu-

Viva Kazan!

'I think of films as self-expression, as a way of saying whatever I feel: a cry of pain, a paean of praise, whatever thrills, whatever anger, whatever longing I've had in my life'

Elia Kazan

Elia Kazanjoglou was born in Istanbul on September 7, 1909. He emigrated to the United States at the age of four, and both he and his name underwent a process of Americanization. In fact, Kazan's models – he idolizes John Ford – and values make him one of the most distinctively American of film directors. No American cineaste has displayed greater reverence for the native idiom, and few have ranged as wide in a critical appraisal of the country's social diversity. Kazan's childhood disruption and ethnic background seem to have made him particularly sensitive to the problems of his adopted society and to its displaced groups and individuals.

The tensions between his basically leftist political sense and his aspiration towards classical artistry have existed from the beginning, and have generally enriched his work. But Kazan's gratitude for America's class mobility – part of the American dream that frequently works – is still in conflict with his perfectionist dismay that it does not work for everybody.

His two early short films – *Pie in the Sky* (1934) and *People of the Cumberland* (1937) – were collaborative efforts. They can be more intelligently viewed as examples of the young intellectual ferment of the Thirties than as personal statements on his part. During this period he was acting under the direction of Lee Strasberg and Harold Clurman with the New York Group Theatre, performing plays by Sidney Kingsley and Clifford Odets. Although Kazan had an opportunity to direct for the stage as early as 1935, it was essentially as an actor that he went to Hollywood in 1940. He appeared in two Anatole Litvak films – *City for Conquest* and *Blues in the Night* (both 1941).

In 1945 Kazan became a fully-fledged movie director at 20th Century-Fox. It was im-

mediately evident with *A Tree Grows in Brooklyn* (1945) that his great strength lay with actors, Dorothy McGuire, playing the Irish girl Katie Nolan, gives the first in Kazan's gallery of great performances, and the otherwise undistinguished James Dunn won an Oscar for his supporting role as the drunken father Johnny Nolan. Kazan acknowledges his limited understanding of the cinematic craft at the time, and he attributes the film's fluidity to the cinematographer Leon Shamroy.

Boomerang (1946), produced by Louis de

Above left: Elia Kazan, the actors' director.
Above right: an early acting role in City for Conquest, *with Frank McHugh and James Cagney. Below: a production shot from* Splendour in the Grass *(1961) which starred Natalie Wood and the then unknown star, Warren Beatty*

Rochemont, began his period of social relevance. Its style aspires towards an American neo-realism, and it foreshadows much of the television drama of the succeeding decade. Semi-documentary in style, *Boomerang's* ensemble cast (including Lee J. Cobb and Karl Malden) moved James Agee to term the acting 'the most immaculate set of naturalistic performances I have seen in one movie.' It is all held together nicely and unpretentiously by the underrated star of many post-war melodramas – Dana Andrews.

Gentleman's Agreement (1947) · brought Kazan enormous success and won Academy Awards for best picture and director. It is ironic and sad that so many of his later and better films – *Wild River* (1960), *America, America* (1963), *The Arrangement* (1969), *The Last Tycoon* (1976) – won him few honours and disappeared virtually unseen. Though lacking

in cinematic values and built around a typically bland Gregory Peck, *Gentleman's Agreement* was esteemed more for its well-intentioned attack on anti-Semitism than for its own merits. Similarly, *Pinky* (1949) – originally a John Ford project scripted by Dudley Nichols and Philip Dunne – had more value as a long-overdue Hollywood plea against racial prejudice than as an intrinsically successful film.

Around this time Kazan became more conscious of the classical cinema which had preceded him, and his films began to open up spatially and show greater concern with imagery. *Panic in the Streets* (1950) a *film noir* shot in the underbelly of New Orleans, has some exemplary location sequences and moments of pure cinema. This flamboyant visual style was to continue for the balance of Kazan's career, pausing only for the poetic eloquence of *A Streetcar Named Desire* (1951).

The play, by Tennessee Williams, is arguably the greatest ever written by an American, and Kazan treated its transfer to the screen with due reverence. His theatrical craftsmanship inspired brilliant performances from Kim Hunter, Karl Malden, Vivien Leigh and Marlon Brando – the only one who did not receive an Oscar. It is impossible to overpraise Leigh's Blanche or Brando's Stanley, and it is difficult to imagine a better amalgam of theatre and cinema. The near-hysterical baroque quality of the drama – inherited from Williams – was to become a Kazan trademark in subsequent films.

At the time of its release *Viva Zapata!* (1952) was Kazan's most personal film to date, even if it suffers from scriptwriter Steinbeck's heavy-handed didacticism. Kazan returned occasionally to Broadway until 1964, but he now saw himself primarily as a film director, and became immersed in the craft of his adopted medium. Brando, playing against his strengths, is less effective here than in his other Kazan films, but Anthony Quinn won an Academy Award.

Kazan finds his anti-communist *Man on a Tightrope* (1953) an embarrassment, and next came the period of his testimony before the

Above: the conditions of impoverished New York immigrants at the turn of the century were re-created for A Tree Grows in Brooklyn. *Left: Jack Palance as Blackie in* Panic in the Streets. *Below: Anthony Quinn, Marlon Brando, Lou Gilbert and Harold Gordon in a scene from* Viva Zapata!

House Un-American Activities Committee, where he testified against some of his colleagues, who inevitably became (and several remain) estranged. The brilliance of *On the Waterfront* (1954) was qualified for many by its defence of informers. Politics aside, Brando's sensitive portrayal of Terry Malloy – the ex-boxer who 'could have been somebody' – provides a few of the great acting moments in the cinema's history. His supporting ensemble – Saint, Malden, Steiger, Cobb – are all excellent, and the net effect is a unique lilting realism quite superior to anything Kazan had achieved before. *On the Waterfront* was showered with Oscars, and Brando's character became a Fifties icon – the prototype of the

alienated hero in subsequent Kazan films.

James Dean in *East of Eden* (1955) owes a great deal to Brando's style, and is a further extension of Kazan's disaffected loner. Kazan has said that Dean 'was himself the boy that he played in the film.' Dean is quite moving, if a bit more mannered in his Method acting than one had remembered. His scenes with Julie Harris are touching and intimate, and Kazan shows great feeling for the values of the family which are central to his later personal works *America, America* and *The Arrangement*. *East of Eden* was his first film in colour and wide screen, and he mastered both easily, with some impressive lighting effects and location work.

Baby Doll (1956) is more cinematic than *A Streetcar Named Desire*, but it is peopled by monsters and lacks both the poetry and poignancy one has come to expect from Tennessee Williams at his best. There are no passing strangers on whose kindness one can depend. The performances are creditable, and Kazan's main effort was aimed at capturing the South as he felt it to be. *A Face in the Crowd* (1957) suffers from a similar grotesquery, with Andy Griffith's Lonesome Rhodes being one of the more loathsome screen creations this side of Erich von Stroheim. Budd Schulberg's script is heavy-handed and simplistic; the acting, except for Patricia Neal and Walter Matthau, is too broad and shrill . . . virtually everything in the film is done to excess. Above all else, there is an air of cynicism about American politics and media, which lacks credibility. The Brando/Dean loner has gone mad with power, but Kazan cannot convey Schulberg's negative vision of America with conviction.

Kazan's richest period began in 1960 with *Wild River*, combining a lyrical romance worthy of D.W. Griffith or John Ford with the natural poetry of Robert Flaherty. He is still in the South, but he has travelled back in time to the muted and mellow landscapes and textures of the Thirties and Roosevelt's TVA project. The film centres on a love affair between outsider Montgomery Clift and wistful, vulnerable Lee Remick – giving the most sensitive female performance in Kazan's *oeuvre* after Vivien Leigh. *Wild River* is languidly placed and lovingly photographed (by Ellsworth Fredericks) and bears little similarity to the freneticism of its antecedents. Kazan had achieved a

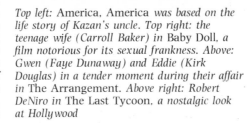

Top left: America, America *was based on the life story of Kazan's uncle. Top right: the teenage wife (Carroll Baker) in* Baby Doll, *a film notorious for its sexual frankness. Above: Gwen (Faye Dunaway) and Eddie (Kirk Douglas) in a tender moment during their affair in* The Arrangement. *Above right: Robert DeNiro in* The Last Tycoon, *a nostalgic look at Hollywood*

command of his craft, a level of maturity, and an authenticity worthy of a major artist.

America, America is Kazan's favourite among his films. It is a sprawling epic account of his uncle's efforts to escape from under the heel of the Turks and reach the United States – a journey filled with passion and vivid imagery. *America, America* is one of the cinema's most extraordinary testaments to a personal morality and cultural legacy. Its power, like that of all great art, comes from an artist wrenching truth from the extreme depths of his own soul. *The Arrangement*, based on the first of Kazan's best-selling novels, is even more personal, being one of the most autobiographical films in history. Kazan draws upon and examines his own mid-life crises, coming to terms with his limitations and failings. It is an eclectic but ultimately very moving work of rare courage and honesty.

Much of the wistful poetry of F. Scott

Fitzgerald's unfinished novel is captured in *The Last Tycoon* – reflecting Kazan's own love-hate relationship with Hollywood. Robert DeNiro's gentle Monroe Stahr recalls Terry Malloy. He is successful and articulate, but equally lonely as a 'somebody'.

Kazan now views himself more as a novelist than a director, but another film is required to fit between *America, America* and *The Arrangement* before the family history is complete. Given the accomplishment and candour of these two works, the dream deserves to be realized.　　　　　　　　CHARLES SILVER

Filmography

1934 Cafe Universal (actor only) (short); Pie in the Sky. **'37** People of the Cumberland (+sc) (short). **'41** City for Conquest (actor only); Blues in the Night (actor only). **'45** A Tree Grows in Brooklyn. **'46** Boomerang. **'47** The Sea of Grass; Gentleman's Agreement. **'49** Pinky. **'50** Panic in the Streets. **'51** A Streetcar Named Desire. **'52** Viva Zapata! **'53** Man on a Tightrope. **'54** On the Waterfront. **'55** East of Eden (+prod). **'56** Baby Doll (+prod). **'57** A Face in the Crowd (+prod). **'60** Wild River (+prod). **'61** Splendor in the Grass (+prod). **'63** America, America (GB: The Anatolian Smile) (+prod;+sc). **'69** The Arrangement (+prod;+sc). **'72** The Visitors. **'76** The Last Tycoon.

Mr Stewart Goes to Hollywood

As the all-American Mr Average, James Stewart has been loved and admired for over four decades. A family man of spotless repute, he has built his career on just such an image. However, in recent years he has displayed an intriguing versatility and revelled in roles revealing the darker side of his nature

Above left: James Stewart as the famous bandleader in The Glenn Miller Story. *Top: Jefferson Smith (Stewart) and his secretary (Jean Arthur) discuss the attractions of the capital in* Mr Smith Goes to Washington. *Above: as Elwood P. Dowd he tries to explain that 'the rabbit just left' in* Harvey

It is possible that no star ever had a better run of pictures than James Stewart did in the four years between 1937 and 1940. There was *Seventh Heaven* (1937), *You Can't Take It With You* (1938), *Mr Smith Goes to Washington*, *Destry Rides Again* (both 1939), *The Shop Around the Corner* and *The Philadelphia Story* (both 1940). It was in these films that his basic screen character – the gulpy voice, gangling walk and sweet, yet principled spirit – was established. His billing might ever be *James Stewart* but he indelibly remains *Jimmy*, the friendly and somehow reassuring diminutive recalling his small-town origins and reiterating his continuing responsibility for personifying the simpler values of a simpler American time.

However, if those films – climaxed in 1946, after a gap in his career for war service, by Capra's cult classic, *It's a Wonderful Life* – established his image, they did not establish his credentials as an actor. That came later, some years after the war, when he self-consciously set about changing his image. *It's a Wonderful Life* was Capra's marvellously sentimental tribute to the verities of American small-town life but was not a success when released, and neither was Stewart's next film, *Magic Town*

(1947). It was obvious that at 34, with a distinguished military record behind him, Stewart was both too old chronologically and too mature emotionally to go on playing juveniles. As he himself put it, too many of the reviews were saying things like: 'Jimmy Stewart is still exuding boyish charm in lethal doses.'

From soft centre to tough nut

He began the process of change in *Call Northside 777* (1948), in which he played a tough but principled Chicago police reporter devoted to clearing an innocent man of a murder charge. In the same year he began his salutary association with Alfred Hitchcock in *Rope*. Here he plays a teacher who comes to realize that his Nazi-like philosophy has led two of his students to motiveless murder. He is therefore obliged to uncover evidence not only of the crime, but also of his own intellectual complicity in it.

If these two films mark the beginning of a turn in Stewart's career, it was the incredible series of Westerns made with Anthony Mann between 1950 and 1955 that established him as an actor to be reckoned with. *Winchester '73* (1950), the story of a man searching for his

father's killer; *Bend of the River* (1952), with Stewart helping a group of pioneers to cross the West; *The Naked Spur* (1953), where he is a bounty hunter; *The Far Country* (1954), in which he plays a 'gritty' cowboy; *The Man From Laramie* (1955), which again sees him as a man out for vengeance – these are among the finest works in the genre. The vision retained of him in these films is of a man in a battered sheepskin jacket with several days stubble on his chin, riding off alone into the high country toward some confrontation – not only with the villain but with his own driving obsessions – that would be cold and lonely.

There was, as critic Jim Kitses has noted, something of the old Stewart in these roles. Mann used the 'charming, bemused side of the actor's talent' in order to make palatable his characters' cynicism and to soften their violent edges. There was also about Stewart a quality that has always endeared him to directors and co-workers – a capacity for disciplined hard work. In interviews Mann would speak admiringly of Stewart's willingness to undergo any hardship (fights were staged under the hooves of horses, the actor permitted himself to be dragged through fire) endure any learning process (he made himself an expert with the

141

Above: Stewart and Maureen Sullavan as the antagonistic shop assistants unaware that they are pen-pals in The Shop Around the Corner. *Above right: with Lee J. Cobb in the film that introduced a tougher image,* Call Northside 777. *Above, far right: as a trigger-happy cowboy in* The Far Country. *Right: as the peaceable part-time sheriff driven to violence in* Firecreek *(1968)*

Winchester rifle through dogged practice) in order to achieve the hard-bitten authenticity that marked these pictures.

By and large they were not expensively produced films, and in this period Stewart alternated his appearances in Westerns with work in more expensive and 'civilized' roles. Yet even in these there seemed to be an attempt by the actor to break his old mould. Occasionally the results were ludicrous – as when he appeared in DeMille's *The Greatest Show on Earth* (1951) as a clown who never dared take off his makeup in case the police should recognize him as a wanted criminal. Sometimes they were merely bland and conventional, as in such biopics as *The Stratton Story* (1949), the life of baseball star Monty Stratton, and *The Glenn Miller Story* (1953); sometimes they were routinely heroic, as in *Strategic Air Command* (1955), in which Stewart was a Lieutenant-Colonel in the US peacetime air force, and *The FBI Story* (1959), the career of an FBI agent through 25 years of service. However, whether ludicrous, bland or routine, they were still very popular and Stewart was often high on the end-of-year exhibitors' list of leading box-office draws.

Days of wine and rabbits

These years also produced much that was far from ordinary. *Harvey* (1950) was the story of Elwood P. Dowd, a gentle alcoholic who has an imaginary rabbit for a companion. Stewart had already appeared in the role on stage in 1947 (and was to return to a stage production in later years) and in the movie he pushed his slight air of befuddlement, always present in

his early portrayals, to epic – yet delicately stated – proportions. Or what about his two finest Hitchcock roles? As the magazine photographer confined to his room by a broken leg in *Rear Window* (1954), Stewart is as sweetly engaging as ever. But he is also, never forget, that unsavoury figure, a dedicated voyeur. In *Vertigo* (1958) he plays a detective not only somewhat unmanned by his fear of heights but obsessed – to the point of derangement by a lost love. Then there was *Anatomy of a Murder* (1959) in which, at first glance, he seems to be playing the grown-up version of one of his old small-town kids until we begin to sense – under all his gargling, gawking and shuffling about – a steely and stubborn mind at work, serving as his own private detective in order to uncover evidence of his client's innocence. That mind is unsheathed in the courtroom sequences where it works fast and tough to best his legal opponent, a big-city prosecutor played by George C. Scott.

The man from Indiana

There was a feeling during those years that 'Jimmy' was deceiving the public by encouraging it to believe that the man it saw was simply the man he was. Certainly what was known of his private life was exemplary. There was never, in the endlessly gossiping Hollywood press, the slightest note of indecorousness. He married late, aged 41, but it was to be a lasting relationship and in 1951 his wife Gloria produced twins. During World War II he had risen from Private to Colonel in the air force and received, among other decorations, the Distinguished Flying Cross for his 23 bombing missions over Germany; after the war he persisted in his military duties, rising in the Reserve to the rank of General. In politics Stewart has always been a conservative Republican, though never strident about it, and has maintained a friendship with Henry Fonda, a determined liberal – which dates back to the time when they were both 'novice'

actors with the University Players theatre group in the early Thirties – precisely because they refuse to discuss politics. And Stewart went around saying, as he still does, that: 'the most important thing about acting is to approach it as a craft, not as an art and not as some mysterious type of religion.' He likes to tell reporters how lucky he was to have come up through the old studio system where young players were worked hard.

Be that as it may, there is something more than mere craft in all those quietly bent strangers, those oddly bedevilled and curiously possessed loners he kept playing. As Stewart got older the press took to calling him an elder statesman; however he did not spend all his time playing kindly uncles and grandpas. He is an out-and-out villain in *Bandolero!* (1968) as the crooked brother of a murderer, and in 1970 he was to be found playing a rancher who comes into some property – a whorehouse – with another old reprobate, played by Henry Fonda, in *The Cheyenne Social Club*. His last

Below: with Richard Attenborough, Christian Marquand and Hardy Kruger in Flight of the Phoenix (1966), *a story of desert endurance. Bottom: the new owner and his friend (Henry Fonda) take over* The Cheyenne Social Club

truly great role in *Fool's Parade* (1971) – about an old convict determined to have his revenge on the people who unjustly sent him to jail – is amazing. The convict has a glass eye which he pops out of its socket and talks to at times of stress, variously frightening or mesmerizing anyone who happens to be nearby. At the end of the picture he walks around with a coatful of dynamite, more than pleased to touch off the fuse and take his enemies along with him to kingdom come if they do not accede to his demands.

This is hardly the behaviour of an air force General, or of the nice middle-class boy born in 1908 whose father owned the hardware store in Indiana. Therefore, it is easy to suspect this model citizen of being a secret subversive, one of those actors who uses stage and screen to work off their private frets and passions, the better to return home and pretend that the job they've been doing all day at the studio is just an exercise in 'craft'.

In his maturity James Stewart has taken great pleasure in displaying his instinctive, brooding and occasionally depressive side. His ability to do so without destroying any affection for his innocent young men of the past has enabled him to make the most difficult of all movie transitions – from guiless juvenile to strong and knowledgeable leading man – without missing a stride. More recently this skill has allowed him to slip gracefully across the line from lead to character actor, and the range of his 'craft' can now be fully appreciated. However, he is perhaps really loved for his duplicity – his insistence that he is just an ordinary fellow.   RICHARD SCHICKEL

Filmography

1935 Murder Man. **'36** Rose Marie; Next Time We Love (GB: Next Time We Live); Wife Versus Secretary; Small Town Girl; Speed; The Gorgeous Hussy; Born to Dance; After the Thin Man. **'37** Seventh Heaven; The Last Gangster; Navy Blue and Gold. **'38** Of Human Hearts; Vivacious Lady; You Can't Take It With You. **'39** Made for Each Other; Ice Follies of 1939; It's a Wonderful World; Mr Smith Goes to Washington; Destry Rides Again. **'40** The Shop Around the Corner; The Mortal Storm; No Time for Comedy; The Philadelphia Story. **'41** Come Live With Me; Pot o' Gold (GB: The Golden Hour); Ziegfeld Girl. **'46** The American Creed (short) (GB: American Brotherhood Week); It's a Wonderful Life. **'47** Magic Town. **'48** Call Northside 777; On Our Merry Way (preview title: A Miracle Can Happen); Rope; You Gotta Stay Happy. **'49** The Stratton Story. **'50** Malaya (GB: East of the Rising Sun); Winchester '73; Broken Arrow; The Jackpot; Harvey. **'51** No Highway (USA: No Highway in the Sky) (GB); The Greatest Show on Earth. **'52** Bend of the River (GB: Where the River Bends); Carbine Williams. **'53** The Naked Spur; Thunder Bay; The Glenn Miller Story. **'54** Rear Window; The Far Country. **'55** Strategic Air Command; The Man From Laramie. **'56** The Man Who Knew Too Much. **'57** The Spirit of St Louis; Night Passage. **'58** Vertigo; Bell, Book and Candle. **'59** Anatomy of a Murder; The FBI Story. **'60** Mountain Road. **'61** Two Rode Together; X-15 (narration only). **'62** The Man Who Shot Liberty Valance; Mr Hobbs Takes a Vacation; How the West Was Won. **'63** Take Her, She's Mine. **'64** Cheyenne Autumn. **'65** Dear Brigitte; Shenandoah. **'66** The Rare Breed; Flight of the Phoenix. **'68** Firecreek; Bandolero!. **'70** The Cheyenne Social Club. **'71** Fools' Parade (GB: Dynamite Man from Glory Jail). **'74** That's Entertainment! (co-narr). **'76** The Shootist. **'77** Airport '77; The Big Sleep. **'78** The Magic of Lassie.

One of the most shocking moments in *Kiss Me Deadly* is when the police detective tells private eye Mike Hammer just what he thinks of him. He tells him that he is a grubby crawler into other people's affairs and underlinen; a man over his head in a situation that is too vast for him to understand. The moment shocks because it reverses the audience's understanding of how it should feel about Hammer.

The average audience would have assumed, however callous and brutal his actions and however sardonically sawn-off his words, that Hammer was somehow on the side of right – as any good private eye in the Chandler tradition ought to be. But Hammer is no Chandleresque knight in tarnished armour walking erect through mean streets; he was created by Mickey Spillane, a writer with an eye for best-selling sadism. In Hammer is the demeaned perpetuation of the private-investigator ethic.

So articulate is the police detective's distaste that it is obvious that the film's director Robert Aldrich and its screenwriter A. I. Bezzerides feel exactly that way about Hammer too. It is not just that he is an anti-hero, but in his arrogant assumption that his amoral might is right, he is a *fascist* hero. It is as though Aldrich and Bezzerides were using the character in order to repudiate him and all he stands for.

This is just one of the many dazzling brilliances in a movie that was of seminal importance for its time, establishing Aldrich as a cult *auteur* with French critics, and later regarded as a classic *film noir*. On the surface, *Kiss Me Deadly* is a roughneck suspense thriller of enormous ingenuity, but on other levels the Cold War concerns of the narrative contain not only a fable for our time, but the echoes of a more ancient myth.

Aldrich's approach to *Kiss Me Deadly*'s brutality is, for him, elegant to the point of fastidiousness (almost as though he were distancing himself and the audience from the film's New York and Los Angeles wastelands) which seems as negative of real emotion as though an atom bomb had already scoured the world. The nuclear hysteria that raged at the time of the film's production is transmuted by the director into powerful deterministic comment.

What begins as a sordid story of underworld intrigue, conspiracy and the search for what is called 'the great whatsit', assumes the irrational nature of nightmare. And there are so many subjective shots from Hammer's point of view – notably when knocked out from behind, and when he is about to open the locker that supposedly contains the answer to all mysteries – that it is evident that, though disclaimed, he is the figure with whom the audience identifies. What he does, he does in our name. As political comment then, *Kiss Me Deadly* daringly persuades its audience – and in 1955, a year of Cold War, it *was* daring – that legalized

thugs like Hammer could hamfistedly seek out radioactivity, leading to climactic destruction. That he was led to it by a woman, Lily Carver, is just another aspect of an ignorant gullibility that is as much part of his sexual nature as his intellect. Ignorance undoes all things; even, in opening the ultimate box, mankind.

Ralph Meeker's performance as Hammer never concedes the slightest shred of decency, as though the actor heroically realized that a one-dimensional character is the only way to set into more defined relief the other perspectives of situation and character. Its connections with the Lemmy Caution of Jean-Luc Godard's *Alphaville*, made ten years afterwards, are only too apparent.

In his book *Film Noir*, Alain Silver has written:

'What distinguishes *Kiss Me Deadly*'s figurative usage from that of other Aldrich films is an explicit aural fabric of allusions and metaphor: the recurring Christina Rossetti poem, *Remember Me*; the Caruso recording . . . they all provide immediate textual reference if not subsidiary meaning.'

Accordingly, and with its necessary undertow of credibility, *Kiss Me Deadly* provides a suitable, realistic context for an allegory – and the film is all the more disturbing in that it is really communicating about the nuclear age in ancient legend. For as Lily Carver opens the box and becomes a column of fire – a pillar of salt? – and Hammer and Velda look backwards from the sea to watch the house mushroom upwards into devastation, so the audience realizes just what has been unleashed by all their separate actions. The totem-words of nuclear armament have already been uttered: 'Manhattan project . . . Los Alamos . . . Trinity'.

The word that is never said, but that is most implicit in all that happens, is Pandora. It is her box that has been breached. The breaking of encasing restraint, the unleashing of the apocalypse, is what those Hammer-blows have achieved. It is more than enough.

TOM HUTCHINSON

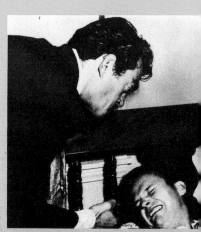

Directed by Robert Aldrich, 1955
Prod co: Parklane Pictures (United Artists). **exec prod:** Victor Saville. **prod:** Robert Aldrich. **sc:** A. I. Bezzerides, from the novel by Mickey Spillane. **photo:** Ernest Laszlo. **ed:** Michael Luciano. **art dir:** William Glasgow. **mus:** Frank DeVol. **song:** 'Rather Have the Blues' by Frank DeVol, sung by Nat 'King' Cole. **ass dir:** Robert Justman. **r/t:** 96 minutes.
Cast: Ralph Meeker (*Mike Hammer*), Albert Dekker (*Dr Soberin*), Paul Stewart (*Carl Evello*), Maxine Cooper (*Velda*), Gaby Rodgers (*Gabrielle/Lily Carver*), Wesley Addy (*Pat*), Juano Hernandez (*Eddie Eager*), Nick Dennis (*Nick*), Cloris Leachman (*Christina*), Marian Carr (*Friday*), Jack Lambert (*Sugar*), Jack Elam (*Charlie Max*), Jerry Zinneman (*Sammy*), Percy Helton (*morgue doctor*), Fortunio Bonanova (*Carmen Trivago*), Silvio Minciotti (*mover*), Leigh Snowden (*girl at pool*), Madi Comfort (*singer*), James Seay, Robert Cornthwaite (*FBI men*), Mara McAfee (*nurse*), James McCallian ('*Super*'), Jesslyn Fax (*Mrs 'Super'*), Mort Marshall (*Piker*), Strother Martin (*truck driver*), Marjorie Bennett (*manager*), Art Loggins (*bartender*), Bob Sherman (*gas-station man*), Keith McConnell (*athletic-club clerk*), Paul Richards (*attacker*).

1

3

4

Driving to Los Angeles at night, private detective Mike Hammer is flagged down by the mysterious Christina (1) and picks her up. 'Remember me', she tells him – a few miles on his car is run off the road and Christina is murdered.

Hammer wakes in hospital where his secretary Velda and a colleague tell him (2) that federal investigators want to question him about Christina. A conspiracy led by gangster Carl Evello tries to

buy Hammer off with the gift of a car, but he and his mechanic Nick discover in time that it has been planted with explosives (3).

Hammer seeks out Lily Carver, Christina's former room-mate, and takes her to his apartment. Shortly afterwards Nick is murdered and Hammer abducted by Evello's hired thugs (4). They take him to Dr Soberin – Christina's killer – who has him restrained (5) and injects him with

pentathol. But Hammer kills one of the heavies and escapes.

Velda has disappeared. But with the help of Lily Carver Hammer decodes Christina's message. It leads them to a morgue where a doctor passes on the key to a locker (6) containing a box. Hammer leaves the box there; Lily meanwhile has gone.

At his apartment the police tell Hammer the box contains radioactive material sought by

foreign agents. Finding the locker empty, Hammer gets Soberin's address off one of his patients' medicine bottles (7). At his beach house, Lily kills the doctor to get the box for herself (8) and shoots and wounds Hammer when he arrives. She opens the box, engulfing herself in flames (9) and starting a nuclear chain reaction. Hammer finds Velda and they stumble into the sea (10) as the house explodes.

6

7

9

10

THE END

A PARKLANE PICTURE

RELEASED THROUGH UNITED ARTISTS

The dictionary defines melodrama as a 'sensational dramatic piece with crude appeals to the emotions'. Or is there more to it than that? Douglas Sirk's torrid melodramas seemed to have been designed to reflect and probe the unspoken hopes and anxieties of the film audiences of middle America in the Fifties

It might be asked why Douglas Sirk, whose career as a director effectively ended in 1959, suddenly became a major focus of attention in Anglo-American film culture in the early Seventies. After years of critical neglect, there appeared an interview book (*Sirk on Sirk*) and a special issue on him in a film-theory magazine (*Screen*, Summer 1971), as well as a retrospective at the Edinburgh Film Festival in 1972 with a book of critical essays on his work to accompany it. His 'rediscovery' resulted primarily from a change in the kinds of films and film directors celebrated in Anglo-American film criticism after the Fifties and the extent to which oppositional critical positions – more favourable to Sirk's kind of cinema – were

finding a voice in the study of films in the Sixties and Seventies.

Douglas Sirk was born Hans Detlef Sierck in Germany in 1900. He studied law, philosophy and the history of art, and worked briefly as a journalist before entering the theatre as a play-reader in 1920. In the next two decades he had a distinguished career as a producer of classical and modern drama and also as a director in the cinema. Fleeing from Nazism, he went to Hollywood in 1939. After a range of low-budget films for various companies – including *Hitler's Madman* (1942) for MGM, *Sleep, My Love* for United Artists and *Shockproof* (both 1948) for Columbia – he settled down in 1950 to almost a decade of productive work with

Universal-International. And it was there, with Ross Hunter or Albert S. Zugsmith as his producer, that he made the melodramas – *Magnificent Obsession* (1954), *All That Heaven Allows* (1955), *Written on the Wind* (1956), *The Tarnished Angels* (1957) and *Imitation of Life* (1959) – on which his critical reputation is founded.

The critical factor

In the twenty years or so following World War II, the dominant critical position in British and American cinema had two main features: the undervaluing of 'commercial' Hollywood movies in favour of the 'artistic' films of the non-English speaking world; and

Douglas Sirk's magnificent obsessions

the celebrating of 'realistic' films that dealt with the lives of ordinary people. On both these counts Sirk's work was, very largely, either ignored or impugned. Most critics of the time found it difficult to take seriously the films of a director who worked recurrently, and often by choice, with Rock Hudson (eight times between 1952 and 1957) and who seemed content to specialize in family melodramas. But a

Below, far left: Sirk's second film, Das Mädchen vom Moorhof *(1935), made in his native Germany. Below left: the filming of* Magnificent Obsession, *with Rock Hudson and Jane Wyman. Below: Hudson in* Taza, Son of Cochise *(1954), Sirk's only Western*

Far left: Sirk relaxes during the making of Lured *(1947) with his star Lucille Ball. Left: the film is a taut thriller about a dancer (Ball) who helps police catch a killer. Above and above right:* Sign of the Pagan *(1954) and* Captain Lightfoot *(1955) were low-budget pot-boilers for both Sirk and Universal*

particular weakness of the dominant critical position of that time was its blindness to *mise-en-scène* (roughly, the arrangement of cinematic effects used to tell a story) and its undervaluing of melodrama as a legitimate artistic form.

The quality of Sirk's Hollywood films was first perceived by French critics, who celebrated rather than disparaged Hollywood and who were much more interested in issues of cinematic *style* than subject matter. These concerns were imported into Anglo-American film culture in the Sixties, most notably in the writings of the American critic Andrew Sarris and the British journal *Movie*, although Sirk's movies did not figure very prominently at first. The interest in him finally surfaced in the Seventies through the work of a group of critics, many of whom were associated with another British journal, *Screen*. Though highly responsive to the formal elements of cinema, these writers deployed a Marxist frame of reference, an important aspect of which was to pose relationships between aesthetic systems and the social systems within which they operate (ie what films mean and how they circulate within particular societies). Sirk, therefore, was a highly congenial figure to this group on several fronts: his left-wing credentials in pre-war Germany; his stress on the *artifice* rather than the realism of cinema; and the way his films offered a critique of bourgeois America. Moreover, through his specialization in the family melodrama in the Fifties, he prophetically explored the stresses in family life and the repression of women – issues that were to become central to radical (especially feminist) politics in the Seventies.

The measure of melodrama
In his films, Sirk seems to have consciously intended both to deliver all the most satisfying

elements of the 'weepie' – glossy bourgeois settings, handsome heroes, suffering heroines – and to operate a critique of that ethos (and thus of bourgeois America itself) by dismantling the form from within. Sirk observed that melodramatic forms, far from being trite or superficial, have been the best indices of the social stress-points within particular societies. He was not unique in charting American social disintegration through melodrama. Nicholas Ray and Vincente Minnelli, for instance, did so with equal intensity if with less self-awareness, *feeling* rather than thinking the process.

Sirk's 'dismantling' of the form of the melodrama from within – rooted in his refusal to align himself, as director, with the sentimental responses that the story-lines of his films demand – is achieved in a variety of ways. Among the most important of these is his relentless insistence on the *fabricated* quality of the films. Thus, the emotional intensity of the 'normal' melodrama is, in many of Sirk's films, pushed to a point of delirious excess which evokes the highly stylized forms of the German Expressionist cinema.

This can be illustrated by sequences from two of Sirk's most accomplished films, *Written on the Wind* and *The Tarnished Angels*. In each, the impression of emotional excess beyond the strict requirements of the story is created by intercutting two separate strands of the narrative until they collide in a crescendo of feeling. Characteristically in Sirk's films, the sexual longings of particular characters are directed at characters whose own sexual longings are directed elsewhere. Thus, in *Written on the Wind*, the wayward daughter (Dorothy Malone) of a rich oil family desires her brother's friend Mitch Wayne (Rock Hudson), who in turn looks to the brother's wife (Lauren Bacall). The daughter, having taken a young petrol-pump attendant to a motel, is brought home to the family mansion by the police. Her father (Robert Keith) confesses to Mitch his disappointment with both his children and then, broken in spirit, moves on up the staircase that dominates the family home. His ascent is intercut with a scene in which the daughter in her room puts on a record and

Hudson and Wyman were reteamed in All That Heaven Allows *(above) following the success of* Magnificent Obsession; *Hudson, tall and handsome, and Wyman, soulful and romantic, were ideal performers for Sirk's melodramas – as were square-jawed Robert Stack and the flamboyant Dorothy Malone who starred in* Written on the Wind *(above right) and* The Tarnished Angels *(right)*

performs what is effectively a striptease in front of a picture of Mitch. As the tempo of the music mounts and her dance becomes an almost abstract pattern of diaphanous red chiffon, the pace of the intercutting with the father's climb up the stairs increases until, at the top, he suffers a heart attack and plunges (dead) to the bottom of the stairs.

In *The Tarnished Angels*, the obsessive interest of the reporter (Rock Hudson) in a troupe of aerobatic performers is guided by his sexual longing for the woman in the troupe (Dorothy Malone), who constantly looks toward her own neglectful husband (Robert Stack). There is a brief moment when, for the 'wrong' reasons – vulnerability and despair – the reporter and the woman come together. This scene is intercut with the scene of a New Orleans Mardi Gras party; just at the moment when the couple are about to engage in their self-deluding kiss, the two scenes come explosively together as the revellers, led by a figure in a skeleton suit, burst into the room, destroying – in an 'overkill' of cinematic effects – the couple's illusory moment.

These sequences indicate the emotional register and the consciously fabricated quality of Sirk's films. Music and objects are made to carry an unusual emotional weight. In another film, *All That Heaven Allows*, the shattering of a piece of pottery, for example, carries resonances far beyond its strictly narrative importance.

Sirk and social insecurity

As the brief description from *Written on the Wind* indicates, the social milieu of Sirk's films is quite often that of the rich bourgeoisie, inevitably emotionally crippled within the parameters of home, family and country club.

This class-analytic element in Sirk's films is perhaps best exemplified in *All That Heaven Allows*, in which Cary Scott (Jane Wyman), a comfortably-off widow, embarks on an affair with her social inferior, gardener Ron Kirby (Rock Hudson), thereby scandalizing her grown-up children and her friends – who attempt to mummify her in the role of bourgeois widowhood. The film also shows that Sirk's work is most fruitfully understood by regarding the *mise-en-scène* rather than by straightforward thematic analysis. The kinds of thematic oppositions set up in *All That Heaven Allows* between the 'natural' world of Ron and the crippled world of Cary (country versus city, casual clothes versus formal clothes, working with nature versus working with money, a gathering at a friend's house versus a gathering at a country club, wine versus cocktails, and so on) constitute ideological oppositions to be found across a whole range of American films. But what is distinctive about Sirk is the extent to which the social decay and atrophy of a particular class is carried beyond the simple thematics of his films so that the form of them poses questions about the kind of art being consumed in Fifties America and what the stance of a thoughtful director should be to that art. And it is this fact that makes Sirk's films as relevant today as when they were made.   COLIN McARTHUR

Filmography

Films made in Germany as Detlef Sierck unless specified: **1935** April, April (co-dir. only on Dutch-language version: 'T Was één April, 1935); Das Mädchen vom Moorhof; Stützen der Gesellschaft (GB: The Pillars of Society). **'36** Schlussakkord (+co-sc) (GB: Final Accord); Das Hofkonzert (+co-sc) (GB: The Court Concert) (dir. only on French-language version: La Chanson du Souvenir, 1936). **'37** Zu Neuen Ufern (+co-sc); La Habanera. **'39** Boef je (+co-sc) (NETH). *All remaining films in USA as Douglas Sirk:* **'42** Hitler's Madman. **'44** Summer Storm (+co-sc). **'45** A Scandal in Paris. **'47** Lured (GB: Personal Column). **'48** Sleep, My Love; Slightly French; Shockproof. **'50** The First Legion (+co-prod); Mystery Submarine. **'51** Thunder on the Hill (GB: Bonaventure); The Lady Pays Off; Weekend With Father. **'52** Has Anybody Seen My Gal?; No Room for the Groom; Meet Me at the Fair. **'53** Take Me to Town; All I Desire. **'54** Taza, Son of Cochise; Magnificent Obsession; Sign of the Pagan. **'55** Captain Lightfoot; All That Heaven Allows; There's Always Tomorrow; Never Say Goodbye (co-dir, uncredited). **'56** Written on the Wind; Battle Hymn. **'57** Interlude; The Tarnished Angels. **'58** A Time to Love and a Time to Die. **'59** Imitation of Life. **'79** Bourbon Street Blues (sup. only).

High noon in the West

The Western took on a new lease of life in the Fifties, using many varieties of colour film and a wider range of themes, including the good Indian

The early history of the Western is largely associated with B pictures and programmers, aside from the relatively small number of prestige productions like *The Covered Wagon* (1923), John Ford's *The Iron Horse* (1924) and *Cimarron* (1931). An upgrading of the genre during 1939–41 proved short-lived as the war film took over, while many leading male stars were lost to the armed services. But a genuine revival began to develop during the immediate post-war period with prestige productions from David O. Selznick (*Duel in the Sun*, 1946) and Howard Hawks (*Red River*, 1948), and a notable series of Westerns directed by John Ford including *My Darling Clementine* (1946) and *She Wore a Yellow Ribbon* (1949). And by the early Fifties the Western was flourishing as it never had before.

High-quality Westerns, mainly in Technicolor, were produced by all the major studios alongside the last of the cheapie programmers in black and white (soon to be killed off by television), while Westerns from the small independent companies like Republic, Monogram and United Artists often exploited the new, cheap, two-colour processes like Cinecolor and Trucolor. There were still 'serious' pictures in black and white like *The Gunfighter* (1950) and *High Noon* (1952). A new respect for the Indian was a feature of 20th Century-Fox's *Broken Arrow* (1950) and MGM's *Across the Wide Missouri* (1951). The more traditional action film also continued to flourish, as represented by the Audie Murphy cycle of Westerns from Universal. The contribution of veteran directors like Ford and Hawks was matched by experienced men like Anthony Mann, Delmer Daves and John Sturges, who had begun their careers during the Forties, along with a group of younger directors coming to maturity, including Robert Aldrich, Budd Boetticher and Nicholas Ray.

Perhaps more than any other genre, the Western during the early and mid-Fifties reflected that this was a period of transition. The political uncertainties of the post-war years – the Cold War, the Korean War and the election of Eisenhower in 1952, the first Republican President for 20 years – contributed to a new American preoccupation with the national past and a reaffirmation of traditional virtues and values, suggesting a need for old-fashioned escapist Westerns newly bedecked in colour, CinemaScope and 3-D. Yet the film audience was more sophisticated than before and demanded a greater complexity and maturity in Western themes and characterization.

The decline of the old studio system coincided with a greater emphasis on location filming of major features in colour making use of authentic settings; the B feature was virtually abandoned. And many leading directors chose a Western for their first venture into colour, including Delmer Daves' *Broken Arrow*, Anthony Mann's *Bend of the River* (1952) followed by *The Naked Spur* (1953) – both starring James Stewart; Don Siegel's *Duel at Silver Creek* (1952, starring Audie Murphy) and George Stevens' *Shane* (1953). Sets and costumes

were generally less expensive than for other types of period picture, while the colourful landscapes and settings were conveniently close to Hollywood.

As for the cheaper colour processes like Trucolor and Cinecolor, outdoor subjects like Westerns were almost a necessity, for their limitations were more apparent when filming interiors with artificial lighting – not surprisingly, the best ever film in Republic's Trucolor process was Nicholas Ray's Western *Johnny Guitar* (1954), starring Joan Crawford. A Western was often used for the 'trial run' in introducing various new colour processes and other technical innovations. For example, MGM's first production in Ansco colour was *The Wild North* (1951), followed by John Sturges' first colour film, *Escape From Fort Bravo* (1953), also shot in a 3-D version.

Similarly, the first films in the new Warnercolor (a version of Eastman Colour) in 1952 were mainly Westerns. And Pathecolor, yet another version of Eastman Colour, was introduced in 1953–4. The first group of 3-D pictures in 1953 included Westerns such as Raoul Walsh's *Gun Fury* and John Farrow's *Hondo* starring John Wayne. The musical Western *Oklahoma!* (1955) was the first production in the new Todd-AO (65 mm) process as well as the first venture into colour by Fred Zinnemann, who had directed the best-known black-and-white Western of the Fifties, *High Noon*. James Stewart starred in the first Technirama production, *Night Passage*, in 1957; and Westerns also proved ideally suited for filming in the other new processes like CinemaScope and VistaVision.

Many of the top male stars who were first discovered and developed by the major studios during the peak years of the Thirties and early Forties had reached an age and maturity by the Fifties which could best be exploited within the Western format. Established Western stars such as John Wayne, Gary Cooper and Randolph Scott appeared in many of their best roles. James Stewart suddenly emerged as a major Western star, after

Top: Jay C. Flippen, Claire Trevor and Kirk Douglas in King Vidor's Man Without a Star *(1955). Douglas gives an aggressive performance as a rugged saddletramp reluctant to recognize that the Old West is dying and that barbed-wire has come to the range to stay forever. Above: in* The Tin Star, *a veteran former lawman (Henry Fonda) tutors an inexperienced sheriff (Anthony Perkins) until he is ready to face the bad guy*

Above: Jessica Drummond (Barbara Stanwyck), ruler of 40 gun-wielding cowboys, and Griff Bonnell (Barry Sullivan) as the frustrated lovers in Forty Guns; *a number of critics have rightly remarked on the close connection between sex and violence in this film. Above right:* 3.10 to Yuma *starred Van Heflin as an Arizona lawman trying against considerable opposition to catch an afternoon train for the state penitentiary with his prisoner (Glenn Ford). Below: in* Westward the Women, *150 would-be brides trek from Chicago to California by wagon train in search of husbands; here one of these hopeful ladies (Hope Emerson) is slugged by another*

appearing in only one previous Western, *Destry Rides Again* (1939). Alan Ladd and James Cagney, previously identified with the gangster or thriller genre, made their mark: Alan Ladd's *Shane* provided one of the archetypal Western heroes of the decade, and the triumphant revival of Cagney's career began with an off-beat Western, Nicholas Ray's *Run for Cover* (1955). Veteran character actors like Walter Brennan and Andy Devine were much in demand, along with a new generation of 'heavies' including Dan Duryea, Richard Boone and Jack Elam. Young, up-and-coming actors were often teamed with older established stars, for example, Jeffrey Hunter with John Wayne in *The Searchers* and with Robert Ryan in *The Proud Ones*, both in 1956, or Anthony Perkins with Henry Fonda in Anthony Mann's *The Tin Star* (1957).

Leading female stars also took to the saddle. Marlene Dietrich totally dominated Fritz Lang's *Rancho Notorious* (1952) although, according to Lang, she was not happy playing an older woman. Jean Arthur made a notable screen comeback as the homesteader's wife in *Shane*. Joan Crawford gave a suitably larger-than-life performance as the tough owner of a gambling saloon in *Johnny Guitar*. But for toughness and self-reliance no-one could rival Barbara Stanwyck, who emerged as a leading Western star during the mid-Fifties in such pictures as *Cattle Queen of Montana* (1954), *The Violent Men* (1955), *The Maverick Queen* (1956) – Republic's first film in the new 'Scope-like anamorphic 'Naturama' – and, most impressive of all, as the ruthless ranch boss of *Forty Guns* (1957), Sam Fuller's much underrated Western, appropriately filmed in black-and-white CinemaScope.

In the landmark year of 1950 there was a major upgrading of the Western genre. John Ford directed *Rio Grande* (the last of his cavalry trilogy) and *Wagonmaster*. This superb tribute to the pioneers who travelled west in wagon trains drew on Ford's stock company of favourite actors, including Ward Bond, Jane Darwell, Russell Simpson, Ben Johnson and Harry Carey Jr.

Another veteran director, Henry King, produced an unexpected bonus from his collaboration with Gregory Peck, sandwiched between the prestige productions of *Twelve O'Clock High* (1949) and *David and Bathsheba* (1951). The theme of the gunslinger unable to live down his past has often been dealt with since, but never more effectively than in *The Gunfighter*, from 20th Century-Fox. Along with

Broken Arrow, it represented a natural extension of Darryl Zanuck's emphasis on the problem picture during the late Forties, which was here combined with his special interest in Americana.

The year 1950 also marked the debut of a number of new Western stars, and directors such as Anthony Mann and Delmer Daves. Mann directed his first three Westerns in 1950: *The Furies*, at Paramount, starring Barbara Stanwyck and Walter Huston; *Winchester '73*, at Universal, with James Stewart in his first mature Western role; and, at MGM, *Devil's Doorway*, in which Robert Taylor played an Indian fighting for the rights of his people. In Delmer Daves' *Broken Arrow*, Stewart played an Indian-scout who falls in love with and marries an Indian girl; Jeff Chandler played Cochise in this first modern Western to portray the Indians with human stature and dignity. William Wellman's

---

Shane was the box-office front-runner, but Mann's Westerns out-drew all opponents with the critics, especially in France

---

Across the Wide Missouri (1951), with Clark Gable, presented an intelligent treatment of the theme of a white trapper and his Indian wife which, although released in a badly shortened version, did well at the box-office.

However, the claim for a new respectability for the Western was firmly established in 1952 with the phenomenal success of *High Noon*. Its director, Fred Zinnemann, said:

'From the time Stanley Kramer and Carl Foreman told me the outline of the story, I saw this film *not* as a comment on the American Western hero, but as an enormously important contemporary theme which happened to take place in a Western setting.'

The tightly constructed script provided Gary Cooper with one of the best roles of his career (and his second Oscar).

The revival of Westerns by 1952 was reflected in their prominence among the top hits of that year. *High Noon* was closely followed in the box-office stakes by *Son of Paleface*, with Bob Hope, and Anthony Mann's *Bend of the River*, which marked a further advance in his collaboration with James Stewart, Raoul Walsh's *Distant Drums*, again with

Gary Cooper, and three pictures from MGM – William Wellman's *Westward the Women, Lone Star* with Gable, and *The Wild North* – all recorded distributors' rentals of over $2 million. But *Shane*, with rentals of over $8 million the following year, was the biggest Western hit of the decade. The fine cast was headed by Alan Ladd, Jean Arthur, Van Heflin and Brandon de Wilde, with Jack Palance as the villainous hired gun brought in to intimidate the homesteaders. The director, George Stevens, was ably supported by A.B. Guthrie's fine script and the Oscar-winning Technicolor camerawork of Loyal Griggs.

Among the many Westerns filmed in the new processes, Robert Aldrich had a big hit in 1954 with *Vera Cruz*, one of the first films in SuperScope. And although Anthony Mann proved in *The Far Country* (1954) that it was still possible to get excellent results from the old format, he finally made the transition to CinemaScope with *The Man From Laramie* (1955), the last of his films with Stewart; all of his subsequent Westerns were in 'Scope. Similarly, John Ford's masterpiece, *The Searchers* (1956), benefitted from the superior photographic quality of VistaVision. The picture presents a harsher, more bitter and sophisticated view of the West than is found in his earlier films.

The black-and-white picture made a temporary comeback during the late Fifties with Delmer Daves' *3.10 to Yuma* (1957) and Arthur Penn's *The Left-Handed Gun* (1958) starring Paul Newman. Both films presented sophisticated and realistic treatments of traditional themes – the lone lawman bringing an outlaw to justice, the story of Billy the Kid – with a modern emphasis on character and relationships on a small scale. The moments of violence develop naturally out of the intensity of personal conflict. Appropriately enough, *The Left-Handed Gun* was in the true Warners tradition of hard-hitting black-and-white pictures featuring a tough hero who dies a violent death in the final reel.

Warners was also responsible for one outstanding Western which brought the decade to a close, Howard Hawks' *Rio Bravo* (1959). Reflecting Hawks' dislike of *High Noon*, the picture may appear conventional on the surface; yet the characters and relationships are observed with great insight and wit while retaining the kind of vitality and spontaneity found in Hawks' earlier pictures:

'I determined to go back and try to get a little of the spirit we used to make pictures with. In *Rio Bravo* I imagine there are almost as many laughs as if we had started out to make a comedy.'

Hawks neatly built on the juxtaposition of old, established Westerners like John Wayne and Walter Brennan with a newer generation represented by Dean Martin and Angie Dickinson. And if the Wayne-Dickinson relationship, a mature man trying to cope with an independent-minded, tough-talking girl, recalls the Bogart-Bacall films of the Forties, this is not surprising, since Hawks was collaborating with two of his favourite scriptwriters from this period, Leigh Brackett and Jules Furthman.

Unfortunately, as the decade drew to a close those qualities developed by directors such as Daves, Boetticher and Hawks during the late Fifties were largely forgotten, and the studios increasingly turned to the overblown, blockbuster Western in the tradition of William Wyler's *The Big Country* (1958). The Sixties began rather unpromisingly with *The Alamo, The Magnificent Seven* – based on *Seven Samurai* – and a disappointing remake of *Cimmaron* (all 1960). These were followed by the scrappy *How the West Was Won* (1962), the first story picture in Cinerama.   JOEL FINLER

Above left: Jack Palance as a hired gunfighter about to kill one of the settlers in Shane. *Above: a showgirl (Sophia Loren) in a touring theatrical troupe joins the gentlemen for a round of poker in George Cukor's* Heller in Pink Tights *(1960). Below, far left: in* Broken Arrow *Jeff Chandler played Cochise for the first but not the last time. Below left: the sheriff (John Wayne) makes his evening patrol in* Rio Bravo. *Below: Glenn Ford and Shirley MacLaine star in George Marshall's* The Sheepman *(1958), a delightful send-up of the archetypal range-war between sheepmen and cattlemen*

JAMES STEWART
in
BROKEN ARROW
Color by Technicolor

JEFF   DEBRA
CHANDLER · PAGET

1

2

3

4

Three years after the American Civil War, Ethan Edwards returns to the home of his brother Aaron, sister-in-law Martha, their two daughters Lucy and Debbie and Martin Pawley (1). Lucy is affianced to Brad Jorgensen, whose family live nearby; his sister, Laurie, is in love with Martin.

Ethan, Captain the Reverend Clayton, Martin and the Texas Rangers ride out to recover some stolen cattle. While they are away, Chief Scar and his Comanche braves attack the Edwards' home. Ethan returns (2) to find that Aaron and Martha have been murdered and that the girls have been kidnapped.

The men embark on a search to find them and have to fight off an Indian attack. When Ethan comes upon Lucy's mutilated body, Brad Jorgensen goes mad with grief. He takes on the Comanches single-handed and is killed.

Ethan and Martin continue to hunt for Debbie. They endure hard winters (3), scorching summers (4) and assaults from white men and Indians. They finally track down Scar and his warriors (5) only to find that Debbie has become one of his squaws (6). She tells Ethan and Martin to leave without her. Ethan tries to kill her but Martin prevents him (7). The Comanches appear and Ethan is wounded fighting them off.

When Scar's new encampment is discovered, Ethan, Martin and the Rangers attack. Ethan finds that Scar has been killed by Martin, who has taken Debbie with him. Ethan scalps the dead chief (8), follows Martin and overpowers him. Just when it seems he is going to kill Debbie, he takes her in his arms (9).

The searchers take the girl back to the Jorgensens' farm. Martin is reunited with Laurie. Ethan lingers outside the door and then wanders off alone (10).

5

6

8

9

Directed by John Ford, 1956
Prod co: C.V. Whitney Pictures Inc/Warner Brothers. **exec prod:** Merian C. Cooper. **ass prod:** Patrick Ford. **sc:** Frank S. Nugent, from the novel by Alan LeMay. **photo** (Technicolor and VistaVision)**:** Winton C. Hoch, Alfred Gilks. **ed:** Jack Murray. **art dir:** Frank Hotaling, James Basevi, Victor Gangelin. **mus:** Max Steiner. **mus orch:** Murray Cutter. **song:** Stan Jones. **sd:** Hugh McDowell, Howard Wilson. **cost:** Frank Beetson, Ann Peck. **prod sup:** Lowell Farrell. **ass dir:** Wingate Smith. **r/t:** 119 minutes.
Cast: John Wayne (*Ethan Edwards*), Jeffrey Hunter (*Martin Pawley*), Vera Miles (*Laurie Jorgensen*), Ward Bond (*Captain the Reverend Samuel Clayton*), Natalie Wood (*Debbie Edwards*), John Qualen (*Lars Jorgensen*), Olive Carey (*Mrs Jorgensen*), Henry Brandon (*Chief Scar*), Ken Curtis (*Charlie McCorry*), Harry Carey Jr (*Brad Jorgensen*), Antonio Moreno (*Emilio Figueroa*), Hank Worden (*Mose Harper*), Lana Wood (*Debbie as a child*), Walter Coy (*Aaron Edwards*), Dorothy Jordan (*Martha Edwards*), Pippa Scott (*Lucy Edwards*), Pat Wayne (*Lieutenant Greenhill*), Bill Steele (*Ranger Nesbitt*), Cliff Lyons (*Colonel Greenhill*), Beulah Archuletta (*Look*), Jack Pennick (*private*), Peter Mamakos (*Futterman*), Chuck Roberson (*Texas Ranger*), Away Luna, Billy Yellow, Bob Many Mules, Exactly Sonnie Betsuie, Feather Hat Jr, Harry Black Horse, Jack Tin Horn, Many Mules Son, Percy Shooting Star, Pete Gray Eyes, Pipe Line Begishe, Smile White Sheep and other members of the Navajo tribe (*Comanches*).

Given the humour, warmth and nostalgia of John Ford's Westerns from *Stagecoach* (1939) to *Wagonmaster* and *Rio Grande* (both 1950), it seemed barely conceivable that he would allow the emergence of the 'psychological' Western in the early Fifties to affect his own roseate vision of the West. *The Searchers*, however, was to prove his most anguished and desperate work.

Whether or not Ford had been influenced by the new trend will never be known, but certainly before *The Searchers* none of his heroes had been permitted to disrupt the complacent celebration of the folk rituals by which he set so much store – at least, not to the extent that the populist philosophy behind them was questioned.

Ethan Edwards, the damned, anarchic hero of *The Searchers*, does just that. There is utter contempt for the customs that bind and sustain society in the way that he cuts short the funeral of his murdered brother and sister-in-law – 'Put an Amen to it' – to begin his relentless pursuit of Scar and Debbie. Later returning home emptyhanded midway through the quest, his arrival completely wrecks the wedding of Laurie Jorgensen and the insipid rancher Charlie McCorry. As a result of this intervention, Laurie resumes her longdistance romance with Martin Pawley, Ethan's fellow searcher. She thus forsakes the homesteader for the wanderer. Ethan is the agent of this treason, and through the film the audience travels with him – away from settlements and civilization – to the brink of the destruction of Ford's hitherto secure moral universe.

Virtually every gesture, every action in *The Searchers* mirrors or mocks Ethan's inner bitterness and obsessions. There is the moment when his brother's wife, Martha, strokes Ethan's cape – a sad indication of their mutual but impossible love. Scar's later violation of Martha seems a perverted expression of Ethan's own frustrated sexual longing. In another scene, Ethan is highly amused when Martin unintentionally purchases a Comanche squaw, Look; this incident ironically functions as the comic obverse of Debbie's miscegenation with Scar, a union that fills Ethan with loathing for her.

The parched desert landscape across which Ethan and Martin trek is itself a metaphor for Ethan's selfdenial and pointless, impotent endurance. The daunting monoliths and wide-open spaces of Monument Valley, the claustrophobic interiors of the cavalry outpost and the dark cave in which the searchers hide out, and the snowbound wastes of winter combine to create a nightmare terrain in which Ethan and Martin go round and round in circles, finally locating Scar and Debbie just a few miles from where they started.

The hunt is carried on in a deceptively relaxed manner; as it progresses, tension and unease mount insinuatingly, making for a breathtaking climax when Ethan catches Debbie defenceless. Two truly terrifying close-ups of Ethan's face – one as he realizes that the Indians are attacking his brother's home, the other when he is confronted with white women who have gone mad after being held captive by Indians – have already indicated the ferocity of his intentions. The film's startlingly bright colours, the climatic extremes of hot and cold, and scenes like Ethan's needless slaughter of the buffalo help to convey his mental instability and the insane nature of his quest.

Calm is suddenly restored when Ethan lifts Debbie into his arms instead of killing her and then returns her safely to the Jorgensens. However, the film's main concern is not for her but for Ethan. Unlike Martin, who is free to settle down with Laurie, he has no place in a civilized, family-based community. Ford, having questioned his traditional values of order and stability, does not ultimately desert them: the final shot is of a door closing on Ethan, who is fated, like the spirit of the dead Indian whose eyes he shoots out earlier in the film, 'to wander forever between the winds'. His search has not ended and never can.
GRAHAM FULLER

7

10

153

Kirk Douglas

Kirk Douglas' energy and magnetism dominate every picture he is in. He seems to challenge audiences with the question – is the hole in his jutting chin a beautifying dimple put there by the Almighty or the imprint of a hoodlum's toecap?

Casting a Giant Shadow

An aggressive vitality, a driving egotism – these are the distinctive qualities conveyed by Kirk Douglas, whose forcefulness repels some cinemagoers as much as it grips others. As an actor who has chosen his own roles since the early Fifties, run his own production company and (more recently) ventured into direction, he has favoured parts in which he can play the brazen individualist, the man out of step with the world around him. His most notable characters are intense, moody, powerful, often tragic – either they are crushed by a society that cannot tolerate them or they destroy themselves through a fatal flaw in their makeup. As the slave leader in *Spartacus* (1960), he is finally captured and crucified (though the real Spartacus died in battle); as the fanatical policeman in *Detective Story* (1951), he destroys his marriage when he cannot forgive his wife for once having had an abortion and effectively commits suicide by stopping a bullet fired by a crazed criminal.

No mercy

Occasionally in his films, others have fallen victim to an oppressive society while Douglas has been cast as a concerned observer. In the powerful *Paths of Glory* (1957), Douglas played a French officer in World War I who tries in vain to prevent four of his men, scapegoats for the failures of the high command, from being executed; a similar situation is given a 'black' twist in *Town Without Pity* (1961), in which Douglas portrays an American Major in World War II who successfully defends four GIs accused of rape by destroying the reputation of the German girl they attacked, driving her to suicide.

But more often Douglas' characters have

been the victims of their own aggression and ambition. The role that established his hard, ruthless image was that of Midge Kelly, the boxer in *Champion* (1949) who fights his way to the top, unscrupulously betraying his associates, and then dies from injuries sustained in the ring rather than accept defeat. Somewhat in the same vein was his newspaperman in *Ace in the Hole* (1951) who whips up the plight of a man trapped in a cave into a

Top: in Spartacus, *Kirk Douglas plays the gladiator who rebels and leads the slave revolt against the Romans. Above left:* Young Man With a Horn *(1950), based on the life of Twenties jazz musician Bix Beiderbeck, was one of Douglas' many biopics. Above: in* The Bad and the Beautiful *he played a film producer who makes his star (Lana Turner) fall in love with him so that she will give a powerful and passionate performance on the screen*

national story, delaying his rescue and causing the man's death.

In *The Bad and the Beautiful* (1952) Douglas brought a saving veneer of charm to the role of film producer Jonathan Shields who uses people but at the same time enables them to realize their own talents: a star (Lana Turner), a director (Barry Sullivan) and a writer (Dick Powell) are burned by their contact with him but at the end of the film are tempted to help him out when he needs them again.

Douglas was even intensely sympathetic in one of his favourite roles, that of the modern-day cowboy in *Lonely Are the Brave* (1962). Attempting to escape on horseback from the

law, he is finally killed crossing a highway by a truck carrying a load of toilet fittings. Douglas' characters court death: his dedicated military commander of *Cast a Giant Shadow* (1966) saves Israel from the Arabs but is senselessly killed by a sentry on his own side when he fails to answer a challenge in Hebrew, a language he does not understand. True to history, it is nevertheless the kind of ironical ending that seemingly delights Douglas.

A marked man

Pain and physical mutilation frequently shape and test the outlook of his screen characters. In *Man Without a Star* (1955) Douglas portrayed

The many faces of Kirk Douglas. Top left: the painter Vincent Van Gogh with Willemein (Jill Bennett) in Lust for Life. *Top: the northwest frontiersman in* The Big Sky. *Above left: the out-of-time cowboy in* Lonely Are the Brave. *Above: the faded film star with his director (Edward G. Robinson) in* Two Weeks in Another Town *(1962).*

another cowboy fleeing the encroachment of civilization (represented by the enclosing of the range with barbed wire). In the film's most intense moment, Douglas rips off his shirt to explain his detestation of the wire, revealing the scars it has left on his body.

In the pioneering saga *The Big Sky* (1952), the Douglas character loses a finger in a sequence pitched for grotesque comedy by the director Howard Hawks. As Vincent Van Gogh in *Lust for Life* (1956), Douglas was thoroughly convincing (apart from the intractable prob-

lem of accent) and conveyed the torment that drove the painter to cut off his ear. As Einar in *The Vikings* (1958), a production of Douglas' Bryna company, he lost an eye to a hawk. In *Scalawag* (1973), Douglas directed himself as a one-legged pirate. Add such incidents as his self-imposed flogging by a black manservant in *The Way West* (1967) and the gruesome end of his dastardly villain, George Brougham, in *The List of Adrian Messenger* (1963) – flung onto the spikes of a concealed plough in place of his intended victim – and his career seems littered with instances of physical suffering that serve as a harsh, but often fitting, reward for the way his characters conduct themselves.

Born under a bad sign

'Virtue isn't photogenic', is the actor's avowed reason for portraying rogues. Even when his violent impulses have a conventional motivation, Douglas' characters have their grief compounded. In *Last Train From Gun Hill* (1959), he plays a marshal pursuing the murderers of his Indian wife. The principal killer turns out to be the son of his best friend.

In *Gunfight at the OK Corral* (1957), Douglas convincingly conveyed the self-disgust that possessed his alcoholic Doc Holliday, just as in *Lust for Life* he vividly rendered the mental anguish that drove Van Gogh to kill himself. More melodramatically, there were his characters in *The Last Sunset* (1961) and *In Harm's Way* (1965) who expiate their sins by inviting certain death in the dignified circumstances of, respectively, a gunfight undertaken with an empty gun and a suicide mission over Japanese waters in World War II.

Even Douglas' patriotic officer of *Seven Days in May* (1964) is afflicted with self-disgust. He reveals a military plot to overthrow the government but he detests being an informer and basically disapproves of the peace-mongering policies of a weak President that have prompted the conspiracy; he is also disturbed at having to recover from a socialite love letters that might be used to blackmail the leader of the conspirators.

Douglas has a reputation for being as forceful off-screen as on. 'I've always insisted on voicing my suggestions with directors,' he has declared, adding, 'The good ones have never objected.' Yet Anthony Mann left *Spartacus* after a disagreement with Douglas (Stanley Kubrick took over) and Robert Aldrich was unable to get on with his star and executive producer when working on *The Last Sunset*

(1961). Indeed, when Douglas made his directorial debut on *Scalawag*, he himself admitted: 'I've been *accused* of directing movies before but now I can be blamed.'

And blamed he was for *Scalawag*; he agreed in retrospect that he had mishandled the picture. However, functioning as director, producer and star of *Posse* (1975), he came up with a surprisingly accomplished and biting Western. He once again played a thwarted self-seeker, whose attempts to make political capital out of the capture of a notorious train-robber rebound on him when the badman lures the posse away and leaves him alone and ridiculed.

Douglas' efforts to play more relaxed parts in contemporary comedies like *Top Secret Affair* (1957) and *For Love or Money* (1963) have made him seem dull, though there was a virile humour to his period rogues of *The Devil's Disciple* (1959) and *The War Wagon* (1967). Douglas needed scope to bring feeling to his parts: the passion to paint he conveyed as no other Hollywood actor ever has in *Lust for Life*. Given a role which he could naturally invest with his own dedication and determination, he has shown himself to be a very considerable performer indeed.　　ALLEN EYLES

Below: Colonel Dax, who rapes a young nurse (Jill Haworth) in In Harm's Way. *Bottom left: the gunman hired to kill Taw Jackson (John Wayne) in* The War Wagon. *Bottom right: the master of disguise receives the tail for the winning ride from the Marquis of Gleneyre (Clive Brook) in* The List of Adrian Messenger

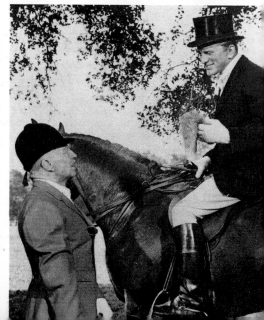

The concrete jungle

Images of violence and conspiracy dominated the gangster movies of the Fifties, together with a certain nostalgia for the good old days of crime – Prohibition-style

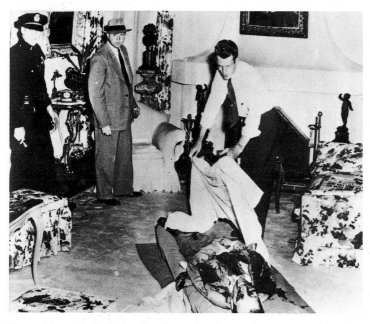

Film critics quite often write about the cinema in terms of the excellence of particular films or the careers of particular directors. Ordinary cinemagoers (including off-duty critics), however, tend to talk about the cinema in terms of the stars and the types of film they like (such as Westerns, musicals, horror movies and so on). It may be that ordinary cinemagoers are closer to the way the cinema actually works as a social process, an essentially industrial/commercial process in which pleasures are produced, marketed and consumed.

To talk about the excellence of particular films is to concentrate on only one aspect of the process, the film as object or individual product, a unique experience labelled by a particular title (*Casablanca*, *Charley Varrick* or *Quadrophenia*, for example). To talk about the careers of particular directors (Nicholas Ray, Don Siegel, Walter Hill) is to suggest that the cinema works primarily through expressing the personality and interests of particular film-makers, a notion that even the most casual cinemagoer knows to be generally false, though the media now tend to push this viewpoint, once largely confined to specialist criticism.

When talking about stars and types (or genres) of film, it is very difficult not to talk also about all the stages of the cinema process, a more inclusive and accurate kind of examination. In particular, such discussion includes consideration of the audience, what it does with the films it sees. The audience once had, and to some extent still has, a habit of cinema-going and this affects how particular films are understood and interpreted. At the very least, it can be said that the audience brings to any individual film its experience of other films.

Since the primary purpose of popular cinema is to deliver a set of particular satisfactions to audiences, there is a sense in which all popular films do the same thing in much the same way. They employ a form of narrative in which one form of stability is shattered by intrusive forces and a new form of stability established at the outcome. The conclusion usually has a strong sense of narrative closure, of having the ends neatly tied up. Within this movement, in itself highly satisfying, the more static satisfactions of the cinema, the opportunity to gaze on particular stars and events, are delivered.

There is, however, a certain tension at the core of the process of recurrent cinema-going. On the one hand, certain *known* satisfactions require to be delivered; on the other hand, the experience is expected to be sufficiently different from previous ones to avoid boredom. This tension between repetition and innovation is central to the way the cinema's genres work and goes a long way towards explaining the process of development and renewal in the genres. A question it will not answer, though, is why particular genres first emerge and then re-emerge at particular historical moments. Such explanations would be very complex, involving discussion of the economic demands of production companies and the ideological and aesthetic needs of film-makers and audiences in particular eras.

As Hollywood entered the Fifties, it inherited a very rich and varied tradition in the crime film. The ensemble of features associated with the classic gangster movie of the Thirties was still in evidence: a particular kind of narrative form (itself a variant of the order/instability/new-order form) which charts the rise and fall of a gangster; an iconography of figures dressed in a particular way, moving through the familiar milieux and engaging in special activities; and set pieces of spectacle, often involving guns or cars. This had been overlaid with and interpenetrated by the qualities of the thriller: a different variant of the order/instability/new-order

Above left: Bugsy Siegel, gangster and friend of several film producers, was shot dead at his Beverly Hills home on June 20, 1947. The real-life photograph is more bloody and horrific than most movies of the period but would not have been unusual in crime magazines of that time. Above: Marilyn Maxwell and Broderick Crawford in New York Confidential, *the story of a big crime-boss who comes to a violent end. Newspaper headlines often feature in gangster movies, both to speed up the narrative and to represent public opinion, the straight world, in the crooks' environment*

narrative form whereby a mystery is solved; forms of lighting derived primarily from the German Expressionist cinema; a different range of figures such as the private eye, the *femme fatale* and the intellectual, sophisticated, Europeanized and often psychologically perverse villain; and an overall awareness of human alienation and cruelty. Overlaid upon both of these major forms were the passion for location shooting, the use of documentary origins of stories and the emphasis on the intricate workings of particular technologies which characterized crime films of the late Forties.

The crucial process of renewal and transformation within the genre can be indicated by comparing the way the elements are handled from one era to another. Thus in *The Public Enemy* (1931) the energy and dynamism of the James Cagney figure are presented as laudable ambition gone wrong and his mother is portrayed as a source of traditional values, while in *White Heat* (1949), Cody Jarrett (James Cagney) is presented as psychotic and his mother as a monstrous harpy goading her son to greater excesses. While the satisfactions delivered by the crime movie (and any other popular form) at any moment invariably involve the following-through of variants on the classical narrative forms

and the opportunity to gaze at stars and spectacle, the crime movies of any era take their subject-matter from what is actually happening, or has recently happened, in American crime. This is one way a genre might be renewed and transformed. Thus after the repeal of the Volstead Act in 1933 which brought an end to Prohibition, labour racketeering occupied a great deal of the attention of organized crime, as in *Racket Busters* (1938), until 1943, when gambling moved to the fore, as in *Force of Evil* (1949).

In the Fifties the gangster movie produced three new strains, one of which took its impulse directly from the reality of American crime at the time. In this first strain there are two characteristic images: one is of a figure, very often a racketeer, testifying, amid considerable media coverage, before a Senate sub-committee; the other is of a group of elderly, sober-suited men sitting around a boardroom table and voting on whether an erstwhile colleague should be murdered. The real events to which both these images relate are the hearings and conclusions of the Senate Special Committee to Investigate Crime in Interstate Commerce, usually called the Kefauver Committee after its chairman. It was the findings of this committee which gave rise to the

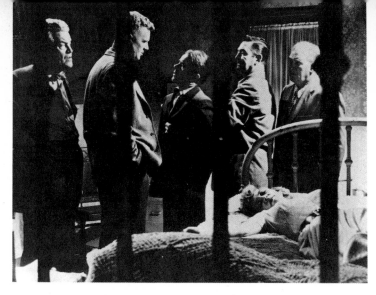

Top far left: John Dall and Peggy Cummins as a couple of young robbers in Joseph H. Lewis' Gun Crazy *(1949). Top left: Richard Wilson's re-creation of Twenties Chicago,* Al Capone. *Far left: another period piece from Richard Wilson, again expertly photographed by Lucien Ballard,* Pay or Die! *was set in New York's Little Italy in 1906. Left: Roger Corman's* Bloody Mama *recounted the violent lives and deaths of Ma Barker (Shelley Winters) and her four sons in the Thirties. Bottom left: Richard Conte as one of* The Brothers Rico *in Phil Karlson's version of a Simenon novel. Above: Jay C. Flippen, Sterling Hayden, Elisha Cook Jnr, Ted de Corsia, Joe Sawyer and (on the bed) Marie Windsor in Stanley Kubrick's* The Killing. *Above right:* My Gun Is Quick *was based on Mickey Spillane's novel. Below: Roger Corman's* The St Valentine's Day Massacre *was a convincingly detailed retelling of Al Capone's most famous crime*

cycle of gangster movies in which 'the Syndicate' (sometimes city-wide, sometimes nation-wide) figured.

In many respects *The Enforcer* (1951) is *the* transitional crime film between the Forties and the Fifties. Dealing with the activities of 'Murder Incorporated', it has some of the features of the so-called 'semi-documentary' film of the Forties but sounds the note which was to dominate the Fifties, the existence of an all-embracing crime conspiracy modelled on legitimate business activity. This cycle includes *Hoodlum Empire* (1952), *New York Confidential* (1955), *The Brothers Rico* (1957) and *Underworld USA* (1960). This motif, more than any other, should have provided the means of offering explanations of crime in terms of social structure rather than personal disposition; but the form of the classical narrative movie, with its emphasis on individual characters, is not well suited to posing questions and explanations in other than personal terms. Similarly, the issues of politics in American movies are displaced on to the terrain of personal action and morality. The Syndicate is usually defeated in this cycle of movies, but almost always through the action of one man motivated by vengeance.

The two central recurring scenes of this cycle are of testimony and conspiracy; there is often a sense, in these movies, of the power of the Syndicate stretching into every area of the characters' lives, as

in *The Brothers Rico*. It is interesting to speculate on the extent to which these images of testimony and conspiracy involving crime were providing the terrain on to which was displaced other kinds of testimony and conspiracy which were quite literally unspeakable in the Hollywood films of the Fifties – those associated with the McCarthy hearings and the aftermath of blacklisting.

The second strain which appeared in the Fifties indicated that Hollywood was beginning to have a conscious sense of its own history, This strain consisted of a series of films set in the Prohibition and Depression periods, the time of the early gangster movies. Very often they took the form of a biography of a notorious criminal. This cycle includes *Baby Face Nelson* (1957), *The Bonnie Parker Story*, *Machine Gun Kelly* (both 1958), *Al Capone* (1959) and continues into the Sixties with *The Rise and Fall of Legs Diamond*, *Pay or Die!* (both 1960), *Portrait of a Mobster* (1961), *Bonnie and Clyde*, *The St. Valentine's Day Massacre* (both 1967) and *Bloody Mama* (1970). The sense that these films offer of Hollywood consciously raking over its own history was pointed up by their stylized, balletic quality and the use of music designed to evoke the Twenties and Thirties.

The third strain which came to the fore in the Fifties had its origins to some extent in the Forties. Films such as *Criss Cross* (1949) and *White Heat* involved carefully prepared robberies which

In the Fifties, gangster movies and thrillers became more conscious of style and history

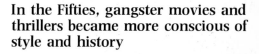

remained a secondary element in these films. *The Asphalt Jungle* (1950) was unique in American cinema for the attention it gave to the preparation for and execution of the robbery. The form which it initiated – the 'caper' movie – is in many respects a celebration of the narrative process of cinema itself. Within this form, a group of disparate individuals comes together to pull off a robbery. The cycle includes *The Killing* (1956), *Odds Against Tomorrow* (1959), *Seven Thieves* and *Ocean's Eleven* (both 1960).

One of the strangest elements in the transition from the Forties to the Fifties in Hollywood was the virtual disappearance of the thriller and *film noir*. Hollywood cinema of the Fifties is generally bright and colourful; even its bleakest films, such as *The Big Heat* (1953), appear bathed in light by comparison with Forties films. The thriller did survive to a limited extent into the Fifties. But virtuous heroes

Above: in The Wrong Man, *Mrs Balestrero (Vera Miles) has struck her husband, Manny (Henry Fonda), resenting the collapse of family life since his wrongful arrest. Maxwell Anderson's book and Hitchcock's film were based on a real-life case of mistaken identity. Below right: a poster for* Strangers on a Train, *based on Patricia Highsmith's first novel, shows Hitchcock's use of his own popular humorous image. Bruno (Robert Walker) does indeed strangle the unwanted wife of a tennis player (Farley Granger) to whom he has proposed a swopping of murders*

like Sam Spade in *The Maltese Falcon* (1941) and Philip Marlowe in *Murder, My Sweet* (1944), *The Big Sleep, The Lady in the Lake* (both 1946) and *The Brasher Doubloon* (1947) gave way to the considerably less virtuous Mike Hammer of the Mickey Spillane adaptations which characterize the decade – *I, The Jury* (1953), *Kiss Me Deadly* (1955) and *My Gun Is Quick* (1957). The change is partly indicated in the casting. While Bogart has a certain toughness, it does not altogether conceal his humour and vulnerability. These qualities are hardly evident in the screen persona of Ralph Meeker in *Kiss Me Deadly*.

If the thriller and *film noir* were largely missing from Fifties Hollywood, their spirit lived on. Nowhere was this more apparent than in the realization of particular acts of violence in the Fifties. In the classic gangster movie of the Thirties, violence tended to be swift, unritualized, unmarked by specific cinematic effects (such as close-ups) and usually executed by firearms. Violence in the thriller and *film noir* of the Forties involved beating, crushing, burning, cutting, disfigurement, pushing from high buildings and poisoning. This more tactile sense of violence is evident, primarily in the Fifties gangster movie and thriller, but also in other Fifties genres such as the Western and the war movie. An example which excited much comment at the time was the shooting of James Stewart's gun hand in *The Man From Laramie* (1955). Among the most disturbing acts of violence in the Fifties gangster movie are those enacted (actually or potentially) on women, such as the disfigurement suffered by Debbie (Gloria Grahame) in *The Big Heat* and the threat of acid to the face of Vicki (Cyd Charisse) in *Party Girl* (1958).

The increasingly disturbing violence of American cinema in the Fifties is perhaps an indication of the sense of unease which underlay the apparent stability of Eisenhower's America. Critics have revealed the presence of a similar sense of unease in the displacement of the nuclear threat into fantasies about mutated monsters in the same period and in the stresses and strains lying just underneath the surface of the family melodrama.

Unease is a key word when discussing a very special variant of the crime film in the Fifties, that type of film in which the focus is less on an account of organized crime or on the solving of a mystery than on the mechanics of suspense.

This type of film is particularly associated with the name of Alfred Hitchcock, for whom the Fifties was a particularly prolific decade. The pattern of the classical Hollywood narrative whereby initial stability is undermined is writ large in Hitchcock's work in the sense that the central figures of his films very often inhabit the most mundane worlds – a tennis player in *Strangers on a Train* (1951), a priest in *I Confess* (1952), a temporarily incapacitated news-photographer in *Rear Window* (1954), an advertising man in *North by Northwest* (1959) – which collapse under their feet, tumbling them into the most nightmarish situations. As critics have demonstrated, these nightmares do not have a *social* basis; they are not concerned with the characters' relations with the outside world. Rather, they are concerned with the fragility of the characters' own personality and identity and with the horrors which may lie in the depths of their own psyches. Thus the priest of *I Confess*, the tennis player of *Strangers on a Train* and the ad-man of *North by Northwest* effectively take on the appearance of guilty men; the policeman of *Vertigo* (1958) becomes a necrophiliac and the temporary invalid of *Rear Window*, a voyeur.

But the bleakest film in Hitchcock's Fifties canon and the film which perhaps best conveys the underlying unease of Fifties America is *The Wrong Man* (1957), in which an unassuming bass player (Henry Fonda) is wrongly identified as an armed robber. Slowly and deliberately, the judicial process locks him into this role, his family disintegrates under the experience and his wife retreats into madness.

It may be that highly stylized genres like the gangster movie, the thriller and the suspense movie offer a better guide retrospectively to the mood of a particular society at a given time than more overtly social films. Certainly they tend to have lasted better when seen again nowadays. COLIN McARTHUR

ALFRED HITCHCOCK
BRINGS YOU 101 MINUTES OF MATCHLESS SUSPENSE!

STRANGERS ON A TRAIN

It begins with the scream of a train whistle... and ends with screaming excitement!

"WILL STILL MAKE YOUR HAIR STAND ON END" NEWS OF THE WORLD

Starring
FARLEY GRANGER   RUTH ROMAN   ROBERT WALKER
with LEO G. CARROLL Screenplay by Raymond Chandler and Czenzi Ormonde   A WARNER BROS. Picture Released through WARNER-PATHE

Above: Farley Granger and Cathy O'Donnell in Ray's directorial debut, They Live by Night. *Left: hands on hips, Ray directs Ava Gardner and Martin Miller in* 55 Days at Peking, *the film that ended his Hollywood career*

Knocking on the Hollywood door

While acting on Broadway in the Thirties, Ray met the producer John Houseman and the director Elia Kazan. He worked with Houseman on radio propaganda programmes during World War II, and when Kazan went to Hollywood in 1945 to make *A Tree Grows in Brooklyn*, Ray accompanied him as an assistant. It was Houseman's television production of the classic suspense thriller *Sorry Wrong Number*, which Ray directed in 1946 (and which virtually established TV drama in the USA), that brought both men to the attention of Dore Schary, head of production at RKO. The result was *They Live by Night* (1948), produced by Houseman (who already had several film credits to his name) and directed by Ray.

They Live by Night immediately established a framework of reference points to which Ray's later movies inevitably return. Based on Edward Anderson's novel *Thieves Like Us* (and remade under that title by Robert Altman in 1974), the movie is the story of the doomed love affair between Bowie Bowers (Farley Granger) and Keechie (Cathy O'Donnell). Bowie is the first of Ray's 'outsiders' – solitary, anguished characters at war with society and themselves. He is an escaped convict – wrongly jailed for murder – who believes quite genuinely that the proceeds of bank robberies can hire him the best lawyer to clear his name. As the title suggests, the world into which the two central characters escape is one of darkness, pessimism and loneliness; yet there they find the love and freedom that has been denied them in the daylight world. Seven years later, in Ray's most famous movie, *Rebel Without a Cause* (1955), the three teenagers played by James Dean, Natalie Wood and Sal Mineo would share similar moments of peace and tenderness in a deserted mansion which for a brief time becomes their own little universe.

In lonely places

This pessimistic, lonely and doomed existence is depicted again and again in Ray's movies, whether it is the harsh, transient world of the professional rodeo circuit in *The Lusty Men* (1952), or one of the last outposts of unspoiled, primitive society like the Eskimo settlement threatened by an encroaching 'civilization' in

Nicholas Ray The Lost Romantic

'If it was all in the script . . . why make the movie?' The words of the director Nicholas Ray enshrine his belief in the purity and power of the cinematic image, a belief he was able to translate into stunning effect with his mastery of colour, composition and performance – vibrantly displayed in his poetic but downcast views of America. But Ray's is a tragic story. Forced for many years to compromise his vision and cater to the bland expectations of Fifties audiences, he finally decided it was better to leave Hollywood and film-making behind and became a lonely wanderer in exile, a rebel without a career, bitterly consigned to an artistic wilderness

Nicholas Ray was always a problem. His career is central to that most difficult of critical conundrums: how great an artist can a director working in the commercial Hollywood system be? Not at all, according to one history of world cinema published in Britain in 1964, which contains just two fleeting references to him. In complete contrast, French critics analysed and eulogized. 'The cinema *is* Nicholas Ray', said Jean-Luc Godard. Although the divergence of opinion on Ray has narrowed over the years, there is a special irony in the

director's own dictum that 'There is no formula for success. But there is a formula for failure; and that is trying to please everyone'.

Ray was born in Wisconsin in 1911. He studied architecture under Frank Lloyd Wright at Chicago University, but chose to become a stage actor and occasionally a director, and at the same time a travelling student of American folklore. Diverse though these four interests might appear, they are combined in the movies he directed – all which bear the indelible stamp of one personality.

161

Ombre Bianche (1959, *The Savage Innocents*).

'I'm a stranger here myself', says Johnny (Sterling Hayden) in *Johnny Guitar* (1954) to explain his diffidence as he watches a bank robbery in progress, and it is an attitude that is at the heart of Ray's world. It suggests both an inner peace of mind, a world of dreams, a means of escape from an unacceptable world outside, and the root of a conflict when that outside world advances threateningly on such a mind. Of these conflicts were the best Ray movies made.

The least interesting of his early movies contain few of these complexities. *A Woman's Secret* (1949), *Born to Be Bad* (1950) and *Flying Leathernecks* (1951) were all to Ray reluctant chores handed out by RKO studio boss Howard Hughes. They were, by Ray's standards, simple movies: two 'women's pictures', with Gloria Grahame (who briefly became Ray's wife) as Susan in *A Woman's Secret*, and Joan Fontaine as Christabel in *Born to Be Bad* – both scheming their way to success by ruthlessly using everyone around them; and a traditional war movie with John Wayne as a marine hammering friend and foe in the national cause.

Of greater interest was *Knock on Any Door* (1949), made for and starring Humphrey Bogart. The huge commercial success of this film helped Ray's career immensely. Its case history of a young hoodlum on trial for the murder of a policeman looks forward to the starting point of *Rebel Without a Cause*. Its polemical condemnation of society, which is deemed as much responsible for the crime as the accused boy, recalls Ray's own involvement in Elia Kazan's radical theatre-workshop groups in the mid-Thirties. Another major ingredient of *Knock on Any Door*, and a recurring interest of Ray's, is the theme of the latent violence in man – a trait that is often only brought to the surface by its opposite, love. Both Ray's best movies of the early Fifties, *In a Lonely Place* (1950) and *On Dangerous Ground* (1951), are depictions of this theme.

On one level, *On Dangerous Ground* is an exciting thriller, the story of a sadistic cop (Robert Ryan) and his relationship with a blind girl (Ida Lupino) who is the sister of a hunted

killer. On another, it is a return to the dark world of *They Live by Night*, but in an urban environment. *In a Lonely Place* has a Hollywood setting with a scriptwriter (Humphrey Bogart) suspected of murder and saved only by the alibi given by his next-door neighbour (Gloria Grahame). The relationship that develops between these two characters provides the basis for Ray's most forceful portrait of an outwardly strong and intelligent man destroyed by his own inner melancholy and his inability to communicate except through terrible fits of violence.

Above: In a Lonely Place *starred Humphrey Bogart as a Hollywood scriptwriter driven by rumour and suspicion to the brink of murdering the girl (Gloria Grahame) he loves. Right: John Wayne as a fighter pilot in* Flying Leathernecks. *Below right: James Mason as the drug addict in* Bigger Than Life. *Below left: the death of a rodeo rider in* The Lusty Men, *with Susan Hayward*

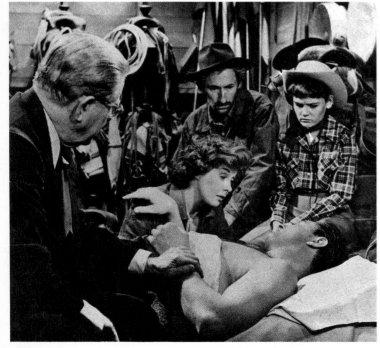

Above: saloon-keeper Vienna (Joan Crawford) faces a lynching at the hands of the mob whipped up by cattle boss Emma Small (Mercedes McCambridge) in Johnny Guitar. Below right: Curt Jurgens in the war film Bitter Victory

Violence, types of and uses

Ray constantly explored this expressive side of violence in his Fifties films. *Johnny Guitar*, possibly the most bizarre Western ever made, concentrates on the psychological and sexual tensions in the relationship between the two main female characters, Vienna (Joan Crawford) and Emma (Mercedes McCambridge), and ends in a savage gunfight between them. Violent outbursts punctuate *Rebel Without a Cause* as Jim Stark (James Dean) is transformed from social misfit to a self-determining adult through the death of the unhappy and unloved Plato (Sal Mineo). In *Bigger Than Life* (1956), the drug cortisone is the metaphor for the change of character in Ed Avery (James Mason) from underpaid teacher (a man forced to work as a taxi-driver after school to maintain his family's standards of living) to virtual madman. Initially he takes the drug to relieve the pain of a fatal nervous disease, but discovers that it offers a freedom that he has never before experienced. His abuse of it leads to paranoid delusions of grandeur and a state of insanity which almost destroys his life and family. Captain Leith (Richard Burton) in *Bitter Victory* (1957) uses the horrors of a World War II desert campaign to satisfy his own masochism. And do these characters add up to a portrait of their creator? They do, admitted Ray in a 1974 interview, 'but it is the role of the poet – and every artist hopes to be a poet – to expose himself. It's the only way he communicates'.

It is also difficult not to see Ray the rebel, the loner and the fighter, as the sheriff played by James Cagney in *Run for Cover* (1955), embarking on a law-and-order campaign based on humanity rather than lynching; or identifying with the misfit outlaw band of *The True Story of Jesse James* (1957); the drunken-teacher-turned-wildlife-preserver (Christopher Plummer) in turn-of-the-century Florida in *Wind Across the Everglades* (1958); the two outsiders of *Party Girl* (1958) – the crooked lawyer trying to go straight (Robert Taylor) and the prostitute who falls in love with him (Cyd Charisse). Another side of Ray can be seen in the anthropological and ecological issues raised by *The Savage Innocents* as Inuk the Eskimo (Anthony Quinn) confronts a scathing portrait of the white man's civilization and rejects it.

Epic farewells

Hollywood and Nicholas Ray rejected each other in 1963 after two big-screen epics, *King of Kings* (1961) displayed more interest in the traitor Judas Iscariot than in Christ, and there were no miracles. Finally, Ray made 55 *Days at Peking* (1963), the story of the Boxer rebellion in China in 1900 starring Charlton Heston, Ava Gardner and David Niven. Like all Ray's movies, it contains some fine performances (including one by the director himself in a cameo role). Indeed, Ray drew some of the finest performances in their careers from such diverse stars as Robert Mitchum, James Mason, James Dean, Joan Crawford and Richard Burton. He embedded these performances in his films with a unique visual style which

even mastered that most cumbersome of screen ratios, CinemaScope. Ray attributed this success to his early architectural training. His work is littered with extraordinary compositions, both of form and colour, which are not just masterly demonstrations of craftsmanship but counterpoints to the actions, emotions and psyches of his characters. Even his worst film, *Hot Blood* (1956), comes alive with some frenetic musical sequences.

The End

Ray spent the last 16 years of his life outside the commercial Hollywood system. He taught film studies at New York State University and made, as a joint project with his students, *We Can't Go Home Again* (1973), a semi-documentary collage of images in which he played a teacher with a death-wish. His health, never good, declined over the years and his only other piece of film-making was a sad segment of an omnibus 'sexploitation' movie, *Dreams of Thirteen* (1974). His final feature-film appearance was as an army general in Miloš Forman's 1979 film adaptation of the stage success *Hair*, but a more satisfying farewell image was his role in *Das Amerikanische Freund* (1977, *The American Friend*). It was directed by Wim Wenders, who later recorded the last few months of Ray's life – he died in June 1979 – in *Lightning Over Water* (1980).

In *The American Friend*, an adaptation of Patricia Highsmith's novel *Ripley's Game*, Ray plays an artist whom the world believes to be dead. The real-life parallel is obvious. To him goes the honour of the movie's closing shot as he turns away from the camera and walks into the distance. Twenty years earlier it was Ray who walked into the final shot of *Rebel Without a Cause*, stopping briefly to admire a flower-bed. At the end of *The American Friend* he walks forcefully on and the scene goes dark. It is a moment of which Nick Ray, for all his pessimism always a great Romantic, must surely have approved.
PETER HOWDEN

Filmography
1945 A Tree Grows in Brooklyn (ass. dir. only). '48 They Live by Night (+co-sc). '49 A Woman's Secret; Knock on Any Door; Roseanna McCoy (add. dir, uncredited). '50 Born to Be Bad; In a Lonely Place. '51 Flying Leathernecks; The Racket (add. dir, uncredited); On Dangerous Ground. '52 Macao (add. dir, uncredited); The Lusty Men; Androcles and the Lion (add. dir, uncredited). '54 Johnny Guitar (+assoc. prod). '55 Run for Cover; Rebel Without a Cause (+co-sc). '56 Hot Blood; Bigger Than Life. '57 The True Story of Jesse James; Bitter Victory (+co-sc). '58 Wind Across the Everglades; Party Girl. '59 Ombre Bianche (GB: The Savage Innocents) (IT-FR-GB). '61 King of Kings. '63 55 Days at Peking (+act). '64 Circus World (co-sc. only) (GB: The Magnificent Showman). '65 The Doctor and the Devils (GB-YUG) (unfinished). '73 I'm a Stranger Here Myself (doc) (appearance as himself only). '73 We Can't Go Home Again (+act). '74 Dreams of Thirteen ep The Janitor (+sc; +act) (GER-NETH). '75 James Dean, the First American Teenager (doc) (appearance as himself only) (GB). '77 Das Amerikanische Freund (actor only) (GER-FR) (USA/GB: The American Friend). '79 Hair (actor only). '80 Lightning Over Water/Nick's Movie (co-dir; +appearance as himself).

Edward G. Robinson

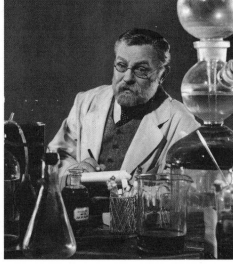

Robinson as Rico down on his luck in Little Caesar *(left), as a scientist in* Dr Ehrlich's Magic Bullet *(above), a framed businessman in* Blackmail *(1939, above right) and a jaded lawyer in* Illegal *(1955, far right)*

Edward G. Robinson, describing the opening of one of his earlier speeches while entertaining the troops during World War II, wrote in his autobiography:

'I began by saying: "I am happy to be here, the most privileged moment of my life, to see the men who are defeating Hitler." . . . I could sense the audience despising me . . . and to stop the buzz of their boos and Bronx cheers, I ad-libbed, "Pipe down, you mugs, or I'll let you have it. Whaddya hear from the mob?" There was an instant burst of high laughter and applause.'

Throughout his book Robinson returns obsessively to a fact that he found incomprehensible; people knew him and wanted to see him primarily as Rico, the title figure in his famous 1930 film *Little Caesar*. The reasons why he found this so surprising have partly to do with

cultural attitudes as to what is important in art – in particular the debate about whether High Art is to be preferred to Popular Art – but in Robinson's case the reasons go deeper. They relate to the time and place in which he was born and raised.

Born Emanuel Goldenberg on December 12, 1893 in Bucharest, Romania, Robinson's family background was based on Jewish discipline and middle-class values. At that time the Jews were denied civil rights in Romania and were subjected to periodic persecution, an important factor in the emigration of the family to the United States in the early years of the century. The moral tone of the Goldenberg family was akin to a certain brand of Protestantism which stressed morality and hard work. However, the Goldenberg family was slightly unorthodox, having a European predisposition

Above left: with Claudette Colbert in The Hole in the Wall *(1929), one of Robinson's earliest gangster roles. Above:* East is West *(1930) featured Lupe Velez and Robinson as an unlikely Chinese pair*

to a highly romantic conception of art.

These elements would have, of themselves, inclined the young Robinson to be hostile to the cinema as a mass art – which was indeed to be the case – but they were reinforced by his choice of career as a theatre actor. During the Twenties Robinson rose to become a considerable figure on the Broadway stage, appearing in a whole range of classic and modern plays and deciding early on that because of his appearance his future was as a character actor rather than as a leading man.

It is often assumed that *Little Caesar* was

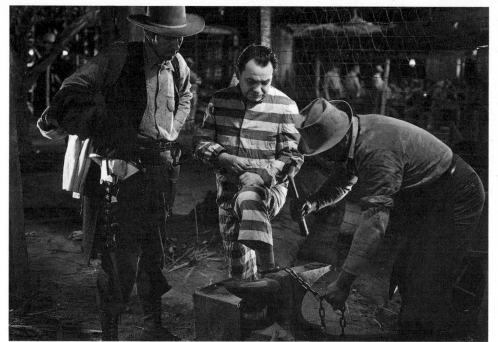

A Master of his Art

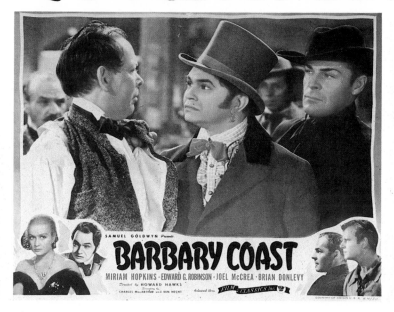

Above: in danger of being typecast, Robinson played a corrupt gangster figure in Barbary Coast *(1935). Above right: a scornful Kitty (Joan Bennett) makes use of her besotted admirer (Robinson) in* Scarlet Street

Robinson's first picture but his stage reputation ensured that he had received offers to go to Hollywood from the early Twenties. The handful of movies he made before *Little Caesar* confirmed for him his intuitive dislike of the medium. Characteristically, while appearing in a theatrical production of *Peer Gynt* he stole off to see himself in his first film, the silent *The Bright Shawl* (1923) – in which he played a Spanish aristocrat – and was appalled.

Little Caesar is regarded as the first of the classic gangster movies and Rico, the Italian immigrant whose rise and fall the film charts, the first of the classic gangster 'heroes' – even to the extent of his lying dead in the street at the end of the film. Robinson never understood its success and his remarks on the film sought to make analogies with Greek tragedy as a way of explaining its popularity:

'He (Rico) is a man who defies society, and in the end is mowed down by the gods and society, and doesn't even know what happened . . . the picture has sustained itself throughout these years because it was constructed as a Greek tragedy.'

His upbringing and training made it impossible for him to appreciate the virtues of pace, simplicity, action and contemporaneity. The paradox is that Robinson became a complete master of the art of screen acting while at the same time regarding most of his film work as beneath contempt. Understand-

ably he was to play in several gangster films as a contract player with Warner Brothers during the Thirties, but he always aspired to roles which approximated more to his conception of 'good theatre'.

He always regarded his finest role as that of Paul Ehrlich – the man who discovered a cure for syphilis – in *Dr Ehrlich's Magic Bullet* (1940) perhaps because of the manifest seriousness of the project. It is significant that the aggressive, lower-class hoodlums he played in the Thirties tended to give way, in the mid-Forties, to articulate bourgeois figures as in *Double Indemnity* (1944), in which he played a shrewd insurance investigator, *Woman in the Window* (1944), which featured him as a psychology professor, *Scarlet Street* (1945), in which he was a clerk who finds in painting an escape from the oppression of the *petit-bourgeois*

milieu in which he lives and works, and *All My Sons* (1948), in which he played a man selling defective airplane parts to the government.

At the same time Robinson seems to have had an odd blindness and lack of sympathy for *Scarlet Street*, given its critical importance as a major film by Fritz Lang and the closeness of its theme – a Sunday painter who produces masterpieces – to an important dimension of his own life. In the debate about High Art or Popular Art Robinson was firmly on the side of High Art. He had built up a renowned collection

of Impressionist pictures and was a considerable painter in his own right, as well as being a confidant of the most illustrious musical figures in America.

If his European background inclined him to an elitist and rather conservative view of art, it predisposed him to an egalitarian and progressive view of politics. Throughout the Thirties and early Forties he lent his name, time and money to a number of progressive causes, a fact which was to cost him dearly during the infamous anti-communist witch-hunts of the late Forties and early Fifties. Though not remotely a communist himself, Robinson's affinity with democratic ideals got him blacklisted for a time.

This and his own early commitment to 'character' roles, meant that his later career was as a supporting actor of great eminence, range and distinction. The more 'theatrical' side of his persona was perhaps best shown in his playing of the temperamental film director in *Two Weeks in Another Town* (1962) and the 'cinematic' side in his role as ace poker player in *The Cincinnati Kid* (1965). There was more than some truth in his final remark to Steve McQueen in the latter: 'As long as I'm around, you're second best; you may as well learn to live with it.'
COLIN McARTHUR

Above left: The Kid (Steve McQueen) and The Man (Robinson), rivals at the poker table in The Cincinatti Kid. *Below: Robinson as an accomplice in the theft of a statue from St Peter's, Rome, in* Operazione San Pietro *(1968, Operation St Peter's). Below right: with Raquel Welch on the set of* The Biggest Bundle of Them All *(1967)*

Filmography
1923 The Bright Shawl. '29 The Hole in the Wall. '30 Night Ride; A Lady to Love; Outside the Law; East is West; The Widow from Chicago; Little Caesar. '31 Smart Money; Five Star Final. '32 The Stolen Jools (short) (GB: The Slippery Pearls); The Hatchet Man (GB: The Honourable Mr Wong); Two Seconds; Tiger Shark; Silver Dollar. '33 The Little Giant; I Loved a Woman; Dark Hazard. '34 The Man With Two Faces. '35 The Whole Town's Talking (GB: Passport to Fame); A Day at Santa Anita (short) (guest); Barbary Coast. '36 Bullets or Ballots. '37 Thunder in the City (GB); Kid Galahad; The Last Gangster. '38 A Slight Case of Murder; The Amazing Dr Clitterhouse; I Am the Law. '39 Confessions of a Nazi Spy; Blackmail. '40 Dr Ehrlich's Magic Bullet (GB: The Story of Dr Ehrlich's Magic Bullet); Brother Orchid; A Dispatch From Reuters (GB: This Man Reuter); Manpower. '41 The Sea Wolf; Unholy Partners. '42 Moscow Strikes Back (doc) (narr only); Tales of Manhattan; Larceny Inc. '43 The Red Cross at War (doc) (narr only); Projection of America (doc) (on-screen narr only); Destroyer; Flesh and Fantasy; Screen Snapshots, Series 22, No 4 (short) (compere only). '44 Tampico; Screen Snapshots, Series 23, No 9 (short) (guest); Double Indemnity; Mr Winkle Goes to War (GB: Arms and the Woman); The Woman in the Window. '45 Our Vines Have Tender Grapes; Journey Together (GB); Scarlet Street. '46 The Stranger. '47 The Red House. '48 All My Sons; Where Do You Get Off? (short) (narr only); Key Largo; Night Has a Thousand Eyes. '49 House of Strangers; It's a Great Feeling (guest). '50 My Daughter Joy (GB) (USA: Operation X); Screen Snapshots (short). '52 Actors and Sin *ep* Actor's Blood. '53 Vice Squad (GB: The Girl in Room 17); Big Leaguer; The Glass Web. '54 Black Tuesday; The Violent Men (GB: Rough Company). '55 Tight Spot; A Bullet for Joey; Illegal; Hell on Frisco Bay. '56 Nightmare; The Ten Commandments. '57 The Heart of Show Business (doc) (co-narr only). '59 A Hole in the Head; Israel (doc) (narr only). '60 Seven Thieves; Pepe (guest). '61 My Geisha. '62 Two Weeks in Another Town. '63 Sammy Going South (GB) (USA: A Boy Ten Feet Tall); The Prize. '64 Good Neighbour Sam; Robin and the Seven Hoods (guest); The Outrage; Cheyenne Autumn. '65 The Cincinnati Kid; Who Has Seen the Wind? (United Nations). '67 Le Blonde de Pekin (FR-IT-GER) (USA: Peking Blonde); The Biggest Bundle of Them All (USA-IT); Ad Ogni Costa (IT-SP-GER) (USA/GB: Grand Slam). '68 Never a Dull Moment; Operazione San Pietro (IT-FR-GER); Uno Scacco tutto Matto (IT-SP). '69 Mackenna's Gold. '70 Song of Norway. '72 Neither by Day or Night (USA-IS); Soylent Green.

Sex and drugs and...

The power of the censors declined as film producers and distributors fought back desperately against the competition of television and suburban leisure

At the end of World War II, Pax Americana reigned. With the Allies decisively victorious over the worst threat ever to their existence and the United States in sole possession of the atomic bomb, millions could now resume the homely ideals and pursuits of 'normal life'. And so could the movies, after years of morale-boosting productions on behalf of the war effort. One eulogy of MGM's Louis B. Mayer sums up the point:

'He revered the sanctity of the home, love of marriage and mother. He didn't believe in perverts, communism, and excessively problem-type pictures.'

The world, in short, was felt to be safe at long last for God, democracy and Andy Hardy.

But this promised millennium very quickly proved to be an illusion, as all kinds of problems and pressures began thrusting themselves to the fore. Anti-communist hysteria fuelled by the rise of the Cold War became rampant during the late Forties and into the Fifties. Soon Russia also had nuclear weapons; wars and crises succeeded one another: Korea, Suez, Hungary, among others. The spectre of total annihilation was now a permanent part of human consciousness.

The same ferment began to disrupt the traditional simplicities and creeds of private life as well. World War II had absorbed national energies, forged unity, distracted attention from other difficulties. Foremost among these was sex. In the United States, the expression of sexuality in the arts had been tightly controlled by an assortment of censorship bodies, religious, municipal or judicial. Hollywood's most teasing, licentious era had ended during the early Thirties when strict enforcement of the Production Code began.

After World War II, this social consensus began to show cracks in its façade. In literature, Edmund Wilson's *Memoirs of Hecate County* scandalized thousands and provoked moral indignation for its supposed degeneracy. Norman Mailer's *The Naked and the Dead*, J. D. Salinger's *The Catcher in the Rye* and Grace Metalious' *Peyton Place* broke into areas previously held to be taboo. Comedians like Lenny Bruce and Mort Sahl began scalding America's puritan sensitivities in their nightclub acts. Jules Feiffer lampooned the all-American mating dance in his Freudian comic strips about neurosis and hypocrisy between men and women. The Kinsey Reports on male and female sexuality (1948 and 1953) rudely dragged into the open the secret lives of ordinary Americans, severely disillusioning those who swore by myths of purity, fidelity and True Love. The successful launching of *Playboy* magazine in December 1953 undermined them further. It seemed to many at the time that, along with Mayer's communists, his 'perverts' were taking over. Pox Americana.

Throughout the Fifties, there appeared several films tagged as 'controversial' – which meant sexually explicit. Lacking anything like England's X certificate (introduced in 1951), American filmmakers had to satisfy the tattered Production Code

to gain the Code Seal. Yet this was not a perfect defence against prosecution by state and local censorship boards or denunciation by the Catholic Legion of Decency. In the United States, political censorship generally attacked specific persons, like the Hollywood Ten and other victims of the blacklist, instead of specific films, in order to muzzle them before they could sneak insidious communist propaganda into American theatres. Violence rarely offended America's censor; Sweden might snip gore from Hammer horror films, but only an occasional youth picture like *The Wild One* (1953) or *The Blackboard Jungle* (1955) stirred up some American moralistic wrath by depicting violence. In America, movies were prosecuted and censored principally for sex.

The key term among the morally righteous was (and still is) 'permissiveness', denoting myriad unspeakable sexual immoralities. Americans have always been ambivalent towards movie stars, on the one hand envying their luxurious lives and fantasizing about their spectacular decadence, on the other mocking them as tinsel creatures and condemning their sexual waywardness. The postwar years provided some juicy scandals to feed this appetite for commingled titillation and indignation: a paternity suit against Charles Chaplin, the adulterous love affair between Ingrid Bergman and Robert Rossellini. When comparable matter found its way into the movies, censors struck back.

After *The Outlaw*, premiered in 1943 but not widely released until 1946, there was apoplexy among the righteous, who had been primed for outrage by years of alluring publicity about Jane Russell and the aerodynamically engineered bra which Howard Hughes was said to have designed

Top: Linda Darnell excelled at portraying ladies of light virtue who were still nice girls at heart. She is seen here as Amber St Clare in Forever Amber, *with Cornel Wilde as Bruce Carleton, a gentleman of King Charles II's time. Above: this witty illustration from the New York* East Village Other *magazine sums up many topics that Hollywood was not allowed to show, according to the Production Code*

Last year's No. 1 best-seller...This year's No. 1 motion picture.

OTTO PREMINGER'S
ANATOMY OF A MURDER

STARRING
JAMES STEWART
LEE REMICK
BEN GAZZARA
ARTHUR O'CONNELL
EVE ARDEN
KATHRYN GRANT

and JOSEPH N. WELCH as Judge Weaver

Polly the pistol... she stayed for breakfast...

Dino-he came to dinner...

THE MIRISCH CORPORATION Presents

DEAN KIM
MARTIN NOVAK
RAY WALSTON

in Billy Wilder's
new comedy

KISS ME, STUPID

Beethoven-he cooked up the whole mess...

THIS PICTURE IS FOR ADULTS ONLY!

Top left: poster for Anatomy of a Murder. *Director Otto Preminger seemed to enjoy upsetting the censors or perhaps he was asserting the freedom of the artist to make a profit; Saul Bass did the memorable poster logo. Top right: in* Kiss Me, Stupid *Kim Novak plays a most amiable prostitute whose job is taken over for one night by a respectable housewife (Felicia Farr). Opposite page, top left: Beatrice Pearson, a talented actress whose career was all too brief, plays a black girl passing for white in* Lost Boundaries – *her second and last film. Opposite page, top right: D. H. Lawrence's novel was still banned in Britain when the French film version of* Lady Chatterley's Lover *was distributed overseas. Though its sex scenes were not very explicit by later standards, the censors rose to the bait of a well-known title. Above: Don Murray as a drug addict, about to 'shoot up', in* A Hatful of Rain, *based on Michael V. Gazzo's play*

for her. Many local censors had various prints of the film trimmed, but it made money anyway and helped to inaugurate the Fifties fashion for bosomy sexpots like Marilyn Monroe, Jayne Mansfield, Anita Ekberg, Mamie Van Doren and Diana Dors. The true joke was that the censors did not even notice the barely-hidden homosexual subtext of *The Outlaw.*

Otto Preminger's *Forever Amber* (1947) allowed its social-climbing minx only five of her original twenty-five lovers in Kathleen Winsor's novel and then deprived her of nearly all pleasure in those five. Even so, according to Preminger, 20th Century-Fox was so afraid of what a Catholic-inspired boycott would do to its $6 million investment that it allowed a priest to censor the final cut before the film opened. Yet *Forever Amber,* too, made a pile. Preminger went on to become the censors' most annoying gadfly. In 1953, he defied the Motion Picture Association of America by releasing *The Moon Is Blue* without a Code Seal, raking in more dollars. His offence? Using the word 'virgin' in his dialogue. *The Man With the Golden Arm* (1956) broke the Code's ban on the depiction of drug addiction, as did Fred Zinnemann's *A Hatful of Rain* (1957). *Anatomy of a Murder* (1959) drove the Chicago police to try in vain to cut the words 'rape' and 'contraceptive' from its soundtrack.

Elia Kazan clashed with censors almost as regularly as Preminger. Warner Brothers bowed to Catholic objections and deleted offensively erotic material from *A Streetcar Named Desire* (1951). Kazan also tackled other formerly forbidden subjects: anti-Semitism in *Gentleman's Agreement* (1947), blacks passing for white in *Pinky* (1949). But his roughest collision with the censors came in 1956 with *Baby Doll,* his Tennessee Williams comedy about a sloe-eyed teenage virgin bride, her seducer and her middle-aged husband. According to the Legion of Decency: 'It dwells almost without variation or relief upon carnal suggestiveness'. *Time* cited it for:

'Priapean detail that might well have embarrassed Boccaccio . . . just possibly the dirtiest American-made motion picture that has ever been legally exhibited.'

Censorial rage included a campaign against the movie fomented by New York City's Catholic Archbishop, Francis Cardinal Spellman, and *Baby Doll* quickly died at the box-office.

Blacks began receiving various kinds of liberal attention. *Lost Boundaries* (1949) joined *Pinky* in dramatizing the agonies of 'passing'. *Home of the Brave, Intruder in the Dust* (both 1949) and *No Way Out* (1950) treated other manifestations of racism. The roll-call of out-of-the-closet subjects came to include miscegenation in *Island in the Sun* (1957),

homosexuality in *Compulsion,* teenage pregnancy and abortion in *Blue Denim,* baroque deviations including cannibalism in *Suddenly, Last Summer* (all 1959) and soft-core nudity in *The Immoral Mr Teas* (1960). In each case the response was the same: loud but transient outbursts of moaning and groaning about how America was going the way of the Roman Empire, and then rapid assimilation into the pop-cultural scene.

In addition, a new breed of sexually forthright 'foreign' (meaning European) film began to make its mark. Accustomed to the sanitization and the innuendoes of Hollywood movies, audiences found themselves alternately shocked and fascinated by European imports which treated sexual matters without such glossiness, or with a glossiness which seemed racier, more chic. Even more than their American counterparts, these examples of Old World 'immorality' roused the censorious to battle.

One of the first *causes célèbres* among them was Roberto Rossellini's *Il Miracolo (The Miracle),* which reached America as a segment of *L'Amore* (1948, Ways of Love). Rossellini had already achieved some popularity in the United States with *Roma, Città Aperta* (1945, *Rome, Open City*) and *Paisà* (1946, *Paisan*); but now he managed to offend on both

European films infuriated the censors by franker treatment of sex than was usual in Hollywood

sexual and religious grounds. His short study of a simple-minded peasant woman who becomes irrationally convinced that her unborn child is Jesus Christ provoked one of the stormiest clamours in the history of American censorship, for both obscenity and blasphemy. Already bedevilled by the House Un-American Activities Committee and its witch-hunt for Reds, Hollywood was terrified of censorship bodies. But Joseph Burstyn, the American distributor of *The Miracle,* decided to fight back after the state of New York banned the film in 1951 for being 'sacrilegious'. The case finally reached the United States Supreme Court, which handed down the momentous decision, *Burstyn vs. Wilson,* in 1952, voiding the ban on *The Miracle* and overturning a 1915 judgment which had denied movies the constitutional protection granted to other forms of speech and expression.

This was a crippling but not a fatal blow to censorship. Various states sought to prohibit or censor with such films as Ophuls' *La Ronde* (1950, The Merry-Go-Round). Sjöberg's *Fröken Julie* (1951, *Miss Julie*). Vadim's *Les Liaisons Dangereuses 1960*

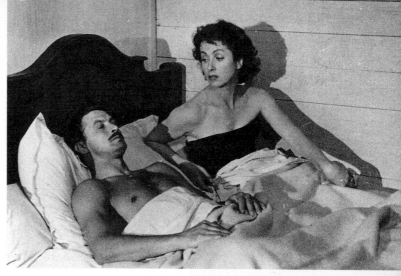

(1959) and Doniol-Valcroze's *L'Eau à la Bouche* (1960, *Game of Love*). Roger Vadim became the stereotypical oh-la-la 'naughty' Frenchman among filmmakers for many Americans, particularly when an earlier film, *Et Dieu Créa la Femme* (1956, *. . . And God Created Woman*) reached their shores in 1958. Again, the offended attacked; clergymen of one city in New York State, for instance, offered to pay a local exhibitor not to book the film; he refused their offer. In 1959, New York tried a different ploy, seeking to ban Marc Allégret's 1955 film *L'Amant de Lady Chatterley* (*Lady Chatterley's Lover*) for portraying adultery 'as a desirable, acceptable and proper pattern of behaviour'. The Supreme Court unanimously rejected this brand of 'thematic' obscenity as fit grounds for censorship.

Cases like these exerted counter-pressure against the strictures of the censors. Besides, the growing influence of television was forcefully impressing upon movie moguls the need to give theatrical films all possible latitude if they were to lure home-bound viewers into theatres. The Production Code underwent a series of revisions in 1956, 1961 and 1966 – until the film industry's present rating board began functioning officially on November 1, 1968. Such subjects as prostitution, homosexuality, miscegenation and drugs slowly became acceptable fare for movies bearing the Code Seal. The *nouvelle vague* films from France and others by such directors as Federico Fellini, Michelangelo Antonioni and Ingmar Bergman further accelerated the decline of censorship in the United States. As late as 1964, the Legion of Decency's C (Condemned) was powerful

enough to cause the financial failure of Billy Wilder's *Kiss Me, Stupid*. But the following year the Legion received scathing criticism after condemning Sidney Lumet's film about a concentration-camp survivor, *The Pawnbroker*, for its images of women's bare breasts. Then, in 1966, *Blow-Up*, with its sex orgy and hints of drugs, became a hit despite another Legion C, and the group quickly lost most of its former influence.

The last major censorial fight of this period began on November 13, 1959, when police arrested Nico Jacobellis, an exhibitor in Cleveland Heights, Ohio, for showing Louis Malle's *Les Amants* (1958, *The Lovers*). Eventually, he was fined $2500 and forced to serve six days in jail. Not until June 22, 1964 did the Supreme Court remove this stain from his record by declaring that *The Lovers* was not obscene. From this point onward, most censorship cases involving films came to centre on hard-core pornography.

Grouping these cases together might give a false impression of constant turmoil in American film circles. In fact, they were relatively rare. Even critics who have been re-evaluating the supposedly comatose Fifties seldom grant much artistic interest to most of the movies which sparked these landmark judicial decisions. Nowadays, for some people at least, imagining a time when such movies were considered obscene, subversive or dangerous is like imagining the era when people actually screamed or fled theatres at the sight of a train entering a station in a Lumière Brothers silent film.

MICHAEL DEMPSEY

Above: the photographer (David Hemmings) gets down to work on a model (Verushka) in Blow-Up. *Below left: poster for* Baby Doll. *Below: Rod Steiger as* The Pawnbroker *is disturbed by a black prostitute (Thelma Oliver)*

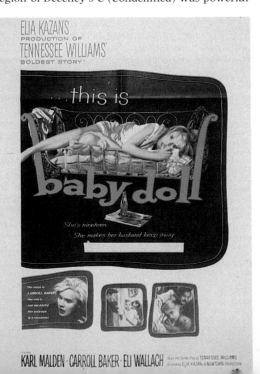

....And Vadim Created Women

Left: on the set of Barbarella *Roger Vadim positions Jane Fonda who plays a sexually naive intergalactic visitor. Above: a portrait of Bardot as the pouting sex kitten that Vadim helped create*

Pretty maids having dangerous liaisons or playing night games are the speciality of director Roger Vadim. The stars he has created and packaged – Brigitte Bardot, Annette Stroyberg, Catherine Deneuve and Jane Fonda – exude a sensuous, self-aware sexuality

Film history is not short of Svengali-like starmakers: Maurice Stiller is legendarily credited with the creation of Greta Garbo, Josef von Sternberg with doing the same for Marlene Dietrich. But Roger Vadim alone can claim repeat status in the role, having successively transformed no fewer than three of the ladies in his life into screen sex symbols.

Firstly, and most famously, there was Brigitte Bardot. Though only 15, she was already a cover girl when Vadim, then an inexperienced screenwriter and assistant to the director Marc Allégret, became infatuated by her in Paris in 1949. They were married in 1952, and by the mid-Fifties Bardot had begun to establish herself in secondary screen roles. Then Vadim persuaded the producer Raoul Levy to let him direct a film with his wife as star: the film was *Et Dieu Créa la Femme* (1956, *. . . And God Created Woman*) – the rest is history.

In her earlier films, Bardot had projected not much more than a conventionally pert sexiness. But in Vadim's CinemaScope opus about a girl from the wrong side of the tracks landing on her feet – and in a succession of beds – amid the Riviera fleshpots, she emerged as something definitively and provocatively new in the way of screen sirens. Sex kitten, the publicists dubbed her: and whilst in some respects Vadim's first movie betrays a lack of assurance, it is uncommonly adroit in heightening Bardot's two-edged, girl-woman ambiguity by weaving a 'child-of-nature' ambience around her. This extends beyond her appearance – her mane of hair in careless disarray, she is repeatedly seen wrapped in a skimpy overall or draped by an even skimpier towel – to the way in which the direction links her to landscape or identifies her with untamed animals.

Bardot's next film with Vadim – his third – *Les Bijoutiers du Clair de Lune* (1958, *Heaven Fell That Night*) brought to a high pitch of intensity her volatile on-screen combination of waywardness and vulnerability (this persona has interesting similarities to that of James Dean). The movie itself, a full-blooded melodrama about fatal passion and smuggling on the Franco-Prussian border, displayed to full advantage the hallmarks of Vadim's directorial personality – his imaginative use of the widescreen format and the glossy presentation of exotic landscape. It is revealing that one of the movies for which he has voiced particular admiration is Elia Kazan's *East of Eden* (1955) with its unabashed emotionalism and pioneering use of the 'Scope frame.

But by 1957, Bardot and Vadim had divorced, though their professional relationship was resumed in 1962 with *Le Repos de Guerrier* (*Warrior's Rest*), with Bardot now – perhaps significantly – cast as the bourgeois socializing force in the life of a nihilistic drop-out (Robert Hossein).

Meanwhile, Vadim was amorously involved with the statuesque Annette Stroyberg, his wife from 1958 to 1961. On the strength of

Top: Jane Fonda in La Ronde. *Above: Catherine Deneuve, Luciana Paluzzi and Roger Vadim prepare a scene from* Vice and Virtue. *Above right: Cindy Pickett in* Night Games. *Above far right: Annette Stroyberg in* Blood and Roses

episode in *Histoires Extraordinaires* (1968, *Tales of Mystery*) where an additional *frisson* was provided among the high-flown love-making by the fact that Jane's leading man was her real-life brother Peter.

Of course, the vociferously politicized Jane Fonda of later years has vehemently repudiated the sex-object status accorded her in the Vadim movies, and in this respect *Barbarella* (1968) is, perhaps, the rock on which their partnership foundered. Based on a comic strip, Vadim's elaborate cocktail of sex and science fiction – not notably witty or inventive, but a big popular hit – uses its leading lady explicitly in fetishistic terms; the very opening sequence, in fact, involves her in an elaborately orchestrated striptease.

Vadim's subsequent film-making career has been active but rather dispirited, though the first of his two American-made films, the black comedy *Pretty Maids All in a Row* (1971), had its admirers, among them Fritz Lang.

Perhaps – as *Night Games* (1979), his second American movie, particularly tends to suggest – he is now in the invidious position of striving to keep up with that very phenomenon of *de luxe* sex films for which his own more interesting early work had paved the way. Or perhaps – sadly – he has simply become a Svengali without a new Trilby, a starmaker lacking the makings of a new heavenly body for the cinematic firmament.   TIM PULLEINE

their relationship, which was surrounded by much ballyhoo, he won for her the chief supporting role in his most prestigious project, a modernized version of a seventeenth-century novel by Laclos, *Les Liaisons Dangereuses 1960* (1959), and subsequently a leading part in a rather different literary adaptation, . . . *Et Mourir de Plaisir* (1960, *Blood and Roses*), based on Sheridan Le Fanu's horror tale *Carmilla*.

The latter was appreciably better suited to Vadim's colour-supplement style – he had filmed *Les Liaisons Dangereuses 1960* in self-denyingly austere black and white – but in neither did Stroyberg emerge as anything more than an elegant exponent of *déshabille*. Later, Vadim said in his memoirs: 'She had no particular gift for acting . . . Her laziness didn't help.' At all events, the relationship came to an end – and so, to a large extent did Stroyberg's film career.

Vadim's next inamorata was Catherine Deneuve, who was in the Sixties largely unknown though she later became an international star on the strength of films like Luis Buñuel's *Belle de Jour* (1967). Deneuve appeared in Vadim's *Le Vice et la Vertu* (1962, *Vice and Virtue*), a rather crass updating of de Sade to the Nazi era, but to Vadim's regret their life together proved short-lived.

It was Jane Fonda who became the third lasting object of his on-and-off-screen desires. Though previously Fonda had appeared in several mediocre American movies, it was in France, and crucially in her films with Vadim – to whom she was married from 1965 to 1968 – that her first star image was set: a mutedly thunderous eroticism crossed with a sprite-like unpredictability.

Fonda played in Vadim's version of *La Ronde* (1964, *Circle of Love*), a major commercial success if hardly comparable aesthetically with Max Ophuls' original. Then came *La Curée* (1966, *The Game Is Over*), Vadim's last really distinctive film, which was based on a novel by Zola. It was followed by his *Metzengerstein*

Filmography

1948 Blanche Fury (ass dir; +co-sc) (GB). '50 Blackmailed (co-sc only) (GB); The Naked Heart (ass dir;+co-sc) (GB). '52 La Demoiselle et son Revenant (ass dir; +co-sc) '53 Julietta (ass dir), '54 Femmina (ass dir) (unfinished) (IT). '55 Futures Vedettes (GB: Sweet Sixteen) (ass dir;+co-sc); Cette Sacrée Gamine (GB: Mam'zelle Pigalle) (co-sc only). '56 En Effeuillant la Marguerite (GB: Mam'zelle Striptease) (ass dir;+co-sc); Et Dieu Créa la Femme (GB: . . . And God Created Woman/And Woman Was Created) (+co-sc). '57 Sait-on Jamais (GB: When the Devil Drives; USA: No Sun in Venice) (+sc) (FR-IT). '58 Les Bijoutiers du Clair de Lune (GB: Heaven Fell That Night) (+co-sc) (FR-IT); Sois Belle et Tais-Toi (GB: Blonde for Danger) (co-sc only). '59 Les Liaisons Dangereuses 1960 (GB: Les Liaisons Dangereuses) (+co-sc); Le Testament d'Orphée (act only). '60 . . . Et Mourir de Plaisir (GB/USA: Blood and Roses) (+co-sc) (FR-IT). '61 La Bride sur le Cou (GB: Please Not Now!) (+co-sc) (FR-IT). '62 Le Repos du Guerrier (GB: Warrior's Rest; USA: Love on a Pillow) (+co-sc) (FR-IT); Les Sept Péchés Capitaux (GB/USA: Seven Capital Sins) (ep: L'Orgueuil) (+sc) (FR-IT); Et Satan Conduit le Bal (GB: Satan Leads the Dance) (prod only;+co-sc); Le Vice et la Vertu (GB/USA: Vice and Virtue) (+prod;+co-sc) (FR-IT). '63 Les Grands Chemins (GB: Of Flesh and Blood) (prod only) (FR-IT); La Reflux (prod only) (film unfinished); Dragées au Poivre (GB/USA: Sweet and Sour) (act only) (FR-IT); Château en Suède (GB: Château in Sweden; USA: Nutty Naughty Château) (+co-sc) FR-IT). '64 La Ronde (USA: Circle of Love) (+co-sc) (FR-IT). '66 La Curée (GB/USA: The Game Is Over) (+prod; +co-sc) (FR-IT). '68 Barbarella (FR-IT); Histoires Extraordinaires (GB: Tales of Mystery; USA: Spirits of the Dead) (ep: Metzengerstein) (+co-sc) (FR-IT). '71 Pretty Maids All in a Row (USA). '72 Hellé (+co-sc). '73 Don Juan 1973 ou Si Don Juan Était une Femme (GB: Don Juan or If Don Juan Were a Woman/Ms Don Juan) (+co-sc) (FR-IT); Ciao! Manhattan (act only) (USA). '74 La Jaune Fille Assassinée (GB/USA: Charlotte) (+prod; +sc;+act) (FR-IT-GER). '76 Une Femme Fidèle (GB: When a Woman in Love) (+co-sc). '79 Night Games (USA).

To Catch a Star

Alfred Hitchcock moulded the screen careers of more than one up-and-coming star. Occasionally his protégés proved difficult to handle, but his choices rarely backfired. Hitch recognized the stuff *real* stars were made of, and he was not afraid to take the best possible compromise between the ideal and the affordable.

Working in Hollywood, at least up to the end of the Fifties, meant working with the star system. But though this was a fact of life, almost no-one but Hitchcock realized its true potential, and embraced it wholeheartedly rather than taking it for granted or treating it like an awful necessity which was best ignored.

As has often been said, Hitchcock directed audiences rather than directing films. His image of the audience was as one vast instrument upon which the film-maker could play, and his fantasy was of a day when it might not be necessary even to make the film – perhaps the seats could just be wired to transmit infinitely sophisticated electrical signals directly to the audience's nervous system, so that they could be made to laugh and cry and gasp absolutely at the director's will. But while films still had to be made, he appreciated to the full the importance of the audience's subconscious, and the use of subliminal effects upon it. Stars, properly used, presented him with a whole arsenal of underlying effects, and he rapidly made himself a master of their use.

After all, a star in a movie works of necessity on at least two levels. On one level, he or she is an actor playing a role, and how well the audience attends depends on how well that role is played, written, directed and generally set up. If the script has the heroine tied to a railroad track in the path of a hurtling express, and the film is staged and edited to build up maximum suspense about whether someone is going to arrive in time to save her, then its viewers duly sit on the edge of their seats and chew their handkerchiefs. But at the same time we have the comforting knowledge that this, after all, is Pearl White – star. And so whatever the immediate indications may be, she will never actually be mangled, because stars never are . . . and anyway she has to survive in order to hang over the edge of a cliff at the end of the next episode.

That is an elementary example. Stars of more complex films produce more complex expectations. When Joan Crawford made a tiny guest appearance in *It's a Great Feeling* (1949), she walked straight on set and slapped Jack Carson's face. 'What did you do that for?' he inquired plaintively. 'Oh, I don't know – I do that in all my movies.' Indeed, Joan Crawford is expected to slap faces, John Wayne to punch the bad guys, Cary Grant to be suave and sophisticated, Jane Wyman to suffer grace-

Left: Hitchcock's second shot at The Man Who Knew Too Much *(he made the first in 1934) had Doris Day playing a retired musical-comedy actress. Below: Marion Crane (Janet Leigh), the short-lived heroine of* Psycho

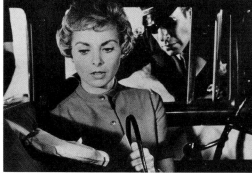

fully . . . and so on. Yet Hitchcock seems to have been the first and only director to recognize this consistently, and then exploit it as part of the means for conditioning audience responses – both by giving his audiences just what they expected, and by cunningly, shockingly, ringing the changes.

Star turns

The most shattering example is the killing of Janet Leigh in *Psycho* (1960). Janet Leigh is, after all, the female star of the film, and as such it is clear what to expect of her and for her. Moreover, the whole film thus far has been concentrated on her, looking through her eyes, and building suspense through concern for her safety. Then, suddenly, half-way through the film, she is attacked in the shower for reasons which have nothing at all to do with what has appeared to be the main plot line – the robbery she has committed – and brutally stabbed to death. Such things never happen to stars in films. Their entrance may be cunningly delayed, but their exit is never so premature and precipitate. A lot of the effect

172

of the murder has nothing to do with the brilliance of its staging: the star system and all its laws are magisterially used by being outrageously flouted.

It was an idea Hitchcock had had in mind for a long time – almost since his arrival in Hollywood. The first time he worked with Cary Grant – at the time one of Hollywood's biggest and most predictable stars – was on *Suspicion* (1941). Hitchcock had a kind of brainstorm. The role was that of a charming man who has seemingly made a habit of marrying rich women and murdering them for their money. But of course, since it is Cary Grant, it is clear from the start that he will be exonerated . . . it will all prove to be a misunderstanding. After all, the audience never ceases to be aware that this is Cary Grant, with all that implies. But, wondered Hitch, what if he were to turn out guilty in the end? Would not that really shock the public? At that point he did not quite dare to do it, but the thought never left him.

And he enjoyed working with Cary Grant so much that Grant became part of his eminent 'stock company'. Since Hitchcock had an obsession with order and controlling every last detail of his films, once he found a congenial and trustworthy collaborator, he liked to work with that person as regularly as possible. This applied all along the line – with cameramen (Robert Burks), art directors (Robert Boyle), costume designers (Edith Head), editors (George Tomasini), composers (Bernard Herrmann) and even, less regularly, writers (John Michael Hayes, Ernest Lehman) – and it was certainly the case with stars. The four important examples in Hitchcock's career were Cary Grant, James Stewart, Ingrid Bergman and Grace Kelly. In the Fifties, when real, proper stars were getting fewer and farther between, he held·on to them all the more tenaciously. Although he never worked again with Ingrid Bergman after *Under Capricorn* (1949) and her cutting loose from Hollywood, his finest uses of Grant and Stewart date from the Fifties, and

Above: a sinister and sensual scene from Notorious *(1946) when Alicia (Ingrid Bergman) realizes she is being poisoned. Above right: Cary Grant the husband, Joan Fontaine the wife in* Suspicion . . . *and the glass of milk she fears will be fatal. Right: Ingrid Bergman and Gregory Peck played psychologists in this 1945 drama. Below right: Grace Kelly as the cool American, Cary Grant as her lover*

naturally his collaboration with Grace Kelly dates from that decade, since her whole meteoric film career was between 1951 and 1956.

Familiarity breeds suspicion
During the Fifties Hitchcock used Cary Grant and James Stewart completely within their established film personae, depending on the context mainly for the interesting sense of disorientation. He lured Grant back from a threatened retirement with the prospect of playing opposite Grace Kelly – the big new sensation – in *To Catch a Thief* (1955). It was a suave and sophisticated role in a glossy comedy-drama about a lady and a jewel thief on the Riviera. But Cary Grant, now in his glamorous fifties, seemed unlikely to be behaving in the ungentlemanly way ascribed to him, perhaps even more unlikely to be hiding an honest idealist under such a smooth exterior, and most unlikely of all to need practically raping by his co-star, who has, it appears, this bizarre fascination with the criminal classes. The next time round – in *North by Northwest* (1959) – he is thrown even more radically off-balance by being an innocent bystander mistaken for a dangerous secret agent who does not in fact exist.

James Stewart had a hardly more predictable time. He had already played once for Hitchcock – as an academic unwillingly turned sleuth in *Rope* (1948) – when he too was offered the come-on of starring with Grace Kelly, in *Rear Window* (1954). Stewart's persona was by this time in his career fixed almost

beyond tampering with – though audiences might be a little surprised by his sexy, slightly risqué lines with a noticeably younger lady in *Rear Window*. But to twist the tail a bit Hitchcock placed Mr Reliable, with his drawling homespun philosophy, in an unexpectedly violent city context. Somehow, the character

Above left: a retired tennis champion (Ray Milland) contemplates the dead body of the assassin he hired to kill his adulterous wife (Grace Kelly). Above: Henry Fonda plays a musician mistakenly suspected of bank robbery – the ordeal ruins his life. Left: James Stewart – witness to a murder through the Rear Window. *Below left: Grace Kelly in the costume-ball denouement of* To Catch a Thief

of the temporarily crippled photographer whiling away his time with a bit of lightweight voyeurism from his own back window took on a new piquancy from having had grafted on to it Stewart's well-loved mannerisms. *The Man Who Knew Too Much* (1956), in which he and Doris Day played the rather conservative parents of a kidnapped child who have to invent their own kind of action in order to get him back, was nearer the norm, but still a certain dislocation was noticeable between the audience's advance expectations and what it in fact got.

During this immensely fruitful decade of his film-making career Hitchcock also used other long-established male stars to some effect: the haunted side of Henry Fonda, which had stood him in good stead when playing victims of fate for Fritz Lang, made him perfect casting as Manny Balestrero, the real-life musician who suffered unjustly at the hands of the law in *The Wrong Man* (1957) – and Ray Milland's easy charm, which had got him through dozens of light comedies, worked very well as a cover for murderous intentions in *Dial M for Murder* (1954). But the most interesting switch of all came with the last film Hitchcock made with James Stewart – *Vertigo* (1958). Stewart played a detective suffering from vertigo and, what is worse, a strange obsession with an elusive woman (Kim Novak) who appears to die and whom he later torments into playing the role of his lost love. Stewart had come a long way indeed from the monosyllabic milksop sheriff of *Destry Rides Again* (1939).

Say it with Grace

On the feminine side, *Vertigo* reads in many respects uncomfortably like an allegory of Hitchcock's own professional life in the Fifties. His fascination with the 'cool blonde' who yet had a paradoxical sizzle of sexuality under the apparently icy-correct surface had been well-known and well-publicized for years, and

many of his earlier American heroines (Ingrid Bergman, Joan Fontaine) had approximated to this ideal. One thing was sure – the Girl Friday brunette or the bouncy redhead in his films, however attractive she might be, was never going to get her man. And with the appearance of Grace Kelly on the scene it seemed as though, like the hero of *Vertigo*, he had at last found his ideal. But then, after three films in immediate succession – *Dial M for Murder*, *Rear Window* and *To Catch a Thief* – she vanished again from show business to become Princess of Monaco, and for years afterwards Hitchcock seemed to be seeking a substitute, and trying, with more or less success, to force the most unlikely ladies into the same mould.

With Grace Kelly it was a perfect coming-together of star and director. In all her films, other than those made by Hitchcock, she tended to appear ill at ease – undeniably beautiful, but rather stiff and decidedly heavy-handed with any humour. But she and Hitch hit it off perfectly from the outset: she was physically and temperamentally just what he had always wanted, and he put her at her ease, knowing how to joke and tease her into relaxation in front of the camera. *Dial M for Murder* is more or less a formula piece, in which she does what little is required of her quite adequately. But in *Rear Window* and *To Catch a Thief* she blossoms into far more than an ice-princess: she is elegant, poised, wears her clothes beautifully, and yet she is also funny and sexy and unexpected – all those things a Hitchcock heroine should be. These films were her finest hour, and no other director ever seemed quite to learn the secret

before her premature retirement prevented them even from trying.

Frenzied females

It is very easy to imagine Grace Kelly in all Hitchcock's subsequent films which feature an obvious, important starring role for a woman – *Vertigo*, *Psycho*, *North by Northwest*, *The Birds* (1963), *Marnie* (1964), even *Torn Curtain* (1966). In fact, the role of Marnie was originally intended for her until considerations of State ruled it out. In *Vertigo* Kim Novak was not even Hitchcock's first choice, and apparently their relations during shooting were none too cordial. But the fact remains that she – the most elusive and often ill-used star of the Fifties – is for once used absolutely right, both as the mysterious dream-like woman of the first part and as the tarty but insecure shopgirl of the second, becoming more and more a passive puppet, manipulated against her will by the man she loves. And in *Marnie*, Hitchcock's discovery and private creation Tippi Hedren – previously rather uncomfortable in *The Birds* – really comes into her own, presenting at the outset the most glacial exterior of all Hitchcock's blondes, and then revealing memorably all the violent passions underneath.

Of the others, Eva Marie Saint in *North by Northwest* ought not to have been right, judging by her Method performances in other films, but somehow miraculously was. Julie Andrews in *Torn Curtain* – every inch a cool lady – ought to have been right but somehow was not. By then, anyway, the real stars were fading from the scene, and the new-style stars

Above: although Hitch's second choice for the part, Kim Novak in Vertigo *brilliantly portrays a cool blonde who mysteriously reappears as a brunette. Below: Sean Connery and Tippi Hedren in* Marnie, *a film whose critical and commercial failure may have been due in part to troubled relations between Hitch and Hedren during shooting*

– for Hitchcock as for the rest of Hollywood – were never quite the same. Hitchcock's last three films were made without stars: ultimately, why did he need them, since he himself was more decisively the star of his films than anyone else could be? The Sixties, after all, was the age of the director as superstar, and Hitchcock was as much a master of that star system as any other.

JOHN RUSSELL TAYLOR

The Taming of Elizabeth Taylor

Audiences came to see Mickey Rooney in *National Velvet* and left talking instead about the young dark-haired beauty who played the winning rider. The dramas of Taylor's life far exceed the fictions of her screen roles. Much married (and maligned for it) the first of the million-dollar superstars continues to delight and amaze

On screen and off, changing her image and her husbands and descending into a defiantly overweight middle-age, Elizabeth Taylor has waged a continuing battle with her extraordinary beauty and fame. She has been expected to live up to the various images created for her by her studio, MGM, since she started making films as a child, and she has rebelled, timidly at first and then with increasing bravura. 'Rapturously beautiful', as James Agee described her in his review of *National Velvet* (1944), made when she was 12, she has had to work hard to prove that beneath the movie-star perfection she has character and wit and temperament.

Though for years she was the world's preeminent star, at the time the highest-paid performer in cinema history, she has never played a *grande dame* on film or appeared like one in her personal life. She has never been queenly – hence her odd, small and unexpectedly appealing performance as the Queen of the Nile in *Cleopatra* (1963). Her characters, for the most part, have sought love rather than power, have been palpably vulnerable and insecure rather than larger-than-life figures of great ambition and assurance. And yet, inevitably, the star's life that she has always led – the attention, the privileges and the often stinging personal and professional attacks launched against her – has left its mark. Despite her resistance to being 'Elizabeth Taylor', despite her evasions, her turnabouts in style and appearance, the fact that she has never had a normal life has made her seem, for all her warmth and earthiness, a little beyond human reach: she is a little mysterious, a little vague, as if she has her secrets; she suffers from a lingering self-consciousness and a touch (not of class, to be sure) of Hollywood artificiality.

Liz and marriage

Her spectacular private life could have been 'written' by someone who grew up on a steady diet of Hollywood melodramas. Keeping pace with her shifting movie images, her marriages seem to have caught her in different moods: as dewy *ingénue* (Mrs Nicky Hilton), dutiful child-bride (Mrs Michael Wilding), boisterous high-liver (Mrs Michael Todd), brazen homebreaker (Mrs Eddie Fisher) and passionate woman of the world (Mrs Richard Burton – twice). Currently, as Mrs John Warner, wife of the Republican Senator from Virginia, she has her most star-like role yet. Presiding over an estate in that state's lush hunt-country and hob-nobbing with politicians, she seems to be living a real-life version of the Southern belles she has played so often and with such flair. In the Elizabeth Taylor story, life and art mingle incestuously in a series of glittering counter-points and parallels.

On screen, as in her private life, she has not been content or able to settle into a single continuing role, but has moved ahead, trying out new ways of relating to the burdens of her beauty and fame. As child actress, adolescent, young woman, scarlet beauty and middle-aged shrew, she discovered a series of images

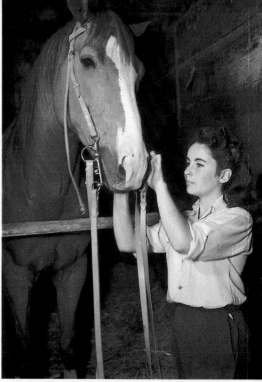

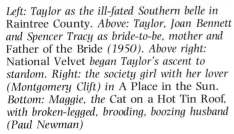

Left: Taylor as the ill-fated Southern belle in Raintree County. *Above: Taylor, Joan Bennett and Spencer Tracy as bride-to-be, mother and Father of the Bride (1950). Above right:* National Velvet *began Taylor's ascent to stardom. Right: the society girl with her lover (Montgomery Clift) in* A Place in the Sun. *Bottom: Maggie, the* Cat on a Hot Tin Roof, *with broken-legged, brooding, boozing husband (Paul Newman)*

that conformed to public expectation but also allowed her to reveal something of her private self as well. From angelic child to braying fishwife, her evolving image demonstrates a greater range than she is often credited with.

Innocence and experience

She was born in London in 1932 and evacuated with her parents to Hollywood at the outbreak of World War II. After a small role in Universal's *There's One Born Every Minute* (1941), she signed for MGM. Elizabeth Taylor the child star – of *Lassie Come Home*, *Jane Eyre* (both 1943) and *National Velvet* – had an ethereal quality that, viewed now in enlightened retrospect, is jarring. Sweet without being sticky, possessed of an almost mystical streak, her little girls were saintly characters. Her sculpted face, with her radiant, piercing eyes, had a grown-up's wisdom, and the young Elizabeth exuded a faintly unsettling pre-conscious sexuality. Her voice, high-pitched and breathy (as it has remained), also had a musical quality, and her remnants of an English accent lent her, in American settings, a dignified air. Strange to say, but as a child actress she had not a trace of vulgarity.

As she grew into adolescence and young womanhood, MGM did not quite know what to do with her dainty, refined, indeed almost otherworldly manner. She clearly was not a typical American teenager, and so she was cast as someone set apart from the American norm, like the society girl Angela Vickers in *A Place in the Sun* (1951).

Throughout the late Forties and early Fifties, Liz played poor little rich girls whose great wealth, or delicate physical condition, or luminous beauty, gave them special distinction. She is surprisingly serene and delicate and

always somewhat remote in these parts. But there were early indications, too, in *Little Women* (1949) for instance, that dainty Taylor had a sly sense of humour and a tongue that could sting; and throughout her la-de-dah *ingénue* period there were portents of the spitfire who blossomed in the mid-Fifties.

Broken-hearted belles

In *Giant* (1956), *Raintree County* (1957), *Cat on a Hot Tin Roof* (1958), *Suddenly, Last Summer* (1959) and *Butterfield 8* (1960), she was seen to act more visibly as she took on a series of wilful, high-spirited, sassy character parts (the last four earned her Oscar nominations in consecutive years). The upper-crust good manners of her young matrons were replaced by increasing doses of the common touch. Her style became harsher as she acquired manner and temperament, as brassiness and sarcasm chipped away at the inaccessible *ingénue* aura that she had never wanted. Interestingly, at the height of her beauty in films like *Raintree County* and *Cat on a Hot Tin Roof*, she played women spurned by men, women bruised and humiliated in the search for love. It is an image – Liz unlucky in love, the great beauty on the

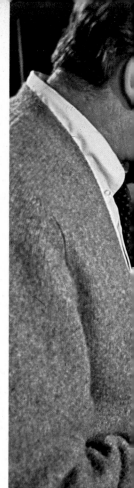

romantic skids – that has stayed with her, off screen as well as on, and at least in movies has been subjected to increasingly baroque variations. Surely she is drawn to these cast-off mistresses and wives, these women tortured by romantic misfortunes, because they reflect aspects of her own insecurity, her very modest self-appraisal, her doubts about who she really is beneath the cosmetic star-packing.

Acknowledged as an actress and finally winning an Oscar, for *Butterfield 8*, Elizabeth Taylor dramatically embarked on a new phase to her career in the early Sixties: the main reasons were Richard Burton, *Cleopatra* and her elevation to superstardom. Her unprecedented million-dollar contracts and her private-life notoriety made it impossible for her to escape herself, and in hollow movies like *The VIPs* (1963) and *The Sandpiper* (1965), she was visibly and awkwardly self-conscious, once again a remote movie star playing fabricated movie-star roles. But her Oscar-winning performance in *Who's Afraid of Virginia Woolf?* (1966) saved her, giving her a new screen persona – one that she has, more or less, held on to ever since. The middle-aged strumpet she played released with full force the bitchy wit and Chaucerian bawdiness that had been struggling for expression in Liz since the time of *Giant*. With her rumbustious performance in *Who's Afraid of Virginia Woolf?* she became a fully fledged Hollywood dame, a West Coast version of the Wife of Bath, coarse, loud, earthy, blowzy and essentially good-hearted. Here was an image she clearly relished; at last she could forget about being beautiful or well-behaved – she was free to burlesque her earlier glamorous persona.

Since then, in films like *The Taming of the Shrew, Reflections in a Golden Eye* (both 1967), *Boom!* (1968), *Zee & Co* (1971) and *Hammersmith Is Out* (1972), she has conducted an ongoing rebellion against the blandness and containment of her earlier MGM image. And as her material has become quirkier and as she

has grown heavier and more shrill, she has seemed to enjoy being a movie star, perhaps for the first time. She has become something of a coterie performer, putting on a whale of a show for dedicated Elizabethans, mocking her sex-goddess, earth-mother image, delivering sarcastic dialogue with a swagger and flourish that the young actress could never have summoned. Her range narrowed, her technique became more mannered as she cultivated a battery of verbal tics – erratic phrasing, stammers, pauses, backtrackings, sudden whoops and dips in pitch and tone – but she acted with zest and abandon. This late, flamboyant phase of her career has a buoyancy, a sense of wicked self-mockery that is endearing.

A Taylor-made image

To many of her fans, the greying of Elizabeth Taylor may seem like the desecration of a national shrine, but to the lady herself it must be a relief to have her days of classic beauty safely behind her. Off screen, she has got herself up in jewellery and teased hair and gaudy tent-like dresses that seem like a parody of old Hollywood theatricality, and her essential good nature and sanity have emerged. Her latest image, with its Rabelaisian and Falstaffian echoes, seems like a final uncovering of her mask – she is letting us in on the uncorseted, fun-loving woman who has always been there beneath the star trappings, though perhaps the star herself has not always been aware of this.

She has certainly been vivid, but she has not had a good part in a good movie for many years. She was miscast, for example, in *A Little Night Music* (1977) because she does not have the diction, carriage or authority to play an autocratic stage actress. But she is still usable, a Hollywood trouper with a ripe personality – a former beauty who has turned herself into a skilful character actress with a wit and a style that are distinctly her own.

FOSTER HIRSCH

Above left: a glorious Cleopatra in the inglorious Cleopatra. *Bottom left: Burton and Taylor as tamer and tamed in* The Taming of the Shrew. *Above: the Burtons antagonizing each other in* Who's Afraid of Virginia Woolf? *Below: in Zee & Co, Susannah York (here with Taylor) plays the 'other woman' threatening an already shaky marriage*

Filmography
1941 There's One Born Every Minute. **'43** Lassie Come Home; Jane Eyre. **'44** The White Cliffs of Dover; National Velvet. **'46** Courage of Lassie. **'47** Cynthia (GB: The Rich Full Life); Life With Father. **'48** A Date With Judy; Julia Misbehaves. **'49** Little Women; Conspirator (GB). **'50** The Big Hangover; Father of the Bride. **'51** Father's Little Dividend; A Place in the Sun; Callaway Went That-a-Way (GB: The Star Said No); Love Is Better Than Ever (GB: The Light Fantastic). **'52** Ivanhoe (GB). **'53** The Girl Who Had Everything; Elephant Walk. **'54** Rhapsody; Beau Brummel; The Last Time I Saw Paris. **'56** Giant. **'57** Raintree County. **'58** Cat on a Hot Tin Roof. **'59** Suddenly, Last Summer; Scent of Mystery/Holiday in Spain. **'60** Butterfield 8. **'63** The VIPs (GB) (USA: International Hotel); Cleopatra. **'65** The Sandpiper. **'66** Who's Afraid of Virginia Woolf? **'67** The Taming of the Shrew (USA-IT); Reflections in a Golden Eye; The Comedians (USA-BERMUDA-FR). **'68** Dr Faustus (GB-IT); Boom! (GB); Secret Ceremony (GB). **'70** The Only Game in Town. **'71** Zee & Co (GB) (USA: X, Y and Zee); Under Milk Wood (GB). **'72** Hammersmith Is Out. **'73** Night Watch (GB); Ash Wednesday. **'74** That's Entertainment! (+conarr); Identikit (IT) (USA/GB: The Driver's Seat). **'76** The Blue Bird (USSR-USA). **'77** Victory at Entebbe; A Little Night Music (USA-A-GER). **'79** Winter Kills (uncredited). **'80** The Mirror Crack'd (GB).

The Preminger Factor

Viennese exile, autocratic producer-director: Hollywood and the critics have long played cat and mouse with Preminger. Or is it the other way round?

Otto Preminger is one of the most controversial figures of the American cinema. Many intelligent critics and audiences refuse to take him seriously as an artist. They all agree that *Laura* (1944) is a masterpiece, but they stubbornly cling to the prevailing theory that his subsequent career, one that spans four decades, is mostly one long decline. Preminger himself encourages and feeds the controversy. His flamboyant, familiar persona smacks more of the showman than the artist. But the aggressive self-promotion that he projects in his media appearances merely suggests that Preminger has shrewdly reconciled himself to the economic realities of Hollywood film-making. He knows only too well that each movie must be sold to enable him to make the next one.

Preminger's instinct for survival has sometimes involved him with mediocre properties, such as the unfortunate kidnap thriller *Rosebud* (1975), which starred Richard Attenborough and Peter O'Toole. But he has never really let that instinct seriously damage or compromise his aesthetic integrity. Even his celebrated, trail-blazing battles with the stifling Hollywood Production Code in the Fifties attest to this integrity, and even his severest detractors acknowledge the importance of his fights against censorship. But, they go on to argue, how can a man whose choice of material is so eclectic be considered a committed artist? Do recurring themes and motifs really appear in movies as seemingly disparate as *Laura*, *Anatomy of a Murder* (1959) and *Advise and Consent* (1962)? These critics also maintain that Preminger's visual style is too cold, too analytical, even anti-humanist. But the most casual viewer will see that his best movies are linked by the recurring theme of obsession. In *Laura*, Mark McPherson (Dana Andrews) is obsessed with the portrait of a beautiful woman he believes is dead. In *Angel Face* (1952), *Bonjour Tristesse* (1958) and *Bunny Lake Is Missing* (1965), the central characters are locked into obsessive and self-destructive incestuous relationships. The quality and nature of the obsession may change from film to film, but the dramatic tension in all comes from the characters' struggles to overcome and survive. In *The Man With the Golden Arm* (1956), an addict's fight to kick his dependence on drugs is successful, while in *Advise and Consent*, a senator's inability to face up to his true social identity ends in tragedy.

Objective cases

What makes Preminger a profound director is the objectivity with which he describes the frequently pathological behaviour of his obsessed protagonists. Jean Renoir's famous credo – that 'everyone has his reasons' – fits Preminger just as well. Like the French master, he refuses to pass any absolute moral judgments on people. And because Preminger appreciates the contradictory nature of human relationships, he delineates characters, actions and issues as impartially as possible.

The director demands a comparable objectivity from his audience. While watching one of his films, it is given the responsibility of sifting and weighing the evidence on the screen, and its responses are constantly being modified. Preminger visually encourages the audience to remain neutral by staging many scenes in long, uninterrupted shots. By cutting as seldom as possible within a scene, he allows the viewer to balance the moral opposites of its dramatic predicaments. This is what makes him the ideal director to tackle such abstract, potentially unwieldy topics as the inner workings of the American judicial system (*Anatomy of a Murder*), the emergence of a nation (*Exodus*, 1960), the US Senate (*Advise and Consent*) and the Catholic Church (*The Cardinal*,

Above: Preminger prepares a scene for Advise and Consent. *Below left:* Laura *(Gene Tierney) encounters detective Mark McPherson (Dana Andrews). Below: Frank Jessup (Robert Mitchum) is drawn into the web of murder by innocent-looking Diane Tremayne (Jean Simmons) in* Angel Face

1963). He brings them down to human scale, interlocking the public and private aspects of the stories and embodying the larger issues in specific personal relationships.

In through the stage door

Preminger was born on December 5, 1906 in Vienna, the son of a prominent Jewish lawyer who encouraged the boy's interest in the theatre with the provision that he finish law school first. But even while he was studying, Preminger was acting in plays at the Josefstadt, Max Reinhardt's Viennese equivalent of his celebrated Berlin theatre. At 19 he decided to concentrate on directing, and in 1932 made his first film, *Die Grosse Liebe* (The Great Love), a melodrama that would be his only foray into the cinema during this period. By 1935 he had become the managing director of the Josefstadt, but he was growing increasingly anxious about the sinister appeal that Hitler had begun to hold for so many of his countrymen. When Joseph M. Schenck from 20th Century-Fox offered him the chance of working in Hollywood, Preminger decided to accept. He left for the United States on October 16, 1935.

His first few years in America were professionally frustrating. Darryl F. Zanuck, 20th Century-Fox's production chief, tested the young director by assigning him to two negligible B movies, *Under Your Spell* (1936) and *Danger – Love at Work* (1937). But the volatile temperaments of the two men soon clashed. After Zanuck dismissed him from a major production – *Kidnapped* (1938) – Preminger found himself outcast from the industry and spent the next few years directing plays on Broadway. And it was one of these, Clare Boothe Luce's *Margin for Error*, that brought him back to 20th Century-Fox in 1943 as a director and an actor – he played the first of his several roles as a singularly convincing Nazi, the most memorable of which was his POW commandant in Billy Wilder's *Stalag 17* (1953).

The success of *Margin for Error* landed Preminger a new contract that enabled him to produce as well as direct. For one of his first productions, he chose a property called *Laura*, but Zanuck, still a bit wary of 'that Austrian autocrat', hired Rouben Mamoulian to direct. When the early rushes proved disastrous, however, Zanuck reluctantly replaced Mamoulian with Preminger – perhaps one of his wisest moves. After a slow start at the box-office, *Laura* became a great success. It is still widely considered Preminger's best film and is certainly one of his finest – a definitive *film noir* whose cool elegance and dark tone the director would sustain throughout much of his subsequent work in the Forties.

Angel Face brilliantly climaxed Preminger's *film noir* period. Like *Laura* and *Fallen Angel* (1945), it is a brooding murder mystery that subordinates conventional suspense to a mood of perverse romanticism. Jean Simmons is superb as a young woman whose enigmatic behaviour and inscrutable mask alternately suggest a saint or the devil. Like Jean Seberg in *Bonjour Tristesse*, she is the quintessential Preminger heroine. Both are driven to perform extreme, arguably immoral acts by impulses that they can neither control nor understand.

In addition to challenging Hollywood's prevailing safeguards of American morality, Preminger's next film, *The Moon Is Blue* (1953), also marked his debut as an independent producer. But the prurient humour of this lightweight sex farce has not aged well and the film lacks any urgency or charm.

Preminger made some of his finest films during the Fifties. He was one of the first directors to explore the expressive possibilities of CinemaScope. He has since stated that he welcomed the elongated frame because the extra space made it easier for him to construct longer sequences that could develop with a minimum of cutting. In early CinemaScope films like *River of No Return* and *Carmen Jones* (both 1954), Preminger used the process to compose lengthy shots with bold framing and complicated camera movements. *Bonjour Tristesse*, *Advise and Consent* and *Bunny Lake Is Missing* are especially eloquent reminders that Preminger instinctively assimilated the dynamics of the wide screen into his style.

Right: Stella (Linda Darnell), the foot-sore victim, and her murderer Mark Judd (Charles Bickford) in Fallen Angel. *Below:* Carmen Jones *(Dorothy Dandridge) having her way with Joe (Harry Belafonte). Bottom: Crown (Brock Peters) abducts the attractive Bess (Dandridge again) in the inspired folk opera* Porgy and Bess

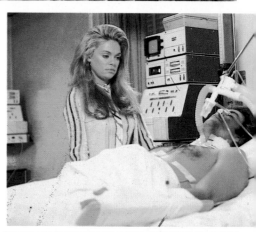

Above: a production shot from Saint Joan *with Jean Seberg at the stake. Above right: in* Exodus, *Kitty Fremont (Eva Marie Saint) and Ari Ben Canaan (Paul Newman) fight side by side. Right: Julie Messinger (Dyan Cannon) discovers her dying husband's secret past in* Such Good Friends

Saint and sinner

Bonjour Tristesse is one of two films that the director made with the late Jean Seberg. An inexperienced unknown from Iowa, she had been chosen by Preminger over thousands of applicants in a national search to find a new star for his 1957 screen adaptation of Shaw's *Saint Joan*. Both film and actress were mercilessly panned, but Preminger persisted and cast his protégée as Cécile, the spoiled adolescent of Françoise Sagan's controversial novella. Although it too flopped at the time, *Bonjour Tristesse* is arguably Preminger's greatest film. In this case Seberg's physical awkwardness and hollow reading of the lines are ideal for her roles as a girl whose amoral father (David Niven) encourages her to pursue pleasure and evade responsibility whatever the moral cost. Preminger transforms Sagan's trifle of a story into a devastating contemplation of time and loss. He develops the tragic relationship between Cécile, her father and his fiancée (Deborah Kerr) in flashbacks, ironically contrasting the sequences in the present, a monochrome portrait of ennui and stasis, with those of the past – a Technicolored evocation of what was or, in typical Preminger fashion, what might have been.

When *Anatomy of Murder*, a courtroom drama, opened in 1959, the director once again found himself in a storm of controversy. Two crucial plot points revolve around the presence, or absence, of sperm in the body of a woman who has allegedly been raped, and an incriminating item of ladies' underwear – the use of the words 'spermatogenesis' and 'panties' in the dialogue set a precedent for screen frankness in 1959. Bolstered by an exceptional cast led by James Stewart, Lee Remick and Ben Gazzara, *Anatomy of a Murder* was one of Preminger's biggest commercial and critical

successes. He followed it with an intermittently inspired version of George Gershwin's folk opera *Porgy and Bess* (1959), and a string of adaptations of pulpy best sellers, including *Exodus, Advise and Consent, The Cardinal, In Harm's Way* (1965) and *Hurry Sundown* (1967). *Advise and Consent* is the only one of these films that can be described as a major achievement, but all of them are models of multi-narrative, multi-character construction that simultaneously transcend their literary sources and elucidate complex themes and ideas. And Preminger is customarily reluctant to judge his characters or to draw any moral conclusions.

In 1965 Preminger directed Laurence Olivier, Carol Lynley and Noel Coward in *Bunny Lake Is Missing*, one of his most powerful studies of obsession and paranoia. In its concentration on a handful of characters and one single thread of action, the film points forward to an important late development in the director's work. In the Liza Minnelli film *Tell Me That You Love Me, Junie Moon* (1970) and *Such Good Friends* (1971), which starred Dyan Cannon and James Coco, he abandons the sprawling structure of his Sixties blockbusters and designs the formal patterns of the stories on a more intimate scale. He continued this distillation of story and character to essentials in *The Human Factor* (1979), which drew on powerful performances by Nicol Williamson and Richard Attenborough. It is a film that may superficially resemble a conventional espionage tale but, like most of Preminger's films, subtly undercuts the audience's expectations of genre. It lacks the tension of the ordinary thriller because the director is typically less interested in describing action than he is in exploring the psychology that provokes it. *The Human Factor* has the resonance and spare quality of a chamber drama. Its seamless fusion of subject and form irrevocably prove that, entering the Eighties, the vastly underrated Preminger had lost none of his creative power.

GEORGE MORRIS

Parts of this article originally appeared in the July 1980 issue of Diversion

Filmography

1932 Die Grosse Liebe (A). **'36** Under Your Spell. **'37** Danger – Love at Work. **'42** The Pied Piper (act. only); They Got Me Covered (act. only). **'43** Margin for Error (+act.). **'44** In the Meantime, Darling (+prod); Laura (+prod). **'45** A Royal Scandal (GB: Czarina); Fallen Angel (+prod). **'46** Centennial Summer. **'47** Forever Amber; Daisy Kenyon (+prod). **'48** That Lady in Ermine (add. dir. only, uncredited). **'49** The Fan (+prod) (GB: Lady Windermere's Fan); Whirlpool (+prod). **'50** Where the Sidewalk Ends (+prod). **'51** The Thirteenth Letter (+prod). **'52** Angel Face. **'53** Stalag 17 (act. only); The Moon Is Blue (+co-prod) (German version: Die Jungfrau auf dem Dach, 1954). **'54** River of No Return (+prod); Carmen Jones (+prod). **'55** The Court Martial of Billy Mitchell (+prod) (GB: One Man Mutiny). **'56** The Man With the Golden Arm (+prod). **'57** Saint Joan (+prod) (GB); The Making of a Movie (doc. about filming Saint Joan) (appearance as himself only). **'58** Bonjour Tristesse (+prod). **'59** Porgy and Bess; Anatomy of a Murder (+prod). **'60** Exodus (+prod). **'62** Advise and Consent (+prod). **'63** The Cardinal (+prod). **'65** In Harm's Way (+prod); The Making of In Harm's Way (doc) (appearance as himself only); Bunny Lake Is Missing (+prod) (GB). **'67** Hurry Sundown (+prod). **'68** Skidoo! (+prod). **'70** Tell Me That You Love Me, Junie Moon (+prod). **'71** Such Good Friends (+prod). **'75** Rosebud (+prod). **'79** The Human Factor (+prod) (GB-USA).

The film director as voyeur

The silken gauze dividing detached sensitivity from passionate sensuality is a flimsier garment than it might at first seem. It all started with what-the-butler-saw machines. Then the peep-show went public. Now we have 3-D sex epics . . .

It may seem arbitrary or forgetful for a history of movies to delay the topic of voyeurism until the Fifties. Yet the dedicated voyeur will appreciate the authority that withholds things as long as possible: striptease becomes an art when languor controls it.

Then again, it is cool cheek to put all the blame on the director. He has seen everything to the point of being stupefied: he foresaw the picture a year before it was shot; he storyboarded it; the precious moment when a peignoir slipped had to be shot 37 times; and then he was three days editing it, running the few seconds of film back and forth until it had lost meaning or magic.

The director hopes never to have to see it again. But when the finished film blooms in the theatre, and a flimsy garment falls away with outrageous originality . . . then it is *we* who are the voyeurs, ranged in rows in the dark, our faces exposed by the flash and shine of the screen.

It was always so. No matter that Marilyn Monroe in *Some Like It Hot* (1959) flaunts more than Theda Bara or Lillian Gish, the earliest movies had little that we would recognize as erotica. They were more chaste than either academic painting or what-the-butler-saw kinetoscopes at fairgrounds. As for those amusement-arcade machines where, as long and as slowly as the viewer's hand turned, so yards of garment unwound from the body of a woman, they were designed for one person to watch at a time. The viewer might be lost in 'iniquity', but he was doing it on his own – *in camera*, so to speak. Society could not see him and the naughty pictures at the same time, so that his illicit satisfaction was not itself a spectacle. However, it was all the sharper a pleasure because he did not feel the guilt of being seen in the act of watching.

Peeping Tom needs Lady Godiva, but he would not go out on the street to inspect her – because his repression fears public recognition, and perhaps because he is just as afraid of Godiva being so moved by his openness that she confronts him with unequivocal sexual love. Voyeurism gets its kicks watching, and is alleged to be a pathological condition . . . until so many people own up to it that it must be reappraised as normality.

Top left: Victorian Lady at Her Boudoir (1896) – *early smoking-room naughtiness by director Esmé Collings. Left: Rear Window is Hitchcock's homage to the voyeur in us all; but the watcher is also watched . . . by the director. Bottom left: as attitudes to sex relaxed, the private peep-show finally went public. Above: Marilyn Monroe – spangles strategically placed – in* Some Like It Hot

That is why the movies are so important in the history of sexual sensibility. No one, of course, believes that nakedness was discovered with photography, or that the sexual act was less varied or vital in the ages of Chaucer or Catullus; but movies were the medium that allowed all of us to watch from the safety of the darkness. Furthermore, they helped to legitimize and reveal voyeurism itself, not just the erogenous zones of the stars. Voyeurism depends on the viewed occupying the same real space that shelters the viewer. In Hitchcock's *Rear Window* (1954), the patterns of voyerism fill one courtyard and one community. A press photographer with a broken leg is forced to sit in his apartment with nothing else to do but watch the lives of the people in the windows he can see from his. But the movie also allows us to watch and fantasize over James Stewart and

How did they ever make a film of LOLITA?

ADULTS ONLY

GOLDWYN MAYER presents in association with SEVEN ARTS PRODUCTIONS JAMES B. HARRIS and STANLEY KUBRICK's LOLITA
JAMES MASON · SHELLEY WINTERS · PETER SELLERS · SUE LYON
VLADIMIR NABOKOV based on his novel 'Lolita' · Directed by STANLEY KUBRICK · Produced by JAMES B. HARRIS · Music composed and conducted by Nelson Riddle · Lolita Theme by Bob Harris

Above: Lolita (1962), *only made possible by a relaxation in censorship. Below:* Inserts (1975) *looks at the left-over lives of a silent-movie star and a has-been director*

"INSERTS"
a degenerate film with dignity.

Top left: Carl Boehm as Mark Lewis, the Peeping Tom, shoots a police detective. Top *right: anguished young men see Jayne Mansfield's true colours in* Too Hot To Handle

Grace Kelly – people we will never meet . . . if we have the luck of the true voyeur.

The first decade of movies coincides with Freud's *Interpretation of Dreams* (published in 1900) and his analysis of scoptophilia in *Three Essays on Sexuality* (published in 1905). The advent of cinema – with its characteristic principle of viewing in the dark – also assists the members of an unbearably large and dense society to live more in their imaginations and less in problematic reality. As cinema became more sophisticated, movie stardom offered the prospect of making love with Jean Harlow or Clark Cable, so the medium made a decisive separation of activity and watching, of actuality and day-dreaming. That in turn threatens the society dependent on the bonds

between love, marriage, sexuality and family.

And that is why it is proper to deal with voyeurism in the movies as a phenomenon of the Fifties, with films such as *The Prowler* appearing as early in the decade as 1951 and *Pushover* in 1954. From the earliest days, film-makers had realized that the camera allowed them to ask young women to take off their clothes. But the 'orgy' was slow in developing because the industry was run by a lower-middle-class piety nearly as devoted to love and marriage as it was to maintaining the business *status quo*. For fifty years, the cinema audience could get its sexual excitement only so long as 'true love' was honoured.

It was a workable bargain, for prudishness and prurience are lodged side-by-side in our soul. From D. W. Griffith onwards, sexual temptation was open country just because the story was so bound to assert happy endings and respectable social solutions. In *Intolerance* (1916) the Miriam Cooper character is clearly doomed, but her 'abandoned' life is arguably the subtlest and most touching thing in the film. Griffith could not have been as sensitive to her without knowing that he would be able to kill her off. And any sexuality in DeMille's work is ultimately recuperated in Christian ideology, The *femme fatale* might have her hour of screen time; she could let several laws and shoulder-straps slip; she sold tickets; but she faced death, disgrace or defeat at the hands of a more wholesome lady.

The compromise came apart in the Fifties and was given up altogether in the Sixties. A quick sketch of the background would disclose greater everyday permissiveness, birth-control devices, censorship yielding to *Lady Chatterley's Lover, Lolita* and *Playboy,* and the atom bomb, for those who care to see that as a metaphor for orgasm.

It was an era in which the limits of acceptable movie erotica were steadily extended. There were no more voyeurs among directors or audiences. Instead, entertainment movies were conscious of changing mores – and the cinema showed greater interest in exploiting the relationship between viewing and sexual arousal, and was insistent that pictures could show sex without having to resort to the wrappings of happy endings.

Literally inch after inch of skin was increasingly revealed, but the censors thought the film-makers had gone too far too soon. The same caution that had drawn up the Hays Code ordained that in one sequence from *Too Hot to Handle* (1960) Jayne Mansfield's costume needed more spangles to disguise what must be her nipples. And so, extra ones were painted on the negative! In *Psycho* (1960), when Janet Leigh entered the shower, a mask was slipped in with her at the bottom of the screen. Presumably it was to protect the viewer from her breasts, but the safeguard only added to the steady, tormenting glee with which Hitchcock had been asking us to imagine them.

In *Some Like It Hot*, when Monroe sings 'I Want to Be Loved By You', there is a momentary wondering whether she will overflow into the camera. It owes something to the precision with which Billy Wilder has the margin between spotlight and shadow fall on the most crucial part of the side area of her bosom. And in *Anatomy of a Murder* (1959) – a movie that asks us whether the Lee Remick character could have been raped – a pair of panties figures in the investigation. Within the film the judge gives warning of this to the courtroom, and tells everyone to get the dirty laughter over with. But the director, Otto Preminger – attempting to demystify the taboo of sex – is giving us the same advice.

By far the most interesting voyeurist movies of the time were *Peeping Tom* (1960) and *Rear Window*. *Peeping Tom* is the story of a focus-puller whose obsession takes the form of killing attractive young women and photographing the fear on their faces as he does so. The recent unavailability of *Rear Window* has made it a sublime ideal for voyeurs; but it is not so much about sexual spectacle as it is about the desire that the act of seeing bestows on anything. Some critics have seen the film as a parable about movies and photography – showing us things so that we begin to make up meanings to explain the appearance, meanings that may not always fit with the feelings of those being watched. Through the eyes of Jeff, the broken-legged press photographer (James Stewart), we are led to think of Thorwald (Raymond Burr) as a monstrous killer. But when he appears, ostensibly threatening to murder, we suddenly realize that he is pathetic and vulnerable. Just

watching without participation leads to making hasty conclusions.

Photography isolates and glamorizes everything it notices. It can cast a kind of erotic glow on an orange as well as a nude, on a starving refugee as well as Brigitte Bardot. The circumstances of the medium encourage our imaginations to cross a forbidden or impossible threshold. We are excited by the intimacy of something that is actually remote.

In recent years John Carpenter's *Halloween* (1978) involved a killer stalking and watching his victims. The spectators of the film could not avoid becoming accomplices in that pursuit. And Brian De Palma's *Dressed to Kill* (1980) – a complete homage to Hitchcock – frequently involves the secret viewer as a participant in the menacing action.

Seeing may be an act in which there is always a trace of that search for pleasure and self-knowledge most intense in sex. The movies have helped us realize this, and made us feel that our brain is something separate from our body, connected by the process of sight. 'Voyeurism' will gradually lose its pejorative associations, but only because we all admit to being spectators.   DAVID THOMSON

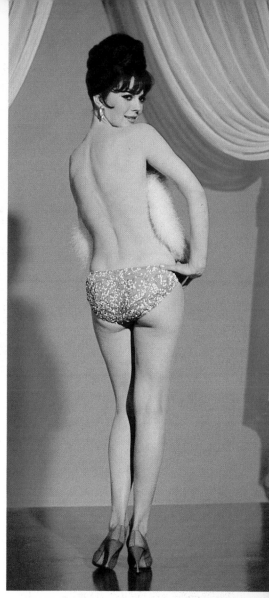

Above: Natalie Wood keeps us guessing – a typical voyeur trick – in Gypsy *(1962). Left: The Prowler peeps in. Below left: recent recruit to the genre of voyeuristic horror – Brian De Palma. Below: rape-case attorney Paul Biegler (James Stewart) holds the incriminating panties as witness Mary Pilant (Kathryn Grant) looks on unruffled in a courtroom scene from* Anatomy of Murder

Tall, dark and terribly handsome

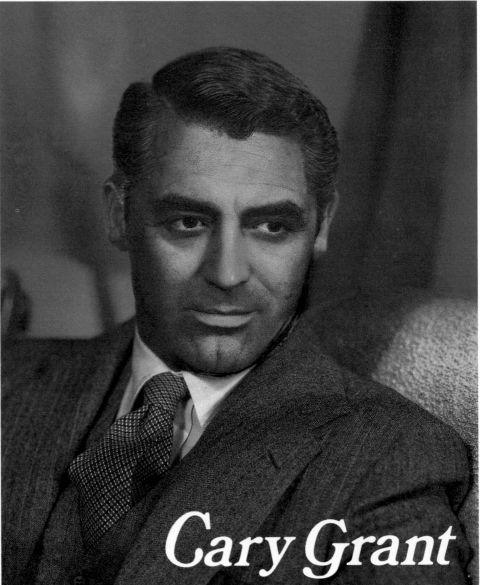

Cary Grant

With his good looks, casual air, wit and extraordinary accent, Cary Grant appears to be the epitome of an English gentleman. However, there is mystery and amusement behind his smile and he is equally capable of becoming a playboy, a male chauvinist or a calculating villain

There have been enough nice guys in movies to make it clear that Cary Grant is much more than handsome, gracious and pleasing. Yet it is easy now, some fifteen years after he gave up pictures, to accept the notion of Grant as the epitome of classy likeability. Everyone feels affection for him. He is not vain or crass; his life seems tidy and rational. There have been four divorces but no woman walked away raging at his impossibility. Instead, they seemed a little wistful that a dream had not quite worked, and absolutely insistent about his decency.

At nearly eighty he remains trim, dashing

Top left: Blonde Venus *gave Grant his opening, opposite Marlene Dietrich, as a romantic lead, Above: a debonair portrait taken by John Miehle in 1945. Left: playing the clown as a man who falls for his fiancée's sister (Katherine Hepburn) in* Holiday

and attractive. He dotes on his daughter, the Los Angeles Dodgers and his business interests with Fabergé. He is modest and retiring, but he laughs a lot and still believes in excellence. In 1979, when Marlon Brando was unable to present a special Oscar to Laurence Olivier, Grant had no qualms about being second choice and glowed with the honour and pleasure of the occasion. That was grace, for the Academy has never given him a Best Actor Oscar, although he was also awarded a special Oscar in 1970 for 'sheer brilliance'.

Grant is, perhaps, the best actor the screen

has ever had, but that could not be said if he were merely a romantic lead beyond compare. He had, and still has, those attributes – no-one else in the movies looked so good and so intelligent at the same time – and he was beautiful in the Thirties, Forties and Fifties, *but* there was always a mocking smile or impatience behind his eyes that knew being beautiful was a little silly. You could never expect narcissism or vanity once you heard him speak. Grant could handle quick, complex, witty dialogue in the way of someone who enjoyed language as much as Cole Porter or Dorothy Parker. Remember his delight when Grace Kelly offers him a leg or a breast at the picnic in *To Catch a Thief* (1955).

Only Fred Astaire ever moved as well as Grant – no wonder, for Grant had been an acrobat, a stilt-walker and a dancer for ten years before he got into pictures – but Grant

moved with more dramatic eloquence while Astaire cherished the purity of movement. Grant could look as elegant as Astaire, but he could manage to look clumsy without actually sacrificing balance or style.

Still, his movements had the same undertone as his looks. Grant is always a little restless on screen and beneath the grace and élan there is a twinge of anxiety. With his accent caught between English and American his tone is uncertain whether to stay cool or let nerviness show. This is more than a perfect dance partner. This is the image of excellence hoping that hidden problems will stay out of sight.

The shadow of a smile

Grant's strength as a screen actor is in giving us a sense of the doubt and dismay that lies behind being 'Cary Grant'. Good looks do not relieve a man of every choice between good and its alternatives. That is why he seems to smile with some inner understanding, and why he is occasionally bitter or malign.

'He smiled understandingly – much more than understandingly. It was one of those rare smiles with a quality of eternal reassurance in

it . . . It faced . . . the whole eternal world for an instant, and then concentrated on *you* with an irresistible prejudice in your favour. It understood you just so far as you wanted to be understood, believed in you as you would like to believe in yourself, and assured you that it had precisely the impression of you that, at your best, you hoped to convey.'

Is that a Hollywood figure of the Thirties on first meeting Grant? No, it is Scott Fitzgerald (through Nick Carraway) describing Jay Gatsby – apparently the ideal host at Long Island parties – a mid-Western kid who had been a gangster and who kept a list of instructions for himself that included 'Practise elocution, poise and how to attain it'.

Gatsby was the essential fake in Americana, the rough become smooth, but never himself convinced by the change. Grant was not a fake, but his quality was ambiguous and intriguing because of a similar transformation.

Destination Hollywood

The immaculate man of the world would seem as smart as Cole Porter's songs and as dry as martinis, but there was a hint of roughneck and a history of enormous social journey.

Above left: despite poor billing, Grant stole the show with his portrayal of a swindler. Above: in this drama he plays a man opposing his wife's family during the American Revolution. Left: in His Girl Friday, *with Rosalind Russell as his ex-wife*

Grant was to marry Barbara Hutton, one of the wealthiest women in the world, but he supported a mother in England who had entered a lunatic asylum when he was 12.

He was born in Bristol in 1904 and christened Archibald Alexander Leach. It was 1920 before he went to America and he had already spent five years working as part of a travelling company of acrobats and comics. He was brought up on patter, somersaults and pratfalls, and he did the same thing in American vaudeville without much recognition. However, by the late Twenties Grant began to get parts on the stage in musical comedy and was 28 when Hollywood, in the person of the producer B.P. Schulberg, thought to give him a chance.

For several years he was not much more than a romantic escort for leading ladies at Paramount, but in his second picture – *Blonde Venus* (1932) – he was very confident and restrained, opposite Marlene Dietrich, as the shady lover. Mae West was another screen goddess who knew how appreciatively he could look at a woman – Grant was always an actor who listened and watched so intently on screen that he was credited with a degree of intelligence and sensitivity that might not exist in the script. He played with West in *She Done Him Wrong* (1933), as an undercover agent investigating white-slave traffic, and in the same year *I'm No Angel*, as the playboy pursued by the vamp, effortlessly catching her risqué association of sex and humour.

By way of a change he was the Mock Turtle in *Alice in Wonderland* (1933), but he then had to do his duty in a run of undistinguished romances. Rescue came in a form that reminded him of his past. He played a charming cockney swindler in George Cukor's *Sylvia Scarlett* (1936). It was also his first movie with Katharine Hepburn, a team usually wittier and more romantically interesting than her celebrated association with Spencer Tracy.

The late Thirties saw Grant coming into his own, principally in comedy, and always playing men amused by the passing scene.

Above: Tracy Lord (Katharine Hepburn) re-marries her ex-husband (Grant) with the reporter (James Stewart) as best man in The Philadelphia Story. *Above right: Grant and Ann Sheridan as newly-weds in* I Was a Male War Bride. *Right: in* To Catch a Thief *as the cat-burglar who comes out of retirement in order to catch his imitator*

However, few of his roles are clear-cut. For instance, the stories in both *The Awful Truth* (1937) and *The Philadelphia Story* (1940) concern themes of divorced couples still in love and allowed Grant to add depths of feeling and melancholy to the comedy. As the ex-husband in *The Philadelphia Story* he is unashamed of his own errors, rakishness and irresponsibility, but still certain that pride and superiority are to be the downfall of Katharine Hepburn's Tracy Lord. These films could not be such searching character studies without Grant's convincing references to the off-screen plot so vital to the central characters' relationship.

Equally in *Bringing Up Baby* (1938), he makes the humanizing of his short-sighted professor as touching as the melting of Garbo's Ninotchka. How generously he allows Hepburn to be the force of the film but how richly he develops his stooge character to the point where the overly sane man is beginning to be liberated by the screwball woman. Further evidence of Grant's skill is apparent in *Holiday* (1938). This film – about an easy-going man who falls in love with his fiancée's sister, a girl much repressed by her surroundings – would not be so good a comedy about snobbery and integrity if it were not for Grant's sensitive use of humour; never for a moment did Grant's comic style suggest that comedy concerned less than the marrow of existence.

Therefore, when a joke is made the audience is aware of the serious man who sometimes needs to laugh at awful and frightening things. That is the essence of his humane toughness in *Only Angels Have Wings* (1939), the Howard Hawks film in which Grant is the leader of a group of pilots who ferry mail in South America. He worked for Hawks again in *His Girl Friday* (1940), a comedy so rapid that it is easy to miss the conniving and ruthlessness in Grant's part. For the first time there was something formidable in his authority and fatalistic attitude. *His Girl Friday* is yet another version of the plot whereby a man regains his ex-wife, played by Rosalind Russell. However in this case it is less easy to believe in a surviving love than in the challenge of conquest. In all these love stories Grant established the idea of an aloof, rather lonely man who could never put all his faith in lasting love.

From Hitch to Hawks

Certainly Alfred Hitchcock noticed the heartless gaiety of *His Girl Friday* and decided to cast Grant in *Suspicion* (1941). Nervousness softened the ending of the film, but Hitchcock had intended it as a black comedy about a wife who is being poisoned by the charming husband she adores. The film dropped that sinister line in favour of the theme of misunderstanding, but for most of the time Grant's debonair smile is masking murderous thoughts – and how well it works on screen. Five years later Hitchcock again explored the darker side of Grant in *Notorious* (1946) – the story of a man who coldly uses a woman (Ingrid Bergman) even though he loves her.

The Forties saw Grant in a lot of praiseworthy movies, although most were less striking than his work for Hawks and Hitchcock. One of his few completely dramatic roles was as

Filmography

1931 Singapore Sue (short). '32 This Is the Night; Sinners in the Sun; Merrily We Go to Hell (GB: Merrily We Go to . . .); The Devil and the Deep; Blonde Venus; Hot Saturday; Madame Butterfly. '33 She Done Him Wrong; Woman Accused; The Eagle and the Hawk; Gambling Ship; I'm No Angel; Alice in Wonderland. '34 Thirty-Day Princess; Born to Be Bad; Kiss and Make Up; Ladies Should Listen. '35 Enter Madame; Wings in the Dark; The Last Outpost. '36 Sylvia Scarlett; Big Brown Eyes; Suzy; Private Party on Catalina Island (short); Wedding Present; The Amazing Quest of Ernest Bliss (GB) (USA: Romance and Riches) (retitling for TV: Amazing Adventure). '37 When You're in Love; Topper; Toast of New York; The Awful Truth. '38 Bringing Up Baby; Holiday (GB: Free to Live/Unconventional Linda). '39 Gunga Din; Only Angels Have Wings; In Name Only. '40 His Girl Friday; My Favorite Wife; The Howards of Virginia; The Philadelphia Story. '41 Penny Serenade; Suspicion. '42 Talk of the Town; Once Upon a Honeymoon. '43 Mr Lucky; Destination Tokyo. '44 Once Upon a Time; None But the Lonely Heart; Arsenic and Old Lace; Road to Victory (short). '46 Night and Day; Without Reservations (uncredited guest); Notorious. '47 The Bachelor and the Bobby Soxer (GB: Bachelor Knight); The Bishop's Wife. '48 Mr Blandings Builds His Dream House; Every Girl Should Be Married. '49 I Was a Male War Bride (GB: You Can't Sleep Here). '50 Crisis. '51 People Will Talk. '52 Room for One More; Monkey Business. '53 Dream Wife. '55 To Catch a Thief. '57 The Pride and the Passion; An Affair to Remember; Kiss Them for Me. '58 Indiscreet; Houseboat. '59 North by Northwest; Operation Petticoat (+prod co). '60 The Grass Is Greener (+prod co). '62 That Touch of Mink (+prod co). '63 Charade. '64 Father Goose (+prod co). '66 Walk, Don't Run (+prod co). '70 Elvis: That's the Way It Is (guest).

a revolutionary fighter in *The Howards of Virginia* (1940), set at the time of the American Revolution, and he was good in two George Stevens films – *Penny Serenade* (1941), a story of marital break-up, and *Talk of the Town* (1942), with Grant as an alleged murderer on the run. He played another cockney drifter in *None But*

Left: as a scientist with 'higher' things in mind Grant is unmoved by the attributes of his secretary (Marilyn Monroe) in Monkey Business. *Below left: the problems of flat-sharing and cocktail-mixing are examined by an industrialist (Grant) in* Walk, Don't Run *(1966). Below: the undercover agent gets his man in* Charade *(1963)*

the Lonely Heart (1944) and Cole Porter in *Night and Day* (1946). However, many of his romantic comedies had lost the sharp edge apparent in his pictures ten years earlier.

It was Howard Hawks who gave him new life in *I Was a Male War Bride* (1949), one of the most brilliant American sex comedies, and successful because of the glee with which Grant approached playing in drag. Three years later in *Monkey Business* (1952) – with Hawks, Ginger Rogers, Marilyn Monroe and the ploy of a rejuvenating drug – Grant was again able to free the boyish energy that was usually kept under wraps.

With the Fifties he let his hair go grey and worked a little less, but there was no difficulty in seeing him as a match for younger women. In *To Catch a Thief* he was very sympathetic support for Grace Kelly and fully at ease in the sophisticated adventure.

His last great fling came in 1959 when he played Roger Thornhill in Hitchcock's *North by Northwest*. In a cornfield pursued by an airplane, in a small train compartment with Eva Marie Saint, at an art auction, on the run, creeping into an occupied hospital room, waking the young woman patient, hushing her screams and being briefly tempted to stay, Grant was at his very best. And he knew all along that Thornhill was a flippant, spoiled baby cad being taught to grow up. *North by Northwest* is a comedy and an adventure, but it is, nevertheless, also a moral tale.

In that year, too, Grant must have known that he had passed into fond folklore when he saw the delicious and very respectful impersonation of him provided by Tony Curtis in *Some Like it Hot*.
DAVID THOMSON

M·G·M presents

CARY GRANT
EVA MARIE SAINT
JAMES MASON

in ALFRED HITCHCOCK'S

NORTH BY NORTHWEST

VISTAVISION
TECHNICOLOR®

Co-starring JESSIE ROYCE LANDIS
Written by ERNEST LEHMAN · Directed by ALFRED HITCHCOCK

AN M-G-M PICTURE

1

3

5

North by Northwest was greeted with sighs of pleasure and relief by those numerous admirers of Hitchcock who were perplexed by the romantic obsession of *Vertigo* (1958). Following *North by Northwest*, Hitchcock made *Psycho* (1960) and viewers were again confronted by a work they did not quite know how to take – as Gothic extravagance, as black comedy or as an appalling lapse of taste.

Superficially, *North by Northwest* is a *divertissement* between two emotionally disturbing films, a colourful spy frolic starring the amiable Cary Grant; a chase movie told with a gleeful disregard for plot but with immense professional skill and good humour. But the film, which Hitchcock described as the culmination of his work in America, contains many darker elements within its genre framework that place it alongside *Vertigo* and *Psycho* as a comment on the char-

acter of American society.

The project came about by chance. Before shooting began on *Vertigo*, Hitchcock was hired by MGM to direct *The Wreck of the Mary Deare* to which screenwriter Ernest Lehman was also assigned. Both men soon realized the problems in adapting Hammond Innes' novel. They began instead on an original story, a spy thriller, which apparently started with Hitchcock's wish to film a sequence on Mount Rushmore. *The Man on Lincoln's Nose* was an early title and Hitchcock conceived an irreverent scene (never shot) in which the hero hides in one of Lincoln's nostrils and gets a sneezing fit.

In the initial stages of preparation it was intended as a James Stewart film but as the main character developed it became a Cary Grant film. This is a crucial element in the film's well-oiled mechanism. Whereas Stewart's persona is one

7

8

9

of integrity and dedication to cause, Grant's is one of cynicism, independence and flamboyance.

Grant's Roger Thornhill is the classic adman: smart and shallow, a believer only in himself, unshakably complacent, unattached and on the make. His personalized bookmatches, inscribed with the initials R.O.T., emphasize the zero in his life. The film charts a moral and spiritual growth by stripping away what identity he has and by forcing him to adopt the identity of someone who does not exist.

Thornhill's commitment at the end is not to the ideals of America, as embodied by the paternalistic head of the CIA (Thornhill already has a dominant mother who keeps a check on his drinking), but to Eve Kendall, another in his long line of women. The survival of this species of American male is a dispiriting prospect just off the edges of the frame.

The opening scenes establish Thornhill as being master of his environment – his ease at commandeering someone else's cab; his relaxed charm in smart cocktail bars. Thornhill is every inch the American man-about-town and, appropriately, it is a man called Townsend who propels him from New York into a world of chaos.

The plot's physical and spiritual trajectory is a north-westerly one and a historical one, with Vandamm's Old World suavity adding a cultural perspective to this satire of the New World. From New York's Plaza Hotel and United Nations building (symbols, respectively, of material success and Utopia) we travel on the *Twentieth Century* to Chicago, with its memories of gangsters (now the CIA and spies). The justly celebrated cropduster sequence, when Thornhill is attacked by the swooping plane, takes place on the wide prairie complete with farmers who might have stepped out of the pages of John Steinbeck. Mount Rushmore's presidents carved in stone is the ultimate symbol of order and tolerance but is used as the setting for betrayals, homosexual jealousies (Vandamm's sadistic henchman) and violence. The American Dream has turned into a horrifying nightmare.

Against this is a palpable background of moral ambiguity and world tension – 'Trouble in the Middle East', cries a prescient New York newsboy. Hitchcock's slow dissolve from the violated United Nations building to the bronze CIA plaque seems now to encompass the cynicism of the Seventies and Eighties and perhaps should not be taken as lightly as Thornhill's flip comment early in the film, 'This is ridiculous'.   ADRIAN TURNER

Directed by Alfred Hitchcock, 1959
Prod co: Alfred Hitchcock/MGM. **prod:** Alfred Hitchcock. **assoc prod:** Herbert Coleman. **sc:** Ernest Lehman. **photo** (Technicolor, VistaVision): Robert Burks. **sp eff:** A. Arnold Gillespie, Lee LeBlanc. **art dir:** Robert Boyle, William A. Horning. **mus:** Bernard Herrmann. **sd:** Frank Milton. **ed:** George Tomasini. **titles:** Saul Bass. **r/t:** 136 minutes.
Cast: Cary Grant (*Roger Thornhill*), Eva-Marie Saint (*Eve Kendall*), James Mason (*Phillip Vandamm*), Jessie Royce Landis (*Clara Thornhill*), Leo G. Carroll (*The Professor*), Philip Ober (*Lester Townsend*), Josephine Hutchinson (*Mrs Townsend*), Martin Landau (*Leonard*), Adam Williams (*Valerian*).

Roger Thornhill, a New York advertising executive, is kidnapped in the Plaza Hotel and taken to see Phillip Vandamm (1), a spy dealing in American secrets who has briefly taken over the home of Townsend, a diplomat. Vandamm believes Thornhill is George Kaplan, a CIA agent, and forces him to drink a bottle of bourbon before putting him blind-drunk in a car.

Instead of crashing as planned, Thornhill is arrested (2) for drunken driving but is released on bail through the charm of his doting mother. Following a clue found in Kaplan's hotel room, Thornhill goes to the United Nations building. He meets Townsend who suddenly falls dead with a knife in his back (3).

Now a prime murder suspect, Thornhill boards a train for Chicago where Kaplan has gone. On the train he meets Eve Kendall (4) who helps him evade the police and arranges a meeting with Kaplan on the open prairie. Whilst Thornhill waits for Kaplan (5), a crop-dusting plane attacks him (6) but Thornhill narrowly escapes and the plane crashes into a passing vehicle (7).

He tracks Eve down to an art auction where she sits with Vandamm. Feeling threatened once more, Thornhill ingeniously escapes by getting himself arrested but this time The Professor, of the CIA, intervenes, explaining that Kaplan is an imaginary agent designed to divert Vandamm's attention away from the real CIA agent, Eve, whose cover Thornhill has virtually blown.

Thornhill flies to Mount Rushmore where, as part of a plan, Eve shoots him with blanks (8) to reassure the suspicious and jealous Vandamm. Thornhill later meets Eve and learns that her duty demands that she leave America with Vandamm. Disobeying orders, Thornhill rescues Eve from Vandamm, who had intended killing her. They nearly fall to their deaths from Mount Rushmore (9) before The Professor's men arrest Vandamm and kill his henchmen.

The microfilm Vandamm was to deliver to the enemy is saved and Thornhill and Eve return to New York by train (10).

Dressed to Thrill

Behind every glamorous film star there stands an ingenious and talented costume designer. Knobbly knees, salt-cellar shoulder-blades, huge hips? Never fear; Adrian or Irene, Jean Louis or Orry-Kelly will be there, with spangles and satin, fur and feathers, to firm and flatter with their fabulous creations

In medieval Europe, fashions were dictated by the royal courts. Only the rich and privileged could afford to import fine silks and brocades from such far-off lands as China and Arabia and transform them into some of the most extravagant, impractical and beautiful clothes the world has ever known.

Extravagant, impractical, beautiful – all words that can equally well be applied to the wonderful world of film costume which reached its zenith in Hollywood in the Twenties and Thirties.

Two directors of the Twenties who must be credited as among the most important of all influences on costume design were D.W. Griffith and Cecil B. DeMille. Indeed DeMille's close attention to detail in his films almost reached the point of obsession: on *The Ten Commandments* (1923), for instance, he made all his staff memorize the Gospels. He turned the back-lots of Hollywood into magnificent towering cities and damask-filled palaces, and unfolded page after page of history, delighting audiences with his exuberant lavishness. Although these films were both silent and black and white, their costumes charged the screen with their bold assurance. Griffith,

on the other hand, made many films with actress Lillian Gish, who personified innocence and relied little on the power of physical adornment to reach the hearts of her public. Nevertheless Griffith's films were no less powerful than DeMille's and his costumes show a scrupulous attention to detail.

World War I did not act as an obvious deterrent to the cinema. The need for diversion was greater than ever, and Hollywood obliged.

It was in the Twenties that the great names of costume design began to make themselves known. The list of men and women who have enhanced film through their clothes is a very long one. The contribution of a handful is dealt with, all too briefly, here. Other names that should be honoured include Helen Rose, Renie, Adele Palmer, Howard Greer, Gwen Wakeling – to mention far too few. But better to concentrate on one or two films, one or two stars, and one or two designers in order to gain some idea of the complexity of this great art and the importance of its contribution to the cinema.

In the late Twenties, with the establishment of Greta Garbo as a major star, there emerged one of the most creative of all costume designers

– Adrian. The magic of Garbo was greatly aided by her favourite cameraman, William Daniels, who knew precisely how to light the magnificent face; her trust in him was complete. Similarly, Adrian, her favourite designer, created for her exquisite costumes. Garbo wore clothes well; though she disliked the endless fittings, she was nevertheless astute enough to realize their power of projection on the screen.

In his book on *Hollywood Costume Design*, David Chierichetti highlights *Camille* (1936) as one of Adrian's greatest successes in interpreting a story through clothes – especially the white chiffon dress sprinkled with stars that encapsulates Garbo's role as Marguerite Gautier – a woman who though a courtesan has great purity of spirit. In the same film, the feathered bonnet Garbo wears in the auction scene is an interesting example of the costume designer's skill. It is a stylized version of the Victorian original, cut away at the sides; an authentic replica would have hidden the famous features. Victorian bonnets are usually 'adapted' in this fashion for the screen.

The Hollywood career of Gilbert Adrian (b. 1903) began when Natacha Rambova (then the wife of Valentino) asked him to design *What Price Beauty?* (1924). In 1928 MGM put him under contract and he stayed with the studio till 1942. In 1930 he worked with DeMille on *Madame Satan*, a designer's dream for the costumes were an endless succession of shimmering fantasies. Spangled stars were a favourite motif, and he used them with

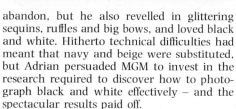

abandon, but he also revelled in glittering sequins, ruffles and big bows, and loved black and white. Hitherto technical difficulties had meant that navy and beige were substituted, but Adrian persuaded MGM to invest in the research required to discover how to photograph black and white effectively – and the spectacular results paid off.

Jean Harlow was one of the great stars of the Thirties whom he dressed – for example *Dinner at Eight* and *Bombshell* (both 1933) and *China Seas* (1935). And Jeanette MacDonald, star of many of the studio's best-loved musicals, never looked more beautiful than when clad by him in whispy chiffons and voiles which had a luminous quality and moved beautifully. With him she made *Naughty Marietta* (1935), *Rose Marie, San Francisco* (both 1936) and *Maytime* (1937).

Many of the stars had problem figures – by today's standards. But Adrian created foundation garments and re-fashioned their figures magnificently while keeping to the authentic lines of the period the film called for.

Many of Adrian's most startling designs were made for Joan Crawford. Conventional clothes did nothing to enhance her broad shoulders. He decided that, rather than conceal them, he would make the most of the star's 'assets'. First he covered them in ruffles, then he went a step further and padded the shoulders of all her outfits. The results were that Crawford's waist looked smaller, and the 'look' made front-page fashion news (and has been in vogue, on-and-off, ever since). Adrian made nearly thirty films with Crawford in his time at MGM.

One of the greatest stars of the Thirties was, of course, Marlene Dietrich. She understood extremely well both how to work with the camera and how to use clothes to enhance her own particular magic. Dietrich made memorable costume movies – the most exotic of which must surely be *Kismet* (1944). Madame Barbara Karinska, who was brought into MGM by Irene, the resident designer, had previously created many costumes for ballets. She had Dietrich's famous legs painted in a special gold substance, her hair was twisted

Opposite page: the treacherous Delilah (Hedy Lamarr) with the Saran of Gaza (George Sanders) in DeMille's sumptuously costumed Samson and Delilah *(1949). Above left: Cleopatra (Theda Bara) – the fashions of Ancient Egypt interpreted by a designer of 1917. Above: Joan Crawford kept to the square-shouldered look Adrian initially designed for her; this version by Irene for* Above Suspicion *(1943) cleverly uses sequins to make her shoulders look even bigger and her legs longer. Above right: Jean Harlow and George Cukor on the set of* Dinner at Eight; *like many Thirties gowns Adrian's dress for Harlow didn't permit her to sit, so these rest-stands were devised. Right and below: Adrian's exquisite designs for Garbo in* Camille *– a mist of tulle and spangled stars for the party, and rich embroidery on velvet (and the artful, face-revealing cut-away bonnet) for the scene at the auction*

and coiffed into elaborate plaits, and her body encased in bejewelled bodices and chiffon veils. The whole effect was designed to amaze, and Dietrich made full use of her costume in projecting both eroticism and sheer bravado.

For Mae West, of the hour-glass figure, costume also played an important part in portraying her own special brand of 'high camp' and overt sexuality. Travis Banton (1894–1958), who worked at Paramount from 1925 to 1938 and designed Dietrich's costumes for her films with the director Joseph von Sternberg, created much of Miss West's wardrobe for such films as *I'm No Angel* (1933) and *Belle of the Nineties* (1934); Miss West pouted and sashayed across the screen in figure-hugging gowns with heavily embroidered trains, and gave a new lease of life to enormous feathered hats and provocative ostrich boas and fans.

In her long career in movies, Bette Davis has worn some of the most beautiful gowns created for the screen. One of the loveliest is the delicately embroidered white tulle dress with which, as *Jezebel* (1938), she tries to win back her man (Henry Fonda). It was designed for her by Orry-Kelly (b. Walter Orry Kelly, 1897–1964) who left Warner Brothers in 1943, returning only to work on Davis' pictures. Designers' work can only be shown to best advantage if the studio contract players can wear the clothes well. Orry-Kelly found his ideal in Bette Davis.

It was not, however, Orry-Kelly but Edith Head (b. 1907) who won an Oscar for dressing Davis and the other stars of *All About Eve*

(1950). This diminutive lady of great ambition became Head Designer at Paramount in 1938 and remained so until 1967 when she joined Universal. Her endless patience and perserverance with a host of major stars earned her praise and fame. She is an enormously versatile designer who can turn her hand with equal assurance to period and contemporary films. *Roman Holiday* (1953), *The Ten Commandments* (1956), *Sweet Charity* (1969) and *The Sting* (1973) are but a few of her great successes. Her strength is in her adaptability,

Top left: gold legs, spun hair and an amazing array of bangles and beads by Madame Karinska for Dietrich in Kismet. *Above: Orry-Kelly's famous ball-gown for* Jezebel *(Bette Davis). Left: one of Edith Head's perfect re-creations – for* Harlow *(Carroll Baker). Below left: Travis Banton's feathers, frills and fans for Mae West in* Belle of the Nineties. *Below centre: a Jean Louis dress that both hides and reveals Rita Hayworth in* Gilda. *Below: Hayworth again in one of the* Cover Girl *dresses created by Gwen Wakeling for the flash back sequences; also working on the film were Travis Banton and Muriel King*

rather than inventiveness – as, for instance, exemplified by the costumes she designed for Carroll Baker in *Harlow* (1965) – re-creations of the body-hugging satin dresses made famous by Harlow herself.

In 1945 the ravishing Rita Hayworth was voted 'favourite pin-up' by the GIs. It isn't difficult to see why. Hayworth was probably at her most alluring in the gowns designed for her by Jean Louis (b. Louis Berthault, 1907) for *Gilda* (1946). Two have gone down in costume history: one the deeply slit, strapless satin sheath in which she sang 'Put the Blame on Mame'; the other an embroidered white two-piece with bare midriff (often a feature of her outfits). Jean Louis was Head Designer for Columbia from 1944 to 1958. Hayworth was obviously an inspiration to him as some of his best work was done in collaboration with her.

Cecil Beaton (1904–1980) was never under a long-term contract to a studio, and only made

a handful of films. But he has made his mark in film history in particular through his costumes for Audrey Hepburn in *My Fair Lady* (1964) and Barbra Streisand in *On a Clear Day You Can See Forever* (1970). His black-and-white creations for the Ascot scene in *My Fair Lady* have the mark of genius, and the Regency gowns and head-dresses that Streisand wore in *On a Clear Day* are an inspiration to all aspiring costume designers. He was master of precision, and a welcome addition to the long array of famous names.

Not every costume film relies on accuracy. There seemed to be a period in the Fifties and Sixties when certain movies paid little attention to costume detail and relied more on the action and blood-and-gore tactics. For example, Virginia Mayo in *King Richard and the Crusaders* (1954), designed by Marjorie Best, has a contemporary hairstyle and a gown sporting a heavy gold chain clasp that had no place in the twelfth century. Similarly the costumes of Margaret Furse (1911–1974) for *Becket* (1964) were more than a century out. The story, set in the late twelfth century, certainly could not have seen the royal women wearing such elaborate head-dresses which were more typical of the court of Henry V more than two hundred years later. Perhaps the reason for this was that the fashions of Henry II's court were not particularly attractive, and the designer felt that audiences would respond better to a more pleasing aesthetic rendition of the period. *Anne of a Thousand Days* (1969), also designed by Furse, although more accurate, still lacks the punch of authenticity. Such discrepancies will, of course, pass largely unnoticed, and will only be disturbing to the serious student of costume.

One of the most exciting costume films of recent decades is Tony Richardson's *Tom Jones* (1963) set in the eighteenth century. Designed by Jocelyn Herbert it not only captures the texture of an old print, but brings to life the 'feeling' and colour of the clothes of that time. You can almost smell the rags Diane Cilento wears. The film marked a turning point in attention to detail and costume precision.

Probably one of the most famous period films ever made is *Gone With the Wind* (1939) starring Vivien Leigh and Clark Gable, and designed by Walter Plunkett (b. 1902), whose distinguished Hollywood career included long spells at both RKO and MGM. The voluminous skirts and tight waists he created for Vivien Leigh influenced the course of fashion. The slinky bias-cut satins that had previously been the rage gave way to organdie and velvet ballgowns with numerous petticoats. For another costume film *Madame Bovary* (1949), also set in the mid-nineteenth century, he designed a no less spectacular wardrobe for Jennifer Jones.

Another period beloved by the costume designer is the reign of Egypt's Queen Cleopatra. The most famous Cleopatras have been Theda Bara in 1917, Claudette Colbert in Cecil B. DeMille's film of 1934, Vivien Leigh in *Caesar and Cleopatra* (1945) – interesting in the fact that its war-time budget was very limited and the maximum effect was achieved by the ingenuity of designer Oliver Messel (b. 1904) – and Elizabeth Taylor in Darryl Zanuck's 1963 production. Taylor's *Cleopatra* was fraught with difficulty, and ran massively over budget, but audiences still marvel at the endless parade of spectacular creations designed for Taylor by Irene Sharaff. The plunging necklines, finely pleated gauze and elaborate wigs were all stylized versions of Egyptian costume, but they were contemporary in feel and the film had a wide and profound influence on women's garments, hair and makeup of the next few years. Sharaff went on to produce equally splendid costumes for Elizabeth Taylor in *The Taming of the Shrew* (1967) in conjunction with Italy's Danilo Donati, one of the most innovative, imaginative and creative costume designers to emerge in the last two decades. His imagination is boundless. He created wonderful jewelled collars and head-dresses made from pasta for *Fellini Satyricon* (1969). He crocheted string and fine rope for Silvana Mangano in Pier Paolo Pasolini's *Edipo Re* (1967, *Oedipus Rex*). Pasolini employed him again for *Il Decameron* (1971, *The Decameron*), *I Racconti di Canterbury* (1971, *The Canterbury Tales*) and *Il Fiore delle Mille e Una Notte* (1974, *Arabian Nights*) each film, bizarre enough in content, is given an extra exotic charge through the magic of Donati's costumes. Those aware of the importance of costume in film can only marvel at his genius – his sense of colouring and his superb stylization of authentic costume which explored new margins in that field.

Another brilliant name who is a force to be reckoned with in Italy is Piero Tosi who, though quieter in mood than Donati, and an expert on the Twenties and Thirties, created for Visconti in *La Caduta degli Dei* (1969, *The Damned*) and *Morte a Venezia* (1971, *Death in Venice*) an array of simple yet exquisite costumes that caught the imagination of the public. Versions of these clothes immediately found their way into the shops. Charlotte Rampling and Ingrid Thulin, stars of *The Damned*, did much to promote the feeling of nostalgia for Thirties style – as did Silvana Mangano in *Death in Venice*, when lace flooded the fashion markets. In film fashion nostalgia reigned supreme in the Sixties and Seventies,

perhaps a reaction against the fear of the new and unknown in a fast-escalating world of change.

One movie that is a particular landmark in fashion influence is *Bonnie and Clyde* (1967) starring Faye Dunaway and Warren Beatty. *Women's Wear Daily* in the United States heavily promoted the clothes from the movie, which were designed by Theadora Van Runkle, with the result that the shops were awash with finely cut tweed skirts, berets, knitted and crocheted sweaters, and Shetland pullovers for men. In contrast to the extravagance that was previously prevalent in Hollywood, the sheer simplicity of costume in *Bonnie and Clyde* was like a breath of fresh air. In a similar vein the clothes worn by Diane Keaton in Woody Allen's *Annie Hall* (1977) did much to promote the trend towards an easy, casual look, and the mode for women to dress in a more masculine fashion; baggy shirts and pants, loosely knotted ties, waistcoats and easy trilbys – a far cry from layers of frothy chiffon.

Another, more off-beat, trend-setting film (costumed by Jacques Fontenay) was Roger Vadim's science-fiction sex saga *Barbarella* (1968) – which may have revitalized the plastics industry. It stars the delectable Jane

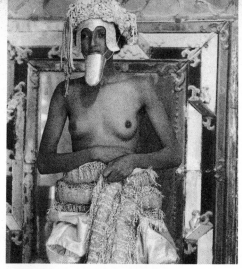

Fonda, legs akimbo in thigh-high vinyl boots and matching body moulds. Only the boots caught on.

Two male stars worthy of mention for their impact on the home wardrobe were Marlon Brando in *The Wild One* (1953) and James Dean in *Rebel Without a Cause* (1955). Brando personified the macho male in leather while Dean gave the T-shirt sex appeal. The looks were widely copied, and are still very much in vogue.

Probably the last memorable 'clotheshorse' who epitomized all that was elegant in the fashions of the day was Audrey Hepburn. Usually dressed by Hubert de Givenchy the French couturier – *Love in the Afternoon* (1957), *Charade, Paris When it Sizzles* (both 1963), *How to Steal a Million* (1966) – the combination of her unique beauty and the stylish simplicity of the clothes gave a new meaning to the word 'chic'. The proverbial little black dress and the string of pearls found its way into many a wardrobe.

Clothes, it is said, are a reflection of the times we live in. Today in 'modern' films, nothing seems comparable to the heyday of Audrey Hepburn – when women wanted to emulate the star. Now, when the clothes in a film are memorable, almost without exception that film is a costume movie. Contemporary fashion in films no longer influences to the extent it did because the fashion-conscious young are there first. However, nostalgia for the earlier decades of the twentieth century still captures the imagination of the public. The Golden Age of Hollywood still lives, and so too the need for escapism. BILL GIBB

Opposite page. Top: in Becket *(left) the court of Henry II (Peter O'Toole) was dressed in the style of Henry V, while in* King Richard and the Crusaders *(right) 'modern' elements crept in. Centre: sketch and still of* Madame Bovary *(Jennifer Jones) designed by Walter Plunkett. Left: Silvana Mangano dressed by Piero Tosi in* Death in Venice

Far left: Irene Sharaff adjusts one of her glorious gowns for Elizabeth Taylor's Cleopatra, *on which she worked with Renie and Vittorio Nino Novarese. This page. Top: Donati's extraordinary designs for* Arabian Nights. *Above: after* Barbarella *appeared, Jane Fonda's boots walked out of the future and into the high-streets*

Above: Audrey Hepburn, here dressed by Pauline Trigere in Breakfast at Tiffany's *(with George Peppard), brought her own elegance to beautiful clothes. Below left:* Bonnie and Clyde *(Warren Beatty and Faye Dunaway) sparked off a fashion trend. Below:* Annie Hall *(Diane Keaton and Woody Allen) elevated crushed cotton trousers to high fashion*

British 'New Wave'

The British 'New Wave' drew on literary sources and the documentary tradition to bring new life to the stagnant waters of British feature-film production

When *Room at the Top* hit the screen in 1959, it signalled the beginning of one of the most exhilarating bursts of creativity in the history of British cinema. During the following five or six years new film-makers with fresh ideas brought to the screen a sense of immediacy and social awareness that had people queuing again after nearly a decade of decline.

These dynamic film developments sprang from the political and social agitation of the period. British imperialism had been dealt a severe body blow by the failure of the 1956 Suez venture in alliance with France against Egypt. Thousands of young people had gathered in London's Trafalgar Square to demand the withdrawal of British troops from Egypt. Thousands more were flocking to join the annual anti-nuclear Aldermaston marches in order to campaign for unilateral nuclear disarmament.

It was a time of protest and demonstrations. Ideas were in the melting pot. Young people were no longer accepting that their elders were necessarily their betters, and in the process of re-examining basic principles they were gaining a new sense of collective identity, which in turn was transforming books, plays and popular entertainment.

Singers like Tommy Steele, Cliff Richard and Lonnie Donnegan were spurning traditional showbiz glamour in favour of a jeans-and-T-shirt image. Authors ultimately as different as John Braine, Alan Sillitoe and Stan Barstow were all writing grittily from working-class and lower-middle-class experience. On the London stage, the 'kitchen sink' era had begun. At the Royal Court Theatre, John Osborne had created the concept of the 'angry young man' and Arnold Wesker was facing West End audiences with East End problems. Joan Littlewood, creator of Stratford Theatre Royal and Theatre Workshop, was bringing a whole new generation of playwrights, actors and actresses into being, to express the questing, socially critical spirit of the times.

Things moved more slowly in the film industry, which is notoriously reluctant to risk its money on anything new. The measures it was taking to counter the catastrophic drop in cinema attendances, caused largely by the upsurge of TV, were mainly commercially opportunist and gimmicky, and this only succeeded in driving more people back home to watch TV.

The first hint of change in feature production came from a modest suspense drama, *The Man Upstairs* (1958), tautly directed by Don Chaffey for ACT Films (the production company of the film technicians' union). Set in a London boarding house, it touched upon many of the vital issues of the day and challenged conventional, cosy attitudes to class relationships and the role of the police. It was a straw in the wind. But it was completely overshadowed by the smash-hit success of *Room at the Top*, released early the next year.

Directed by Jack Clayton, and based on the John Braine best seller – a key book in the new-style

literature – *Room at the Top* was, in fact, a transitional film. Its starry cast, its steamy sex scenes and its depiction of life at the top belonged to the past. But its Northern setting and its candid exploration of the social barriers, corruption and palm-greasing of class-divided Britain signposted the future. Its enormous popularity at home and abroad brought fresh confidence to the film industry and helped to shake some of its more entrenched notions of what draws people to the cinema.

Meanwhile, back at the National Film Theatre, a group of youngish, independent film-makers, including Karel Reisz, Tony Richardson, Lindsay Anderson and cameraman Walter Lassally, were showing each other and young audiences the documentary films they had made with small grants from the British Film Institute or at their own expense, in a series of programmes they called *Free Cinema*.

The stated aim of the group was, by adopting far more personalized styles, to break away from the approach to documentary film-making established by John Grierson in the Thirties. Most of their films were free-flowing observations of work and play among young working-class people; and in retrospect they are more striking for their continuity with the Grierson tradition than for their rejection of it. Anderson looked at a Margate amusement arcade in *O Dreamland* (1953); at life in a school for deaf children in *Thursday's Children*, which won an Oscar in 1954; and at the people of Covent Garden market in *Every Day Except Christmas* (1957). Richardson's *Momma Don't Allow* (1955) observed young people at a jazz club; and Reisz's *We Are the Lambeth Boys* (1959) was about a South London youth club.

The 'personalized' view was sometimes patronizing or snobbish. The standard of the films was

Top: the success of John Osborne's Look Back in Anger *at the Royal Court Theatre in 1956 started a fresh movement in British drama. The film version retained the play's claustrophobic force, despite location filming in Romford market. Above: the Free Cinema documentarists had to eke out a living in television, advertising and the theatre while awaiting the chance to make feature films*

THE FILM THAT HIT THE HEADLINES!

SATURDAY NIGHT and SUNDAY MORNING

Top: the subject of school obviously inspires Lindsay Anderson; Thursday's Children *(co-directed by Guy Brenton) is a fine documentary in which deaf children are taught to speak by various ingenious methods, including feeling the vibrations of sound in a balloon. Top right:* Saturday Night and Sunday Morning *had the best press of any 'New Wave' film; as the Sixties went on, pop music dominated the media more than new films. Above: Joan Littlewood, best known for her lively work in the theatre, directed only one film,* Sparrows Can't Sing, *which starred Barbara Windsor, James Booth and George Sewell as an East End love-triangle*

uneven; but the best of them had a freshness and sense of urgency which was a taste of things to come. They stimulated discussion in the pages of the serious film journals; Lindsay Anderson argued for the recognition of the relationship between art and society in his much-discussed article, 'Stand Up! Stand Up!', published in *Sight and Sound*, Autumn 1956. The enthusiasm generated by the group in its search for contemporary styles to match contemporary attitudes helped to open up new possibilities for feature production.

First to the starting post was Tony Richardson, who had produced John Osborne's plays on the stage, and joined him to form Woodfall Films with a view to adapting them for the screen. Neither *Look Back in Anger* (1959), with Richard Burton as Jimmy Porter, the original 'angry young man', nor *The Entertainer* (1960) with Laurence Olivier as the has-been stand-up comic, was as successful as they had been on the stage, largely, perhaps, because Osborne had been addressing himself to middle-class theatre audiences.

It was not until Woodfall linked up with a working-class writer, Alan Sillitoe, that it was able to launch the cinematic equivalent of the theatre's 'kitchen sink' revolution, with the screen version of Sillitoe's best seller, *Saturday Night and Sunday Morning* (1960), directed by Karel Reisz.

Despite the ripples made by *Room at the Top*, Woodfall had a long and difficult struggle to raise the finance for a film with a factory worker as 'hero'. Few believed that it could succeed. In the event, it beat all former box-office records for a British film and proved that there need be no contradiction between artistic integrity and commercial success. The ripples then grew into a flood-tide; and for the next few years British cinema rode on the crest of the 'New Wave' which, for a time, freed a section of it from Hollywood financial and cultural domination.

The new film-makers, like the pioneers of the 'Grierson school' before them, rejected studio sets in favour of location shooting in the back streets, waterways and working-class homes of industrial cities. The black-and-white photography, mainly with natural lighting, gave rise to the 'grainy realism' which was the typical visual style, and the influence of recently developed TV techniques helped achieve a sense of immediacy.

The star system was abandoned, and leading roles were taken by new or up-and-coming players (Albert Finney, for example, was virtually unknown outside London theatre circles before *Saturday Night and Sunday Morning*). Many had been trained at Theatre Workshop. The characters they played were close to life, complex – like real people rather than standard 'heroes' and 'heroines'; the contemporary mood of social protest was expressed less through what they said on the screen than through the close relationship that was depicted between their frustrations and rebelliousness and the specific context of their environment.

Most of the films were based on books and plays by authors with personal experience of working-class life in the provinces (very few of the films were made from original scripts). This contrasted with the rather condescending view of working-class life that had been adopted in earlier feature films. For the first time, typical cinema audiences were able to feel a strong sense of identity with what was happening on the screen.

Over-reliance on novels and plays made the new start precarious and unlikely to last the course

Woodfall Films, with the backing of the British Lion subsidiary, Bryanston Films, continued to lead the field. Tony Richardson brought Shelagh Delaney's Theatre Royal play, *A Taste of Honey*, to the screen (1961), with Rita Tushingham as the pregnant schoolgirl and Murray Melvin (from Theatre Workshop) as the lonely homosexual with whom she shares a brief spell of contented domesticity. Richardson followed it with *The Loneliness of the Long-Distance Runner* (1962), based on Alan Sillitoe's remarkable short story, with Tom Courtenay as the young delinquent in Borstal who demonstrates which side he is on by deliberately losing the race that, if won, would have brought great prestige to the Borstal authorities. Much underrated by critics at the time, it has proved to be among the most enduring films of the period. Both these films gained much from Walter Lassally's brilliant camerawork.

It was not until 1963 that Lindsay Anderson made his first feature film, *This Sporting Life*, based on a David Storey novel. At one level, it explored a miserably stormy relationship of two lovers (Richard Harris and Rachel Roberts); at another, it exposed the corruption and commercialism of Rugby League as a business. It was highly acclaimed by most critics; but its fragmented flashback structure and rather heavily emphatic symbolism – a departure from typical 'New Wave' directness – operated against commercial success; it was six years before Anderson was able to make his second

and more successful feature film, *If . . .* (1968).

Woodfall also launched Desmond Davis as a director; his two films based on Edna O'Brien stories – *The Girl With Green Eyes* (1964) and *I Was Happy Here* (1966) – were late contributions to the no-longer-new trend.

One of the key directors of the period was John Schlesinger who, after gaining attention with his Waterloo Station documentary, *Terminus* (1961), teamed up with the Italian producer Joseph Janni to make *A Kind of Loving* (1962), in which he explored the effect of upper-working-class puritanism – and the housing shortage – on the uncertain relationship between a young couple, played by Alan Bates and June Ritchie. His second feature film was *Billy Liar* (1963) with Tom Courtenay as a young office worker who lives in a fantasy world and Julie Christie, in a small but important role, as the girl who helps him to face reality.

The young Canadian director, Sidney Furie, probed deeply into current social issues among working-class youngsters in *The Boys* (1962) and *The Leather Boys* (1963). He injected a crisp, contemporary style into British musicals with *The Young Ones* (1961) and *Wonderful Life* (1964), both featuring Cliff Richard. The 'pop' scene was also the launching pad for Richard Lester, who captured the changing spirit of the times in *It's Trad, Dad!* (1962) and in the first of his two films with the Beatles, *A Hard Day's Night* (1964).

Among the screen versions of the key stage plays of the period were a poor adaptation of Brendan Behan's *The Quare Fellow* (1962) and a good,

straightforward version of Wesker's *The Kitchen* (1961), directed by James Hill for ACT Films. Joan Littlewood herself, whose Theatre Workshop at Stratford was supplying so many new faces and new ideas for the screen, made a brief but lively excursion into cinema with the perky and resilient cockney comedy, *Sparrows Can't Sing* (1963), adapted from the Theatre Royal play by Stephen Lewis – another much underrated film.

In 1963, over a third of the films generally released dealt with aspects of contemporary life in Britain. It was a vintage year for the 'New Wave' – but it spelled the beginning of the end. Ironically, it was Woodfall Films, prime mover in freeing British cinema from Hollywood domination, which unwittingly handed it back.

The 'New Wave' films had not been costly. But Tony Richardson needed a bigger budget for *Tom Jones* (scripted by John Osborne from Henry Fielding's classic novel) which was to be shot in colour, with expensive costumes. When British Lion declined to take the risk, United Artists stepped in. Despite its period setting, the film's racy, rumbustious spirit and strong social comment – together with Albert Finney's roistering central performance – hit the contemporary mood. It was a fabulous success – and it opened the floodgates for American capital to pour into British production. The 'New Wave', with its regional nuances and its lack of star value and glamour, was an early victim of the Americanization process. British cinema lost much of its native character and again became part of transatlantic movie culture.   NINA HIBBIN

Top left: Tom Courtenay's bony, melancholy face was his fortune in The Loneliness of the Long-Distance Runner, *which set him on the path to stardom. Top: a girl (Rita Tushingham) about to become an unmarried mother tries to develop some maternal feelings with the dubious help of a plastic doll, while her flat-mate (Murray Melvin) looks on uneasily in* A Taste of Honey. *Above: Rita Tushingham plays a young girl in love with an older man (Peter Finch) in* The Girl With Green Eyes. *Left: a little boy feels lost in* Terminus. *The film's director, John Schlesinger, had previously worked mainly in TV documentary, notably for the arts programme,* Monitor

Juke Box Jungle

The Beatles were on their way, the Rolling Stones were being born, and British rock'n'roll was taking its first unsteady steps towards the cinemas. But this was the Fifties – good-clean-fun and all-round-entertainment were just what the kids wanted

When rock'n'roll music started figuring in the planning schedules of film producers in the USA, it was already a key ingredient in the pop-music world, having moulded its own sub-culture involving artists, fans and fashions. It was far from hitting any kind of excitement peak, but it was there.

Then, in 1955, the feature film *The Black-board Jungle* appeared. It was a pretty straightforward classroom drama but it had a headline-making extra – Bill Haley and his Comets playing 'Rock Around the Clock' over the credits. To the near-worldwide sound of audiences' stomping feet and the slashing of seats, cinematic rock was on its way. Elvis Presley emerged next as rock's first solo super-star in a feature film which was to have been called *The Reno Brothers*, but became *Love Me Tender* (1956), the title of the main vocal theme.

This flurry of American action, which included *The Girl Can't Help It* (1956), starring the pneumatic Jayne Mansfield and a host of Top 50 singers, as the first major colour film to feature rock, created wide interest in Britain.

Stage package shows, generally featuring near unknowns, rocked round Britain, and the record companies started cashing in. The British film industry finally woke up to the potential of rock on celluloid in 1957, but it took up the challenge with severe self-doubt, an obvious lack of know-how and a hit-or-miss philosophy.

Stainless Steele
Two of the earliest contenders for the title of Britain's Elvis were Tommy Steele and Frankie Vaughan – the first a one-time merchant seaman and the other a dead ringer for Victor Mature. Steele (b. 1936) – whose career was masterminded from coffee-bar singing to starring at the London Palladium by Larry Parnes, a refugee from the rag trade, and John Kennedy, a gimmick-conscious photographer – was initially a genuine rock superstar. Yet, strangely enough, he had comparatively few hit records, and by 1960 had turned his back on rock and become an early example of the all-round-entertainer syndrome.

Steele's rags-to-riches saga was celebrated in *The Tommy Steele Story* in 1957. It was originally planned as a documentary on British rock'n'roll, but that was before the producers fell prey to the persuasive powers of the Parnes-Kennedy team; skiffle, calypso and traditional jazz were added. The toothy singer went on to films like *The Duke Wore Jeans* (1958) and *Tommy the Toreador* (1959), but it was soon apparent that his heart was not in trying to become a Presley-patterned performer.

Find-a-Presley
There were very real (but short-lived) hopes that Frankie Vaughan (b. 1928) would be Britain's home-grown rock superstar. He made his debut on screen in 1957 in *These Dangerous Years* – a song-studded story about law-defying Liverpool teenagers – co-starring with Carole Lesley. And for a while, in the British 'find-a-Presley' campaign, it seemed Terry Dene (b. 1938) might fill the bill. 'White Sport Coat' was his only big hit record, but his lower lip curled in Elvis style, the hips moved freely

Top: Serious Charge – *Cliff plays it cool in a coffee bar, perfect venue for the juke-box beat. Below left: Joe Brown (on bar) in* Three Hats for Lisa *(1965). Below: despite the 'sensation', Frankie Vaughan quickly took a back seat in the race to stardom*

201

Above: ageless Cliff Richard taking a hip Summer Holiday. Above left: Tommy the Toreador – a bravura Spanish fantasy comes to life for seaman Tommy. Left: another dual identity for Tommy Steele as the cockney double of a young Duke in The Duke Wore Jeans. Bottom left: Claire Gordon, Shirley Ann Field, Gillian Hills, Adam Faith in 'Beat' Girl. Only Faith continues to act rather than sing

and he was good on stage. So Dene was hustled into a movie – *The Golden Disc* (1958) – along with such contemporary pop performers as Denis Lotis, Nancy Whiskey, Sheila Buxton and disc-jockey David Jacobs.

Steele rejected rock; Vaughan became more of a housewives' choice; but Dene just was not cut out for the life. He was over-exposed and harried to the point of nervous collapse. Called into the Army for two years' National Service, he found the pressure too much for him, and was abruptly discharged. His career collapsing under him, Dene turned to fervent street-corner evangelism.

Bachelor boy

This confusion in British movie rock circles left space for Cliff Richard (b. 1940), who really was in the Presley mould, though his emergence – into a mixed world of successful movies and hit records – was by no means straightforward.

His career actually began in *Serious Charge* (1959), directed by Terence Young, starring Anthony Quayle and Sarah Churchill. The film boasted a serious topic – an alleged sex offence. Richard had only a small role but, with a group of session musicians he also sang 'Living Doll'

Above: life was cruel to Terry Dene, and even this star appearance in The Golden Disc *failed to guarantee success. Right: 6.5 Special moved from TV to film to encapsulate the frenetic rhythm of the whole beat era*

which Lionel Bart had written for the soundtrack. It was later recorded first as part of a movie-linked EP record, then put out as a single at a slower tempo and with Richard's own backing group – then The Drifters, now The Shadows. The single sold a million, and decisively changed his career from rocker to versatile all-rounder.

Expresso Bongo (1959) was a parallel key movie in the Cliff Richard story, a film version of a Wolf Mankowitz stage hit. Richard played Bongo Herbert, an up-and-coming singer, and one of his songs – 'Voice in the Wilderness' – was a huge hit, despite the star's intense dislike of it.

Cliff Richard's status in the area of rock-movie action grew steadily. *The Young Ones* in 1961 had him with The Shadows, Robert Morley and Carole Gray, plus a powerful score that included the hits 'Bachelor Boy' and 'Summer Holiday'. This film was publicized as 'the first film ever to have three tunes in the Top 10'. And Cliff gained even more credibility as a box-office draw with *Summer Holiday* (1963) directed by Peter Yates, featuring The Shadows, Una Stubbs, Lauri Peters and Melvyn Hayes.

You gotta have Faith
But events have surely proved that Adam Faith (b. 1940) – a vocal contemporary of the emergent Cliff – is the best actor of all the early British rock artists. His first film foray was 'Beat' Girl (1960) co-starring with Shirley Ann Field. It contained the hit 'Someone Else's Baby', itself melodically emphasized by the pizzicato string backing laid down by John Barry. The film had Faith playing a beatnik kid in a storyline that earned it an X certificate, and he agreed with the critics that it was 'no epic'. It was banned in many territories: in Singapore, incidentally, because it showed a

young girl being rude to her parents.

Faith's second movie – *Never Let Go* (1960) with Richard Todd, Peter Sellers and Elizabeth Sellars – actually came out first, because at the time there was a queue of X-rated films waiting to get out on the cinema circuits. Faith has stuck with his acting, of course, on television as Budgie, in *Stardust* (1974), and more recently with Roger Daltrey in *McVicar* (1980).

Artful Anthony
As British celluloid rock sought acceptance at a reasonably serious level internationally, the Anthony Newley episode emerged to provide an element of farce. Newley (b. 1931) – an actor since he was 15, regularly in films, spotlit for playing the Artful Dodger in *Oliver Twist* (1948) – took on a character role in *Idle on Parade* (1959) as Jeep Jackson, a rock singer enlisted by accident into the British Army's crack regiment. For most Newley viewers this was the first time he had actually sung in public. From getting maybe one or two letters from fans a week as a respected actor, he got a hundred a day as a rock singer. Newley was then only 28.

Newley, of course, went seriously into the music world, collaborating with Leslie Bricusse, and inspiring big-stage successes like *Stop the World – I Want To Get Off*. Today he is a Las Vegas-based musical entertainer. But his entry into the rock world of 1959 and subsequent television exposure on shows like *6.5 Special* and *Drumbeat* were purely accidental.

And the stars wore jeans
The television success of *6.5 Special*, with its fast-paced format, led to a full-length cinema

production, out in 1958, and starring among many others the young Jim Dale. Dale (b. 1935) was another part-time British rock singer who figured in the movie scene of the late Fifties. He went on to work in the Carry On series, and had remarkable success as a stage actor both with Olivier's National Theatre and later on Broadway.

Actor-turned-singer John Leyton was showcased in the short *The Johnny Leyton Touch* (1961) and was another Presley successor who did not quite succeed, despite appearing briefly in *It's Trad, Dad!* (1962). This was predictably strong on traditional jazz (Chris Barber, Acker Bilk, Kenny Ball, The Temperance Seven), but also included the rock brigade, notably Craig Douglas, Chubby Checker and Gary Bonds from the USA. Joe Brown was another established pop name who showed potential in the whole crazy mixed up world of British teenage talent coming of age in movies good, bad and indifferent.

Many observers of the scene felt that Billy Fury should have been bigger than most. *Play It Cool* (1962) featured his moody aggression alongside Helen Shapiro, Danny Williams and one Shane Fenton, later to make the charts all over again as Alvin Stardust. And through the whole hectic era, Elvis Presley was turning out two or three movies a year, as regular as clockwork.

The Beatles, Dave Clark and the others were just around the corner. Ideas of presenting authentic British rock'n'roll music were to become creatively and dynamically more sound. But the first fumbling, stumbling efforts to get the music into cinematic formats will long be fondly remembered.　PETER JONES

Considering Britain's position as a major industrial nation, British film companies were remarkably slow to recognize that the realities of working-class life could attract mass audiences. They were convinced that people went to the pictures 'to get away from it all'.

When Tony Richardson sought finance to produce the film version of *Saturday Night and Sunday Morning*, he therefore met with considerable resistance. Even the comparatively modest sum required (its final cost was only £116,000) seemed too much to risk on a film about a factory worker, to be shot in black and white in the backstreets of an industrial Midlands city (Nottingham), with no big stars and no glamour.

Richardson's confidence and persistence, however, were fully justified by the result. Much to the industry's surprise, the film, released in 1960, was a stunning success, both commercially and artistically. It changed the whole face of British cinema by proving that audiences enjoyed seeing their own life-styles on the screen – when the film-makers got it right. Adapted for the screen by Alan Sillitoe from his own best seller, and sensitively directed by Karel Reisz, it was the first British film to present an inside view of working-class life.

In the first half of the film – its 'Saturday night' – the high-spirited young factory worker, Arthur Seaton, is mainly interested in beer and women. He is out for kicks – his secret affair with Brenda is all the more exciting to him because Brenda's husband, Jack, works alongside him at the factory. But Arthur, unlike the Michael Caine character in *Alfie* (1966), for example, is not an incorrigible rogue with predictable responses to every situation thrown up by the plot. He is in active rebellion against those forces in society which restrict pleasure and self-fulfilment; and he is undergoing a process of change and growth.

The film is episodic in structure and many of the incidents are designed to identify the influences which Arthur is determined to resist: television, for instance, when he teases his TV-addicted father, who is too engrossed to notice the joke at his expense; bigotry, in the shape of gossipy neighbours; the notion of an engagement ring, which his prim new girl-friend, Doreen, insists upon as a precondition for sex. The army uniforms of the men who beat him up represent a further force of oppression; and Freddie Francis' grimly realistic photography of the cramped houses and back alleys suggests constriction and limitation.

Above all, it is Arthur's work which shapes his outlook. When the film opens, he is shown, tense and tight-lipped at his lathe, inwardly defining his aim. He will work just hard enough, he tells himself, to earn a good time, but not so hard as to become a wage-slave. His watchword is: 'Don't let the bastards grind you down.'

Brenda's pregnancy is the first

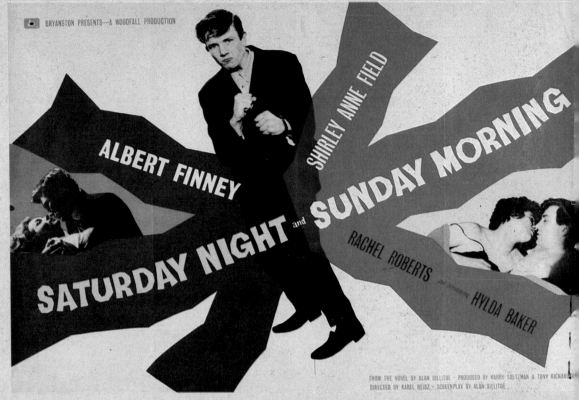

indication to Arthur that what brings pleasure to him can bring pain to others – and ultimately to himself, as well, when the soldiers, on behalf of Brenda's husband, beat him up. In his 'Sunday morning' mood, he begins to understand that his relationship with Doreen has to be give-and-take on both sides.

The problem for Arthur – and for the film – is how to view the prospect of conventional marriage without capitulating to conformity. Arthur's final defiant gesture could be seen as a futile knock against the inevitable. But through its various episodes, the film has laid a trail which, in conjunction with Albert Finney's brilliant use of character

development, could suggest that his rebellious spirit, purely self-centred at first, is now maturing into some social – and perhaps even political – awareness. This leads to a more positive interpretation of the conclusion – to the effect that there's a lot of good fight left in him.

Even so, in today's social climate, the ending might appear to lack real challenge. But *Saturday Night and Sunday Morning* was very much a film of 1960. Doreen's sexual reserve and Brenda's unwanted pregnancy had special relevance at a time of change when 'permissiveness' was in its infancy, the contraceptive pill was just beginning to become available, the

women's liberation movement had not yet brought the whole concept of conventional marriage under scrutiny, and abortion was still illegal.

The film's open discussion of abortion had a startling – even sensational – effect and may have contributed to its box-office success. The overriding element in its popularity, however, was its extraordinary accuracy of perception, together with amazingly close-to-life performances from the entire cast. Audiences could identify not only with the people and places on screen but also with the particular quality of Arthur's social protest, which exactly captured the spirit of the times.   NINA HIBBIN

Directed by Karel Reisz, 1960
Prod co: Woodfall. **exec prod:** Harry Saltzman. **prod:** Tony Richardson. **sc:** Alan Sillitoe, from his own novel. **photo:** Freddie Francis. **ed:** Seth Holt. **art dir:** Ted Marshall. **mus:** Johnny Dankworth, played by the Johnny Dankworth Orchestra. **lyr:** David Dearlove. **sd:** Peter Handford, Bob Jones. **sd ed:** Chris Greenham. **ass dir:** Tom Pevsner. **prod man:** Jack Rix. **r/t:** 89 minutes.
Cast: Albert Finney (*Arthur Seaton*), Shirley Anne Field (*Doreen*), Rachel Roberts (*Brenda*), Hylda Baker (*Aunt Ada*), Norman Rossington (*Bert*), Bryan Pringle (*Jack*), Robert Cawdron (*Robboe*), Edna Morris (*Mrs Bull*), Elsie Wagstaffe (*Mrs Seaton*), Frank Pettitt (*Mr Seaton*), Avis Bunnage (*blowzy woman*), Colin Blakeley (*loudmouth*), Irene Raymond (*Doreen's mother*), Louise Dunn (*Betty*), Anne Blake (*Civil Defence officer*), Peter Madden (*drunken man*), Cameron Hall (*Mr Bull*), Alister Williamson (*policeman*).

7

While Arthur Seaton is working at his machine in a large Midlands factory, his mind is on the good times ahead. He is pacing himself carefully. He needs money to spend on beer and women but he has no intention of working himself into the ground (1).

After a heavy session in the pub at the weekend, he slips into Brenda's house through the back while her husband, Jack, is away

for the night (2). His affair with Brenda looks even more promising when Jack is transferred to the night shift (3), but his ardour cools a little when he meets a younger girl, Doreen, in the pub (4) and begins to date her. Doreen, less sexually free than Brenda, wants to be sure of Arthur's future intentions before agreeing to make love (5).

When Brenda tells Arthur that

she is pregnant by him, he takes her to visit his aunt to seek help for an abortion (6), but the attempt is unsuccessful. After taking Doreen to a fairground, Arthur is badly beaten up by two aggressive soldiers, one of whom is Jack's brother (7, 8).

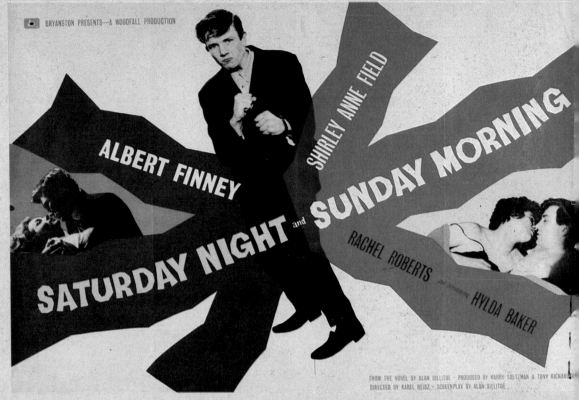
Poster for the film: ALBERT FINNEY · SHIRLEY ANNE FIELD · SATURDAY NIGHT and SUNDAY MORNING · RACHEL ROBERTS and introducing HYLDA BAKER · BRYANSTON PRESENTS — A WOODFALL PRODUCTION · FROM THE NOVEL BY ALAN SILLITOE · PRODUCED BY HARRY SALTZMAN & TONY RICHARDSON · DIRECTED BY KAREL REISZ · SCREENPLAY BY ALAN SILLITOE

1

2

3

4

5

6

His experiences make him feel more responsible towards Doreen. They become engaged and visit a housing estate where they might soon live (9). Arthur huris a stone at a hoarding in front of the houses. 'This won't be the last one I throw,' he says.

8

9

All the Angry Young Men

At the time when the hopefully labelled 'New Wave' in British films appeared in the late Fifties, a lot of fuss was made about its supposedly unprecedented aspects. British theatre, it was alleged, had always been set in the drawing-rooms of the rich until John Osborne showed otherwise with *Look Back in Anger*. The British novel had always been genteel and reverential to the Establishment until the working-class heroes of John Braine and Alan Sillitoe found room at the top and showed sexual efficacy on Saturday night equal to their ability to fight their way through life on Sunday morning, or a multitude of Lucky Jims showed their disaffection by cocking a comical snook at everything their middle-class training had always stood for.

As for films, the same pundits claimed that there had never before been anything like a working-class cinema in Britain, and the new concern for the working-classes (from film-makers of impeccably middle-class background and education, let it be noted) was going to transform the whole British film industry and alter forever notions of what did and did not go to make a star. And admittedly, the shapers of such wild and wayward generalizations were perhaps closest to the mark when talking about films than they were in the other areas.

Career opportunities

The heroes of *Room at the Top* (1959), *Saturday Night and Sunday Morning* (1960), *A Kind of Loving* (1962), *This Sporting Life* and *Billy Liar* (both 1963) were, therefore, in the cinema at least, an almost unprecedented phenomenon. And it is understandable that when exciting new actors came forward to play them, they were at once hailed as a new kind of star. Subsequent experience, however, tends to indicate what might have been guessed all along: they were not a new kind of star, but just the old kind of star playing a new kind of role. As long as the roles were offered they

They portrayed to perfection sullen yet vulnerable working-class lads, staring out of grimy windows at the damp oppressive horizons of the industrial provinces, yearning for their place in the sun. Richard Burton, Albert Finney, Richard Harris, Alan Bates and Tom Courtenay all went on to achieve varying degrees of international stardom, but many of us will always remember them best for their films of the late Fifties and early Sixties

would play them, and when other kinds of role were more in vogue they would, quite understandably, play those too.

It is not surprising, with hindsight, to discover that nearly all the angry young men of the British screen proved to be birds of passage, shaped by the time and the circumstance of their first appearances, but not limited by them. In no case has this been more obvious than with the first two, Laurence Harvey and

Richard Burton. Both had been stars already in very different kinds of film before their 'angry' debuts, and the only difference between them in that particular respect was that while nobody ever worried very much where Laurence Harvey was – London or Hollywood – or quite saw him shaping up as a working-class hero (despite his relative success in *Room at the Top*), Richard Burton did at least provoke some excited speculation.

Far left: Albert Finney with Liza Minnelli as his willing secretary in Charlie Bubbles, *his first film as director. Left: the seedy life of a Liverpudlian private eye who models himself after Bogart in* Gumshoe. *Below: Finney as factory worker and Rachel Roberts as his mate's wife whom he makes pregnant in* Saturday Night and Sunday Morning

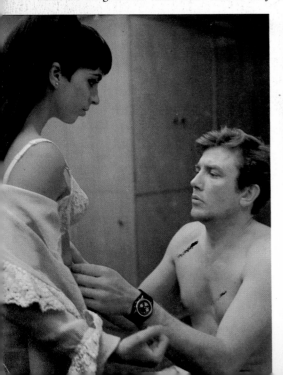

Far left: Richard Burton as Jimmy Porter, the prototype angry young man, bitter in sentiment, sharp of tongue, feeling hopeless, trapped and isolated in Look Back in Anger, with the woman who is his mistress – and his wife's best friend (Claire Bloom). Left: putting his undeniable skills as a powerful actor into Becket, the martyred archbishop

Finney on the wing

Look Back in Anger was the first feature made by stage director Tony Richardson. His second, The Entertainer (1960), also based on a play by Osborne, had the incidental distinction of introducing, in small roles, two future stars of some importance in the history of the British cinema, Albert Finney and Alan Bates. Finney (b. 1936) went from this unobtrusive debut to his first great moment of glory in Saturday Night and Sunday Morning, made almost immediately afterwards. As the lusty young factory worker Arthur Seaton, his rough-hewed appearance ('iron-faced', the script says) and unselfconscious masculinity found their perfect vehicle: where Laurence Harvey and Richard Burton were only play-acting, this was the real, unadorned working-class

hero a generation had been so eagerly looking for. The fact that Finney was embodying a Lawrentian myth of the working class and the industrial Midlands did not really matter. It was time for new myths to replace the old, just as it was time for new star images. And because that element of roughness is built into Finney's stage and screen personality, he has stayed closer to the working-class hero than any of the other angry young stars.

His next big hit, Tom Jones (1963), transferred his established screen character to a period context. Thereafter he tended to play Arthur Seaton in glossier surroundings – as in Two for the Road (1966) – or, naturally, as he himself matured, to show what happened to such characters later on with a little education. Thus in Charlie Bubbles (1968), he directed himself as an ex-working-class writer who has acquired a lot of the neuroses of the rich and famous; but less successfully was a provincial, would-be detective who has fantasies of being Humphrey Bogart in Gumshoe (1971). Later still he followed his mentor Charles Laughton into elaborate character parts, playing the title-role in Scrooge (1970) and Hercule Poirot in Murder on the Orient Express (1974).

Looking back on Burton

Burton's early career fed a particularly British myth: that of the serious Shakespearean actor tempted away from the austere satisfactions of the Old Vic by the glittering prizes of Hollywood. It was understandable that a young man might have his head turned in this way, but would he be able to live with himself in the morning? Born in Wales in 1925, he had made his film debut – playing a Welshman – under the direction of his mentor Emlyn Williams in Korda's modest The Last Days of Dolwyn (1949). Despite Korda's subsequent interest, Burton avoided long-term contracts and continued to play small roles in minor films while he went from strength to strength in the theatre.

Then in 1952 he went to Hollywood to appear in a Daphne du Maurier romantic drama, My Cousin Rachel, which did lead to a long-term contract – with 20th Century-Fox – and CinemaScope stardom in the likes of The Robe (1953), Prince of Players (1954) and The Rains of Ranchipur (1955). He did, however, return between these assignments to play Hamlet and Coriolanus at the Old Vic, and in 1959 starred in Look Back in Anger. It may have seemed he was being imported as a Hollywood star to improve the film's box-office prospects, but in fairness Burton was highly effective as Jimmy Porter; his great Welsh voice and the uncomfortable, abrasive side to his screen personality admirably suited Osborne's rebellious hero, especially in his savage rhetoric.

This early identification with the burgeoning 'New Drama' in Britain might have led to something more for Burton, and for it. But no, back to Hollywood he went, and Cleopatra (1963) and Elizabeth Taylor and all that was only just around the corner. A handful of later roles – in Becket (1964), The Spy Who Came in From the Cold (1965), Who's Afraid of Virginia Woolf? (1966) – served to remind audiences of the actor he might have become had he stayed in Britain. But never again did he tangle with working-class heroes.

Man in the middle

At least Finney stayed with the kind of role that made him famous longer than did Alan Bates (b. 1934). Bates' big chance on the screen came in John Schlesinger's A Kind of Loving, one of the last and perhaps best of the slice-of-life school of British films. In it he played a young working man trapped into a drab conventional existence by getting a casual girl-friend (June Ritchie) pregnant, and did so with great simplicity and feeling.

But Nothing But the Best (1964) showed him ruthlessly climbing out of the working class – indeed, very much like the young British playwrights and novelists whose own social

climb was matched by the increasingly middle-class preoccupations of their works. Bates accordingly played middle-class heroes in several screen adaptations: in Peter Nichols A Day in the Death of Joe Egg (1972), as a father trying to cope with a spastic child; in Simon Gray's Butley (1974), as a disillusioned academic; and in David Storey's In Celebration

Above: longing for new horizons, Vic Brown (Alan Bates) finds that life consists of compromises, especially when he gets his girl friend (June Ritchie), pregnant in A Kind of Loving. The girl's shrill and bullying mother was marvellously played by Thora Hird

Above: Frank (Richard Harris, the most volatile of the angry young men) offers his love in This Sporting Life *and begs for it to be returned by his frigid, hate-filled landlady (Rachael Roberts). Below: the delinquent in* The Loneliness of the Long-Distance Runner *who asserts his independence by purposely losing the big race*

(1975), as one of a group of successful, educated brothers returning uncomfortably to their working-class background.

Bates' career thus continued to mirror social developments in Britain during the Sixties and Seventies with a recognizable consistency, though he did play different types of roles in different kinds of film. He appeared in period adaptations like *Far From the Madding Crowd* (1967), *Women in Love* (1969, with the famous nude wrestling scene (and *The Go-Between* (1971); subjects that showed the classless Englishman abroad, *Zorba the Greek* (1964) or *The Rose* (1979); and eventually went on to grand character roles like Diaghilev in *Nijinsky* (1980).

Mad dogs and Irishmen

In all these films Bates was essentially different from Richard Harris (b. 1933), whose starring role in Lindsay Anderson's film *This Sporting Life*, based on a faintly autobiographical novel by David Storey, seems at this distance of time like a trick of fate, quite divorced from the rest of his acting career. Like Richard Burton he started with distinct regional affiliations, though in this case Irish instead of Welsh, and in three of his first four films – *Alive and Kicking* (1958), *Shake Hands With the Devil* (1959) and *A Terrible Beauty* (1960) – he played Irishmen and bade fair to be typed forever within this local definition. At least in *The Long and the Short and the Tall* (1961), adapted from an angry play by Willis Hall, he played rather effectively a stereotyped bullying corporal in support of Laurence Harvey, and established his most distinctive feature as an actor – a sort of mad-dog intensity which suggested he might be dangerous to know and would not hesitate to apply extreme solutions.

By the time he made *This Sporting Life*, he had already appeared in a couple of international co-productions, *The Guns of Navarone* (1961) and *Mutiny on the Bounty* (1962), and seemed set to become a major star. In *This Sporting Life* he played a rowdy, emotionally obsessed Rugby League professional, a role that gave perfect expression to his own special personal qualities. Immediately afterwards he went into *Deserto Rosso* (1964, *Red Desert*), one of Michelangelo Antonioni's icy studies of urban malaise, in which he was dubbed in Italian, but then, alarmed perhaps by what he had done (and the two films' lack of commercial success), went straight back to conventional Hollywood movies appearing in *Major Dundee* (1965), a Western with Charlton Heston; *Hawaii* (1966), an emotional drama with Julie Andrews; *Caprice* (1967), a secret-agent spoof with Doris Day; and *Camelot* (1967), a musical with Vanessa Redgrave. Nothing he has done since has even slightly recalled his brief moment of youth and anger and artistic ambition.

Courtenay behaviour

Tom Courtenay (b. 1937) has escaped all of this for better or worse, by never really becoming a Hollywood-type star in the first place. Like so many of his generation (including the nearest Britain had to an angry young working-class heroine, Rita Tushingham) he was given his first chance in films by Tony Richardson, in another Alan Sillitoe subject, *The Loneliness of the Long-Distance Runner* (1962). His puny physique and air of being undernourished made Courtenay ideal casting as the Borstal boy who deliberately refuses to win the race that would do credit to the establishment rather than to him. But although his appearance suited him to this particular role, it seemed unlikely in the long run to help him become a major (let alone romantic) star. He did manage to exploit it playing rather similar roles as soldiers, rebellious or downtrodden, in *Private Potter* (1962), *King and Country* (1964) and *King Rat* (1965).

His consecration though came in John Schlesinger's film of the Keith Waterhouse-Willis Hall play *Billy Liar*, about a weedy young Northerner who regularly fantasizes himself out of his own humdrum life. Albert Finney had created the role on stage and Courtenay had taken over from him, but there was no doubt that the latter was better casting for the film. For the moment it made him a star.

Billy Liar also demonstrated that Courtenay had a real gift for comedy. It was further revealed in *Otley* (1969), a spy spoof that was kept in touch with reality mainly by his performance as an ordinary Londoner suddenly involved in a series of extraordinary situations. Otherwise Courtenay's later career has consisted of filling character roles in films like *Doctor Zhivago* (1965) and *The Night of the Generals* (1967) with distinction. But in any case, by the time he achieved his short-lived screen stardom tastes were already changing. The Swinging Sixties had already begun and social concern and gritty realism were coming to seem a bit old-fashioned. Suddenly films were again looking for actors – and stars – who could be smooth and grand and play gentlemen when required. Michael Caine, Michael York and James and Edward Fox were waiting in the wings, and angry young men were about to be shuffled unceremoniously off the stage, never to return except as interesting period-pieces in a world they had helped to change.

JOHN RUSSELL TAYLOR

Moments of choice

The director is the key figure in film-making; his decisions determine the feel and texture of the film, as well as its overall character and development

Orson Welles filmed the sleigh-ride scene for *The Magnificent Ambersons* (1942) neither in a studio nor on location. He insisted on building his set inside the largest available refrigeration plant. The landscape he required could have been simulated at RKO just as convincingly and much cheaper. What could justify such costly self-indulgence? What gain could it possibly bring to the film? Were Welles' actors so incompetent that they needed to be frozen stiff before they could bring conviction to a winter scene?

There is an answer, and it is visible on the screen. In sub-zero conditions, unlike those on a hot sound-stage, the breath of players (and ponies) freezes in the air to a visible vapour. That is an important effect, since it goes with the soft white landscape to make the scene felt as one of natural purity. The sharp freshness of its air, made present in this way, provides an all-the-more telling site for the appearance of the horseless carriage. Here, in a scene whose nervous jollity is only touched with foreboding, it is a joke that the vehicle sullies the countryside with racket and filth. But there is nothing frivolous about the contrast between the heavy black fumes of the machine and the silvery human breaths that vanish on the air. It states the vulnerability of the complacent small-town aristocracy to the impact of a new technology.

The very breath of an actor can be made significant when the director places it in an expressive relationship with the other aspects of the scene. It can contribute to the effectiveness of the moment – building the sense of a threatened and fleeting purity – and it can establish a visual theme: the Amberson life-style is progressively submerged in an industrial wilderness of smoke, metal, speed and mechanical din. Though the choices are seldom as costly (and only sometimes as rewarding) as Welles' here, directing a film is always about making choices of this kind – hundreds of them every day and at every stage in the translation from script to screen.

Many of the choices are matters of craft. The director works to make the scenes vivid and varied, so as to achieve an arresting presentation of the characters and their story. Flaws in the casting may

have to be disguised. Dull spots in the writing and sagging passages in the construction of the screenplay may need to be enlivened. Cunning may be required to stretch limited resources: in *Letter From an Unknown Woman* (1948), Max Ophuls had to construct the living world of late nineteenth-century Linz on the back-lot set that Universal had been keeping going as an all-purpose Mittel-Europa exterior since *All Quiet on the Western Front* (1930).

The most promising script, judiciously cast, will still fall flat if the director is unable to get all the elements of the production working together – either in harmony or in lively contrast – so that the end result flows when it is played to an audience. If it does not work on the screen, we are likely to think that there was not much of a story or that the performances were lacking. But often the fault lies in the director's inability to find a style that brings the material convincingly to life. Just as often, it is

Below: Joseph Cotten as an inventor taking his home-made car for a spin in The Magnificent Ambersons. *Although his hopes of marrying a widow are ruined by the snobbish jealousy of her son, the industrial development which he foreshadows comes to dominate the Indiana town previously run by a few wealthy families such as the Ambersons. Bottom: the outdoor sets originally built for* All Quiet on the Western Front *(left) were refurbished for the Linz sequences of* Letter From an Unknown Woman *(right), of which the main action takes place in an equally inauthentic Vienna*

the director who should take the credit for our belief that we have seen a credible and forceful story with colourful and engaging characterization. In terms of the package and its ingredients, there is not much that separates *The Reckless Moment* (1949), *Johnny Guitar* (1954) or *Written on the Wind* (1956) from dozens of mediocre products of the Hollywood machine. The crucial factor is the direction of Max Ophuls, Nicholas Ray and Douglas Sirk.

Old Hollywood was well aware how much its product stood to gain, as entertainment, from a style that rendered its drama effectively and made it look, move and sound as if it had a *sense of direction*.

It expected directors to be capable production managers and to complete their work on time, on budget and without major damage to studio morale. But it also valued and rewarded the ability to control performance, image and editing so as to create moods and viewpoints through which the story could persuade and grip the audience.

Very seldom would a director's career suffer from a noisy insistence on getting a particular fabric for the set, a particular lens for the camera or a particular casting for an apparently insignificant role. Directors were paid to believe that every little thing mattered – and to prove it by their results.

One minor instance is the choice of props. At the start of Nicholas Ray's gangster movie, *Party Girl* (1958), chorus-girl prostitutes are paid for their services at boss Rico Angelo's party with a gift of powder compacts. The glittering cases are discarded as soon as they have been emptied of the $100 bills inside. Later Rico settles accounts, at a presentation dinner for his 'ambitious' underling, Frankie Gasto,

by beating him about the head with a gold-plated miniature pool-cue inscribed 'From Rico to Frankie'. At the film's climax, Rico's threat to disfigure the heroine is teasingly developed as he unpicks the tinsel and tissue wrapping from a bottle of acid. Throughout the picture, then, elaborate gift-wrapping serves as a cover for payments, bribes, assaults and threats. Ray presents an image of gangland Chicago as a world of disguise whose characters are constantly hiding the true nature of their transactions from themselves as well as from others. The props are one means through which he was able to remodel a fairly routine gangster assignment into a film about pretexts.

If objects may be dressed, performers nearly always are. Dress offers the characters' conscious or unconscious self-presentation and may define social role or financial circumstance. A fur coat provides Max Ophuls with an image for the rewards and limitations of the role of bourgeois housewife in *The Reckless Moment*. Although the coat is 'her own', Mrs Harper (Joan Bennett) cannot dispose of it at a point when she is in desperate need of cash. It is too much part of her uniform, her identity, as the wife of a successful architect. A vital moment is conveyed when she manages to persuade her hitherto rebellious daughter to borrow it: she has at last cast her offspring into the 'womanly' role of decorative servitude. The daughter can now be sent out into the world – or to the movies with the 'boy next door' – as a replica of her dutiful mother.

The same director, in *Caught* (1948), uses three different coats to depict the options open to his indecisive heroine: the extravagant mink of a Long Island hostess; a plastic mac for the poor-but-honest nurse; and a 'sensible' cloth coat, warm and becoming but not showy, for the unassumingly loyal doctor's wife. The use of dress here goes beyond working as a simple but effective visual presentation of changing circumstances. It helps also to define an attitude to those changes. What is

important is that none of the garments represents the heroine's 'natural' character. Each of them gives her a role which she will try, or be forced, to live in.

Dress is a vital element in deciding how the film will look. But it is only one element, and its design needs to be related to the visual context determined by the choice of locations and the construction of sets. In *Some Came Running* (1958), the textures and colours of the decor stake out three different worlds in which the hero moves. In the downtown section, the director Vincente Minnelli said, he wanted the audience to feel that it was living inside a juke-box. The design yields a raucous contest between harsh metallic colours.

A justly famous scene in *La Règle du Jeu* (1939, *The Rules of the Game*) gains much of its effect from Renoir's use of decor. At the start of a country-house party, the aristocratic hostess, Christine, is obliged to confront the gossip surrounding her relationship with a young aviator, André Jurieu. She does this by introducing him to her other guests as a group with a speech in praise of pure friendship. The scene is set in the château's entrance hall and the decor is a perfectly credible arrangement of doors, pillars and open space. But Renoir's dis-position of his actors and camera turns the space into a theatrical arena as Christine takes André 'centre stage' to present him to the others, grouped at a little distance to constitute the audience, while her husband and his friend look on anxiously and at last proudly from 'the wings'. The sense of Christine's performance as one governed by strict rules, where a wrong move threatens disaster, emerges from another visual parallel that the decor permits:

the camera sees the floor, with Christine and André moving across its black-and-white marble tiles, as a chess-board. The power of the scene largely derives from the tension between Christine's nervously awkward sincerity and the demand implied by the theatre/chess-game image for the precise execution of a delicate manoeuvre.

Physical aspects of production like decor and dress can help the actors to feel themselves into their roles. But the detail of performance that brings the characters to life – movement, gesture, into-nation, rhythm – has to be established on the set. Here the director's job is, particularly, to hold each and every moment of performance within a vision of the scene as a whole so that the impact and effectiveness of *today's* scene is not achieved at

the expense of what was filmed last week or what remains to be shot. The continuity of the end product is, most often, an impression that has to be constructed and protected in spite of the radically discontinuous method of shooting. (The first day's work may be on scenes from the final pages of the script, and the leading man may be speaking his lines to an off-screen heroine who is due to join the production in a fortnight's time.) The pacing of a scene may seem just right in itself, but how will it look when the audience reaches it halfway through the film? Directors work in the knowledge that nothing is right 'in itself' but only in relation to the developing design. Balance and proportion are crucial.

The task here begins with the casting. The famous Hollywood 'chemistry' was usually pub-licized as an aspect of star teams like Hepburn and Tracy; but it applies to all casting, right down to the smallest roles. When the young fugitives get married in Nicholas Ray's *They Live by Night* (1948), the scene exploits, in systematic parody, all the elements of the conventional presentation of a white wedding. The casting of Hawkins, the local justice, whose business is marriage, is clearly crucial. Greed – extortionate greed leaning towards but never quite toppling over into criminality – is what the character must mainly evoke. Conven-tional casting would therefore suggest a fat man whose figure could represent an unrelentingly capacious appetite. By giving the role against type to scrawny, piping-voiced Ian Wolfe – a starved sparrow rather than a satiated vulture – Ray shades the notion of greed away from indulgent avarice and makes it an anxious habit born of insecurity.

The casting of the star parts is a matter on which the director might or might not be consulted. For instance, Max Ophuls did not first agree to direct *Letter From an Unknown Woman* and then decide that the heroine's role should be offered to Joan Fontaine. He had to decide whether he wanted to make the film, given that Fontaine was to play the lead. In case of conflict, the producer carries more weight over casting decisions than the director: Ray had to accept Germany's top star, Curt Jurgens, as a British officer in his World War II film, *Bitter Victory* (1957). More often than not, the director's notion of ideal casting for leading parts will be compromised by the constraints of schedule and budget.

Once on the set, however, directors have all the

Above: Bowie (Farley Granger) marries Keechie (Cathy O'Donnell) in They Live by Night; *Hawkins (Ian Wolfe) officiates at the hasty wedding. Ray's first film was given a delayed release in America and recognition of its merits was due to the efforts of French and English critics. Robert Altman remade the film as* Thieves Like Us (1974). *Left: Mervyn LeRoy pins up June Allyson's dress while discussing a production problem with an assistant during the making of* Little Women (1949). *LeRoy both produced and directed; the film reveals his great care for detail*

Above: Mrs Danvers (Judith Anderson), the sinister housekeeper of Manderley, startles the second Mrs de Winter (Joan Fontaine) by her sudden apparition in Rebecca. *Right: the same gesture, a hand on the shoulder, can be patronizing, friendly or contemptuous, reflecting the many sides of the hero played by Humphrey Bogart. Dorothy B. Hughes' original novel, also called* In a Lonely Place, *makes the hero guilty of murder; the film version exonerates him from actual guilt, but still attributes violent impulses to him*

freedom that their imagination, tact and persuasiveness can provide. Large statements can be made with small gestures. In the opening scene of *Caught*, the car-hop heroine is apparently sharing a harmless dream with her flat-mate when she fantasizes a chance meeting with a handsome young millionaire. But what is calculating and predatory in this innocence is conveyed by her punctuating her words by making idle passes with a fly-swat while lying open-legged on the bed. What is blind in her calculation, too, emerges from her complete inattention to her own gestures and their evident meanings.

Suppose that you were planning the first few minutes of a film whose central issue is to be the uncertainty of emotion, a story of passion dogged by mistrust in which only the strength of feeling (not its nature) remains constant. You want to establish that neither hero nor heroine is sure whether the man's embrace is protective and loving or threatening, murderous.

That was Ray's problem at the start of *In a Lonely Place* (1950). His answer was to give the same gesture to three different characters within the brief space of the scene that establishes the film's Hollywood setting: each of them approaches another character from behind and grasps his shoulders with both hands. The first time, it is a perfunctory and patronizing greeting whose pretense of warmth is a bare cover for the assertion of superiority. Then, between the hero and an old friend, it conveys intimacy and genuine regard. Finally, when a large-mouthed producer uses the shoulders of the hero himself as a rostrum from which to publicize his latest triumph, it is seen as oppressive and openly slighting. These moments are significant in their own right, but their deeper purpose is – in a perfectly ordinary context – to dramatize the ambiguity of gesture itself.

The work of film direction, as it has so far been considered, is not fundamentally different from that of directing for the stage. But in movies everything is designed to be filtered through the eye of the camera and remade in the patterns created on the cutting bench. Just how far a characterization may result from the director's control over camera – even when the role is as well cast and expertly played as Judith Anderson's menacing housekeeper, Mrs Danvers, in *Rebecca* (1940) – is nicely indicated by Hitchcock's description of his design.

He said that the figure of Mrs Danvers: '. . . was

rarely shown in motion. If she entered a room in which the heroine was, what happened is that the girl suddenly heard a sound and there was the ever-present Mrs Danvers, standing perfectly still by her side. . . . To have shown Mrs Danvers walking about would have been to humanize her.'

The camera's frame and the editor's scissors provide the means whereby the director carves a particular path through the world constructed on the set. Thus at the start of Ray's rodeo picture, *The Lusty Men* (1952), we are shown a selection of the displays in the opening-day parade through the centre of a modern Texan town. The camera's viewpoint constantly encompasses the solid fronts of banks, shops and offices as the permanent background of the passing show. Then, in ordering the succession of images, Ray moves systematically back through time, taking us from tractors and decorated lorries, through covered wagons and mule trains, to a band of fancy-dress Indians war-dancing along the city streets. When we get to the rodeo itself, the film has set it up as a show that attempts to extend the life of images from the past in a drastically transformed present.

Selection and sequence are the keys to viewpoint

212

that the director controls. It is a strategic decision, for instance, never to identify members of the rodeo's audience as individuals but always to view the spectators distantly as an anonymous mass. The place that might be occupied by shots of audience reaction is taken by images of the professionals in the commentary box, and of the harshly impersonal metallic cones of the arena's

loudspeaker system. The audience becomes one large component of a machine whose appetite is spectacle and danger, and which runs without regard for the particular human material it devours.

Cutting and camera movement are both means through which direction shifts and manipulates viewpoint. Yet their effects, the kinds of statements they make, are very different. To cut from one object to another is to assert continuity across a chopped-up time and space. Hitchcock does this spectacularly in *Strangers on a Train* (1951). His montage makes a single sequence out of contrasted events in two towns and on different time-scales: the hero's battle in a tennis tournament is intercut with the villain's struggle to regain possession of an incriminating cigarette lighter.

To shift the frame via camera movement, on the other hand, is to impose an order of perception on objects which exist in a continuous time and space so that they could, in principle, be seen all at once. In *The Lusty Men*, Ray introduces his rodeo-star hero in a shot which starts with the camera looking in through the gate of a bull-pen. The animal charges along its track to halt at the gate with its eyes glinting in fierce close-up. At this the image tilts upwards to frame Mitchum above the animal, preparing to mount. A direct contrast is drawn between two kinds of strength – the power of a natural force, and the force of human determination. But the camera's movement links these two images in comparison as well as contrast. For all his apparent mastery, as we look up to him outlined against the sky, Robert Mitchum is like the bull in being contained within the structures of the rodeo: his image, too, is framed, hemmed in, by the wooden posts of the bull-pen.

The movement and angle of the shot give a precisely calculated degree of overstatement to the assertion of mastery. Within fifteen seconds Mitchum will be floundering, injured, in the dirt of the arena. His previous inward smile of self-satisfaction at the commentator's tribute to his prowess, his pose of confident virility as he tightens his belt on the words 'one of the all-time rodeo greats', are opened up to irony by the camera's too hearty endorsement of his supremacy.

Ironic overstatement like this is a possibility for the director because the expressiveness of a film style is so much a matter of balance, of what happens when you put together, in a particular

way, a posture, a facial expression, an off-screen voice and a camera viewpoint. At the very centre of the director's job is this task of co-ordination. Direction works with the various talents of highly-skilled artists to ensure that their contributions meet in a coherent design. The photographer may devise ingenious ways of lighting a confined space so as to give it a sense of room and air. The ingenuity will yield little if the designer has been working to develop an image of claustrophobia.

In post-war Hollywood, directors often enjoyed considerable freedom *within* their assignments – much more than their freedom to choose and develop subjects or to initiate production. So long as they were thought to be making the best possible job of the given package of story, stars and resources, they were likely to meet with little resistance to their ideas about how a film should look, sound and move.

But even this freedom had strict limits. Those were still the days of the classic approach which valued formal design only so long as it supported the spectator's involvement, understanding, pleasure and belief in the narrative. Moreover, quite strict notions of what was appropriate were in play.

A brasher, gaudier array of colour was thought suitable for musicals than for, say, light comedy. Melodrama which aimed to carry its audience over the top, with heightened situations and excessive passions, offered a corresponding licence to explore the possibilities of a flamboyant visual rhetoric.

Many directors seem to have lived quite happily within these prescriptions, being ready to exert their skills within a range of genres to achieve effective versions of the accepted manner. The limitation of such adaptable know-how was that it would seldom carry a film beyond the qualities of the package originally handed down by the studio. A movie directed by, say, Michael Curtiz would be neither more nor less than the sum of its carefully blended ingredients. Sometimes that was enough. It is no mean praise to say that *Casablanca* (1942) was as good as its script and cast.

But it is probably fair to claim that Curtiz's best films achieve a dramatically effective *manner*, rather than a style. The various elements of the film are harnessed only to a reliable judgement of what will make the story work. More is possible. The films of Ophuls, Ray and Sirk, among others, are there to demonstrate how, with no sacrifice of movie-craft, the director can bind the movie together in a design that offers a more personal and detailed conception of the story's significance, embodying an experience of the world and a viewpoint both considered and felt. At this point, manner becomes style.
VICTOR F. PERKINS

Above left: Robert Mitchum as a too-assured rodeo rider, about to be thrown, in The Lusty Men. *The low angle deliberately exaggerates his confidence.*
Above: Elia Kazan, a founder of the Actors' Studio, prepares the cast of Splendour in the Grass *(1961). Zohra Lampert and Natalie Wood seem attentive to their guru, but Warren Beatty is less than enthralled*

INDEX

216